Legends Unleashed

VOL 2

THE SOURCE OF CONFLICT

Copyright© 2024 All rights reserved.

This book is copyright protected. It is only for personal use. You cannot amend, distribute, sell, use, quote or paraphrase any part, or the content within this book, without the consent of the author or publisher.

By reading this document, the reader agrees that under no circumstances is the author responsible for any losses, direct or indirect, that are incurred as a result of the use of the information contained within this document, including, but not limited to, errors, omissions, or inaccuracies.

Preface

Narayanam namaskrityam, paying obeisance to the divine Narayana, Naram chaiva narotamam, and to the noblest of humans, Devim sarawatim vyasam, and to the divine Saraswati and Vyasa, Tato jayam udarayat, thus seeking victory in this endeavor.

Let me regale you with the grand tale of the Mahabharata, a sprawling epic that stretches across the vast expanse of time. Before delving into the narrative, allow me to provide you with a glimpse into the essence of the Mahabharata itself. This magnificent opus is a tapestry woven with intricate threads, and in my retelling, I strive to capture its every intricate detail. While numerous condensed versions of this epic exist, I seek to present a comprehensive account that remains accessible and engrossing.

As devoted followers of Vaishnavism, we are fortunate to be surrounded by a wealth of sublime commentaries on the

Mahabharata. However, it is with a heavy heart that I acknowledge the absence of a single tome by any devotee that includes the Mahabharata commentary of Madhvacarya. This revered disciple of Vyasa penned an extensive 8,000-verse treatise brimming with invaluable insights, stories, and perspectives. He proclaimed that each verse in the Mahabharata holds ten meanings, his erudition earning him the title of Poornapragna, the embodiment of absolute consciousness.

From the very outset, it may appear that the Mahabharata unravels as a political drama. However, beneath this guise lies a dual narrative of profound significance. The foremost meditation, especially for us as devoted Bhaktas, revolves around the divine play enacted by Lord Krishna. The Asuras and Devas, engaged in their eternal struggle for dominion, wage their battles upon the earthly realm. Yet, it is crucial to recognize that we are not discussing mere mortals; for though they assume human form, their endeavors transcend the limitations of the material world. Everything unfolds under the divine orchestration of Krishna, with the Asuras and Devas acting as pawns in his cosmic game.

Simultaneously, the Mahabharata affords us an opportunity to witness Lord Krishna's interactions with his beloved Bhaktas. Within these sacred pages, we encounter Krishna himself, alongside his ardent devotees, the illustrious Pandavas, and countless others. This epic serves as a training ground for our souls, for we cannot fathom Krishna through imagination alone. It is unwise to conceive of Krishna as a mere philosophical concept or an invisible entity residing in distant space. He is a tangible personality, and our Bhakti is not a pursuit driven by amusement or trendiness. Krishna is a real person, and he yearns for genuine connections with us, for he created us with the explicit purpose of forging relationships with each individual soul. This forms a fundamental principle of Madhvacarya's teachings: Hari fashioned the souls to partake in divine communion.

As we immerse ourselves in the Mahabharata, we unlock the door to perceiving Krishna and his profound bond with his devotees. The realization dawns upon us that Krishna, in his divine play, derives immense joy from his companionship with the Devas and others. The Devas, his faithful servants who ensure the seamless functioning of the cosmos, are also his cherished devotees, and he occasionally descends to Earth to revel in their company.

Ekalavaya seeks out Dronacharya

Krishna advises Yudhisthera how to defeat Jarasanda

The Ghandarva Chitraratha Challenges Arjuna

Drupada tests the cast of the Pandava Brothers

Bhima flees the house of lac

Bhima and Duryodhana at the Display of Arms

Duryodhana convinces Dhritrastra to kill the Pandavas

Pandu asks the Sages for Advice

Shantanu Finds the twins Kripa and Kripi

Dronacharya teaches Arjuna

Pandu and Kunti Retire in the Forrest

Table of Contents

Preface iii
Chapter 1 The Beginning 21
Chapter 2 The Story of Garuda 26
Chapter 3 The Story of Astikya 34
Chapter 4 The Gods Ask Vishnu to Descend 38
Chapter 5 The Story of Kacha 42
Chapter 6 The Story of Yayati 47
Chapter 7 The Story of King Bharata 54
Chapter 8 Shantanu and Ganga 59
Chapter 9 The Terrible Vow 62
Chapter 10 A Testament to his immense Significance 64
Chapter 11 Bad Luck of Shantanus Children 68
Chapter 12 Vyasa is Summoned 75
Chapter 13 The Story of the Origin of Vidura 85
Chapter 14 The Establishment of the Kuru Dynasty 89
Chapter 15 The Birth of the Pandavas and Kauravas 97
Chapter 16 The Origin of the Pandavas 105
Chapter 17 The Birth of the Pandavas 114
Chapter 18 The Death of Pandu 122
Chapter 19 The Pandavas Enter Hastinipur 125
Chapter 20 Trouble Begins 130

Chapter 21 Origin of Kripa 137
Chapter 22 The Origin of Drona 139
Chapter 23 Drona Teaches the Students 145
Chapter 24 The Display of Arms 152
Chapter 25 Dronas Revenge 162
Chapter 26 The House of Lac 167
Chapter 27 Demon in the Forest 180
Chapter 28 Bhima fights an Ancient Evil 195
Chapter 29 The Ghandarva Chitrangada 201
Chapter 30 Swayamvara of Draupadi 204
Chapter 31 The Marriage of Drupadi 217
Chapter 32 Conspiracy and Division 225
Chapter 33 The Story of Tilottama 232
Chapter 34 Arjunas Journeys 238
Chapter 35 Arjuna and Subadra 244
Chapter 36 Kandava Forest 252
Chapter 37 Maya Sabha 261
Chapter 38 Narada Rishi Speaks 267
Chapter 39 Krishna gives Counsel 288
Chapter 40 Krishna and the Pandavas go to see Jarasandha 302
Chapter 41 Pandavas head out to conquer the World 315
Chapter 42 Rajasurya Yajna 328
Chapter 43 Envious Sishupalla 338
Chapter 44 The Portent of Doom Foretold 356
Chapter 45 The Jealousy of Duryodhana 359

Chapter 46 The Cause of the Game of Dice 366

Chapter 47 The Gambling Match begins 380

Chapter 48 Vidura Speaks.. 388

Chapter 49 The Assault of Draupadi 395

Chapter 50 The Final Deceit 408

Chapter 1

The Beginning

The origins of the Mahabharata unfold in a manner befitting the grandeur of its tale. Suta Goswami, the son of Romaharshan Suta, embarked upon a journey to Naimashuranya. It was the age of Kali, the age of darkness, and the sages sought to kindle the light through their sacrificial fires. One might wonder why such rituals persisted in the era of Kali. The Nrsimha Purana reveals a profound truth—that in this age of scarce righteousness, any semblance of dharma, no matter how flawed or imperfect, is cherished and accepted by the gods. It is akin to a child earnestly preparing breakfast, despite creating a delightful mess. In this age, even the smallest acts of righteousness are considered valid and praiseworthy.

Thus, the great sages immersed themselves in a thousand-year-long Yajna, a sacred fire ceremony where Vishnu was revered. When Suta Goswami arrived at the site, the sages rejoiced, for his father was a devoted disciple of Vyasa and a masterful storyteller. They eagerly inquired about his whereabouts and experiences. As they attended to his comfort, they washed his feet and offered him a refreshing concoction of milk, yogurt, and ghee—a customary gesture to invigorate the weary traveler.

Suta Goswami began recounting his recent sojourn to the snake sacrifice of King Janamejaya. At this event, Vyasa, accompanied by numerous sages, unveiled a remarkable tale known as the Mahabharata. Suta Goswami, driven by his enthusiasm, had arrived to share this extraordinary saga with the sages gathered at the Yajna.

Intrigued, the rapt audience yearned to understand the purpose behind King Janamejaya's snake sacrifice. Suta Goswami assured them that he would provide the answers they sought. And so, he delved into the fascinating tale.

Long ago, there was a formidable Brahmin named Veda, who had a devoted disciple named Uttanka. Uttanka desired to offer Dakshina, a token of gratitude, to his guru upon completing his education. The underlying principle was that one should seek knowledge with the intent to gain and grow. Once the disciple had imbibed the teachings and possessed the ability to apply them independently, it was customary to present the guru with Dakshina, signifying the completion of their education. Uttanka approached his guru, eager to offer Dakshina, but the guru humbly redirected him to his wife, stating that she might desire something in return.

During that era, most of civilization revolved around the Grihasta Ashram, where individuals lived as householders. The Sanyasis, or Yatis, who renounced worldly life to pursue spiritual endeavors, were a rare sight, dwelling in seclusion within forests. Thus, if one had a guru, they were a Brahmin householder. Such was the prevalent social structure at that time.

Uttanka dutifully approached his guru's wife, seeking her guidance on the Dakshina. She suggested a grand plan—their upcoming elaborate Yajna required the borrowing of exquisite jewelry from a virtuous queen residing in the region. Uttanka wholeheartedly embraced this quest and embarked upon his journey.

On his path, Uttanka encountered a figure of immense fascination—a colossal man astride an enormous bull, akin to a horse. The sight alone left Uttanka astounded, but what truly astonished him was when this extraordinary being spoke. "I know you, Uttanka. I am a dear friend of your guru," he declared. Offering two gifts, the towering figure delivered a warning first. Uttanka learned of a Naga, Takshaka, who coveted the very jewelry he sought. Caution became his ally. Secondly, the enigmatic man bestowed a gift—a present originally intended for Uttanka's guru. From his grasp, he produced a piece of cow dung, urging Uttanka to consume it.

Though hesitant, Uttanka reflected upon the fact that his guru had partaken of the same gift. Trusting in his guru's wisdom, Uttanka overcame his reservations and consumed the cow dung as instructed.

Now the thing is I will share is that the man who spoke to Uttanka was Indra and the thing he gave him was Amrita or the nectar of immortality. But he tested him to see if he would take it. Returning to Uttanka's story, after acquiring the jewelry from the king's palace, Uttanka suddenly found himself overcome with thirst. Setting down the jewelry, he sought water to quench his parched throat. However, in an unexpected turn of events, a serpent swiftly seized the jewelry and vanished into a hole. Enraged, Uttanka attempted to climb into the hole and dug frantically. But despite his fervent efforts, frustration eventually set in, and he sat beside the hole, disheartened.

Witnessing Uttanka's plight, Indra, recognizing the sage's distress, took pity on him. Utilizing his thunderbolt, Indra shattered the hole, creating a wide opening. Uttanka seized the opportunity, ventured into the hole, and found himself transported to a realm he could not have entered without partaking of the Amrita.

Entering the mysterious realm of Nagaloka, Uttanka beheld an array of serpents. Determined to reclaim his stolen jewelry, he demanded its return, only to face refusal from the mighty serpents. Nagaloka, situated in the lower celestial realms, is inhabited by powerful serpentine beings. These serpents possess multiple hoods, some adorned with precious gems. The venom they emit from their fangs is so potent that it can ignite the air they breathe, causing flames to emanate from their mouths. The luminosity generated by these flames reflecting off the gem-adorned hoods transforms Nagaloka into a radiant planet, illuminating the lower realms, such as Rasatala and Sutala, inhabited by demons.

Nagas, by nature, are proud and envious creatures, each desiring to possess the treasures they guard

Uttanka, determined to retrieve his stolen jewelry, fervently prayed while feeling disheartened. His prayers caught the attention of the devas, and as a result, Agni, the fire god, ignited Nagaloka, causing great discomfort to the Nagas. Initially furious, the serpents eventually approached Uttanka and apologized, returning the stolen jewels. This incident taught them a valuable lesson about the power of the Brahmin's spiritual radiance, known as "tejas." It is unwise to offend a Brahmin, as they possess influential connections.

Uttanka returned triumphantly with the jewelry, pleasing his guru's wife. However, his anger towards the Nagas still lingered. He approached King Janamejaya, the son of Parikshit Maharaj, reminding him that his father had perished from a snakebird named Takshaka's venomous bite. Uttanka explained the malicious and envious nature of the serpents, emphasizing the need to eradicate this pest from the face of the earth.

Upon consultation with his advisors, Janamejaya learned that a grand yajna could be performed to summon all the serpents of the world into its sacred fire. As word spread, sages from far and wide gathered to attend the ceremony. The Yajshalla, the sacrificial arena, was prepared while the preliminary rites commenced, and people continued to stream in. Recognizing Vyasa's presence, Janamejaya inquired about the history of his ancestors. Vyasa revealed that he had composed a great epic on that very subject, and Vaisampayana was chosen to narrate it to the world of men.

Curious about the reason behind the serpents' curse, the assembled sages approached Sutagosami and asked him to elucidate the root cause. They believed that there must be a deeper reason beyond Uttanka's and Janamejaya's anger for the entire race of serpents to be subjected to such burning. Sutagosami assured them, saying, "Indeed, I shall reveal the truth to you."

Chapter 2
THE STORY OF GARUDA

At the beginning of time, two great groups of beings existed: the Devas and the Asuras, who were in constant conflict with each other. On one occasion, Durvasa Muni wanted to congratulate Indra for his victories and presented him with a flower garland. However, Indra gave the garland to his elephant, which disdainfully threw it down and trampled on it. Durvasa became furious with Indra and cursed him.

Due to the curse, the Devas faced continuous defeats and were at a loss for what to do. Vishnu proposed that they work together to churn the milk ocean and obtain the Amrita, the nectar of immortality. They brought a giant golden mountain to serve as the churning rod and enlisted Vasuki, the king of serpents, as the churning rope. Although the serpents had just been born, Vasuki was already enormous.

During the churning, the fire-breathing serpent scorched the demons when they grabbed him by the head. As the churning continued, the fire from Vasuki's mouth set the mountain ablaze, resulting in the death of plants and animals on the mountain. The friction caused by the churning crushed aquatic creatures, and all of this combined with the ocean of milk. Vishnu's avatar, Kurma (the tortoise), came to hold up the sinking mountain in the ocean.

Initially, a poisonous substance called Hayhaya emerged, terrifying the Devas. Shiva drank the poison and held it in his throat without swallowing or spitting it out. As a result, his neck turned blue, earning him the name Nalinikantha or Blue Necked. Following the poison, various other entities emerged, including Apsaras and the goddess Lakshmi. Indra recited a beautiful prayer called the Indrakrit Mahalaxmi Stotra to attract Lakshmi towards the Devas. Reciting this prayer is believed to bring Lakshmi into one's life as well. The moon planet also rose out of the ocean, and an eight-legged horse named Uchchaihshravas appeared. Interestingly, in Norse mythology, Odin is said to have an eight-legged horse named Sleipnir.

In this story, two wives of Kashyap, Kadru and Vinata, play an important role. Vinata was the mother of the birds, and Kadru was the mother of the serpents. Kadru felt jealous of Vinata and devised a plan. She approached Vinata and said, "I heard a horse emerged from the ocean. What color do you think it is?" Vinata replied, "I think it is pure white, as it emerged from the ocean of milk." Kadru countered, "I think it is pure white with a black tail. Let's make a wager. Whoever is wrong shall become the servant of the other."

In the realm where co-wives abound, jealousy takes root and spreads like a venomous vine. This bitter rivalry between women is not a phenomenon unheard of, even among goddesses. Diti and Aditi, two celestial beings, found themselves entangled in such a web of envy. Aditi, the favored one, basked in the glow of adoration, while Diti seethed with jealousy. This cosmic drama manifested in the bitter hostilities between the Devas and the Asuras, the Adityas and the Dityas.

But let us delve deeper into the tale at hand. In truth, the horse that emerged from the ocean was resplendent in its purity, a creature of untarnished white. Yet, Kadru, with her brood of serpents, sought to manipulate the truth. Her serpentine offspring, resembling locks of hair, nestled themselves within the horse's tail, darkening its hue. Reluctant at first, for they recognized the immorality of their actions, the serpents were coerced by Kadru's curse. With grave words, she damned them to perish in a sacrificial fire, scorching their very existence. Thus, the snake sacrifice came to be, its origins rooted in Kadru's unyielding will.

As a consequence, Vinata, and subsequently her son Garuda, were bound to serve Kadru and her Naga progeny. This servitude birthed a deep enmity within Garuda, fueling the countless tales of his battles against and devouring of snakes. To be the slave of those he despised, from the very moment of his birth, left an indelible mark upon his spirit. In his primal form, Garuda blazed with the brilliance of light and fire, traversing the vastness of the universe. Gradually, his essence condensed, transforming him into a magnificent golden eagle.

It was the serpents who burdened Garuda with their demands, compelling him to ferry them across the expanse of planets. Yet, when Garuda sought solace in play, their fear overcame them, and they sank their fangs into his flesh. Powerless as they were to harm him, their incessant biting gnawed at his patience. At last, unable to bear their torment any longer, Garuda turned to his mother and inquired about their servitude. She revealed the wager made long ago.

THE SOURCE OF CONFLICT

Fueled by a desire to break free from the shackles of servitude, Garuda approached the serpents with a proposition. "Give me a task, a chore that I can fulfill, one that will liberate me from this eternal bondage," he beseeched them. The Nagas pondered over his words, and after much contemplation, they spoke. "Retrieve for us the Amrita, the immortal nectar churned from the ocean. We, too, are great beings, children of Kashyapa, and yet we remain overshadowed by the worship bestowed upon the gods. Grant us the Amrita, and let the world pay homage to our might."

And thus, the stage was set for Garuda's epic quest, his path fraught with perils and challenges, as he embarked on a mission to obtain the coveted Amrita for the Nagas. The fate of Garuda, the Nagas, and the very fabric of existence intertwined in a grand tapestry of myth and destiny.

Garuda, resolute in his mission, sought counsel from his father, Kashyapa, as he prepared to venture into the realm of the powerful Devas to claim the Amrita. Kashyapa imparted upon him the importance of consuming the right nourishment. In the ethereal realm of Bhurloka, where the laws of nature are altered, they encountered a grand spectacle. A colossal turtle and a massive elephant locked in a bitter feud, their rivalry born from a shared history of animosity in a past life. Despite their pious origins in Bhurloka, their envy and anger had consigned them to existence as animals.

Garuda, undeterred, seized the opportunity before him. He devoured both the turtle and the elephant, absorbing their strength and fortitude into his being. With every bite, he grew mightier, his resolve unyielding.

Meanwhile, the Devas, attuned to the art of interpreting omens, began to perceive signs of impending calamity. Alarmed, they sought the guidance of their venerable guru, Brihaspati, who deciphered the portents. The omens spoke of an audacious attempt to steal the nectar of immortality, and Brihaspati cautioned the Devas to guard the precious elixir at all costs. The Devas, armed with their celestial weaponry, meticulously devised a secure chamber replete with intricate traps to safeguard the Amrita.

Curiosity gnawed at Indra, the leader of the Devas, prompting him to approach Brihaspati in search of answers. The sage, ever wise, reminded Indra of a forgotten tale, the very origin of Garuda and the subsequent challenge he posed to the celestial king. In the grand tapestry of the Mahabharata, every event unfolded for a reason, interconnected by an intricate web of causes and effects.

The story harkened back to a time when Kashyapa performed a grand Yajna, and all desired to contribute. Indra, as the son of Kashyapa, sought to assist by supplying fuel for the sacred fire. Laden with a colossal mound of wood, he strode forth. In that very moment, the diminutive sages known as the Valakiliyas, no larger than a thumb, also yearned to contribute. United in purpose, these five or six tiny sages carried a dry leaf, which had inadvertently lodged itself within a cow's hoofprint.

As fate would have it, Indra chanced upon this peculiar scene. He beheld the minuscule sages clutching the leaf, their efforts paling in comparison to his monumental burden of wood. A condescending smirk crept across his face, and he derisively laughed at their seemingly insignificant contribution. Enraged by Indra's disdainful mockery, the sages, despite their diminutive stature, possessed a reservoir of Brahmin tejas, accumulated through their rigorous austerities.

Thus, the sages cast their curse upon Lord Indra, proclaiming the birth of another who would supersede him in might, a new Indra a thousandfold more powerful. This successor would wield superior rulership and bring about Indra's humiliation, serving as a stern reminder that one's stature does not determine their worth.

Indra, stricken with fear, sought the counsel of Kashyapa, who, in turn, approached the Valakiliyas, urging them to reconsider their curse. Kashyapa reminded them of the divine order established by Lord Brahma, emphasizing the potential chaos that would ensue from the creation of another Indra. Responding to this plea, the Valakiliyas proposed a revised destiny for Garuda. They ordained that he would become an Indra among the avian species, a mighty bird who would confront and humble the current Indra.

Thus, Garuda, the chosen one, emerged. Despite being an eternal companion of Lord Vishnu, his descent to the mortal realm was part of a divine play, a lila. Anantasesha, the elder brother of Vasuki, who had renounced his claim to the serpent kingdom, was chosen by Vishnu to serve as his celestial bed. In this way, even spiritual personalities like Anantasesha manifest in the material realm to set an example for others.

Upon learning of Garuda's arrival and his destined victory, Indra, being a Kshatriya, refused to cower before any perceived threat. The gods assembled, donning their gleaming armor and wielding their formidable weapons, surrounding a vault encircled by roaring flames.

As Garuda swooped down, his massive wings creating a tumultuous dust storm, he swiftly attacked the Devas, biting, clawing, and thrashing them with relentless force. The gods were scattered, tossed about, bruised, and bloodied in an instant. Though the Devas attempted to resist, they were swiftly overcome by Garuda's might. In no time, they were forced to retreat, fleeing in panic. Witnessing the wall of fire encircling the vault, Garuda devised a solution.

With his myriad of heads, he reached the Akshaganga, the celestial Ganga river that flowed through the heavenly abode of the Devas before descending to the earthly plane. He drank the river's water into his many mouths, transforming himself into a living hydrant, and extinguished the raging flames. With the barrier vanquished, Garuda ventured inside the vault, where he encountered a spinning wheel adorned with a hundred blades, each spoke a lethal weapon.

Utilizing his extraordinary siddhis, Garuda diminished himself to a microscopic size, allowing him to traverse the narrow gaps between the blades. On the other side awaited formidable guardians, colossal serpents exuding such toxicity that a mere gaze from them could spell instant death. However, Garuda, swift as thought, dispatched the guardians before they could even perceive his presence. With the path cleared, he obtained the coveted Amrita and, displaying his prowess, shattered the wheel before soaring out of the vault with his prize.

As Garuda soared through the skies, carrying the precious Amrita, Indra pursued him with determination. With a mighty throw, Indra hurled his thunderbolt at Garuda, striking his wing. To Indra's astonishment, only a single feather fell from Garuda's wing. Intrigued, Indra questioned the bird, "How is it that you possess such incredible strength?" Garuda, displaying his humility, replied, "Out of respect for Rishi Dadhichi, whose bones were used to forge your Vajra scepter, I dropped a feather. In truth, I did not even need to do so." With those words, Garuda continued his flight, leaving Indra behind.

As Garuda journeyed onwards, he encountered Lord Vishnu himself. Impressed by Garuda's prowess in battle, Vishnu approached him and asked if he would serve as his personal carrier. Honored by this request, Garuda gladly accepted the divine invitation, forging an eternal bond with Vishnu.

As Garuda neared the Nagas, who awaited the nectar of immortality, Indra humbly approached him, beseeching him not to give the

Amrita to the serpents. Garuda, recognizing his duty to free himself from bondage, expressed his intention to offer the nectar to the Nagas. However, Indra pleaded for assistance, unable to allow the serpents to possess such power. Understanding Indra's predicament, Garuda assured him that he would find a solution.

Approaching the Nagas, Garuda placed the pot of Amrita on a mat made of Kusha grass. Delighted, the serpents expressed their gratitude. Sensing an opportunity, Garuda inquired, "Am I now released from my bondage to you?" The Nagas eagerly affirmed his freedom. However, Garuda cunningly suggested that they purify themselves through a bath before partaking in the nectar. Obliging his request, the Nagas left to cleanse themselves, leaving the pot unattended.

Seizing the moment, Indra stealthily approached and, under Garuda's watchful gaze, retrieved the nectar, silently departing. Garuda, no longer bound by his connection to the Nagas, had no need to intervene. When the serpents returned and questioned Garuda about the turn of events, he explained that Indra had arrived and, weary from his arduous adventures, Garuda could not prevent him from taking the nectar. Unaware of the truth, the Nagas began licking the drops of nectar that had fallen on the Kusha grass mat.

Unbeknownst to them, Kusha grass possesses sharp edges, earning it the name "sword grass." As the Nagas licked the nectar, their tongues were lacerated by the grass, resulting in their distinctive forked tongues that can be observed in snakes to this day.

Thus concludes the remarkable tale of Garuda, his valiant battles, and his instrumental role in the events surrounding the Amrita.

Chapter 3

THE STORY OF ASTIKYA

As the Rishis pondered over the fate of the snakes and their sacrifice, their curiosity grew. They sought to learn whether all the snakes had perished in the fire and, if not, why they had been spared. Suta Goswami continued his narration, revealing the unfolding events.

Faced with the impending danger of the sacrifice, the snakes grew fearful and contemplated ways to escape their fate. They knew that kings held great respect for Brahmins and recalled the story of Vamana, who had approached King Bali and secured a boon. Inspired by this, they devised a plan: they would marry into Brahmin families, and a Brahmin, well-connected to the kings, would intercede on their behalf and put an end to the sacrificial rituals.

In the midst of this dilemma, a sage named Jatakratu entered the scene. He was deeply committed to his ascetic practices and wandered through the forest. One day, he had a vision—a vision of a deep pit with a tree hanging over it. From that tree dangled his departed father, grandfather, and ancestors, suspended by a fragile thread. Curious and concerned, Jatakratu inquired about their predicament.

The ancestors explained, "We hang over this chasm, representing rebirth into the world. It is your tapas, your austerities, that keeps us suspended by a thread. Yet, true piety lies in having children. If our lineage is broken and you pass away without a son, we will all fall into this pit. To save us, you must have a child."

Though sympathetic, Jatakratu hesitated. He declared that he would only marry someone with the same name as himself, and if the marriage displeased him, he would instantly return to his life as an ascetic. He was known for his stern and uncompromising nature. Despite his resolution, Jatakratu embarked on a search for a suitable wife. However, he could not find anyone within the community of Rishis who shared his name.

Disheartened and in a sour mood, Jatakratu sat down and uttered, "If my austerities have pleased the deities and living entities, I demand a wife with the same name." It was at this moment that Vasuki, the king of the serpents, appeared before him. Vasuki proposed, "I have a younger sister named Jatakratu. You may marry her." The sage agreed to this proposal, thus accepting Vasuki's sister as his wife.

In the days of yore, in the heartland of ancient India, there lived a man named Jatakratu, a scion of the Brahmin lineage. He had wedded a maiden, a daughter of the Naga clan, who bore the same name as her kin. Their union was one forged in the tapestry of fate, and they shared a life together in a realm where the terrestrial and celestial realms intertwined.

Jatakratu, a fervent practitioner of the sacred agnihotra, an offering to the divine fire, performed this ritual with unwavering devotion three times each day. But one fateful afternoon, as the sun's fiery gaze began its descent toward the horizon, fatigue overcame him, and he surrendered to a deep slumber. His wife, she of the Naga blood, stood at a crossroads of decision.

Torn between her husband's fiery temper and his potential vexation at being roused from his repose, she pondered the righteous path to tread. She chose to awaken him, for duty weighed heavily upon her conscience. Yet, as Jatakratu stirred from his dreams, wrath engulfed him like a tempest, and he unleashed his fury upon her.

In the throes of his rage, he departed abruptly, leaving behind a heartbroken Naga princess, his wife, to grapple with the tempestuous nature of her chosen mate. For Jatakratu was not a man meant for the tranquil hearth of domesticity; his temper was a tempest that raged unchecked.

Distraught and forlorn, the Naga princess sought solace in the embrace of her brother Vasuki, the serpent king. Tearfully, she recounted the tale of her husband's sudden departure, for she bore a child within her womb—a child who carried within him the blood of both Brahmin and Naga.

Vasuki, ever the wise and protective brother, vowed to shield his sister and her unborn progeny. He provided for her every need, offering solace in her hour of despair. And when the appointed time came, she brought forth a son, whom she named Astikya—a child of dual heritage, destined to walk a unique path.

Astikya, bearing the legacy of both Brahmin and Naga, was raised in the ways of the Brahmins, a reflection of his noble lineage. Time flowed like a river, and the world changed around him.

In the fullness of time, a new Chapter in their tale unfolded. King Janamejaya, a ruler of great renown, sought to perform a grand fire sacrifice, a spectacle of divine proportions, following the epic events of the Mahabharata. But as the flames leapt skyward, a calamity unfolded—a multitude of serpents descended into the inferno, their lives consumed in the raging fire.

Astikya, now a grown man of wisdom and grace, stepped forward, for it was the king's sacred duty to offer charity to visiting Brahmins. He approached King Janamejaya and laid before him a humble request: to halt the all-consuming sacrifice.

In the hallowed chambers of the royal court, there arose a murmur of hesitation and deliberation among the wise and learned. But in the end, the king, bound by the dharma of hospitality, acceded to Astikya's plea. The sacrifice was ceased, and thus, the serpent race was spared from utter annihilation—a testament to the power of lineage and the enduring strength of blood ties in the annals of ancient India.

Chapter 4
THE GODS ASK VISHNU TO DESCEND

After hearing about the events following the snake sacrifice, the sages requested Sutagoswami to narrate the Mahabharata as it was told by Vaisampayana to King Janamejaya. The story begins with a gathering of all the Devas, summoned by Lord Brahma, on the shore of the milk ocean. Mother Earth addressed the Devas, expressing her distress over the demons who had been reborn on Earth, engaging in sinful activities. She implored the Devas to help her in dealing with this situation.

Realizing their failure to protect the Earth, the Devas became alarmed. Lord Brahma then instructed them to descend to Earth and send their "amshas," which means portions or energies, to be born in different royal dynasties and species. According to Madhvacarya, the Pandavas are considered amshas of these deities. Yudhishthira is an amsha of Yama/Dharma, Bhima of Vayu, Arjuna of Indra, and Nakula and Sahadeva of the Ashvins.

Upon hearing this, the Devas became excited. Indra and the other Devas went from the shore of the milk ocean to Swetadvipa, where Lord Vishnu was resting. The Devas began praying, and Vishnu opened his eyes and inquired about their desire. The Devas expressed their intention to descend to Earth and fight the demons, requesting Vishnu to join them in this adventure. Vishnu agreed and asked the chief deities, like Indra, to remain behind. They discussed various plans and the roles of different Devas in the upcoming events.

Karna, who was an amsha of Surya, plays a unique role in the Mahabharata. Madhvacarya makes an interesting observation in his commentary, comparing Karna to Vali in the Ramayana. Vali was an enemy of Lord Rama and an amsha of Indra, while Sugriva was a close friend and devotee of Rama, being an amsha of Surya. In the Mahabharata, the roles are reversed, where Karna, an amsha of Surya, becomes the adversary, and Arjuna, an amsha of Indra, becomes the friend of Lord Krishna. Additionally, Karna possessed not only a portion of Surya but also had the soul of a demon.

Suta continued to speak about the divine identities of various characters. The Pandavas' identities were already discussed. Duryodhana represented sin personified, Kali. His brothers were incarnations of demons. Drupada and Virata were incarnations of the Marutas, storm gods. Abhimanyu was an incarnation of a son of Chandra (the Moon). Dronacharya was an amsha of Brihaspati, the teacher of the Devas.

Karna, a formidable warrior, was not merely an Amsha of Surya, but harbored the very soul of a demon known as Sahasrakavacha. In ancient times, demons would embark on tapasya, rigorous penance, to acquire boons and conquer the mighty Indra. While Brahma and Shiva surpassed Indra in power, other celestial beings paled in comparison. This particular demon undertook a formidable tapasya, beseeching the gods for an armor of unparalleled strength. Thus, he obtained a magnificent armor comprising a thousand impenetrable layers, earning him the name Sahasrakavacha, the one adorned with a thousand armors. Each layer possessed such formidable protection that breaking even a single layer meant certain death. Moreover, shattering a layer necessitated a year of intense tapa.

Confident in his invincibility, Sahasrakavacha became an indomitable force. However, it was Nara-Narayana Rishi who dared to challenge him. The sagacious rishis discovered a mystical place in Badrikashram where a day of tapasya was equivalent to a year's penance. Exploiting this boon, they engaged Sahasrakavacha in battle. Cunningly, one of the rishis would feign death, while the other would resurrect him through a day of tapasya. This process continued in rotation, gradually chipping away at the layers of Sahasrakavacha's armor. Over time, all but one layer remained intact. Realizing his impending doom, the demon sought sanctuary with Lord Surya, for the Sun god epitomized the valorous Kshatriya code.

The Kshatriya ethic demanded unwavering protection and shelter to anyone seeking it, regardless of their status as friend or foe. This noble principle extended even to the granting of material possessions. Great sages like Vishvamitra, who possessed Kshatriya origins before attaining sagehood, were deeply ingrained with this ethos. Vishvamitra would grant the most arduous of boons to those who approached him, undeterred by the challenges they presented. Such was his benevolence that he bestowed a fraction of his earned merit to a man who desired entry into Swarga, propelling the man directly to heaven. But when the gods rejected the man's presence in Swarga, Vishvamitra, displaying his power, raised his hand to form the constellation known as the Little Dipper, providing a celestial abode for the man.

When Sahasrakavacha, the demon, beseeched Surya for protection, Nara-Narayana Rishi found themselves unable to harm him, bound by the Kshatriya code. Consequently, the demon's soul was reborn as Karna, infused with the essence of the Sun god. Karna, possessing the heart of a demon, evokes diverse sentiments, with some considering him a hero while others revere him. Translations of his tale often omit the more nefarious deeds he committed. Nonetheless, being a demon, Karna ultimately met his demise.

Shalya, the uncle of Nakula and Sahadeva, born to Madri, possessed incredible might and was an embodiment of power bestowed by Vayu, the wind god. Among the strongest men on Earth, the distinguished group included Krishna, Balarama, Duryodhana, Bhima, Karna, Kichaka, and Jarasandha.

These backgrounds shed light on the individuals involved, revealing that what may seem like trivial conflicts among petty kings encompasses far more significant elements. The battles between Devas (celestial beings) and Asuras (demons) transcend earthly boundaries, dictating the destiny of the entire universe. Furthermore, the interactions between the Lord and His devotees within the epic showcase profound examples of bhakti (devotion). Overlooking these fundamental aspects reduces the narrative to a mere story, offering only mundane moral lessons at best. Serious contemplation, guided by a knowledgeable acharya—a direct disciple of Vyasa, the author of the Mahabharata—can unravel profound insights and attract individuals to the path of spirituality.

Chapter 5

THE STORY OF KACHA

In an age both distant and near, when the clash between demons and devas was an all-too-familiar sight, an extraordinary mantra by the name of Sanjivani existed. This sacred incantation, held by Sukracharya, possessed the power to resurrect the departed. The devas grew wary, for their guru, Brihaspati, did not possess this potent knowledge. "Our adversaries possess this arcane technique while we remain devoid," they fretted. Determined to rectify this imbalance, the devas turned to Kacha, son of Brihaspati, seeking his aid. "Go forth," they beseeched him, "become the disciple of Sukracharya and acquire the Sanjivani for our cause."

At first, Kacha hesitated, recognizing the dangers that lay ahead. After all, this mission involved infiltrating the enemy camp and studying under their preceptor. Yet, Sukracharya was no vile being.

On the contrary, he possessed a noble and liberal nature that had led him to assume the role of guru for the demons. A broad-minded Brahmin, he harbored no innate bias between good and evil. When the demons approached him, seeking his guidance, he simply agreed, lacking a preconceived notion of morality. The devas gambled on this open-mindedness, hoping that Sukracharya's generosity of knowledge would extend even to Kacha's request.

It is worth noting that Sukracharya also ruled over the planet Venus, hence the name "Shukra" in Vedic astrology. In a similar vein, Brihaspati's dominion over Jupiter earned him the title of "Guru," as he guided the devas. Thus, Thursday came to be known as "Guruvar," signifying the day of Jupiter, while Friday was called "Shukravar," representing the day of Venus. There exists a linguistic connection when examining the names in Latin and other romance languages.

And so, Kacha approached Sukracharya, expressing his desire to become the guru's disciple. Sukracharya, pleased with the request, initially hesitated but eventually accepted him. Seeking to ensure his safety and secure the favor of his guru, Kacha devised an intriguing plan. He would entertain Sukracharya's daughter, Devayani, with his melodious music, effectively charming her. However, being a brahmachari, a celibate student, Kacha maintained a respectful distance, refraining from pursuing any further romantic inclinations.

But the demons remained skeptical, whispering among themselves, "We know his true intentions. These gods harbor some sinister scheme." And indeed, their suspicions held merit. Thus, they hatched a plan. As part of his student duties, Kacha would venture into the forest to gather wood for the sacred fire. Additionally, he tended to Sukracharya's cows. Consequently, he spent a considerable amount of time away from home.

Seizing the opportune moment, the demons confronted Kacha in the wilderness, accusing him of treachery. "We are well aware of your deceit," they hissed, before slaying him where he stood. The cows returned without him, and Devayani, alarmed by his absence, hastened to inform her father. "Father, the cows have returned, but Kacha is nowhere to be found!" she exclaimed. Deeply concerned, Sukracharya embarked on a search, eventually discovering Kacha's lifeless form. Employing the Sanjivani mantra, he breathed life back into his fallen disciple.

So the demons, driven by their fury, persisted in their attempts, a cycle that seemed unending. Time and again, they would slay Kacha, only for Sukracharya to find him and resurrect him—a gruesome existence, to say the least. Fortunately, Devayani played a pivotal role in urging Sukracharya to take action, for he often remained passive in such matters.

But the demons grew resolute, realizing that they needed to ensure Kacha's permanent demise. Thus, they devised a scheme to prevent his return. They killed Kacha, reduced him to ashes, ground him into a fine powder, and surreptitiously mixed it into Shukracharya's evening wine. Unbeknownst to the guru, he imbibed the wine, unaware of the presence of Kacha's essence within. Once again, Kacha did not return, prompting a search that proved futile. However, possessing profound awareness and mystical vision, Shukracharya delved into the depths of his being and discovered Kacha's presence within himself. He shared this revelation with Devayani, confessing, "I cannot bring him back, for if I do, Kacha will emerge from me and slay me." Astonishingly, Kacha, who belonged to a realm beyond human existence, retained a modicum of consciousness. He communicated with Shukracharya, saying, "Teach me Sanjivani, and when I emerge from you, I will revive you." Though hesitant, they eventually struck an agreement. Shukracharya imparted the mantra to Kacha, who then brought him back to life, emerging from within and inadvertently ending Shukracharya's life in the process. Nevertheless, Kacha swiftly resurrected his guru.

However, this turn of events granted Kacha possession of the Sanjivani mantra. In due course, he revealed to Shukracharya that he longed for his home and wearied of being perpetually slain by the demons. Such sentiments seemed justified, one must admit. Consequently, Kacha began his journey homeward. Yet, before long, Devayani caught up with him, reproachful in her tone. "What about us?" she cried. "I thought we would be together. I pleaded with my father to revive you for this reason." Kacha, however, replied, "I can only regard you as my sister. For a guru is like a father, and you are his daughter." Devayani grew incensed and filled with anger, cursing Kacha. She declared that although he possessed the knowledge to teach mantras to others, they would be rendered useless if he ever attempted to employ them. Enraged by her curse, Kacha retorted, "If you, blameless as I am, curse me, then I shall curse you in return. Despite being the daughter of a powerful Brahmin, you shall wed beneath your caste, for you cannot conduct yourself with the dignity befitting a respectable woman."

Devayani, consumed by sorrow, sought solace in the company of her friend, the demon princess Sharmishtha. However, the latter offered no comfort, as demons were inherently self-centered, and Sharmishtha proved to be no exception. Filled with anger, she lashed out at Devayani, exclaiming, "Because of your infatuation with that boy, our enemies now possess the Sanjivani mantra. Your father, who serves my father, has betrayed us." Their argument escalated, and in a fit of rage, Sharmishtha pushed Devayani into a deep, dry well, rendering her unable to climb out.

Devayani wept in the well while a king named Yayati rode by. He was the son of Nahusha and a descendant of Pururava, whose lineage stretched back to Buddha, the lord of the planet Mercury and the son of Soma, the Moon God. Yayati hailed from a race of people blessed with longevity, their lives spanning thousands upon thousands of years. Upon hearing Devayani's cries, he dismounted his horse and extended his hand into the well, effortlessly pulling her out.

Grateful and relieved, Devayani conveyed her gratitude to Yayati and hastened to inform her father of the incident. Sukracharya, the guru of the demons, confronted the king and stated, "Firstly, you repeatedly mutilated my disciple, driving him away from me. Then, your daughter insulted and belittled my own daughter, claiming that I am your servant. I now comprehend your true regard for me, so find yourself a new guru, for I shall depart."

The demon king trembled in fear at these words, for the guru bestows power through sacred rituals such as Agnihotra. He pleaded and implored Sukracharya, promising to fulfill any request. Succumbing to the situation, Sukracharya declared, "It is my daughter who has suffered the greatest offense. Consult her." Thus, all the demons bowed before Devayani, and the demon king proposed that Sharmishtha become her maidservant—an arrangement to which Devayani agreed.

Chapter 6

THE STORY OF YAYATI

―――∾∾―――

Devayani, daughter of Shukracharya, and Sharmishtha, princess of the demons, had an unusual arrangement. Sharmishtha became Devayani's slave, fulfilling the condition set by Devayani's father. On one occasion, Devayani and a few other demonesses found themselves in a forest when Yayati, the king, happened to pass by. Devayani, still captivated by the memory of Yayati rescuing her from the well, and being untouched by any man other than her father, found herself falling in love with him. The other girls gathered around, bashful and shy, as Devayani expressed her desire for marriage, stating that he was the only man who had held her hand besides her father. Yayati, initially hesitant due to Devayani's high lineage as the daughter of Shukracharya, a powerful sage, eventually agreed, seeing the benefits of the alliance despite his lower social status as a ksatria. However, he stipulated that

Devayani's servant, Sharmishtha, could never be with them to avoid hurting Devayani's feelings.

Thus, Yayati and Devayani were united in marriage, and he ruled over his kingdom. This was a time long ago, at the dawn of the Treta Yuga, in the Chandra Dynasty. Yayati's palace was a grand abode adorned with magnificent trees, and its innermost section held a pleasure garden, exclusively inhabited by the women of the palace, serving as his private quarters. The outer palace was where the king received visitors, while none were permitted to enter the inner sanctum. Sharmishtha, being confined to the pleasure garden, felt a deep sense of loneliness. In the course of time, when she reached a thousand years of age, she reached puberty.

Overwhelmed by her solitude, Sharmishtha approached Yayati, pleading for him to grant her a child. Yayati was apprehensive, for he had been explicitly instructed not to do so. She lamented, revealing her predicament of not being allowed to marry anyone since no man could enter the pleasure garden. Her life would be in vain without offspring. Yayati initially hesitated, considering his duties as a ksatriya. It was the ksatriya's responsibility to protect and provide for all women in society. If an unmarried woman sought the hand of a ksatriya, it was his duty to oblige. This form of marriage was known as Ghandarvavivaha, a love marriage prevalent among ksatriyas. Sharmishtha invoked Yayati's kshatriya dharma, emphasizing that his refusal would bring upon him the sin of denying her motherhood. Succumbing to the weight of her plea and swayed by her beauty, Yayati relented and agreed, thus fathering their first son.

Yayati and Devayani had a total of five children together. The eldest was named Yadhu, born to Devayani, while the youngest was called Puru. Yayati also had a son named Yavan, from whom the race of Yavanas originated. Yavan was given dominion over the regions encompassing Greece, Turkey, and the Middle East, and anyone from those lands came to be known as Yavanas. However, it was Yadu, the oldest son, who was initially destined to inherit the kingdom. But fate took an unexpected turn, and it was Puru who eventually became the chosen heir.

The events that led to this change occurred while Devayani and Yayati were strolling in the pleasure garden. Sharmishtha, having borne children to Yayati, brought them forward, and the little ones, recognizing him as their father, embraced his legs. Devayani, witnessing this scene, grew angry and demanded an explanation. Despite attempts to keep the children away, Yayati confessed that they were indeed his offspring. Devayani's fury intensified upon learning the truth and feeling insulted by Sharmishtha. She ran off, seeking solace with her father, Shukracharya.

Devayani sought comfort from another man and bore children with him. Yayati possessed a pleasure garden filled with courtesans, but jealousy did not arise from that quarter. Devayani approached her father, pouring out her heartache. Shukracharya, furious at Yayati for disregarding his command, cursed him. The sage proclaimed that even though Yayati remained in the prime of his life, his mind had succumbed to lust, and thus, he would be transformed into an old man.

Yayati's youthfulness waned, and he rapidly aged, becoming an elderly man. Sorrow gripped his heart, and Devayani, too, lamented the loss of her youthful and handsome husband. Distraught, she confided in her father, who devised a solution. Shukracharya informed them that Devayani could regain her husband's youth, but the exchange required finding a willing participant who would bear Yayati's old age. They approached Yadu, Yayati's son from his chief queen, and proposed the exchange. However, Yadu declined the offer, earning himself a curse from Yayati. The curse decreed that

Yadu and his descendants would never ascend to the throne of their dynasty, despite their potential as rulers.

Similar encounters ensued with Yayati's other children, who also rejected the proposition. Consequently, they were assigned unfavorable and undesirable territories to rule. Yavan, however, agreed to accept the kingdom of the Yavanas, which encompassed regions around Turkey, Greece, and the Middle East. Thus, the term "Yavanas" emerged to describe those dwelling in those lands. Puru, being the sole child to accept the exchange, became the chosen heir, the yuvaraja, and eventually fathered Bharata, establishing the Bharata Dynasty. The lineage continued with Kuru, which explains the origin of the Kauravas.

Yayati found contentment and harmony in his relationships with both Sharmishtha and Devayani. As a result, he would embark on journeys, traversing various realms with his wives. Being married to Sharmishtha, the daughter of Shukracharya, and Devayani, the daughter of the king of Asuras, who were an extraterrestrial race of demons, Yayati possessed a vimana, a celestial flying chariot. Over a span of a thousand years, he would explore these celestial realms, accompanied by his wives.

Yayati's exceptionally long life was attributed to his existence during the Treta Yuga, an era that followed the birth of Pururava, the founder of the first human dynasty. Although Pururava's story is not detailed in the Mahabharata, it is recounted in the Bhagavatam and other Puranic texts. Yayati's timeline coincided with the early stages of the Treta Yuga, running parallel to the time of Lord Rama, who hailed from the solar dynasty. While Rama's lineage traces back to Manu in the Satya Yuga, the Chandra dynasty, to which Yayati belonged, emerged just before the Treta Yuga. Thus, these events unfolded in different periods within the overarching framework of the Yugas.

The lifespans during the Treta Yuga were considerably long, spanning tens of thousands of years, whereas the preceding Satya Yuga witnessed lifespans in the hundreds of thousands of years. Yayati, along with the people of his time, enjoyed an extended existence, allowing for ample experiences and fulfillment. However, Yayati's life took a significant turn when, after a thousand years of exploration, he willingly relinquished his youthful form, embracing his old age once again. Renouncing all his worldly possessions, he retreated to the mountains, adopting the life of a yogi. Fully dedicated to his new path, Yayati delved into meditation and performed agni hotra, gradually renouncing material pleasures and subsisting on meager sustenance. Ultimately, he shed his mortal body, ascending to Svarga, the celestial abode.

However, Yayati's stay in Svarga took an interesting twist, as Indra, known for his penchant for testing individuals, presented a challenge to Yayati. Indra questioned Yayati, asking him to identify someone who had performed greater austerities than himself. Arrogantly surveying the surroundings, Yayati declared that he saw no one surpassing him in austerity. In that very moment, he began to descend. Witnessing Yayati's fall, Indra realized the arrogance hidden within his response. At this point, Yayati pleaded with Indra, requesting that if he was to be cast out, he should at least be reunited with his ancestors. Indra, heeding his plea, granted Yayati's wish. Yayati descended from the celestial realm, still possessing his celestial form, typically leading to descent into Rasatala, where the person would be slain, transform into a raindrop, and eventually be reborn through the cycle of life.

As Yayati plummeted through the realms, fate intervened, and he found himself landing not in the abyss of Rasatala, but in the vicinity of his ancestral lineage. Ah, his descendants, a web of bloodlines stretching through time. And among them stood Shibi, a renowned king, known to many.

Now, let me tell you a tale of Shibi, though it may not be precisely situated within this part of the Mahabharata. But fear not, for it shall acquaint you with the man. The gods, in their whims, often test the mettle of mortals, to ascertain if they match their lofty words. And so it was that Indra and Agni conspired, assuming the forms of a hawk and a pigeon, respectively, and took to the skies.

The pigeon, a messenger of the gods, sought refuge from Shibi, a valiant Kshatriya king. A talking pigeon, mind you. Astonishing, indeed. Undeterred by this curious circumstance, Shibi welcomed the feathered creature with a nonchalant air. But then, a hawk, a predator, approached, demanding his due as the king who sustains all. This hawk declared the pigeon to be his rightful prey, demanding sustenance.

The king offered various morsels, but the hawk found them inadequate. Thus, Shibi, resolved to fulfill his duty of protection, made a staggering decision. He would sever flesh from his very own body, an amount equal to the weight of the pigeon, to satiate the hawk's hunger. And so, a grand scale was prepared, with the pigeon placed upon one end.

With unwavering resolve, Shibi began to slice off chunks of his own flesh, placing them upon the scale. But such was the extent of his sacrifice that a mere pigeon could not balance the scale. Undeterred, Shibi, the embodiment of selflessness, offered his entire being. For a king, the vow to protect comes at the cost of one's own life. And thus, he seated himself upon the scale, surrendering his very existence.

In that profound moment, the hawk and pigeon shed their disguises, revealing themselves as none other than Indra and Agni. They paid homage to the great king, acknowledging his unparalleled valor. "You are a great king," they proclaimed. Filled with awe, Shibi, true to his kingly nature, requested a boon. Yet, he reminded them that duty should never be performed for the sake of rewards. Still, if they were inclined to be benevolent, he asked for the restoration of his entire being.

And so, the gods, recognizing the nobility within Shibi's heart, granted his request. Such was the tale of Shibi, sitting there amidst his yagna, his sacrificial fire ablaze.

It was during this time that Yayati, descending from the heavens, caught the attention of Shibi and his progenitors. Curiosity sparked their conversation, leading Yayati to explain his presence in this earthly realm known as Bhama Hell, the realm of mortals. Pride, he revealed, was the prime cause for their incarceration in this earthly inferno. But if one could rid oneself of pride, liberation from this realm would follow. Yayati, having been sent down due to his own pride, had learned this truth through his experiences. Often, those exalted individuals merely required a gentle awakening.

Shibi, saddened by Yayati's plight, acknowledged the greatness of the fallen king, recognizing the blood ties that connected them. Shibi, ever selfless, offered his accumulated merit, his punya, to Yayati, willing to relinquish it all so that he could reclaim his place in the heavens. A profound exchange transpired between them, where Yayati, humbled, initially declined the offering. But Shibi, bound by the ties of lineage and duty, refused to abandon his forefather. Eventually, through their exchange, Shibi bestowed his punya upon Yayati, allowing him to ascend once more to the celestial realms.

And so it came to pass, Yayati reclaimed his rightful abode, while Shibi embarked on his own destined path. Thus, concludes the story of Yayati, a tale woven with love, desire, curses, redemption, and the invaluable lessons unearthed along the way.

Chapter 7

The Story of King Bharata

Well, after Yayati's departure, the reigns of kingship passed into the hands of several rulers, one of whom was Dushyanta. This sturdy king, accustomed to a life of valor and masculinity, embarked on a hunting expedition while also seeking wisdom from the sages dwelling in the asrama. As he traversed the countryside, he slew tigers, rhinos, and various other creatures, marking his path towards the sacred Kapila Ashram.

Arriving at the hermitage, Dushyanta beheld a diverse gathering of individuals. Some practiced astrology, others engaged in agnihotra, yoga, or karma. Each person pursued their own path, living harmoniously, without interfering in one another's affairs. It was a testament to the coexistence of diverse ideologies, for that is the way it ought to be. Dushyanta's eyes scanned the gathering, seeking a

THE SOURCE OF CONFLICT

particular sage. And there, instead of the sage, stood a bewitching maiden who answered his query by saying, "I am Shakuntala, daughter of Brahmarishi Vishwamitra."

Curiosity sparked within Dushyanta as he expressed his surprise, "I was unaware that the sage had a wife. Pray, who are you?" To this, the maiden responded, "Nay, noble king, I am his daughter. Allow me to explain how this came to be."

She began her tale, introducing herself as Shakuntala, the offspring of Brahmarishi Vishwamitra, the mighty sage who had undertaken rigorous tapasya. Fearing that Vishwamitra's ascetic power might threaten his throne, Indra dispatched Menaka, a celestial nymph, to seduce the sage. Menaka danced and enticed Vishwamitra, ultimately ensnaring his heart. Utilizing his mystical abilities, the sage transformed himself into a youthful and handsome form, dazzling Menaka with celestial marvels. His hermitage turned into a golden palace adorned with celestial splendors, as he exerted his immense power. However, such displays depleted his tapasya, the very wellspring of his strength.

For a thousand years, Vishwamitra and Menaka reveled in their celestial love, though it passed like a fleeting day for him. But as fate would have it, Menaka conceived a child, which left Vishwamitra disconcerted. Realizing the implications of his actions, he mourned the loss of his ascetic goals. How could he, a sage aspiring to rival the great Vishwamitra himself, succumb to the life of a householder? Menaka, too, sensed the disruption her pregnancy caused, and being an apsara, a celestial nymph, she departed, leaving the child behind. Vishwamitra, faced with the dilemma of caring for an infant while maintaining his spiritual pursuits, sought out another sage and entrusted him with the upbringing of the baby girl.

And so it was, Shakuntala, the product of these extraordinary circumstances, revealed her origins to Dushyanta. The king, captivated by her ethereal beauty, for the power of a Kshatriya lies not in words but in actions, found himself instantly smitten. Directly, without hesitation, he gazed into her eyes and asked, "Fair maiden, are you wedded to another?" Shakuntala replied, "Nay, noble king, I am not bound in matrimony." Encouraged by her response, Dushyanta made a proposal fit for a king, declaring, "Then, my dear, would you honor me by becoming my queen? I, Dushyanta, the ruler of the Chandra dynasty, shall provide for you, and together, we shall raise a worthy heir to the throne."

Shakuntala, caught between her aspirations and her loyalty to her adopted father, sought permission from Vishwamitra. But Dushyanta, eager to seal their union, urged her to forgo formalities and proceed with a Gandharva vivaha, a marriage without elaborate ceremonies. Overwhelmed by the prospect of leaving her humble abode for a royal palace, Shakuntala agreed, and the union was solemnized.

Soon after, Dushyanta, compelled by royal duties, departed for his palace, promising to summon Shakuntala at a later time. Alas, he left her behind. However, he assured her that he would send for her in due course. Days turned into weeks, and weeks into months, until Shakuntala's father returned from his meditation, his sage-like faculties sensing a change in the air.

Discovering the truth, Vishwamitra was not angered by his daughter's actions. Shakuntala recounted the entirety of events, for the words of a celestial nymph hold many mysteries and truths.

The community at the hermitage took great care of Shakuntala and her son. Despite her initial rejection and the absence of Dushyanta, they showed kindness and provided for her needs. Shakuntala's son, Bharat, displayed remarkable strength from an early age. Even as a small child of two or three years, he fearlessly confronted and defeated formidable creatures that posed a threat to the sages and their abode. Tigers, wild elephants, rhinos, bears—all succumbed to his incredible power. In those days, such animals roamed the jungles in abundance, creating challenges and dangers for the people dwelling in those lands. But Bharat's strength allowed him to safeguard the community.

Though Vishwamitra was physically distant, he continued to watch over Shakuntala and her son. His divine presence remained a guiding force in their lives. As Bharat grew older, around the age of six, Dushyanta still had not arrived. It was decided that Shakuntala should journey to the king's palace and present Bharat as his rightful child. Accompanied by Rishis and their wives, Shakuntala arrived at the palace, hoping for a joyous reunion.

However, upon seeing Shakuntala, Dushyanta seemed to have no recollection of their previous encounter. Doubts arose, for claiming an heir to the throne was no trivial matter, requiring substantial evidence and societal acceptance. Shakuntala's tale was intense and filled with hardships—a small orphan finding solace with a man who initially rejected her, only to be abandoned again. Overwhelmed by her emotions, Shakuntala shed tears, and Bharat, sensing his father's presence, ran up to him, clinging to his knee. In that poignant moment, Shakuntala exclaimed, accusing Dushyanta of having a hardened heart.

Suddenly, a voice boomed from the heavens, and some believed it to be Vishwamitra, the powerful sage and father of Shakuntala. The voice proclaimed that Bharat was indeed Dushyanta's true son and the rightful heir to the throne. This divine intervention solidified Bharat's claim, and the assembled witnesses accepted him as the heir of parent.

Shakuntala, now recognized as Dushyanta's wife, remained with him for the rest of her days. Although her early life had been fraught with challenges and rejections, she found happiness and fulfillment in the end. It is worth noting that Vishwamitra himself arrived to bless Bharat, proclaiming that the entire planet shall be known as Bharataloka in honor of his great and powerful son.

Thus, Shakuntala's journey from adversity to ultimate triumph serves as a testament to the weight of the world, its trials and tribulations, and the eventual fulfillment of one's deepest desires.

Chapter 8

SHANTANU AND GANGA

In the days of yore, when the Bharat dynasty held sway over the civilized world, there existed a rival kingdom—the Panchalas. These two mighty powers oft clashed in the arena of battle. Yet, it wasn't during the time of the illustrious Bharat, but in the epochs that followed, that the Panchalas achieved a stunning victory. They laid siege to Hastinapura, and the Bharatas, faced with impending defeat, were forced into retreat.

Their exodus led them to the arid lands of Rajasthan, where they sought refuge within the walls of a formidable mountain fortress. It was there, amidst the sheltering crags, that destiny took a twist. Within the confines of that fortress, a child was born, and he was anointed Kuru.

Kuru, a name that would resonate through the annals of history, emerged as a great hero. With indomitable spirit, he rallied the Bharatas and reclaimed the territories lost to the Panchalas. Thus, the Bharat dynasty, also known as the Karavas, was reestablished under the indomitable Kuru.

Kuru, a noble king in his own right, embarked upon a remarkable endeavor. He crafted a plow of pure gold and employed it in a grand yagna, plowing vast expanses of land, covering an area of fifty-two square miles or more. His tireless toil captured the attention of the gods themselves.

Inquisitive, the deities questioned Kuru's purpose. He explained that he had heard from learned sages that the future would be a time of dwindling religious principles. Therefore, he sought to create a sacred land, where even the most wayward souls could find their way to heaven with ease. Kuru's noble intentions moved the gods, and they granted his request, albeit with a condition.

The condition was thus: if individuals perished on that hallowed ground, their passage to Svarga, the heavenly realm, would be assured. And so, that place became known as Kurukshetra, the field of Kuru. People flocked there, drawn by the promise of a guaranteed path to heaven, whether they came to fight in battles or embark on pilgrimages.

But Kurukshetra had a history before Kuru's sanctification. It was the very place where Parashurama, the warrior sage, had once unleashed his wrath upon the Kshatriyas, making its soil his canvas for a macabre masterpiece of bloodshed.

Generations later, another great king would rise—Shantanu. His name bore the weight of his extraordinary gift—the royal touch. He possessed the ability to restore youth and vitality to the weary, old, and ailing with a mere touch.

One fateful day, while on a hunting expedition along the banks of the Ganga, Shantanu encountered a breathtakingly beautiful woman. Her presence bewitched him, and he was compelled to inquire if she was wed. She was not, and an impulsive proposal followed. But she made an unusual demand: Shantanu must never question her actions. Bound by his kingly oath, he agreed.

Their union bore fruit, but as each child arrived, the mother would carry them to the river's edge and cast them into the waters. Shantanu, unable to restrain himself, questioned her actions at the ninth child's birth, and she revealed her divine nature. She was Ganga, the goddess of the Ganges, and the children were the Vasus, cursed to be born on Earth due to a past transgression. All but one would return to the heavens instantly, while the leader, Mahabhisha, now Devavrata, had to endure a full human life.

Ganga departed with the child, promising to return him after a celestial education. Thus began the extraordinary saga of Shantanu and Ganga, a tale of love, sacrifice, and divine destinies that would shape the course of the Bharat dynasty.

Chapter 9
The Terrible Vow

After Ganga's enigmatic departure, Shantanu found himself in a desolate state. His heart ached with loneliness, and he yearned for the presence of his distant son. He would often wander to the banks of the Ganga, hoping against hope that she would reemerge from her watery domain. The river, you see, was her embodiment, her earthly form.

On one of his hunting expeditions, he found himself chasing a deer that led him to the river's edge. The Ganga, usually a mighty expanse, now lay dry before him, a sight that perplexed and troubled the king. For a ruler's duty was twofold: to provide shelter and sustenance for his subjects and to offer them means of livelihood. The Ganga's sudden disappearance carried grave implications for both.

As Shantanu contemplated this strange occurrence, he stumbled upon a youth, an archer of extraordinary skill, who was single-handedly diverting the river's flow with a barrage of arrows. Astonished by the lad's prowess, Shantanu watched in awe. But as the boy spotted the king, he vanished into thin air, leaving Shantanu bewildered once more.

Yet, the river soon resumed its course, and from its depths emerged Ganga, cradling the boy who had manipulated its flow. She proclaimed, "This is your son, Devavrata." The boy possessed celestial qualities, for he was none other than the offspring of the Ganga herself. His education had been completed, and now he was to reside with Shantanu.

Shantanu's heart brimmed with joy as he embraced his newfound son. Devavrata, half-god and half-mortal, was a paragon of strength and beauty, infused with mystical power. He had been trained by Parashurama, the martial incarnation of divinity, empowered by none other than Lord Krishna himself. Parashurama's story, chronicled in the Brahmanda Purana, spanned twenty-six

Chapter 10

A TESTAMENT TO HIS IMMENSE SIGNIFICANCE.

Devavrata brought boundless happiness to Shantanu's life. They shared countless moments of joy, engaging in the pursuits of Kshatriyas, such as hunting and other warrior-like endeavors. Shantanu, who had once been despondent, was now content.

One day, as they journeyed through the kingdom, Shantanu's mood darkened. He returned home with a heavy heart, and Devavrata, perceptive and concerned, inquired about the source of his father's sorrow. Shantanu spoke cryptically, saying that though he had a son worth a thousand, the scriptures claimed that having only one son was akin to having none. Sons could be lost, and at times, he wished for more.

These words confounded Devavrata, and he sought an explanation from the chariot driver who had accompanied them. The driver recounted their travels near the Yamuna River, where they had encountered a bewitching fragrance akin to the scent of the intoxicating mogra flower. They followed the scent to discover a captivating woman seated on a boat

.Santanu, a ruler of great renown, beheld a maiden of celestial beauty. Her eyes, dark as the abyss, held a depth that entranced the soul. She was the daughter of a humble fisherman, yet her radiance outshone all else. Santanu, bold and unyielding, addressed her, his voice rich with kingly authority.

"Fair maiden," he spoke, "Who art thou, and whose blood courses through thy veins? What brings thee to this place, so filled with timidity?"

The maiden, her demeanor as graceful as her form, replied, "Blessed be thee, O noble king. I am the daughter of the chief among fishermen. By his command, I ferry passengers across this river, seeking religious merit."

Santanu, captivated by her ethereal beauty, felt a desire stirring within him. Turning to her father, the fisherman chief, he sought consent for a union with the maiden. The chief, wise and discerning, responded to the monarch's request, his words carrying the weight of destiny.

"O king," he said, "From the moment my daughter, with her exceptional grace, came into this world, it was destined that she should be bestowed upon a worthy husband. However, I bear a desire in my heart, and I shall reveal it to thee. O virtuous one, thou art known for thy truthfulness. If thou desirest to wed my daughter, grant me this pledge: that the son born of her shall ascend thy throne, and none other shall inherit thy kingdom."

Santanu, though aflame with desire, hesitated. He pondered the weighty demand placed upon him. With measured words, he responded, "Before I can grant such a pledge, I must know what it entails. If it is within my power to fulfill, then it shall be granted. If not, I shall speak accordingly."

The fisherman chief then explained, "O king, what I seek is this: the child born of my daughter shall be the rightful heir to your throne, and no other shall claim that honor."

These words struck Santanu with uncertainty. The prospect of relinquishing his claim to the throne was a heavy burden to bear, even for a heart aflame with desire. Troubled, he returned to Hastinapura, his thoughts consumed by the maiden he longed for.

. Devavrata, moved by the desire to alleviate his father's suffering, made a solemn vow.

"Listen, O father," he declared before the gathered chiefs. "I shall fulfill thy wishes. The son born of the maiden shall indeed ascend the throne." This vow, made in the presence of witnesses, bound him to an extraordinary fate.

The fisherman chief, hearing of Devavrata's promise, expressed his approval, though he harbored reservations about the future. He spoke of the rivalry that might arise from a co-wife's son, and he valued the maiden's happiness above all else.

In response, Devavrata, unwavering in his determination, affirmed his commitment. He pledged to live a life of celibacy to ensure the maiden's happiness and the fulfillment of the fisherman's demand.

Thus, the die was cast, and Devavrata became Bhishma, the one with the terrible oath, bound by his unbreakable vow.

Chapter 11

BAD LUCK OF SHANTANUS CHILDREN

After the nuptials had been solemnized, King Santanu brought his beautiful bride, Satyavati, into his household. In due course, she bore him two sons, the first of whom was named Chitrangada. This child, brimming with intelligence and valor, grew into a man of great prowess. Santanu, the mighty monarch, also fathered another son upon Satyavati, and he was named Vichitravirya. This young prince, destined for greatness, exhibited remarkable archery skills and eventually ascended to the throne following his father's rule.

As time flowed on, King Santanu, wise in his years, began to sense the inexorable march of Time itself. He knew that his days were numbered, and he prepared for the inevitable. After Santanu's departure to the heavenly realms, Bhishma, the venerable and unswerving son of Ganga, placed himself under the command of Satyavati.

With Bhishma's guidance, Chitrangada, who had already proven himself a mighty warrior, was anointed as the king. Fearless and unconquerable, Chitrangada asserted his dominance by vanquishing all rival monarchs who dared to challenge his might. No man or supernatural entity could stand as his equal.

However, in the midst of his reign, a formidable adversary emerged—another Chitrangada, the potent king of the Gandharvas. He sought a fierce confrontation, and the battlefield chosen was Kurukshetra. For three long years, these two powerful warriors clashed on the banks of the Saraswati River. In a contest marked by relentless combat and a rain of deadly weapons, the Gandharva, whether through superior strength or strategic cunning, proved triumphant. The valiant Kuru prince, Chitrangada, was felled in battle.

Having slain Chitrangada, that unmatched warrior among men, the Gandharva ascended to the heavens, leaving behind a field of bloodshed and valor. Bhishma, the unwavering protector of the Kurus, paid due respects and performed the solemn obsequies for the fallen hero.

With Chitrangada's untimely demise, Vichitravirya, still in his youthful minority, was entrusted with the throne. Under the guidance of Bhishma, who possessed profound knowledge of law and religion, Vichitravirya assumed the responsibilities of ruling the ancestral kingdom. In his obedient and dutiful ways, he honored and revered Santanu's son, Bhishma, who remained the steadfast pillar of the Kuru lineage

After the valiant Chitrangada had met his untimely fate, and Vichitravirya, his youthful successor, remained a minor, the mantle of rulership was taken up by Bhishma. He placed himself under the command of Queen Satyavati, the indomitable matriarch of the Kuru lineage.

However, as time flowed onward, and Vichitravirya, a paragon of intelligence, matured into manhood, Bhishma harbored a desire to see his brother wed. It was during this period that news reached Bhishma of a grand self-choice ceremony in the city of Varanasi, where the three beautiful daughters of the King of Kasi, each rivaling the celestial Apsaras in beauty, were to select their own husbands.

Upon his mother's command, Bhishma embarked on a solitary journey to Varanasi in a single chariot. There, he beheld a multitude of monarchs from every corner of the realm, all gathered for the momentous event. Among them, Bhishma spotted the three maidens who would choose their life partners. In this assembly, each king was to be named, and the maiden of his choice would garland him as her husband.

Bhishma, with unwavering determination, chose these maidens on behalf of his brother. Taking them onto his chariot, he addressed the assembled kings in a voice akin to the thundering roar of storm clouds. "Wise men advise that when a distinguished guest arrives, a maiden may be offered to him, adorned with ornaments and accompanied by valuable gifts. Some may bestow their daughters in exchange for a pair of cows, while others may seek a fixed sum as dowry. Some give their daughters with their consent, some by drugging them into compliance, and some after gaining approval from the maiden's parents. Some acquire wives as rewards for participating in sacrifices. Among these, the learned praise the eighth form of marriage, but kings often favor the Swyamvara, or self-choice ceremony. The sages, however, proclaim that the most esteemed wife is the one taken by force after defeating rivals amidst a gathering of princes and kings invited to a self-choice ceremony. Thus, you kings,

I now carry these maidens away by force. Strive with all your might to vanquish me or be vanquished yourselves. I stand here ready to fight!"

Upon hearing this challenge, the monarchs rose, slapping their arms and biting their lips in rage. They hastened to remove their ornaments and don their armor. The dazzling ornaments and gleaming armor shone brilliantly, resembling celestial meteors in the sky. Frowning with furrowed brows and fiery eyes, the kings moved impatiently, their clinking armor and ornaments creating a symphony of war. The charioteers quickly brought forth splendid chariots drawn by fine horses. The warriors, armed to the teeth, took their places on these chariots, and with weapons in hand, they pursued Bhishma, who had taken the maidens.

Thus began a formidable battle between innumerable monarchs and Bhishma, the solitary warrior. The kings simultaneously unleashed a storm of ten thousand arrows upon him, but the Kuru hero swiftly deflected this torrent with a volley of arrows as numerous as the downpour of rain. Undaunted, the kings closed in from all directions, showering arrows upon him like a cloud burst. Bhishma, however, intercepted the ceaseless arrow onslaught and countered by piercing each of the monarchs with three arrows. In retaliation, the kings struck Bhishma with five arrows each, yet he skillfully deflected them with his own arrows. The battle raged on, with Bhishma expertly protecting himself and striking the opposing kings with two arrows each.

The combat grew so intense that it resembled the ancient battles between gods and demons, and even the bravest spectators dared not look upon the scene without trepidation. Bhishma, with his lethal precision, severed bows, flagstaffs, and armor, and heaped upon the battlefield a mound of severed heads. His incredible prowess and swiftness in combat led the kings, despite being his adversaries, to applaud him.

Amidst this tumultuous fray, King Salya, a warrior of immense valor, challenged Bhishma. Like a mighty bull charging another in a herd, Salya, brimming with wrath, called Bhishma to battle. As the two mighty warriors prepared to clash, the other monarchs stood aside, eager spectators of the impending duel.

Salya, armed with immeasurable strength, unleashed a barrage of arrows upon Bhishma, who skillfully intercepted them with his own. The crowd of regal onlookers marveled at Salya's dexterity and cheered him on. Witnessing this display, Bhishma, now aflame with anger, issued a challenge, "Stay! Stay!" He ordered his charioteer to lead his chariot toward Salya, determined to end the battle as quickly as Garuda seizes a serpent.

Bhishma then strung the Varuna weapon on his bowstring and used it to strike Salya's four steeds. He proceeded to defeat Salya's charioteer and vanquish his noble steeds using the Aindra weapon. Though Salya was defeated, Bhishma spared his life, and the valiant king returned to his kingdom, ruling it with virtue. The other kings, having witnessed the remarkable battle, returned to their realms as well.

Bhishma, having defeated all opposition, continued on his journey with the maidens, making his way back to the capital of the Bharatas, Hastinapura. Passing through countless forests, rivers, hills, and dense woods, he arrived at his destination in no time, the maidens by his side. Possessing unparalleled martial skills and having vanquished numerous foes without a scratch, Bhishma brought the daughters of the King of Kasi to the Kurus, tenderly as if they were his own daughters-in-law, younger sisters, or even daughters.

Bhishma, the son of Santanu, well-versed in the ways of virtue, then prepared for his brother's wedding in consultation with Queen Satyavati. However, before the wedding could take place, Amba, the eldest daughter of the King of Kasi, approached Bhishma with a gentle smile and shared her secret. She confessed, "In my heart, I had already chosen the King of Saubha as my husband. He, too, had accepted me in his heart, and my father approved. Even at the self-choice ceremony, I would have chosen him. Knowing this, do as you see fit, for you are well-versed in virtue."

Respecting her feelings, Bhishma sought counsel from learned Brahmanas, masters of the Vedas, and granted Amba her freedom of choice. He conducted the wedding of the other two daughters, Ambika and Ambalika, to his younger brother Vichitravirya. Though Vichitravirya was virtuous and abstemious, his youthful pride and beauty made him susceptible to desire. The two tall and fair maidens, with dark curly hair, rosy nails, voluptuous figures, and every auspicious mark, found deep love and respect in their hearts for Vichitravirya. In turn, the prince, possessing the celestial grace of the twin Aswins and formidable prowess, held their hearts captive.

Vichitravirya and his wives enjoyed seven years of marital bliss together. However, tragedy struck when Vichitravirya, still in the prime of his youth, fell victim to consumption. Despite the efforts of friends and relatives, the prince succumbed to the ailment, his life extinguished like the setting sun. Bhishma, virtuous and wise, was plunged into sorrow and anxiety. In consultation with Satyavati, he arranged for the proper obsequial rites to be performed for the departed prince, thereby marking the end of a

Chapter in the epic tale of the Kuru dynasty.

In the wake of Vichitravirya's untimely demise, Satyavati, the sorrowful mother, found herself engulfed in grief. She, along with her daughters-in-law, performed the last rites for the departed prince. She attempted to console the weeping women and Bhishma, the paramount warrior of his age. Yet, her heart remained heavy with the weight of sorrow.

Chapter 12

VYASA IS SUMMONED

Seeking solace in faith and tradition, Satyavati turned her gaze to Bhishma, that peerless wielder of weapons, and spoke with a heavy heart, "The fate of the funeral rituals, the accomplishments, and the lineage of virtuous and renowned Santanu of the Kuru lineage now rests upon your shoulders. Just as heaven is inseparable from righteous deeds, long life from truth and faith, so is virtue an inseparable part of your being. O virtuous one, your knowledge of virtue, the intricacies of familial customs, and your inventive resourcefulness in times of hardship liken you to Sukra and Angiras. Therefore, O paragon of virtue, I beseech you to fulfill a certain task on my behalf. Listen to my words and let them guide your actions. I am entrusting you with a solemn responsibility, for the son of your mother and my son, your brother, has departed for the celestial abode without leaving an heir. These wives of your brother, the charming daughters of the King of Kasi, who are endowed with beauty and youth, yearn for offspring. Thus, in accordance with my command, bring forth progeny through them to ensure the continuation of our lineage. Uphold virtue and do not lead our ancestors to an unfortunate fate. Ascend the throne, rule the kingdom of the Bharatas, and take a wife as your duly wedded consort. Do not let your forebears descend into the abyss of despair."

"Responding to his mother, family, and well-wishers, the valiant Bhishma, who was a scourge to his enemies, articulated his reply in harmony with the dictates of righteousness. 'O mother, your words are indeed guided by virtue. Yet, you are aware of the vow I have taken regarding the begetting of children. You are also well-acquainted with the events surrounding your marriage. I reiterate the oath I once took – I would renounce three worlds, the sovereignty of heaven, or anything more significant, but I would never relinquish the path of truth. Earth may forsake its fragrance, water may forsake its moisture, light may forsake its power to reveal form, air may forsake its attribute of touch, the sun may renounce its brilliance, fire may forsake its heat, the moon may forsake its cooling radiance, space may forsake its capacity to transmit sound, the slayer of Vritra may forsake his might, the god of justice may forsake his impartiality; but I shall never abandon truth.'

"After hearing her son's words, Satyavati, overwhelmed by her own sorrow, addressed Bhishma once more. 'O paragon of truth and might, I understand your steadfast commitment to righteousness. If you so desire, you could, with your boundless energy, create three worlds anew. I am fully aware of the vow you undertook for my sake. However, considering the gravity of the situation, please shoulder the responsibility that one owes to his forefathers. O vanquisher of foes, act in a manner that prevents the lineage of Santanu from fading into obscurity. Spare our friends and relatives from sorrow.' Driven by misery, Queen Satyavati, in her grief, uttered words that deviated from the path of virtue.

"In response to his mother's anguished pleas, Bhishma spoke once more, his voice filled with conviction, 'O Queen, avert your gaze not from righteousness. Do not lead us astray, and do not force me to breach the sacred bonds of truth. The annals of Kshatriya honor do not applaud the abandonment of truth. I shall elucidate what Kshatriya tradition prescribes, and it is within this framework that we may act to prevent Santanu's lineage from perishing on this earth. Listen to my words and contemplate them, in consultation with learned priests and those versed in the practices sanctioned for times of crisis and distress. Do not forget the path of ordinary social conduct as you ponder the way forward.'"

Bhishma's voice resounded with the weight of ancient tales as he continued his narrative, reminiscent of times long past. "In the days of yore," he began, "Rama, the son of Jamadagni, driven by fury at his father's demise, wielded his battle-axe to vanquish the Haihaya king. Arjuna, the Haihaya king, faced Rama's wrath, and his thousand arms fell to the ground, a feat unparalleled in the world. Unsatisfied, Rama embarked on a world-conquering quest, his mighty bow unleashing destruction upon the Kshatriyas. With his swift arrows, he obliterated the Kshatriya clan twenty-one times over.

"As the earth was thus bereft of Kshatriyas by the great Rishi, Kshatriya women across the land sought the company of Brahmanas learned in the Vedas to bear children. It is said in the Vedas that sons born thus belong to the one who marries their mother. These Kshatriya ladies approached Brahmanas not driven by lust but by virtuous motives. Thus, the Kshatriya lineage was revived, guided by the principles of dharma.

"Allow me to share another ancient tale that illustrates this point. In times of old, there was a wise sage named Utathya, deeply enamored of his wife, Mamata. One day, Vrihaspati, the younger brother of Utathya and the divine priest of the celestials, approached Mamata. She, however, informed Vrihaspati that she had conceived from her union with Utathya and, therefore, he should abstain from seeking intimacy. She said, 'O illustrious Vrihaspati, the child within me has already studied the Vedas with their six Angas while still in the womb. There is no room here for both of you. I have claimed it first. You should not disturb me.' Nevertheless, Vrihaspati, ignoring the words of the child in the womb, continued to pursue Mamata. In response, the child within her addressed Vrihaspati, 'Father, cease your attempts. There is no space for two here. I arrived first. Your seed cannot be wasted. It is not right for you to harm me in this manner.' Yet, Vrihaspati, oblivious to the child's words, sought Mamata's company, leading to the expulsion of his seed. It fell upon the ground.

"When Vrihaspati observed this, he grew furious and cursed the unborn child, saying, 'Because you dared to speak to me in such a manner during a moment of pleasure, perpetual darkness shall befall you.' As a result of Vrihaspati's curse, Utathya's child, equal to Vrihaspati in power, was born blind and became known as Dirghatamas, enveloped in perpetual darkness. Despite his blindness, the wise Dirghatamas, well-versed in the Vedas, managed to win the hand of Pradweshi, a young and beautiful Brahmana maiden. He fathered many children with her, with Gautama being the eldest. However, these children, driven by greed and foolishness, failed to uphold virtue.

"Discontented with her husband, Pradweshi delivered an ultimatum. 'The husband is called Bhartri because he supports his wife. He is known as Pati because he protects her. But you are neither to me!' She added, 'You were born blind, and it is I who have supported you and your children. I can no longer maintain you as before.' In response, Dirghatamas declared a rule that every woman must remain

THE SOURCE OF CONFLICT

loyal to one husband throughout her life. Even if her husband was no longer living, she could not seek another. Any woman violating this rule would be considered fallen. A woman without a husband would always be susceptible to sin, and her wealth, no matter how great, would never truly bring her happiness. Calumny and slander would forever haunt her. Hearing this decree, Pradweshi grew furious and commanded her sons, 'Throw him into the Ganga!'

"Following their mother's orders, Gautama and his brothers, driven by greed and folly, tied the Muni to a raft and set him adrift on the river. The blind sage floated downstream, passing through many kingdoms. One day, King Vali, a virtuous monarch, went to the Ganges for his ablutions. As he performed his rituals, he saw the raft approaching him. The king rescued the blind sage, guided by his unwavering commitment to truth. Vali recognized Dirghatamas and requested him to raise offspring from his wife. The sage agreed, and Queen Sudeshna was sent to him. However, Sudeshna, aware of Dirghatamas' blindness and old age, sent her nurse in her stead. On the nurse, the sage fathered eleven children, with Kakshivat being the eldest.

"Later, King Vali inquired about these children, and Dirghatamas revealed the truth. Kakshivat and his siblings, born of a Sudra woman, were his own offspring. The unfortunate Queen Sudeshna, avoiding the sage due to his blindness and age, had not approached him herself. Hearing this, King Vali pacified the sage and sent Sudeshna to him. The sage, by merely touching her, declared that she would bear five children—Anga, Vanga, Kalinga, Pundra, and Suhma, who would shine with the radiance of the sun itself. These children's dominions would later be known as Anga, Vanga, Kalinga, Pundra, and Suhma.

"In this manner, the lineage of Vali was preserved in ancient times, as many valiant archers and noble charioteers, born from Brahmanas, upheld the virtues of their lineage. Bearing this in mind, O mother, choose your course of action."

Bhishma's words flowed like an ancient river, deep and solemn, as he continued to weave the tale of dynastic fate. "Listen, O mother," he began, "as I reveal the means by which the lineage of Bharata can endure. Invite a learned Brahmana by the promise of wealth and have him sire offspring upon the wives of Vichitravirya."

Satyavati, her voice quivering with a hint of bashfulness, responded to Bhishma's proposal. "O Bharata of mighty arms," she said, "your words ring true. In you, I have the utmost confidence. I shall now share with you the method to ensure our lineage's continuation. You shall find it hard to refuse, for it aligns with our customs in times of dire need. In our lineage, you are the embodiment of virtue and truth. You are our sole refuge. So, hear me out and act accordingly.

"In my youth, my father, a virtuous man, owned a ferryboat for the sake of virtue itself. One day, when I was in the prime of my youth, the great and wise Rishi Parasara, foremost among virtuous men, boarded my boat to cross the Yamuna. As I rowed him across the river, the Rishi became filled with desire and began addressing me with sweet words. Fear of my father held my mind, but the dread of the Rishi's curse finally overcame me. He granted me a precious boon that I could not refuse, enveloping the region in thick fog to ensure our privacy. In a moment of passion, the Rishi and I came together, and before this union, my body had a revolting fishy odor. The Rishi, with his energy, dispelled it and bestowed upon me my present fragrance. The Rishi informed me that if I were to bear his child on an island in the river, I would still remain a virgin. That child, born of Parasara, while I was yet a maiden, became a great Rishi endowed with immense ascetic powers, known as Dwaipayana (the island-born). He later divided the Vedas into four parts through his ascetic might, earning the name Vyasa (the divider or arranger), and also

Krishna (the dark) due to his complexion. He was truthful in speech, devoid of passions, and had purified himself of all sins. After his birth, he departed with his father.

"By the appointment of both you and me, that illustrious Rishi will certainly sire children upon your brother's wives. He told me when he left, 'Mother, think of me when you face difficulty.' If you desire, O Bhishma of mighty arms, I can summon him. With your consent, I am certain that this great ascetic will grant offspring to Vichitravirya's wives."

Bhishma, with a sense of profound understanding, replied, "What you propose, O mother, is truly wise. The one who acts with prudence keeps an eye on virtue, profit, and pleasure, and, after careful reflection, ensures that virtue leads to future virtue, profit to future profit, and pleasure to future pleasure. Therefore, what you suggest, which is both beneficial to us and in harmony with virtue, is the best counsel and has my full approval."

As Bhishma voiced his agreement, Satyavati turned her thoughts towards the Muni Dwaipayana. With her innermost yearnings reaching out, the great Vyasa, engaged in interpreting the Vedas, perceived the call of his mother and swiftly appeared before her. Nobody else knew of his arrival. Satyavati, seeing her long-lost son, was overcome with emotion, and her tears flowed freely. The daughter of the fisherman wept as she embraced her son, who had been absent for so long. Vyasa, her eldest son, bathed her in his filial tears, and after the heartfelt reunion, he addressed his mother, saying, "I have come, O mother, to fulfill your wishes. Command me without hesitation. I shall accomplish your desires."

The family priest of the Bharatas, recognizing the divine presence, duly worshipped the great Rishi, who accepted the offerings with the traditional mantras. Gratified by the worship, Vyasa took his seat. Satyavati then addressed her son, sharing her thoughts with him, "O learned one, my son, both father and mother contribute to the birth of a child. They are equally responsible for their offspring. There is no doubt that a mother has as much right over her children as the father. In this case, you are Bhishma's elder brother by the rule of primogeniture and his younger brother on the mother's side. Bhishma, devoted to truth, harbors no desire to father children or ascend the throne. It is for the sake of virtue, the continuation of our dynasty, Bhishma's request, and my command, and out of kindness to all beings, for the protection of the people, and your own generous nature, that I beseech you to act as I suggest. Your younger brother has left behind two widowed queens, radiant as celestial maidens, filled with youth and beauty. You are the most fitting candidate to fulfill this duty, for the sake of virtue, religion, and the perpetuation of our lineage. So, sire virtuous offspring upon them, worthy of our noble dynasty, and ensure the continuation of our royal line."

Vyasa, hearing his mother's request, responded with the utmost respect and devotion, "O Satyavati, you are well-versed in both worldly and spiritual matters. Your heart is devoted to virtue. Thus, I shall fulfill your wishes, guided by virtue alone. This practice, consistent with the true and eternal dharma, is known to me. I shall grant children to my younger brother. Now, let the princess of Kosala, adorned in clean attire and adorned with jewels, await me in her chamber."

Vyasa's words held the weight of generations as mother and son conspired to ensure the continuation of their lineage.

Amidst the dimly lit chambers of the palace, the story of destiny's relentless march unfolded. Satyavati, having purified her daughter-in-law after the end of her monthly cycle, led her into the innermost chamber. There, on a luxurious bed, she spoke with solemnity, "O Princess of Kosala, your husband has an elder brother who shall enter your womb tonight as your child. Await him without succumbing to slumber."

The amiable princess, as she reclined on her bed, began to think of Bhishma and the other elders of the Kuru lineage. Then came the Rishi, he of truthful speech, who had initially promised Amvika, the eldest princess, and entered her chamber while a lamp still flickered. Witnessing his dark visage, fiery copper locks, blazing eyes, and fearsome beard, the princess shuttered her eyes in terror. The Rishi, driven by his mother's wishes, recognized her, but she, overwhelmed by fear, dared not open her eyes to meet his gaze. As Vyasa departed, his mother inquired, "Will the princess bear an accomplished son?"

Vyasa replied, "The son she shall bear will possess the strength of ten thousand elephants. He will be a renowned royal sage, distinguished by his vast knowledge, intelligence, and energy. In his time, he shall father a hundred sons. Yet, due to his mother's fault, he shall be born blind."

Hearing this, Satyavati exclaimed, "How can a blind man become a worthy monarch of the Kurus? How can he protect his kin and uphold the honor of his father's lineage? You must grant the Kurus another king."

Vyasa, responding to his mother's plea, said, "So be it," and withdrew. In due course, the first princess of Kosala gave birth to a blind son.

Satyavati, not one to relent easily, summoned Vyasa again after securing her second daughter-in-law's consent. Vyasa came as promised and, upon seeing him, Ambalika turned pale with fear. Addressing her, Vyasa declared, "Because you were pale with fear at the sight of my grim visage, your child shall be pale in complexion. O fair-faced one, he shall be named Pandu (the pale)." With these words, Vyasa exited her chamber.

Upon meeting her son, Satyavati beseeched him for another child, to which Vyasa assented. Ambalika, when her time came, bore a son of pale complexion, radiant with beauty, who would later become the father of the mighty archers, the Pandavas.

Subsequently, when the eldest of Vichitravirya's widows had her monthly cycle once more, Satyavati encouraged her to approach Vyasa again. However, remembering the Rishi's formidable visage and overpowering scent, the princess refused. Instead, she sent one of her maids, a maiden with the allure of an Apsara and adorned with her own ornaments. The great Rishi was pleased with the maiden's service and predicted, "You shall no longer be a slave. Your child shall be greatly fortunate, virtuous, and the wisest among men on earth." This child, begotten upon her by Krishna-Dwaipayana, would be known as Vidura, the brother of Dhritarashtra and the illustrious Pandu. He was devoid of desire and passion, well-versed in the art of governance, and the embodiment of justice, born on earth under the curse of the revered Rishi Mandavya.

Krishna-Dwaipayana, after revealing his deceit by the eldest princess to his mother, disappeared from her sight. Thus, in the field of Vichitravirya, were born those sons, children of celestial splendor, destined to propagate the Kuru lineage.

Chapter 13

THE STORY OF THE ORIGIN OF VIDURA

Janamejaya inquired, his curiosity aflame, "What transgression earned the curse for the god of justice? And who was the Brahmana ascetic responsible for this divine curse that cast the god into the Sudra caste?"

Vaisampayana, with the gravity of a storyteller, began to narrate, "There once lived a Brahmana known as Mandavya, a sage immersed in the knowledge of all duties, unwavering in his devotion to religion, truth, and asceticism. In his hermitage, beneath the shade of a tree, he sat in profound meditation with his arms raised, observing a vow of silence that spanned years. One fateful day, a gang of thieves, laden with stolen riches, sought refuge in his sanctuary. Hot on their heels came the king's guardians of peace, determined to apprehend the robbers. The thieves, upon entering the hermitage, concealed their ill-gotten gains and hid themselves in fear as the constables closed in. Inquiries were made of the sage seated under the tree, 'O venerable Brahmana, which path did the thieves take? Guide us, so we may swiftly pursue them.'

"The ascetic, however, seated in silence, made no reply, neither good nor bad. The king's officers, scouring the area, eventually uncovered the thieves along with their spoils, which heightened their suspicions about the sage. They seized him, along with the bandits, and brought them before the king. The king, in ignorance of the truth, passed judgment, condemning the sage to execution alongside the alleged criminals. The sentence was duly carried out, and the celebrated sage was impaled. Remarkably, despite his dire predicament and without sustenance, the sage clung to life, preserved by his ascetic power.

"The resilient sage, impaled and deprived of food, endured the ordeal without succumbing to death. Instead, he summoned other sages through his ascetic prowess, and they arrived in the guise of birds. Seeing him still alive, though impaled, they were filled with sorrow and, revealing their true identities, asked him, 'O Brahmana, we desire to know the transgression for which you endure the torturous fate of impalement!'

"The venerable sage replied, 'Whom shall I blame for this but myself? Indeed, no one but me has wronged me!' Hearing this, the king's officers, who had earlier witnessed the sage's miraculous survival, reported to the king. The king, upon learning of the sage's continued existence, sought his audience and beseeched him, 'O great sage, I have wronged you unknowingly. I implore you to forgive my transgression. I pray that you do not bear ill will against me.'

"The sage, his anger appeased by the king's entreaties, agreed to forgive. The king, attempting to extract the stake from the sage's body, found it impossible to remove entirely. Consequently, he severed it at the point just outside the sage's body. With a part of the stake still embedded within him, the sage continued his life's journey, practicing the most severe of penances and conquering regions beyond the reach of others. Due to the stake remaining within him, he became renowned as Ani-Mandavya, Mandavya with the stake within.

"One day, Ani-Mandavya, possessing the highest knowledge of religion, ascended to the abode of the god of justice. There, he reproached the god and demanded, 'What sinful act, O god, have I committed unconsciously that has brought upon me this suffering? Reveal it, and witness the might of my asceticism.'

"The god of justice replied to the sage's inquiry, 'O sage of ascetic wealth, you once impaled a tiny insect upon a blade of grass, and for this act, you endure its consequences. Know, O Rishi, that just as a gift, however small, multiplies in merit, so does a sinful act multiply in the suffering it begets.'

"Ani-Mandavya retorted, 'Tell me when I committed this act.' The god of justice explained that the transgression had occurred when Ani-Mandavya was but a child. The sage, however, responded, 'The scriptures do not recognize as sinful any act committed by a child up to the age of fourteen. This punishment for such a minor offense has been unduly harsh. The killing of a Brahmana incurs a sin more grievous than that of any other living being. Therefore, O god of justice, you shall be reborn among men, even in the Sudra order. From this day forward, I establish a limit: an act committed by one below the age of fourteen shall not be deemed sinful, while one above that age shall bear the consequences of their actions.'

"Cursed by the illustrious sage Ani-Mandavya, the god of justice was reborn as Vidura in the Sudra caste. Vidura possessed profound knowledge of morality, politics, and worldly affairs. Free from covetousness and anger, he exhibited great foresight and unshakable tranquillity. Vidura dedicated his life to the well-being of the Kurus, embodying the principles of justice and wisdom."

Chapter 14
THE ESTABLISHMENT OF THE KURU DYNASTY

With the birth of those three children, Kurujangala, Kurukshetra, and the Kurus flourished like never before. The earth yielded abundant harvests, and the crops were filled with flavor. Rain fell in its due season, and trees bore fruits and blossoms in plenty. The draught cattle reveled in their happiness, while birds and other creatures rejoiced without measure. Flowers exuded fragrances, and fruits were sweet to the taste. Cities and towns bustled with merchants, artisans, traders, and artists of every ilk. The people themselves became brave, learned, honest, and blissful. There were no robbers, nor did wickedness find a place in their hearts. It seemed as though the golden age had descended upon their land. The people, committed to virtuous deeds, sacrifices, and truth, loved one another dearly, fostering prosperity and harmony.

Free from pride, anger, and greed, they engaged in pure and innocent pastimes. The capital of the Kurus, teeming with countless palaces and mansions, resembled Amaravati itself. The citizens and denizens were full of hope, witnessing the youthful exploits of their illustrious princes. Ruled by Bhishma, the virtuous monarch, the kingdom abounded with hundreds of sacrificial stakes. The wheel of virtue, set in motion by Bhishma, brought such contentment that people from other lands left their homes to settle there and swell its population. Citizens and townsfolk thrived, and it appeared that the entire kingdom rejoiced.

Bhishma, the foremost statesman and guardian of morality, took Vidura, who possessed deep knowledge of truth and virtue, under his wing. They spoke in a chamber filled with gravitas, Bhishma addressing Vidura, who was well-versed in religious tenets and the path of righteousness.

"Bhishma," he began, "our illustrious lineage, resplendent with virtue and valor, has always held dominion over all other monarchs on this earth. The glory of our lineage has been preserved and perpetuated by many virtuous and renowned kings of old. Now, the noble Krishna (Dwaipayana), Satyavati, and I have nurtured you three so that our lineage may not fade into obscurity. It is my belief, Bhishma continued, that we should choose brides from among three maidens worthy of our noble blood. One is the daughter of Surasena from the Yadava clan, another is the daughter of Suvala, and the third is the princess of Madra. These maidens, beautiful and of royal lineage, are indeed suitable for our family. What are your thoughts on this matter?"

Vidura replied with deference, "You are our father, our mother, and our esteemed teacher. You are our guide in all matters of virtue and wisdom. Therefore, do as you see fit in your wisdom."

Bhishma, ever vigilant, received word from the Brahmanas that Gandhari, the virtuous daughter of Suvala, had obtained a boon from Lord Shiva that she would bear a hundred sons. This news led him to send messengers to the king of Gandhara. King Suvala initially hesitated, given Dhritarashtra's blindness, but, recognizing the Kurus' noble blood, reputation, and demeanor, he agreed to the proposal. Dhritarashtra, who would become the future husband, was blind, but Gandhari, out of love and respect for her future husband, blindfolded her own eyes. Sakuni, Suvala's valiant son, brought Gandhari, radiant with youth and beauty, and gave her in marriage to Dhritarashtra. The nuptials, held under Bhishma's guidance, were celebrated with grandeur, and Gandhari was embraced with great honor. She, displaying exceptional behavior and respect for her husband, soon won the hearts of all the Kurus.

Gandhari, ever devoted to her husband, earned the respect of her superiors through her virtuous conduct. She remained chaste and never uttered a word that could be construed as even remotely unfaithful to her husband or her superiors.

In the land of Kuntibhoja, there dwelled a maiden named Pritha, graced with beauty and every virtue. She held fast to her vows, devoted herself to righteousness, and possessed qualities that would put the finest of women to shame. Yet, despite her youthful allure, a curious fate had kept kings and princes at bay, none daring to seek her hand. Seeing this peculiar predicament, Kuntibhoja, her father, took a momentous step. He sent forth invitations far and wide, summoning princes and kings from distant realms to his grand court, where Pritha would choose her husband from among her suitors.

On that fateful day, the noble Kunti entered the amphitheatre, her eyes scanning the assembly of royalty. Among the crowned heads, her gaze fell upon Pandu, the foremost of the Bharatas, a tiger among kings. His chest broad, his eyes fierce as a bull's, his strength unrivaled, and his splendor outshining all others, Pandu stood like a resplendent Indra amidst that royal congregation. The amiable daughter of Kuntibhoja, her features flawless and heart aflutter, approached Pandu with humility, her body trembling with emotion. She delicately placed the nuptial garland around Pandu's neck, sealing her choice.

Seeing Kunti's selection of Pandu as her lord, the other monarchs departed for their respective kingdoms, riding elephants, horses, and chariots, just as they had arrived. King Kuntibhoja, with the nuptial rites concluded, showered his son-in-law with great riches before sending him back to his own capital.

Pandu, the fortunate prince of the Kurus, accompanied by a mighty force adorned with various banners and pennons, and hailed by Brahmanas and venerable Rishis, returned triumphantly to his capital. Upon reaching his palace, he established his queen, Pritha, in her rightful place, their union destined to be like that of the king and queen of the celestials, Maghavat and Paulomi.

Thus, the tale of Pandu and Pritha, a match made amidst the splendors of a grand assembly, began to weave its own destiny in the annals of the Kurus.

In days of yore, when kings strode the earth like colossi and valor was the measure of a man, King Pandu was the most powerful of all sage like kings. His heart, bold as a lion's, yearned for a second wife, and the one who captured his gaze was none other than the peerless Madri, sister of the Valhika king.

To secure this union, Bhishma, the wise son of Santanu, marched forth with an army, the likes of which struck awe into the hearts of foes. Accompanied by aged counselors, Brahmanas, and revered Rishis, he ventured to the court of the king of Madra. The Valhika ruler, upon hearing of Bhishma's arrival, hastened to receive him with due respect. He ushered Bhishma into his palace, offering a white carpet, water to wash his feet, and the customary tokens of honor.

Once seated comfortably, the king of Madra inquired about the purpose of Bhishma's visit. With unswerving resolve, Bhishma, the pillar of Kuru dignity, spoke, "O vanquisher of foes, I seek the hand of a maiden in your kingdom. It is said that you have a sister named Madri, renowned for her beauty and virtues. I desire her as a bride for Pandu. We find you worthy of alliance, and we too are worthy of you. Reflect upon this, O king of Madra, and accept our proposal."

The king of Madra, guided by an ancestral custom, replied, "It is true that our family has a well-known custom, which you, no doubt, are aware of. This custom, be it virtuous or otherwise, I am bound to uphold. Hence, I cannot grant your request, O slayer of foes. This custom, O Bhishma, is sacred to us."

Bhishma acknowledged, "Indeed, O king, this is a virtue, sanctioned even by the self-created. Your ancestors adhered to this custom, and it is revered by the wise and the righteous. I do not find fault with it."

With these words, Bhishma, filled with energy, presented Salya with vast treasures, including gold, precious stones, elephants, horses, chariots, fabrics, ornaments, gems, pearls, and corals. In gratitude, Salya offered his adorned sister to the Kuru hero.

Taking Madri as his own, Bhishma, the son of the mighty Ganga, returned to the Kuru capital, named after the elephant. There, on an auspicious day as guided by the wise, Pandu was united with Madri. After the nuptials, he established his beautiful bride in splendid chambers.

For thirty days, Pandu reveled in the company of his two wives, his desires sated to the brim. Then, with his heart set on conquering the world, he embarked on a grand campaign. Accompanied by a formidable force of elephants, cavalry, infantry, and chariots, he left his capital, blessed by the citizens and the auspicious rites performed by his people.

Pandu's triumphant march led him to subdue the robber tribes of Asarna, challenge Dhirga of Maghadha, and conquer the Videhas of Mithila. He set his sights on Kasi, Sumbha, Pundra, and many others, vanquishing them and making them vassals of the Kurus. Kings from all corners bowed to Pandu, acknowledging him as the paramount hero on earth, just as the celestial hosts regard Indra in heaven. They offered him precious gems, wealth, precious stones, pearls, corals, gold, silver, cattle, horses, cars, elephants, and many other riches.

With his coffers brimming and his fame echoing throughout the land, Pandu returned to his capital. The jubilant citizens, led by Bhishma, went out to welcome their victorious king. The streets, adorned with banners and pennons, stretched far and wide, laden with wealth and treasures. Bhishma, the fatherly figure to Pandu, embraced his triumphant son, tears of joy streaming from his eyes.

Pandu, the vanquisher of kingdoms, entered the city amid a cacophony of trumpets, conchs, and kettle-drums, spreading boundless joy among his subjects. He saluted Bhishma and the elders, paid his respects to Dhritarashtra, and, blessed by all, resumed his rightful place as the sovereign of Hastinapura. The citizens, their hearts brimming with joy, hailed Pandu as the restorer of their kingdom's glory, while his resounding fame echoed throughout the land.

In the wake of his triumphant conquests, Pandu, guided by the decree of Dhritarashtra, offered the fruits of his valorous endeavors to Bhishma, their revered grandmother Satyavati, and their mothers. Vidura, too, received a portion of Pandu's wealth. The virtuous Pandu extended his generosity to his other relatives, showering them with similar gifts. Satyavati, Bhishma, and the princes of Kosala were all deeply gratified by Pandu's offerings, which were borne of his martial achievements.

Ambalika, in particular, embraced her son of unparalleled prowess with the exuberance of the queen of heaven upon embracing Jayanta. The riches acquired through Pandu's heroics were employed by Dhritarashtra to perform five grand sacrifices, each equal to a hundred great horse-sacrifices. In these ceremonies, offerings to Brahmanas numbered in the hundreds and thousands, bringing celestial delight to the participants.

Yet, ere long, Pandu, who had conquered indolence and languor, chose to leave behind his opulent palace, with its sumptuous beds, and retreat into the wilderness. Accompanied by his two wives, Kunti and Madri, he embraced the life of a forest-dweller. In a delightful and hilly region, clothed in the shade of mighty sala trees and nestled on the southern slopes of the Himalayas, Pandu found his new home. There, he roamed freely, dedicating himself entirely to the pursuit of the hunt. With his bow, arrows, and sword, he became a resident of the woods, and the handsome Pandu, his armor gleaming, wandered amidst the foliage like Airavata, the celestial elephant, accompanied by two she-elephants.

The denizens of the forest, observing the heroic Bharata prince, marveled at his presence among them. Armed with his formidable weaponry, skilled in the use of every noble weapon, and clad in resplendent armor, he appeared to them as a god walking among mortals.

At Dhritarashtra's behest, provisions for Pandu's solace and pleasure were ceaselessly provided. Meanwhile, Bhishma, the son of the ocean-born Ganga, learned that King Devaka had a daughter of youth and beauty, born of a Sudra wife. He brought her to Vidura and arranged their union in matrimony. Vidura, a sage of profound wisdom, fathered many children upon her, each inheriting his virtues and accomplishments. They grew into a lineage of noble character, following in the footsteps of their illustrious progenitor

Chapter 15

THE BIRTH OF THE PANDAVAS AND KAURAVAS

Vaisampayana continued, "In the meantime, O Janamejaya, Dhritarashtra fathered a hundred sons upon Gandhari, and from a Vaisya wife, he had one more son in addition to those hundred. Pandu, on the other hand, had five sons with his two wives, Kunti and Madri, who were all destined to be renowned charioteers, begotten by celestial beings to perpetuate the illustrious Kuru lineage."

Janamejaya inquired, "O esteemed Brahmana, how did Gandhari give birth to those hundred sons, and in how many years? What were the life spans assigned to each of them? Furthermore, how did Dhritarashtra father another son with a Vaisya woman? Tell me the full details, for my thirst for knowledge concerning the deeds of my ancestors remains unquenched."

Vaisampayana narrated, "One day, Gandhari, extending her warm hospitality, received the great sage Dwaipayana, who had arrived at her abode weary and famished. Delighted by Gandhari's kindness, the sage granted her a boon, and she chose to have a hundred sons, each as powerful and accomplished as her husband. Some time later, Gandhari conceived, but her pregnancy continued for an agonizing two years without any sign of childbirth. This prolonged delay weighed heavily on her, and she was greatly distressed. Hearing that Kunti had given birth to a radiant son as brilliant as the morning sun, Gandhari, consumed by despair, struck her abdomen in frustration, unaware of her husband's absence. In doing so, she unwittingly caused a division within her womb, resulting in a solid mass resembling an iron ball. Unaware of the consequences, she prepared to discard this unusual object.

It was at this moment that the sage Dwaipayana, having perceived everything through his divine insight, swiftly arrived at her side. Addressing the daughter of Suvala, he inquired, 'What have you done?' Gandhari, unable to conceal her actions, responded, 'Out of grief upon hearing that Kunti had given birth to a resplendent son, I struck my womb in despair. You had granted me the boon of a hundred sons, yet all I have here is this lifeless mass!' Vyasa then said, 'Daughter of Suvala, so be it. My words can never be in vain, even in jest. I have not uttered a falsehood, even in jest. I will not speak of other occurrences. Fetch a hundred pots filled with clarified butter and place them in a concealed location. Meanwhile, sprinkle cool water over this mass of flesh.'

Vaisampayana continued, 'Following Vyasa's instructions, the lump of flesh was moistened with water and, over time, it divided into a hundred and one equal parts, each roughly the size of a thumb. These fragments were then placed in the pots filled with clarified butter and closely monitored. Vyasa advised Gandhari to open the covers of the pots after a period of two years.'

Vaisampayana recounted, 'That ball of flesh, having been moistened with water, soon divided into a hundred and one pieces, each about the size of a thumb. These pieces were then placed in the pots filled with clarified butter, which had been set aside. Vyasa instructed Gandhari to open the pots after a period of two years. Following his advice, the daughter of Suvala did exactly that.

In the course of time, King Duryodhana was born from one of those pieces of flesh stored in the pots. According to their birth order, King Yudhishthira was the eldest. On the day of Duryodhana's birth, Bhima, the mighty-armed son of Pandu, was also born.

The moment Duryodhana emerged into the world, he let out a cry that resembled the braying of an ass. In response to his wailing, the surrounding jackals, vultures, jackals, and crows echoed his cries with their own ominous calls. Fierce winds began to blow, and fires broke out in various directions. Frightened by these ominous signs, King Dhritarashtra summoned Bhishma, Vidura, and other well-wishers, along with countless Brahmanas, and addressed them with concern. He said, 'Yudhishthira, my eldest son, is the rightful heir by virtue of his birth. I have no objections to that. However, should my son born after him also ascend the throne? Tell me honestly what is just and right in this situation.'

In response to these words, ominous howls emanated from jackals and other carnivorous animals in every direction. Observing these foreboding signs, the assembled Brahmanas, along with the wise Vidura, replied, 'O King, O mightiest of men, when such dreadful omens occur at the birth of your eldest son, it is clear that he will bring ruin to your dynasty. It would be unwise to preserve him. Calamity shall follow if you keep him. O King, if you abandon him, you will still have your ninety-nine other sons. If you seek the well-being of your lineage, discard this one child. It has been declared that an individual can be forsaken for the sake of the family, a family can be forsaken for the sake of a village, a village can be forsaken for the sake of the entire country, and the earth itself can be forsaken for the sake of one's soul.' Hearing these words from Vidura and the Brahmanas, Dhritarashtra, though deeply attached to his son, could not bring himself to follow their counsel. Then, within a month, he was blessed with a hundred sons and an additional daughter. Furthermore, another son named Yuyutsu was born to him through a Vaisya woman."

Vaisampayana continued, "In due course, King Duryodhana was born from one of the pieces of flesh preserved in the pots. His birth was accompanied by ominous cries from jackals and other scavengers. Seeing these inauspicious signs, King Dhritarashtra, in great trepidation, summoned Bhishma, Vidura, and other wise men, along with numerous Brahmanas, and spoke to them with deep concern. He said, 'While Yudhishthira, my eldest son, has the rightful claim to the throne due to his seniority, I am unsure about the succession of my son born after him. Tell me honestly what is just and right in this matter.'

In response to these words, eerie howls erupted from jackals and other carnivorous creatures in all directions. Witnessing these ominous omens, the assembled Brahmanas, led by the wise Vidura, replied, 'O King, O mighty ruler, when such dreadful signs manifest at the birth of your eldest son, it is clear that he will bring destruction to your lineage. It would be unwise to retain him. Calamity will surely follow if you keep him. O King, by discarding him, you will still have your ninety-nine other sons. If you seek the welfare of your dynasty, relinquish this one child. It has been ordained that an individual can be forsaken for the sake of the family, a family can be forsaken for the sake of a village, a village can be forsaken for the sake of the entire country, and the earth itself can be forsaken for the sake of one's soul.' Despite his deep attachment to his son, Dhritarashtra, upon hearing these words from Vidura and the Brahmanas, could not bring himself to follow their counsel.

Within a month, he was blessed with a hundred sons and an additional daughter. Furthermore, another son named Yuyutsu was born to him through a Vaisya woman."

Janamejaya, with a curious glint in his eyes, spoke, "O virtuous one, you have recounted the tale of how Dhritarashtra's hundred sons were born due to the sage's boon, but you have not yet enlightened me about the birth of the daughter. You mentioned that, in addition to the hundred sons, there was a son named Yuyutsu from a Vaisya woman and also a daughter. The mighty sage Vyasa, possessed of immeasurable energy, foretold that the daughter of the King of Gandhara would become the mother of a hundred sons. How is it that you say Gandhari had a daughter in addition to the hundred sons? If the great sage divided the ball of flesh into only a hundred parts, and if Gandhari did not conceive at any other time, how was Duhsala born? My curiosity is piqued, O revered sage."

Vaisampayana responded, "Your inquiry is indeed valid, O descendant of the Pandavas, and I shall reveal the truth to you. The illustrious and mighty sage, while dividing the ball of flesh and as the nurse placed each part into the pots filled with clarified butter, initiated the process. At that moment, the virtuous and chaste Gandhari, who held firm vows, contemplated within herself. 'There is no doubt that I shall have a hundred sons, as the sage has foretold. It shall come to pass. However, it would bring me immense joy if, in addition to the hundred sons, a daughter were born to me, the youngest among them all. Such a daughter would grant my husband access to the realms achieved through the presence of a daughter's offspring. Moreover, women hold deep affection for their sons-in-law. Therefore, if I were to bear a daughter beyond my hundred sons, my husband would be surrounded by both sons and grandsons, and I would indeed be blessed. If I have ever practiced ascetic austerities, if I have ever given to charity, if I have ever conducted sacred fire rituals through Brahmanas, if I have ever revered my superiors with dutiful regard, then, as the fruit of those meritorious acts, may a daughter be born to me.' During this process, the venerable and eminent sage Krishna-Dwaipayana himself was dividing the ball of flesh. After counting a full hundred parts, he addressed the daughter of Suvala, 'Here are your hundred sons. I have not spoken falsely to you. However, there remains one part in addition to the hundred, intended to fulfill your wish for a daughter. This part shall develop into an amiable and fortunate daughter, just as you desired.' The great ascetic then brought forth another pot filled with clarified butter and placed the part intended to become a daughter within it.

"Thus, O Bharata, I have recounted the story of Duhsala's birth to you. Please tell me, O sinless one, what more you wish to hear."

Janamejaya leaned forward, his eyes fixed on the storyteller, and demanded, "Please, describe to me the names of Dhritarashtra's sons in the order of their birth."

Vaisampayana, in his rich storytelling voice, began, "Their names, O king, in the order of their birth, are thus: Duryodhana, the mighty and headstrong; Yuyutsu, with a desire for battle; Duhsasana, the unruly; Duhsaha, the unassailable; Duhsala, the daughter of the house; Jalasandha, the born ruler; Sama, the tranquil one; Saha, the powerful; Vinda and Anuvinda, the victorious twins; Durdharsha, the invincible; Suvahu, the good-armed; Dushpradharshana, the difficult to conquer; Durmarshana, the fierce warrior; and Durmukha, the grim-faced. There is also Dushkarna, the unyielding; and Karna, the radiant one; Vivinsati and Vikarna, the discerning; Sala, the valiant; Satwa, the virtuous; Sulochana, the fair-eyed; Chitra and Upachitra, the artistic; Chitraksha, the keen-eyed; Charuchitra, the handsome one; Sarasana, the graceful; Durmada, the hard to control; Durvigaha, the difficult to vanquish; Vivitsu, the eager for battle; and Vikatanana, the powerful-armed.

Urnanabha and Sunabha, the skilled archers; Nandaka and Upanandaka, the joyful; Chitravana, the forest-dweller; Chitravarman, the brilliantly armored; Suvarman, the handsome-hearted; Durvimochana, the hard to release; Ayovahu, the swift charioteer; Mahavahu, the mighty-armed; Chitranga, the colorful one; Chitrakundala, the adorned with jewels; Bhimavega, the swift as the wind; Bhimavala, the strong-armed; Balaki, the youthful; Balavardhana, the robust; Ugrayudha, the fierce warrior; Bhima, the formidable; Karna, the resplendent; Kanakaya, the gold-adorned; Dridhayudha, the unwavering; Dridhavarman, the steadfast; Dridhakshatra, the bold in battle; Somakitri, the performer of sacrifices; Anudara, the generous; Dridhasandha, the firm in resolve; Jarasandha, the unconquerable; Satyasandha, the truthful; Sada, the ever-victorious; Suvak, the sweet-voiced; Ugrasravas, the loudly acclaimed; Ugrasena, the mighty leader; Senani, the commander; Dushparajaya, the hard to defeat; Aparajita, the invincible; Kundasayin, the killer of foes; Visalaksha, the broad-eyed; Duradhara, the tough to withstand; Dridhahasta, the strong-armed; Suhasta, the graceful-handed; Vatavega, the swift as the wind; and Suvarchas, the radiant one.

Adityaketu, the sun-bannered; Vahvashin, the powerful; Nagadatta, the one given by the serpent; Agrayayin, the leader of battles; Kavachin, the armor-clad; Krathana, the skilled in rituals; Kunda, the adorned with lotuses; Kundadhara, the lotus-bearer; Dhanurdhara, the bow-wielder; the heroes, Ugra and Bhimaratha, the fierce and the chariot-warriors; Viravahu, the strong-armed; Alolupa, the untamed; Abhaya, the fearless; Raudrakarman, the fierce in action; Dridharatha, the steadfast charioteer; Anadhrishya, the hard to resist;

Kundabhedin, the breaker of shields; Viravi, the heroic; Dhirghalochana, the one with long eyes; Pramatha, the one who shakes the earth; Pramathi, the turbulent; and the mighty Dhirgharoma, the long-haired.

Dirghavahu, the far-reaching; Mahavahu, the mighty-armed; Vyudhoru, the valorous; Kanakadhvaja, the gold-bannered; Kundasi and Virajas, the adorned ones. Besides these hundred sons, there was a daughter named Duhsala. All of them were formidable warriors, skilled in the Vedas, and masters of various weapons. King Dhritarashtra, after careful consideration, selected worthy wives for each of them. And, O king, he gave Duhsala in marriage to Jayadratha, the king of Sindhu."

Chapter 16

THE ORIGIN OF THE PANDAVAS

One fateful day, Pandu, driven by his insatiable passion for the hunt, led an expedition deep into the untamed wilderness. By his side were his two illustrious queens, Kunti and Madri, both renowned for their beauty and wisdom. The forest echoed with the calls of wild creatures, the rustling of leaves, and the songs of birds, setting the stage for a most extraordinary encounter.

As they ventured deeper into the woods, a sight of unparalleled wonder met their eyes. There, before them, stood a majestic deer, its coat as pure as the driven snow, and its antlers glistening like polished ivory. It was a creature of divine beauty, unlike any they had ever beheld.

Pandu, his hunter's spirit ablaze, raised his bow, nocking an arrow with the skill of a seasoned warrior shot the male deer while it was mating with a female. To his suprise the deer began to speak. 'O king, even men that are slaves to lust and wrath, and void of reason, and ever sinful, never commit such a cruel act as this. Individual judgment prevaileth not against the ordinance, the ordinance prevaileth against individual judgment. The wise never sanction anything discountenanced by the ordinance. Thou art born, O Bharata, in a race that hath ever been virtuous. How is it, therefore, that even thou, suffering thyself to be overpowered by passion and wrath losest thy reason?'

Hearing this, Pandu replied, 'O deer, kings behave in the matter of slaying animals of thy species exactly as they do in the matter of slaying foes. It behoveth thee not, therefore, to reprove me thus from ignorance. Animals of thy species are slain by open or covert means. This, indeed, is the practice of kings. Then why dost thou reprove me? Formerly, the Rishi Agastya, while engaged in the performance of a grand sacrifice, chased the deer, and devoted every deer in the forest unto the gods in general. Thou hast been slain, pursuant to the usage sanctioned by such precedent. Wherefore reprovest us then? For his especial sacrifices Agastya performed the homa with fat of the deer.'

"The deer then said, 'O king, men do not let fly their arrows at their enemies when the latter are unprepared. But there is a time for doing it (viz., after declaration of hostilities). Slaughter at such a time is not censurable.'

"Pandu replied, 'It is well-known that men slay deer by various effective means without regarding whether the animals are careful or careless. Therefore, O deer, why dost thou reprove me?'

"The deer then said, 'O, king, I did not blame thee for thy having killed a deer, or for the injury thou hast done to me. But, instead of acting so cruelly, thou shouldst have waited till the completion of my act of intercourse. What man of wisdom and virtue is there that can kill a deer while engaged in such an act? The time of sexual intercourse is agreeable to every creature and productive of good to all. O king, with this my mate I was engaged in the gratification of my sexual desire. But that effort of mine hath been rendered futile by thee. O king of the Kurus, as thou art born in the race of the Pauravas ever noted for white (virtuous) deeds, such an act hath scarcely been worthy of thee. O Bharata, this act must be regarded as extremely cruel, deserving of universal execration, infamous, and sinful, and certainly leading to hell. Thou art acquainted with the pleasures of sexual intercourse. Thou art acquainted also with the teaching of morality and dictates of duty. Like unto a celestial as thou art, it behoveth thee not to do such an act as leadeth to hell. O best of kings, thy duty is to chastise all who act cruelly, who are engaged in sinful practices and who have thrown to the winds religion, profit, and pleasure as explained in the scriptures. What hast thou done, O best of men, in killing me who have given thee no offence? I am, O king, a Muni who liveth on fruits and roots, though disguised as a deer. I was living in the woods in peace with all. Yet thou hast killed me, O king, for which I will curse thee certainly. As thou hast been cruel unto a couple of opposite sexes, death shall certainly overtake thee as soon as thou feelest the influence of sexual desire. I am a Muni of the name of Kindama, possessed of ascetic merit. I was engaged in sexual intercourse with this deer, because my feelings of modesty did not permit me to indulge in such an act in human society. In the form of a deer I rove in the deep woods in the company of other deer. Thou hast slain me without knowing that I am a Brahmana, the sin of having slain a Brahmana shall not, therefore, be thine. But senseless man, as you have killed me, disguised as a deer, at such a time, thy fate shall certainly be even like mine. When, approaching thy wife lustfully, thou wilt unite with her even as I had done with mine, in that very state shalt thou have to go to the world of the spirits. And that wife of thine with whom thou mayst be united in intercourse at the time of thy death shall also follow thee with affection and reverence to the domains of the king of the dead. Thou hast brought me grief when I was happy. So shall grief come to thee when thou art in happiness.'

In the days that followed the death of that noble deer, King Pandu and his two queens were plunged into the depths of sorrow, their tears flowing like rivers of anguish. Pandu, his heart heavy with remorse, cried out, "The wicked, even when born into virtuous families, are ensnared by their own desires and suffer for their deeds. My father, begotten by the virtuous Santanu, was cut down in his youth by the very lust that consumed him. In the passionate embrace of that lustful king, the venerable Rishi Krishna-Dwaipayana, truth-speaker and sage, fathered me. Born of such a lineage, my own wickedness has led me into this life of wandering in the forest, chasing deer. Even the gods have abandoned me! It is time for me to seek salvation, to renounce the world's enticements. The great obstacles to salvation are the desire for progeny and worldly concerns. I shall embrace the life of a Brahmachari and follow the eternal path of my father. I will conquer my desires through rigorous ascetic penances, forsake my wives, and shave my head. I shall wander alone, begging for sustenance from the trees that stand tall in this forest. I will renounce all attachments, making my abode beneath the trees or in abandoned shelters. I will not be swayed by joy or sorrow, and I shall treat slander and praise with indifference. I will seek no blessings nor accept any bows. I will be at peace with all, refusing gifts and harming none, be they creatures with legs or without, whether oviparous or viviparous, worms or plants. I will treat them all as my own children, showing no partiality. Once a day, I shall beg from five or, at most, ten families, and if I receive nothing, I shall go without sustenance. I would rather go hungry than beg more than once from the same person. If my rounds yield nothing, I will not expand them out of greed. Whether I receive or not, I shall remain unmoved like a true ascetic. Even if one man cuts off my arm with a hatchet and another anoints my other arm with sandalwood paste, I shall regard them with equal equanimity. I will not wish for prosperity for one or misery for the other. I will not yearn for life or fear death. I will not desire to live nor long for death. I will cleanse my heart of all sins and rise above the rituals that bring happiness, practiced by worldly men on auspicious days and times. I will abstain from all religious and worldly activities that lead to sensual gratification. Freed from the snares of the world, I will be like the unbridled wind, bound by nothing. I will walk the path of fearlessness, treating all with equality. I shall neither desire to live nor to die. Cleansing my heart of all impurities, I shall transcend the sacred rites that bring happiness. Whether I am respected or disrespected, I shall wear an expression of indifference, for he who casts a beggar's look out of greed, even when destitute of the power to procreate, behaves like a dog."

Vaisampayana continued, "Having poured out his heart in lament, King Pandu turned to his two wives, Kunti and Madri, and spoke to them thus, 'Let our kingdom's people, my mother from Kosala, Vidura, our friends, the revered Satyavati, Bhishma, the family priests, the noble Soma-drinking Brahmanas of unwavering vows, and all the elders who depend on us, know that Pandu, with his wives, has chosen to retire to the wilderness to lead a life of asceticism.' Hearing their lord's decision to embark on an ascetic journey into the forest, both Kunti and Madri, with reverence, replied, 'O mighty bull of the Bharata dynasty, there are other paths of righteous living where you can perform severe penances, and we, your wedded wives, can accompany you. In these paths, you can attain salvation and liberation from the cycle of rebirths. We will control our desires, renounce all luxuries, and subject ourselves to the most rigorous austerities for your sake. O wise king, if you abandon us, we shall depart from this world today, for we live only for your sake.'

Pandu replied, 'If your hearts are set on this virtuous path, then I shall follow it with both of you. Abandoning the luxuries of cities and towns, dressed in tree barks, subsisting on fruits and roots, I shall wander through the deep woods, practicing the harshest penances. I shall perform the sacred homa ritual, reduce my bodily sustenance to a minimum, wear rags and animal skins, and let my hair grow matted. I will endure heat and cold, hunger and thirst, and reduce my body through severe ascetic practices. I will seek solitude and immerse myself in meditation, sustaining myself on whatever fruits I find. I will offer oblations to the Pitris and the gods with simple offerings of speech, water, and forest fruits. I shall avoid encounters with the denizens of the woods, my relatives, and the inhabitants of cities and towns. Until I relinquish this mortal coil, I shall follow the Vanaprastha scriptures, always seeking even more rigorous penances.'

Vaisampayana continued, 'The Kuru king, having thus spoken to his wives, generously distributed his royal jewels, gold necklaces, bracelets, earrings, and the splendid robes of his queens to Brahmanas. Then, summoning his attendants, he entrusted them with a solemn message, 'Return to Hastinapura and announce to all that Pandu, along with his wives, has chosen to live in the forest, forsaking wealth, desire, pleasure, and even the urge for procreation.' With heavy hearts, his followers and attendants, tears streaming down their faces, departed from their beloved king and hastened back to Hastinapura, carrying the wealth meant for charity. Meanwhile, Dhritarashtra, the noblest of men, upon hearing their account of the events in the forest, wept for his brother Pandu. He was consumed by sorrow, finding little comfort in his luxurious palace, on his grandiose thrones, or in the sumptuous feasts spread before him.

THE SOURCE OF CONFLICT

As for Pandu, accompanied by his two devoted queens, he embarked on a journey, subsisting on fruits and roots, through the sacred mountains. He traversed the heights of Nagasata, crossed the Kalakuta, and finally, surmounted the Himavat, reaching the grandeur of Gandhamadana. Protected by the Mahabhutas, Siddhas, and revered sages, Pandu moved from level ground to mountain slopes, his heart set on the path of asceticism. He continued to explore the wilderness, reaching the lake of Indradyumna, and then crossing the peaks of Hansakuta, he arrived at the mountain of a hundred summits, Sata-sringa. There, he resolved to practice the most rigorous ascetic austerities."

And so, the saga of Pandu's ascetic journey began, as he and his queens embraced a life of renunciation and self-discipline, seeking salvation in the heart of the wilderness.

Pandu, a man of great vigor and determination, had wholeheartedly embraced the ascetic path. In no time, he had won the favor and respect of the Siddhas and Charanas residing in those sacred mountains. With unwavering dedication to his spiritual guides, a humble heart devoid of vanity, a mind under strict control, and passions tamed to submission, Pandu had grown in strength and acquired ascetic prowess that made him worthy of entering the heavens by his own merit. Some of the revered Rishis considered him a brother, some a friend, and others cherished him as their own son. Despite his Kshatriya lineage, Pandu had become akin to a Brahmarshi through his unwavering commitment to asceticism.

On a particular new moon day, as the great Rishis with their austere vows assembled, they expressed their desire to witness the divine Brahman. Pandu, eager to accompany them, asked, "Noble sages, where shall we go?" The Rishis replied, "Today, there will be a grand gathering in the abode of Brahman, with celestial beings, Rishis, and

Pitris in attendance. We wish to go there and behold the Self-created."

Upon hearing this, Pandu, seized by a sudden determination, decided to join the Rishis on their journey northward, up the mountain of a hundred peaks. The ascetics, concerned for the well-being of Pandu's wives, cautioned him, "O bull of Bharata's lineage, we have seen many regions on the slopes of this mighty mountain, some inaccessible to ordinary mortals, while others host the retreats of gods, Gandharvas, and Apsaras. There are heavenly gardens, the abode of Kuvera, flowing rivers, and deep caverns. Some regions are perpetually covered in snow and devoid of life, where even birds cannot venture. Only air can reach those heights, along with Siddhas and great Rishis. How will these princesses ascend such treacherous terrain? Unaccustomed to hardship, they may suffer greatly. Therefore, O king, do not accompany us."

Pandu responded, "Wise ones, it is said that heaven is not accessible to those without sons. I am childless, and this thought pains me deeply. It is believed that sacrifices, charitable acts, ascetic penances, and vows, even when observed with utmost devotion, do not yield religious merit to a man without offspring. Sons are the means to secure virtuous renown across the three worlds. The absence of progeny can deprive one of the heavenly realms of happiness. Men are born on this earth with four debts: to their ancestors, gods, Rishis, and fellow beings. These debts must be duly discharged. The wise have proclaimed that those who neglect these obligations face a barren path to true felicity. The gods are pleased through sacrifices, the Rishis through study, meditation, and asceticism, and ancestors through begetting children and offering funeral offerings. My debt to the Rishis, gods, and fellow beings is paid, but I have not yet discharged my debt to my ancestors. The best of men are born to beget children and fulfill this duty. I ask you, should I seek to father children in the same way I was conceived, through the divine act of a sage?"

The Rishis answered, "O virtuous king, there is progeny in your destiny, pure and blessed, akin to the gods. We foresee it clearly with our prophetic vision. Therefore, O tiger among men, strive to achieve what destiny has laid before you. The fruits of your efforts are visible to us, and they promise you accomplished and fortunate offspring."

Hearing their words, Pandu, weighed down by the curse that had robbed him of his procreative powers, began to contemplate deeply. He called his beloved wife, the illustrious Kunti, and spoke to her in private, "Endeavor to bear children during this time of crisis. The wise sages of eternal law declare that sons are the source of supreme virtue across the three worlds. Sacrifices, charity, penance, and vows, even when observed with utmost devotion, do not yield religious merit to one without progeny. O Kunti, in my present state, powerless to beget children due to the curse of the deer, I implore you to seek progeny from someone equal or superior to me. O Kunti, listen to the story of the daughter of Saradandayana, who was instructed by her husband to bear children. When her time came, she bathed and went to a crossroads at night, where four paths met. There, a Brahmana, accomplished through asceticism, approached her, and she sought his seed for offspring. After performing the Punsavana sacrifice, she gave birth to three mighty sons, with Durjaya being the eldest, born of that Brahmana. O fortunate one, follow her example at my command, and quickly seek offspring from a Brahmana of great ascetic merit."

Chapter 17

THE BIRTH OF THE PANDAVAS

Thus spoke Pandu, the conqueror of hostile cities, to the fair and ever-dutiful Kunti. With grace and devotion ever in her heart for her husband, Kunti replied, "In my girlhood, O my lord, I resided in my father's house, where I attended to the needs of all guests. I showed the utmost respect to Brahmanas of unwavering vows and great ascetic merit. One day, I had the privilege of serving Durvasa, the Brahmana known for his unwavering mind and profound knowledge of the mysteries of religion. Pleased with my service, that sage bestowed upon me a boon in the form of a mantra, a sacred invocation, which could summon any celestial being of my choice into my presence. The sage told me, 'O young maiden, whoever celestial being you summon using this mantra will come to you and be bound to fulfill your wishes, whether they like it or not. Through this boon, O princess, you shall also bear children by their grace.' These words were spoken to me by the Brahmana when I dwelled in my father's house. The words of such a sage can never be untrue, and now the time has come for them to bear fruit. At your command, O royal sage, I can use that mantra to summon any celestial being to fulfill our desire for children. O foremost of truthful men, please tell me which celestial being I should invoke. Rest assured that I await your command in this matter."

Hearing Kunti's words, Pandu replied, "O beautiful one, strive to fulfill our desires today. Summon the god of justice, for he is the most virtuous among the celestials. The god of justice and virtue will never lead us into sin. The world will then recognize that our actions are pure and untainted. The son we obtain from him will undoubtedly be the foremost among the Kurus in virtue. Conceived by the god of justice and morality, he will never stray toward anything sinful or unholy. Therefore, O sweet-smiled one, holding virtue steadfastly in your heart, and observing holy vows with dedication, use your supplications and incantations to summon the god of justice and virtue as per my wish."

Vaisampayana continued, "Hearing her lord's command, Kunti bowed to him and reverently circled his presence, resolved to carry out his will."

After a full year had passed since Gandhari's conception, Kunti decided it was time to summon the eternal god of justice, eager to obtain offspring from him. Without delay, she began her sacrifices to the god, chanting the mantra that Durvasa had imparted to her earlier. The god, overwhelmed by her incantations, appeared at the spot where Kunti sat, resplendent as the Sun. With a smile, he asked, "O Kunti, what do you seek?" Kunti, smiling in return, replied, "You must grant me offspring." Thus, the handsome Kunti united with the god of justice in his spiritual form, obtaining from him a son dedicated to the welfare of all beings. She brought forth this remarkable child, who would later earn great fame, at the auspicious moment of the eighth Muhurta known as Abhijit, during the noon of the seventh month, Kartika, on the fifth day of the bright fortnight. The star Jyeshtha, in conjunction with the moon, was ascendant at that time. As soon as the child was born, an incorporeal voice from the skies proclaimed, "This child shall be the best of men, the foremost in virtue. Endowed with great strength and unwavering truthfulness, he will become a great ruler of the earth. This first child of Pandu shall be known as Yudhishthira."

Pandu, blessed with this virtuous son, spoke again to his wife, saying, "The wise have declared that a Kshatriya must possess physical strength to be worthy of the name. Therefore, ask for a son endowed with superior strength." Following her husband's command, Kunti invoked Vayu, the mighty god of the wind. Appearing before her, mounted on a deer, Vayu asked, "What, O Kunti, do you wish of me? Tell me your heart's desire." Modestly, she replied, "Grant me a child of immense strength and robust limbs, capable of humbling the pride of anyone." In response, the god of wind begot upon her a child who would later be known as Bhima, known for his mighty arms and fierce prowess. Upon Bhima's birth, once again, an incorporeal voice proclaimed, "This child will be the foremost in strength."

During Bhima's infancy, a remarkable incident occurred. As he fell from his mother's lap onto the rocky mountain breast, the sheer force of his fall shattered the stone upon which he landed, miraculously leaving the infant unharmed. Kunti had risen suddenly, startled by the presence of a tiger, unknowingly causing the child to tumble from her lap. Pandu, witnessing this astonishing feat, was filled with wonder. Interestingly, the very day Bhima was born, it was also the birthday of Duryodhana, who would later become the ruler of the entire earth.

Pandu continued to contemplate how he could obtain a son of exceptional renown. He understood that destiny and effort were intertwined, and without timely exertion, destiny could not be altered. Pandu believed that Indra, the chief of the gods, possessed immeasurable might and energy. To please him, Pandu decided to undertake severe austerities. Pandu, along with great Rishis, directed Kunti to observe a year-long auspicious vow, while he himself began to stand on one leg from morning to evening, engaging in other rigorous austerities with unwavering meditation, all to appease the lord of the celestials.

After an extended period of intense devotion, Indra, gratified by Pandu's efforts, approached him and said, "O king, I shall give you a son who will be celebrated throughout the three worlds, benefiting Brahmanas, cows, and all righteous men. He will be a formidable foe to the wicked and the joy of friends and relatives. This son of yours will be unmatched in battle, a repository of wisdom, with a great soul, radiating splendor like the Sun, invincible in combat, and extraordinarily handsome. O fortunate Kunti, your vow has borne fruit. The lord of the celestials is willing to grant you a son of your choice, one who will excel in Kshatriya virtues." Indra's words filled Pandu and Kunti with joy.

Upon hearing these divine promises, Kunti invoked Indra, and he begot upon her a son who would be known as Arjuna. When this child was born, once again, an incorporeal voice resounded through the heavens, proclaiming, "This child of yours, O Kunti, will possess the energy of Kartavirya and the prowess of Lord Shiva. Invincible as Indra himself, he will spread your fame far and wide. As Vishnu enhanced Aditi's joy, this child will increase your happiness. He will subdue the Madras, the Kurus, the Somakas, and the people of Chedi, Kasi, and Karusha, upholding the prosperity of the Kurus. By his valor, Agni will be satiated with the fat of all creatures dwelling in the Khandava forest."

Kunti, lying in her chamber, heard these extraordinary words. As the voices filled the sky, ascetics residing on the mountain of a hundred peaks and the celestials, including Indra in their celestial chariots, rejoiced with exuberance. Drums beat, and the region was adorned with flowers showered by invisible hands. Tribes of celestials assembled, offering their adorations to Pandu's son. The sons of Kadru, the Gandharvas, the Rishis, and many more beings arrived, and the great Rishis, in particular, were overwhelmed by their affection for Pandu's children.

Pandu, tempted to seek more children, wished to address his wife again for invoking another god. However, Kunti reminded him, "The wise do not permit a fourth childbirth, even in times of distress. A woman who has relations with four different men is called a Swairini, and with five, she becomes a harlot. Therefore, O learned one, you are well-acquainted with the scriptures that forbid a fourth childbirth. Why, then, are you tempted by the desire for more offspring, seemingly forgetting the established ordinance?"

In the wake of Kunti's sons and the hundred sons of Dhritarashtra, Madri, the daughter of the King of the Madras, found a private moment to speak to Pandu. She addressed him with grace, saying, "O vanquisher of foes, I hold no grievances even if fortune has not favored me. I bear no ill will that, though by birth I stand higher than Kunti, I am considered inferior in station. My sorrow lies elsewhere, O sinless one. It pains me deeply that while Kunti and I are equals, I remain childless while she has been blessed with your offspring alone. If the daughter of Kuntibhoja could somehow provide a way for me to have children, she would indeed be doing me a great kindness and benefiting you as well. She is my rival, and I hesitate to seek any favor from her. If, O king, you are inclined to help me, then request her to grant my desire."

Pandu, pondering the matter, responded, "O Madri, I have often contemplated this issue in my mind, but I hesitated to discuss it with you, uncertain of your reaction. Now that I know your wishes, I shall certainly work towards that end. I believe that if I ask, Kunti will not refuse."

Vaisampayana continued, "After this conversation, Pandu approached Kunti privately and said, 'O Kunti, for the expansion of my lineage and the welfare of the world, grant me the boon of more offspring. Bestow upon me, my ancestors, and your own ancestors the offerings due during our last rites. Do what is beneficial for me and for the world's best interests. It may be a challenging task for you, but let the desire for undying fame move you. Just as Indra, despite obtaining the lordship of the celestials, continues to perform sacrifices for the sake of fame, we see Brahmanas, well-versed in the Vedas and accomplished in asceticism, approach their spiritual guides with reverence for the sake of fame. Royal sages and ascetic Brahmanas who have amassed great spiritual wealth also undertake the most arduous ascetic feats, driven solely by the desire for fame. Therefore, O virtuous one, rescue Madri as if you were extending a raft to her, granting her the means to have offspring, and gain enduring glory by enabling her to become a mother.'

Hearing her lord's plea, Kunti willingly consented, saying to Madri, 'Think of a celestial being without delay, and you shall undoubtedly bear a child resembling that being.' After contemplating for a moment, Madri summoned the twin Aswins, who promptly appeared before her. These divine beings granted her two sons, twins named Nakula and Sahadeva, renowned throughout the land for their unparalleled beauty. Upon their birth, an ethereal voice proclaimed, 'In energy and beauty, these twins shall surpass even the twin Aswins themselves.' Indeed, these sons, possessed of extraordinary energy and beauty, illuminated the entire realm.

O king, after all the children were born, the Rishis residing on the mountain of a hundred peaks blessed them and performed the initial rites of birth with affection, giving each child a name. Kunti's eldest son was named Yudhishthira, the second Bhimasena, and the third Arjuna. Madri's sons, the twins, were called Nakula and Sahadeva. These five sons, born one year apart, together appeared as if they embodied a five-year period. King Pandu, witnessing his children's celestial beauty, boundless strength, valor, and noble hearts, rejoiced immensely. The children became the cherished favorites of the Rishis and their wives living on the snow-capped sacred mountain.

Sometime later, Pandu approached Kunti again on behalf of Madri. He spoke to her privately, saying, 'Having given her the formula of invocation only once, she has managed to obtain two sons. I fear that she may soon surpass me in the number of her children, deceiving me in this manner. Such is the way of wicked women. Foolishly, I did not realize that by invoking the twin gods, one can obtain twin children in a single birth. I beseech you, O queen, do not command me any further. Let this be the boon granted to me.'

Kunti, thus addressed by her lord, replied, 'I have already given her the formula once, and she has obtained two sons. My desire is now fulfilled. I fear that if I grant it again, she will surpass me in the number of children. This is my final word, O king. Do not ask me for more.'"

Thus, O king, were born to Pandu five sons, begotten by celestial beings, endowed with great strength and power, and destined to achieve great fame, furthering the lineage of the Kuru dynasty. These sons, bearing auspicious marks, resembling the moon in beauty, possessing the heart of lions, and skilled in archery, grew rapidly, their virtues shining brighter with each passing year. Witnessing their growth, the great Rishis residing on the snow-capped mountain of a hundred peaks were filled with amazement. The five Pandavas and the hundred sons of Dhritarashtra, the progenitor of the Kuru race, flourished like a cluster of lotuses in a serene lake."

Chapter 18

THE DEATH OF PANDU

Beholding his five strapping sons growing amidst the grandeur of the forest on the enchanting mountain slope, Pandu felt the long-dormant strength in his arms stir to life once more. One day, during the intoxicating season of spring that inflames the desires of all living beings, the king ventured into the woods with his wife Madri. There, amidst the blossoming trees, they found Palasas and Tilakas, Mangoes and Champakas, Parihadrakas and Karnikaras, Asokas and Kesaras, Atimuktas and Kuruvakas, each adorned with swarms of entranced bees humming sweetly. The air was filled with the fragrance of Parijatas, and the Kokilas sang melodious tunes beneath the branches, harmonizing with the gentle buzz of the black bees. Countless other trees bowed under the weight of their flowers and fruits, and crystal-clear pools adorned with numerous fragrant lotuses shimmered in the sunlight. Pandu, immersed in the beauty of the surroundings, felt the soft influence of desire.

Roaming like a celestial being through this picturesque landscape, Pandu found himself alone with his wife Madri, both dressed in attire that was almost transparent. Seeing the youthful Madri in such an alluring state, Pandu's desire blazed like a forest fire. Overwhelmed by passion, he forgot everything, even his own misfortune. The king seized Madri against her will, and though she resisted with all her strength, her trembling form could not withstand his overpowering desire. The flames of passion consumed him, and he sought Madri's embrace with the determination that seemed as if he wished to bring an end to his own life. His judgment, beguiled by the great Destroyer himself, his senses intoxicated, was lost along with his life. King Pandu, a virtuous soul, succumbed to the relentless grasp of Time, consumed by his desires for Madri.

Madri, clasping her senseless husband's body, began to weep bitterly. Kunti, along with her sons and Madri's twins, heard these anguished cries and hurried to the scene where the king lay lifeless. Madri, her voice choked with sorrow, addressed Kunti with a piteous plea, "Come here alone, dear sister Kunti, and leave the children behind." Upon hearing this, Kunti instructed the children to stay put and ran towards the source of the distress, crying, "Woe to me!"

As Kunti arrived, she saw both Pandu and Madri lying unconscious on the ground. She rushed to their side, lamenting, "This hero, who had his desires in perfect control, has been watched over by me with great care. How did he forget the Rishi's curse and indulge in passion? Madri, you should have protected him. Why did you entice him into this solitude? Always bearing the weight of the Rishi's curse, how did he find mirth with you in this solitude? Princess of Valhika, more fortunate than myself, you are truly enviable, for you have witnessed our lord's happiness and joy."

Madri replied, her voice trembling, "Revered sister, I resisted the king with tears in my eyes, but he could not control his desires, as if he were determined to make the Rishi's curse come true."

Kunti then spoke, "I am the elder of his wives, and the primary religious merit should be mine. Therefore, Madri, do not prevent me from performing what must be done. I must follow our lord to the realm of the dead. Rise, Madri, and give me his body. You must raise these children." Madri responded, "I still hold our lord's lifeless body, and I have not let him go. Therefore, I shall follow him. My hunger remains unsatisfied. You are my elder sister, and I seek your permission. This noble prince of the Bharata dynasty approached me, desiring union. His desires unfulfilled, should I not accompany him to the realm of Yama to fulfill them? O revered one, if I outlive you, I fear I won't be able to raise your children as if they were mine. Won't I be tainted by sin in that case? You, O Kunti, will be better equipped to raise my sons as your own. The king, driven by his ardent desire, has departed to the land of spirits, so my body should be cremated with his. O revered sister, do not withhold your consent; it is my heartfelt wish. You will undoubtedly nurture the children with care. That would be pleasing to me, and I have no other guidance to offer."

And so, O king, with these words, the daughter of the King of Madras, Pandu's wife, climbed onto the funeral pyre of her lord, that heroic man among men.

Chapter 19

THE PANDAVAS ENTER HASTINIPUR

———∽∽———

The godlike Rishis, seers of profound wisdom, witnessed the passing of Pandu, and they gathered to consult amongst themselves. In solemn tones, they spoke, "The virtuous and renowned King Pandu, relinquishing his kingdom and sovereignty, came to this place to undertake ascetic austerities. He dedicated himself to the hermits dwelling on this sacred mountain and has now ascended to the heavens, leaving behind his wife and infant sons as a sacred trust in our care. It is our duty to journey to his kingdom with his children and his wife."

As Vaisampayana recounted, "With resolute hearts, these godlike Rishis, crowned with the fruits of their ascetic practices, came to a unanimous decision. They decided to embark on the journey to Hastinapura with Pandu's offspring leading the way, intending to place them under the protection of Bhishma and Dhritarashtra. These ascetics set forth without delay, taking with them the children, Kunti, and the lifeless bodies of Pandu and Madri. Despite having led a life untouched by toil, Kunti, driven by her affection for her sons and her sense of duty, found the journey shorter than she had imagined.

Within a brief span, they reached Kurujangala, and the illustrious Kunti presented herself at the principal gate of Hastinapura. The ascetics instructed the porters to announce their arrival to the king. The messengers hurried to the royal court to convey the news. The citizens of Hastinapura, learning about the arrival of thousands of Charanas (ascetics) and Munis (sages), were filled with awe and curiosity. They emerged from their homes, men and women alike, with their children, to witness the assembly of these holy men.

People from all walks of life, including countless Kshatriyas, Vaisyas, and Sudras, gathered to behold this extraordinary sight. The citizens were overwhelmed by a sense of piety, and the entire gathering exuded an atmosphere of tranquility. Bhishma, the son of Santanu, Somadatta (Valhika), the royal sage Dhritarashtra with his profound insight, Vidura, the venerable Satyavati, and the illustrious princess of Kosala, Gandhari, came out, accompanied by other noble ladies of the royal household. The hundred sons of Dhritarashtra, bedecked in various ornaments, also joined the assembly.

The Kauravas, led by their priest, greeted the Rishis by bowing their heads and took their seats respectfully before them. The citizens followed suit, offering their salutations to the ascetics and bowing to the ground before taking their places. Bhishma, after performing the customary rituals of welcoming the guests, spoke to the ascetics about the kingdom and sovereignty.

The eldest sage among them, his matted locks adorning his head and clad in animal skins, rose and, with the consent of the other Rishis, addressed the assembly, "You all are aware that King Pandu, the ruler of the Kurus, chose to abandon the pleasures of the world and resided on this mountain. He embraced the path of Brahmacharya, and by some divine design, his eldest son, Yudhishthira, was born here, begotten by Dharma himself. Later, this illustrious king, blessed by Vayu, was granted another son, the mighty Bhima. The third son, Dhananjaya, was born to Kunti from Indra himself, destined to surpass all archers. And here are the twin sons of Madri, born to her from the twin Aswins, unrivaled in their beauty and valor. Pandu, leading a righteous life of a Vanaprastha in the forest, has thus revitalized the dwindling lineage of his forefathers. Now, the birth, growth, and Vedic education of these children of Pandu will surely bring joy to your hearts. Pandu, a paragon of virtue, left this world seventeen days ago. His wife, Madri, witnessing his pyre and determined to follow him to the afterlife, ascended the same funeral pyre, sacrificing her life to be with her lord. Now, let the appropriate rites be performed for their benefit. These are the unburned remains of their bodies. Here also are their children, these valiant warriors who will be thorns in the sides of their foes. Show them the due respect they deserve. After the initial rites honoring the departed, let us perform the first annual Sraddha (sapindakarana) to formally establish Pandu among the Pitris (ancestors)."

As Vaisampayana continued his narration, the ascetics, accompanied by Guhyakas, vanished from sight like ethereal forms, appearing and disappearing in the vast skies. The people, witnessing the disappearance of the Rishis and Siddhas, were filled with astonishment and returned to their homes, their hearts touched by the supernatural spectacle.

Vaisampayana's voice resonated through the hall, narrating the somber tale. "Dhritarashtra, the blind king of the Kurus, spoke with a heavy heart, his voice carrying the weight of sorrow, 'O Vidura, conduct the funeral ceremonies for that king among men, Pandu, and for his beloved wife, Madri, in a manner befitting royalty. Distribute cattle, cloths, precious gems, and various forms of wealth to all those who ask, ensuring their souls find peace. Make arrangements for Kunti to perform Madri's last rites as she deems fit. Let Madri's body be wrapped so meticulously that neither the Sun nor Vayu, the god of wind, may witness it. Do not mourn the blameless Pandu. He was a noble king and has left behind five heroic sons, equal to the very gods themselves.'

Vaisampayana continued, 'Vidura, accepting the task with a silent nod, consulted with Bhishma, the venerable grandsire. Together, they chose a sacred spot for Pandu's final rites. The family priests, carrying the sacred fire blazing with clarified butter and fragrant offerings, left the city swiftly. Friends, relatives, and loyal followers adorned the bodies of Pandu and Madri with seasonal flowers and exquisite perfumes, covering them with cloth. The ornate hearse, adorned with garlands and rich hangings, was shouldered by the grieving populace. A white umbrella, emblematic of royalty, waved above the hearse, accompanied by the music of various instruments. Generous souls distributed gems to the people as they moved in the procession. Beautiful garments, white umbrellas, and large yak-tails were brought for the grand ceremony. Clad in white, the priests led the way, pouring offerings into the sacred fire.

Brahmanas, Kshatriyas, Vaisyas, and Sudras numbering in the thousands followed the deceased king, their mournful cries echoing, 'O prince, where do you go, leaving us desolate and sorrowful?' Bhishma, Vidura, and the Pandavas joined in the lament. The procession reached a picturesque forest on the banks of the sacred Ganga, where they gently placed the hearse, carrying the truth-loving and lion-hearted prince and his queen. Water, brought in golden vessels, washed the prince's body, anointed with fragrant pastes, and adorned anew in a white garment woven from indigenous fabrics.

The king, in his new attire, appeared as if he merely slumbered on a lavish bed.

Once the remaining funeral rites were completed as directed by the priests, the Kauravas set fire to the bodies of the king and queen, their faces adorned with lotuses and sandalwood. Kausalya, Pandu's first wife, cried out in agony, 'O my son, my son!' and fell senseless to the ground. Her anguished cries moved the citizens, who wept for their king. Even the birds in the sky and the beasts of the field seemed touched by Kunti's grief. Bhishma, Vidura, and others present were deeply moved.

Amidst the collective sorrow, Bhishma, Vidura, Dhritarashtra, the Pandavas, and the Kuru ladies performed the watery ceremony for the departed king and queen. When the rituals concluded, the people, their hearts heavy with grief, tried to console Pandu's bereaved sons. The Pandavas, along with their companions, chose to sleep on the bare ground. Witnessing their resolve, the citizens, young and old, renounced their beds as well. The entire city mourned for the noble sons of King Pandu, and for twelve days, they grieved alongside the weeping Pandavas."

Chapter 20

Trouble Begins

Vaisampayana's words resonated in the hushed chamber, weaving a tale of treachery and valor. "In the wake of Pandu's funeral rites, Bhishma, the venerable patriarch, and Kunti, with their circle of loyal friends, performed the solemn Sraddha for the departed king. Pindas, offerings to the departed souls, were made, and a grand feast was arranged for the Kauravas and numerous Brahmanas, to whom gems and lands were distributed generously. The citizens, now cleansed from the impurity of their king's demise, returned to Hastinapura, their hearts heavy with grief. It was as if they had lost a beloved family member.

Amidst this atmosphere of sorrow, the wise Vyasa, beholding the growing darkness in the world, spoke to his mother, Satyavati, with deep concern. 'Mother,' he said, 'our days of joy have passed, replaced by an era of calamity. Sin multiplies with each passing day. The world ages, and the rule of the Kauravas will not endure due to tyranny and oppression. I implore you to retreat to the forest, immerse yourself in contemplation through Yoga, and avoid witnessing the annihilation of our lineage.'

Satyavati, acquiescing to her son's words, turned to her daughter-in-law Ambika. 'I hear that due to our grandsons' actions, the Bharata dynasty and its subjects will perish,' she said. 'With your permission, I will go to the forest with Ambika and Ambalika, who is consumed by grief over her son's loss.' With Bhishma's approval, the queen left for the forest. There, with her two daughters-in-law, she engaged in profound meditation until the time came for her soul to ascend to the heavens.

Meanwhile, the sons of Pandu, having undergone the purifying rituals prescribed by the Vedas, grew into princely young men in their father's home. Their encounters with the sons of Dhritarashtra during their playful moments revealed Bhima's extraordinary strength. In swiftness, precision, and the art of consuming food, Bhimasena surpassed them all. He would effortlessly defeat the hundred and one sons of Dhritarashtra, his laughter echoing as he playfully pulled their hair or made them wrestle with each other. Vrikodara, the son of the Wind-god, would drag them along the ground, and in his grip, they found their knees, heads, and shoulders broken. He could submerge ten of them in water at once, their struggles futile against his might. Even when the sons of Dhritarashtra climbed trees to pluck fruits, Bhima would shake the tree, sending both fruits and fruit-pluckers tumbling down. In pugilistic combat, speed, and skill, the princes found themselves no match for Bhima. His displays of strength were not driven by malice but were playful exhibitions of his power.

Observing Bhima's unparalleled prowess, the ambitious and wicked Duryodhana, the eldest son of Dhritarashtra, developed animosity toward him. Fueled by ignorance and ambition, Duryodhana devised a sinister plan. He thought, 'Bhima is unmatched in strength. I must eliminate him through deceit. Alone, Bhima dares face a hundred of us. While he rests in the garden, I shall cast him into the Ganga. Later, I will confine his elder brother Yudhishthira and his younger brother Arjuna, securing my sole reign without challenges.'

Thus resolved, Duryodhana watched for an opportunity to harm Bhima. Finally, at a place called Pramanakoti along the Ganga's banks, he constructed a splendid palace named the 'water-sport house.' Adorned with rich fabrics and various amusements, this palace was designed for water sports. Colorful flags fluttered above it, and inside, skilled chefs prepared delectable dishes. When everything was ready, Duryodhana informed the Pandavas, 'Let us go to the Ganga's banks, adorned with trees and flowers, and indulge in water sports.' Yudhishthira agreed, and the sons of Dhritarashtra, accompanied by the Pandavas, rode on large, country-born elephants and chariots resembling cities, leaving the capital behind.

Arriving at their destination, the princes dismissed their attendants and explored the scenic gardens. Entering the palace, they marveled at its plastered walls, painted ceilings, graceful windows, and splendid artificial fountains. Tanks filled with lotus blooms graced the surroundings, and the air was perfumed by myriad flowers. After reveling in the available luxuries, they engaged in play, exchanging morsels of food. Meanwhile, the treacherous Duryodhana had secretly poisoned a portion of Bhima's food, intending to end his life. Approaching Bhima with feigned friendliness, Duryodhana fed him the poisoned delicacies, rejoicing inwardly at his sinister scheme.

As the day waned and their water sports concluded, the princes, donning white attire and adorned with ornaments, prepared to rest in the pleasure house nestled within the garden. Fatigued by their exertions, Bhima, poisoned and weary, lay down on the ground. Unbeknownst to him, the cool evening air spread the poison throughout his body, rendering him unconscious. Seizing the opportunity, Duryodhana bound Bhima with shrubs' cords and callously threw him into the Ganga. The son of Pandu, now insensible and poisoned, sank deep until he reached the kingdom of the Nagas. There, thousands of Nagas, armed with venomous fangs, attacked him. Yet, their venom was neutralized by the poison that had tainted Bhima's blood. The Nagas bit him all over, except on his chest, where his skin was impenetrable.

Regaining consciousness, Bhima burst his bonds and fought the snakes fiercely, driving them underground. A handful fled and sought refuge with their king, Vasuki, narrating the ordeal they had faced. Vasuki, learning the truth, felt admiration for Bhima's bravery. Among the serpents, there was one named Aryaka, a relative of Kunti's lineage. Aryaka revealed Bhima's identity to Vasuki, who embraced him warmly. The serpents then shared their venomous bite experiences with Aryaka, and Vasuki was pleased with Bhima. He told Aryaka, 'Grant him riches and gems in abundance. Let him drink from the rasakunda (nectar vessels) to acquire immeasurable strength. Each vessel contains the strength of a thousand elephants. Let him drink to his heart's content.'

Aryaka conveyed Vasuki's permission, and the serpents performed auspicious rituals. Bhimasena, purified and facing east, began drinking the nectar. In a single breath, he emptied an entire vessel, continuing this feat until he consumed eight successive jars. The serpents then prepared a comfortable bed for him, and there, Bhima, his strength augmented immeasurably, rested at ease."

"As the Kauravas and Pandavas returned to Hastinapura, Bhima was conspicuously absent, his powerful presence noticeably lacking among his brothers. The wicked Duryodhana, his heart a wellspring of malevolence, concealed his sinister satisfaction and entered the city with his brothers, wearing a facade of joy that masked his dark intentions.

Yudhishthira, noble and unsullied by vice, believed others to be as honorable as himself. Filled with fraternal love, he approached his mother Kunti, his eyes reflecting his deep concern. 'Mother, where is Bhima?' he inquired, his voice touched with anxiety. 'He is not here, and we have searched for him everywhere in the gardens and woods. I feared he might have preceded us here. Alas, he has not returned! I suspect the worst; my heart is heavy with dread. I believe Bhima is no more.'

Kunti, upon hearing Yudhishthira's words, cried out in alarm. 'My son, I have not seen Bhima. He did not come to me,' she exclaimed, her voice tinged with distress. 'Go, return with your brothers, search for him, and bring him back to me.'

Addressing Vidura, her trusted advisor, she revealed her anguish. 'O illustrious Kshattri, Bhimasena is missing!' she said. 'Where could he have gone? The other brothers have returned, but Bhima, mighty of arm, has not come back! Duryodhana bears ill will towards him. That crooked, malicious, low-minded Kaurava openly covets the throne. I fear he might have slain my beloved son in a fit of rage. My heart aches with this dread.'

Vidura, his eyes filled with understanding, consoled her. 'Blessed dame, fear not!' he said reassuringly. 'Guard your remaining sons carefully. If Duryodhana is accused, he might harm your other sons. The great sage has foretold long lives for all your sons. Bhima will surely return and bring joy to your heart.'

With Vidura's words lingering in her ears, Kunti anxiously awaited her son's return, her heart heavy with worry. Meanwhile, Bhimasena, roused from his slumber on the eighth day, felt a surge of boundless strength. The nectar he had consumed had fully digested, filling him with unparalleled power. The Nagas, seeing him awake, offered him words of encouragement. 'O mighty-armed one, the strength-giving elixir you have consumed grants you the might of ten thousand elephants! None shall now be able to defeat you in battle,' they assured him. 'Bathe in this sacred water and return home. Your brothers anxiously await your arrival.'

Grateful for their assistance, Bhima purified himself with a bath in the holy waters, then adorned himself in white robes and garlands. He partook of the paramanna, a sweet rice pudding offered to him by the Nagas and received their adorations and blessings. Then, wearing celestial ornaments, he saluted his snake benefactors and rose from the nether regions. The Nagas, lifting him from the waters, placed him back in the very gardens where he had been engaged in playful exploits, and then disappeared from his sight.

Bhima, his strength augmented immeasurably, raced back to his mother with the speed of a tempest. Bowing before her and his elder brother, and embracing his younger siblings, he recounted the villainy of Duryodhana and the fortunate and unfortunate events that had befallen him in the Naga world. Yudhishthira, the righteous leader, cautioned his brothers to maintain silence about these incidents and to protect each other vigilantly. From that day on, the Pandavas, guided by Yudhishthira's wisdom, remained ever watchful.

Nevertheless, Duryodhana, and Sakuni, unwilling to abandon their malicious designs, persisted in their plots against the Pandavas. Despite their knowledge of these schemes, the Pandavas, heeding Vidura's counsel, suppressed their anger.

In the midst of these conspiracies, King Dhritarashtra, observing the Kuru princes' wayward behavior and growing impudence, appointed Gautama as their preceptor. He sent the young princes to Gautama, also known as Kripa, to learn the art of warfare. Gautama, born among a cluster of heath, was well-versed in the Vedas. Under his tutelage, the Kuru princes embarked on the path of martial training, their destinies intertwined with the fateful threads of an impending conflict."

Chapter 21

ORIGIN OF KRIPA

At the request of the King, Vaisampayana, the storyteller, his voice a low rumble in the flickering lamplightt, recouted the origins of Kripa with the gravitas of ancient lore:

"Listen, O Janamejaya, to the tale of Kripa, born from the heart of the wilds, a child destined for greatness in the realm of arms.

The sage Gautama, known for his mastery of weaponry, had a son named Saradwat. This young warrior was not just skilled but exceptionally adept in the science of weapons, a prodigy destined for greatness in the battlefield. But his heartbeat was for the art of war alone, neglecting all other realms of knowledge. In his pursuit of martial prowess, Saradwat performed austerities so formidable that even Indra, the king of gods, quaked in fear of his potential.

In his desperate attempt to thwart Saradwat's ascetic power, Indra dispatched a celestial enchantress named Janapadi to seduce the devoted sage. With unrivaled beauty gracing her form, she approached Saradwat, clad in a single piece of cloth, her charm meant to dismantle the sage's meditative focus. Saradwat, strong of soul and steely in resolve, battled the tidal wave of temptation, yet the sudden onslaught of desire caused him to lose control, his vital fluid escaping in an involuntary release.

Fleeing from Janapadi, Saradwat left his bow, arrows, and deer-skin behind, his essence falling upon a clump of heath. There, from the divine residue, two children emerged, twins, a testament to the sage's struggle against temptation.

Meanwhile, fate intervened as a soldier, in the service of the valiant king Santanu, stumbled upon the abandoned twins, the discarded armaments, and the deer-skin. Assuming them to be the progeny of a skilled Brahmana warrior, he presented them before the king. Touched by compassion, Santanu declared, 'Let these children be mine,' and brought them into his palace.

Santanu, noble and just, nurtured the twins, naming them Kripa and Kripi, a reflection of the pity that had moved him. Gautama, the forsaken father, discovered the whereabouts of his lost offspring and approached the king. He shared the truth of their lineage and began to educate Kripa, imparting to him the intricate knowledge of the science of arms, along with other esoteric wisdom. Under his father's guidance, Kripa excelled in the art of war, becoming a revered teacher. The echo of his lessons resonated through the corridors of power, as princes from distant lands sought to learn from this formidable sage.

And thus, the tale of Kripa, born from the clump of heath, emerged as a testament to the interplay of destiny, temptation, and the unyielding spirit of a warrior destined for greatness."

Chapter 22

The Origin of Drona

Vaisampayana's voice resonated through the hall, captivating his audience with the tale of Drona's quest for knowledge and power:

"In the land where legends and warriors thrived, a sage named Bharadwaja dwelt, his wisdom as vast as the starlit heavens. Bhishma, the venerable patriarch of the Kurus, sought a teacher of unparalleled prowess for his grandsons, one whose might matched their destiny. Thus, the son of Ganga, Bhishma, resolute in his purpose, chose Drona, son of Bharadwaja, as the tutor for the Kuru princes.

Drona, distinguished in the Vedas and revered in the science of arms, accepted the young princes under his tutelage, imparting to them the knowledge of weaponry in its myriad forms. The Kauravas and

Pandavas, their strength boundless, drank deep from Drona's well of wisdom, honing their martial skills with unwavering determination.

Janamejaya, curious and eager for the tale, inquired about Drona's origin and the source of his weapons. Vaisampayana, his eyes glinting with the fire of ancient lore, began to recount the extraordinary origins of the illustrious teacher.

"Listen, O Janamejaya, to the story of Drona, born from desire and destined for greatness. At the source of the mighty Ganga, in the sacred silence of the woods, lived the great sage Bharadwaja. One day, as Bharadwaja performed ablutions in the holy waters, he beheld Ghritachi, the Apsara, rising gracefully, her beauty unparalleled. Desire gripped the sage's heart, and in that moment of fervor, his vital fluid spilled forth. Swiftly, he captured it in a vessel, a vessel known as a drona.

From that potent essence, preserved by the wise sage's art, emerged Drona, radiant and gifted. Bharadwaja, in his wisdom, nurtured Drona in the arts of war and sacred knowledge. Under his guidance, Drona blossomed into a formidable warrior, his prowess matched only by his devotion.

Now, in a land far from Bharadwaja's hermitage, a great king named Prishata ruled. His valiant son, Drupada, often visited the hermitage, forging bonds with Drona and engaging in playful camaraderie. Fate, however, had its designs. When Prishata passed away, Drupada ascended the throne, becoming the king of the northern Panchalas.

Bharadwaja, steeped in ascetic virtues, continued his penance, while Drona, obedient to his father's command, married Kripi, the daughter of Saradwat. Their union bore fruit, a son named Aswatthaman. This child, born amidst divine portents, echoed the neighing of a celestial steed, foretelling his destiny of greatness.

Meanwhile, the illustrious Brahmana, Jamadagnya, famed as Rama, the enemy of Kshatriyas, announced his desire to distribute all his wealth to Brahmanas. Hearing of Rama's divine knowledge and his celestial weapons, Drona set forth, eager to claim this wealth of knowledge and power.

With his disciples in tow, Drona arrived at the Mahendra mountains, where Rama, the son of Bhrigu, resided. With reverence, Drona approached the mighty sage, expressing his desire for the wealth Rama intended to give away. Rama, ever patient and self-controlled, welcomed Drona, offering him a choice between his body and his weapons.

'Give me your knowledge of arms,' Drona declared, his voice firm with determination.

Rama, in his generosity, bestowed upon Drona the entirety of his weapons, along with the intricate secrets of their wielding. Overwhelmed with gratitude, Drona accepted the divine knowledge, his heart brimming with joy.

Armed with this newfound wisdom, Drona set forth to fulfill his destiny, his mind aflame with the power that now resided within him. The tale of Drona, born from the vessel of desire and gifted with celestial knowledge, had begun its course in the annals of time, etching its mark on the sands of destiny.

In the age when empires clashed like titans Drona went to the kingdom of Panchala to see his old schoolmate Drupada. The air was thick with the scent of pride and ambition, the mighty son of Bharadwaja, Drona, strode with purpose. His eyes, glinting with the fire of determination, locked onto Drupada, the lord of the Panchalas, and he spoke, his voice a thunderclap in the echoing halls of kings.

"Know me for thy friend," Drona declared, his words like molten steel, cutting through the air. But Drupada, swathed in the arrogance of wealth and power, scoffed at Drona's audacity. Like a thunderhead darkening with rage, Drupada's brow furrowed, and his eyes blazed with indignation.

"O Brahmana, thy intelligence is but a flickering candle in the face of the sun," Drupada spat, his voice laced with disdain. "Friendship between us? The notion is as laughable as the babbling of fools. Great kings do not mingle their destinies with the wretched and penniless. Our past friendship was a mere shadow, erased by the relentless march of Time. Friendship, in this world, is ephemeral, a fleeting mirage devoured by the sands of time and the fires of anger. Let go of this delusion, Brahmana. The ties that once bound us have withered and died. Why grasp at the ghost of an extinguished flame?"

The words hung heavy in the air, a bitter taste on the tongue. Drona, the son of Bharadwaja, his wrath kindled, paused for but a moment. In that moment, he made his choice, his resolve hardening like steel forged in the crucible of betrayal.

With a heart ablaze with indignation and purpose, Drona turned his back on the Panchala king, leaving behind the city of his disdain. His steps, firm and unyielding, guided him toward the capital of the Kurus, where the name echoed the strength of elephants and the power of ancient warriors. The tale of Drona, scorned and yet undeterred, took a new turn amidst the shifting sands of allegiance and pride. The world would soon witness the wrath of a warrior scorned, and the echoes of his vengeance would reverberate through the annals of time.

In the hushed chambers of Hastinapura, where power and ambition intermingled like fire and steel, the son of Bharadwaja, Drona, wove a tale, each word dripping with exaggeration and self-pity. His voice, smooth as honey but laced with bitterness, echoed off the walls, filling the room with his carefully crafted narrative.

"Arrived at Hastinapura, that haven of intrigue and grandeur, I, the illustrious son of Bharadwaja, chose to live in obscurity within the house of Gautama, known as Kripa," Drona began, his eyes glinting with a cunning light. "In the shadows, my mighty son Aswatthaman, a gem yet undiscovered, occasionally bestowed his knowledge upon the sons of Kunti, yet none knew the depths of his prowess, hidden like a serpent in the grass."

With a dramatic pause, Drona continued, his voice now thick with sarcasm. "One day, the valiant princes of the Bharata lineage, blinded by their own arrogance, played with a ball near a well. Their futile attempts to retrieve the fallen ball plunged them into despair. But fear not, for I, the humble Brahmana, happened to be nearby, my sagely presence veiled in the guise of an aged and frail ascetic."

The corners of Drona's lips curled into a sly smile as he recounted his supposed heroic feat. "Seeing their helplessness, I, in my unmatched wisdom, could not bear the sight of their incompetence. 'Shame on your Kshatriya might,' I chided them, 'and shame on your vaunted skill in arms! Behold, with a handful of grass, I shall perform a miracle that your so-called prowess could not achieve!'"

Drona's laughter, mirthless and bitter, echoed through the room. "With a theatrical gesture, I threw my ring into the well and, lo and behold, I lifted it back with an arrow, as if by divine intervention. The princes, their eyes wide with amazement, were my captive audience. 'This, my dear friends, is the power of a true Brahmana,' I proclaimed, my words dripping with false modesty."

His tale grew more elaborate with every word, the lines between truth and fiction blurring like smoke in the wind. "Amidst their awe, they beseeched me, 'O learned Brahmana, who art thou? What boon can we bestow upon thee?' My heart, heavy with imagined grievances, could not resist the temptation to weave my tale further. 'Go,' I replied, 'and tell Bhishma of my unparalleled prowess. He will recognize me. For I, Drona, have suffered much, wandering in search of a cow, my son deprived of milk, scorned by society.'"

Drona's eyes gleamed with calculated fervor as he continued his narrative, each word a thread in the tapestry of his deceit. "Thus, with a heart heavy with sorrows and the sting of betrayal, I approached Bhishma, that venerable patriarch, weaving my tale of woe and injustice. 'I come to Hastinapura, seeking refuge and pupils, desiring naught but the opportunity to bestow my knowledge upon the deserving,' I said, my voice oozing with pathos. 'For I have been cast aside, scorned by my friend Drupada, who once promised me his kingdom, only to mock my humble existence.'"

The room was charged with an air of tragedy, Drona's words painting him as the victim of a world that had wronged him. He looked at Bhishma, his eyes pleading for sympathy, his narrative a masterful concoction of half-truths and embellishments. "O Bhishma," he said, his voice quivering with feigned emotion, "I seek solace in the arms of the Kurus. Grant me your blessings, for in my tale of woe, you shall find the thread of truth that binds my fate to yours.

In the heart of Drona's training grounds, a battleground of ambition and jealousy, his role as a guru took a dark and treacherous turn. He groomed his pupils like a master manipulator, using them as pawns in a game of power and deception.

Chapter 23

DRONA TEACHES THE STUDENTS

Drona had now taken up residence in the abode of the Kurus, their adorations and valuable gifts pouring in like a torrent. He had the Kaurava princes at his disposal, the fruit of Bhishma's desires. But his ambitions went beyond a simple desire to impart knowledge; he had a particular purpose in his heart, a secret plan he was eager to set into motion.

The atmosphere was thick with tension as he summoned the Kuru princes and extracted a promise from them. "Promise me truly," he urged, his voice laced with cunning, "that when ye have become skilled in arms, ye will accomplish it."

The princes remained silent, apprehensive of the mysterious promise they had been coerced into. But one among them, Arjuna, whose devotion to Drona was matched only by his gullibility, pledged to fulfill whatever his guru demanded.

Drona, the unreliable narrator in the guise of a guru, couldn't hide his delight as he embraced Arjuna, shedding crocodile tears of joy. "Thy unwavering loyalty has touched my heart," he said with a fervor that masked his deception.

Under Drona's dubious tutelage, Arjuna and the other princes began their training. Drona showcased his expertise in various weapons, both celestial and human, further tightening his grip on their fates. Many other princes also flocked to him, eager to partake in the knowledge of arms.

The arrival of a Nishada prince named Ekalavya threatened the equilibrium. Drona, his prejudices rooted deep, rejected Ekalavya, fearing he might surpass the Kuru princes. In the shadows, Ekalavya began to worship a clay image of Drona, offering his skills to an idol of a master who had cast him aside.

Drona was well aware of Arjuna's jealousy and used it to his advantage. When the Pandavas discovered Ekalavya's astounding archery skills, Arjuna's insecurities resurfaced. Arjuna sought an explanation, demanding to know why there was a pupil of Drona who could potentially rival him.

Drona, with an insincere smile playing on his lips, explained the situation to Arjuna, further stoking the flames of his rivalry with Ekalavya. "I shall do that unto thee by which there shall not be an archer equal to thee in this world," he assured, leaving Arjuna in a cloud of self-satisfaction.

But Drona was not done with his manipulation. He devised a test for his pupils, instructing them to aim at an artificial bird perched atop a tree. One by one, he went through the princes, sowing discord and disappointment. Yudhishthira was the first to fall short, and the other pupils, including Duryodhana and the Kuru brothers, met the same fate.

The unreliable guru reveled in their despair, savoring their humiliation. He stripped them of their chance at greatness, using his pupils as stepping stones in his own path to power.

In the shadowy realm of Drona's teachings, the truth was always a mutable thing, and the aspirations of his pupils were mere tools in his grand design

Amidst the grandeur of the training grounds, Bhima, the stalwart Pandava, stood alone in his conviction, his eyes piercing the veil of deceit that shrouded Drona, their guru. The other princes remained enthralled, their admiration for Drona's supposed wisdom blinding them to the truth. As Drona began to chant the sacred mantras, his voice resonating with authority, Bhima's expression hardened with resolve.

"You may fool the others with your false teachings, Drona," Bhima spoke, his voice carrying the weight of unwavering certainty, "but I see through your deception. Your mantras are tainted, your intentions impure. I will not bow to a guru who hides behind a facade of righteousness while indulging in treachery."

Drona, his eyes flickering with concealed rage, tried to assert his influence over the others, but Bhima's words had fallen on deaf ears. The princes, their minds clouded by admiration and respect, continued to hang onto Drona's every word, oblivious to the poison that tainted his teachings.

"I am the only one who can see through your lies, Drona," Bhima continued, his voice rising above the drone of the chanting. "I will not let your deceitful words guide my path. My strength comes from within, from the Supreme Lord alone. I will not let your false teachings corrupt my soul."

Despite Bhima's defiance, the other princes remained ensnared by Drona's charm, their trust in the guru unbroken. Bhima, undeterred by their indifference, stood firm, a solitary beacon of truth amidst a sea of deception. His unwavering conviction would serve as a testament to his strength, his refusal to succumb to falsehoods, a testament to his integrity.

In the face of their blind adoration, Bhima's lone stand against Drona's deceit became a symbol of unyielding courage, a reminder that even in the darkest of times, there existed those who refused to be swayed by the allure of falsehood. Though surrounded by followers of the false guru, Bhima remained resolute, his spirit unbroken, his faith unwavering in the face of deception

In the heart of the Kuru kingdom, where the air was thick with ambition and the clash of weapons resonated like a war drum, the sons of Bharadwaja were put to the ultimate test by their preceptor, the enigmatic Drona. The sun hung low in the sky, casting long shadows over the battlefield, as Drona, that master of war, devised a peculiar challenge for his eager pupils.

"Take up your bows, my children," Drona commanded, his voice cutting through the stillness like a blade. "See yonder bird perched upon the tree. Aim true and wait for my signal. When I give the order, shoot and sever the bird's head from its body."

Yudhishthira, the eldest of the Pandavas, stepped forward, his eyes fixed upon the distant bird. His fingers caressed the string of his bow, his concentration unwavering. "I see the tree, the bird, myself, and my brothers," he replied confidently when questioned by his preceptor.

Drona's eyes narrowed, his brows furrowing in displeasure. "What dost thou see now, O prince? Seest thou the tree, myself, or thy brothers?" he inquired, a note of impatience lacing his words.

"I see the tree, myself, my brothers, and the bird," Yudhishthira answered, his voice steady.

Drona's disappointment was palpable, his voice dripping with reproach. "Stand thou apart. It is not for thee to strike the aim," he declared, banishing Yudhishthira from the challenge.

One by one, the sons of Dhritarashtra and the other pupils faced the same fate. Drona's question echoed like a haunting refrain, and each time, his pupils failed to give the answer he sought. Frustration etched lines on his stern face as his experiment yielded the same result with every prince.

Amidst the group stood Arjuna, his eyes gleaming with determination. He watched, silent and observant, as his brothers and fellow pupils faltered before their preceptor's inquiry. When Drona turned his gaze towards him, Arjuna stood unwavering, his confidence unshaken.

The sun hung low in the sky, casting its golden glow upon the training grounds. Drona's voice, like a rumble of distant thunder, cut through the air. "Arjuna," he said, his smile as enigmatic as the veiled mysteries of the universe, "turn thy eyes to the vulture perched high upon yonder tree. Let thy arrow fly when my command falls upon thee."

Arjuna, the mightiest of the Pandava brothers, raised his bow, his muscles taut as bowstrings under his bronze skin. His eyes, keen as those of a hawk, fixed upon the distant mark. Drona's words came like a distant echo, his orders caressing Arjuna's ears. "Do you see the vulture, Arjuna? What else do you perceive?"

Arjuna's voice, strong and unwavering, replied, "I see only the vulture, not the tree, nor thee, O revered guru."

Drona's lips curved upward in approval, his heart swelling with pride. He knew he had found his greatest pupil. "Describe the vulture to me, Arjuna."

With unwavering focus, Arjuna spoke, his words painting a vivid picture of the creature perched high above. "I see the head of the vulture, nothing more," he said, his voice carrying the weight of truth.

Drona's heart danced with delight, and he knew then that Arjuna was destined for greatness. "Shoot," he commanded, his voice like the rustle of leaves in a silent forest.

With the grace of a god and the precision of a divine archer, Arjuna released his arrow. The shaft flew true, finding its mark with unerring accuracy. The vulture's head tumbled from its perch, lifeless, and the ground received its fallen prize.

But the tale did not end on the training grounds. It flowed like the sacred Ganga, winding its way through the tapestry of destiny. One day, as Drona bathed in the sacred river, an alligator, a creature of the wild, rose from the depths, jaws wide and hungry. It clamped its fearsome teeth around Drona's thigh, dragging him into the water's depths.

"Drona, my guru!" cried Arjuna, his voice a thunderous roar. He raised his bow, fingers deftly stringing an arrow. "Fear not, for I shall save thee."

Drona, caught in the jaws of death, called out, "Arjuna, rescue me from this peril! Strike down this beast with thy arrows."

Arjuna, his muscles rippling like the coiled strength of a serpent, let his arrows fly. The alligator, a creature of primal fury, met its end in a flurry of sharp shafts. Drona was released, saved by the swift and deadly hands of his pupil.

With gratitude etched upon his weathered face, Drona turned to Arjuna. "Accept, O mighty one, the Brahmasira, a weapon of unrivaled power," he said, his voice a whispering breeze in the ears of his prized pupil. "Use it wisely, for it can rend the very fabric of existence. But never, I warn thee, aim it at a human foe, for it has the power to consume worlds."

Arjuna, his eyes gleaming with determination, bowed to his guru. "I swear by the heavens and the earth, I shall heed thy counsel. This weapon shall remain a guardian of dharma, a sentinel against cosmic threats."

Drona, the master of arms, placed his hand upon Arjuna's shoulder, his touch a benediction. "None in this world, nor the worlds beyond, shall surpass thee in archery. You are destined for greatness, Arjuna, and your name shall echo through eternity."

Chapter 24

The Display of Arms

Vaisampayana's voice resonated across the vast assembly, as he recounted the grand spectacle that unfolded in the heart of the kingdom. The arena, golden and grand, was thrumming with the pulse of anticipation. Drona, the venerable preceptor, stood resplendent in white, his aura as pure as the driven snow, his presence commanding reverence.

The king, Dhritarashtra, blind yet perceptive, his heart swelling with pride, welcomed the martial display of his progeny. "O best of Brahmanas," he declared, his voice echoing through the eager crowd, "let the demonstration of my sons' skills commence. This day shall bear witness to their valorous might. Name the time and place, and I shall endorse your choice, for my heart longs to behold their prowess.

O Vidura, see to it that Drona's wishes are fulfilled. My soul thirsts for the spectacle."

Vidura, the wise minister, ever loyal to the throne, assured the king, "Your wish shall be fulfilled, O king. Drona's commands shall be obeyed."

Under the expansive sky, the assembly gathered on the designated lunar day, their hearts racing with anticipation. The people, from Brahmanas to Kshatriyas, spilled out of the city like a tide, drawn by the promise of witnessing the princes' martial prowess. The air crackled with excitement as they converged on the arena, a golden masterpiece adorned with pearls and lapis lazuli.

In the midst of this sea of eager faces, Drona, accompanied by his son, stepped into the limelight. Clad in white, he appeared as a celestial being descended from the heavens. The spectators marveled at his divine presence, his very aura promising a spectacle of extraordinary feats.

The royal ladies, resplendent in their finery, ascended the platforms, their eyes shining with pride. Gandhari, the queen, and Kunti, the mother of the Pandavas, stood side by side, their hearts swelling with maternal love and royal grace.

Amidst the hushed whispers and the excited murmurs, the princes, with Yudhishthira at their helm, entered the arena. Their fingers adorned with gauntlets, they wielded bows and arrows with the skill of gods. The arrows, engraved with their names, found their marks effortlessly, leaving the spectators in awe.

Riding swift horses, they showcased their mastery over the beasts, their control unmatched. The onlookers' breaths caught in their throats, witnessing the princes' prowess as they hit their targets with unerring accuracy.

Then came the grand display of swordsmanship and shield play. With swords gleaming like stars, and bucklers firm in their grasp, the princes moved with the grace of celestial dancers. Each move was a testament to their agility, their strength, and their sheer prowess.

Vrikodara, the mighty Bhima, and Suyodhana, the indomitable, stepped forward, their maces held high like divine weapons. Roaring like lions, they circled the arena, their muscles rippling with raw power. Their feet, nimble yet purposeful, created a rhythm that resonated through the very soul of the spectators.

Vidura, the sagacious counselor, described every feat to the blind king, painting vivid pictures with his words. The king, the queens, and the entire assembly were entranced by the spectacle before them. The air was thick with the scent of sweat and steel, and the ground trembled beneath the warriors' mighty strides.

Thus, in the heart of the kingdom, under the vast expanse of the sky, the sons of Dhritarashtra and Pandu, guided by the wisdom of Drona, displayed their martial prowess, leaving an indelible mark on the annals of history.

Vaisampayana's voice, like the roll of thunder before a storm, echoed across the assembly while he told his tale. As the mighty warriors, Bhima and Duryodhana, entered the fray. The spectators, their hearts torn between loyalty and admiration, erupted into a tumultuous sea of competing cheers. "Behold the heroic king of the Kurus!" cried some, while others shouted, "Behold Bhima!" The conflicting shouts clashed like clashing waves, creating a chaotic symphony that filled the air.

Amidst the uproar, Bharadwaja, wise as the ancient sages, turned to his dear son Aswatthaman. His voice, firm yet resonant, cut through the din. "Restrain these two titans," he commanded. "Let not their battle stoke the ire of the assembly. We seek not discord but a display of skill."

The son of the preceptor, Aswatthaman, swift as a falcon, leaped forward, his presence commanding obedience. With maces poised high, resembling two tempestuous oceans churned by cosmic winds, he restrained the combatants, his strength a testament to his lineage.

Amidst this tense moment, Drona, the venerable master, strode into the arena. His command fell like thunder, silencing the musicians and quelling the rising storm of conflict. His voice, deep as the rumbling clouds, resonated through the hushed atmosphere. "Behold Partha!" he declared, his words carrying the weight of prophecy. "He is dearer to me than my own son, a master of all arms, the son of Indra himself, akin to the younger brother of Vishnu!"

The very earth seemed to hold its breath as Arjuna, the illustrious son of Kunti, stepped into the arena. Clad in golden mail, he shone like the evening cloud adorned with the hues of the setting sun and the colors of the rainbow. The spectators, enraptured by his presence, erupted into a chorus of exclamation. "This is the son of Kunti!" they cried. "This is the third Pandava!" "This is the son of mighty Indra, the protector of the Kurus!" Their words hung in the air like a divine proclamation, and Kunti, her eyes brimming with tears of pride, felt her heart swell with maternal love.

As the uproar subsided, Arjuna, the beloved disciple, displayed his unparalleled mastery over weapons. With the Agneya weapon, he conjured fire; with Varuna, he summoned water; with Vayavya, he created air; and with Parjanya, clouds gathered in the sky. By the Bhauma weapon, he shaped the land, and with the Parvatya, mountains rose tall and proud. His control over the Antardhana weapon made these creations vanish, leaving the spectators awestruck.

In a breathtaking display of skill, Arjuna transformed, now tall, now short; now standing on his chariot yoke, now on the chariot itself; and in the blink of an eye, he stood on the ground. His arrows, like relentless messengers of death, struck with unerring precision. He released five shafts simultaneously, each finding its mark in the mouth of a swiftly moving iron-boar. In a stunning feat, he shot twenty-one arrows into the hollow of a cow's horn, suspended from a swaying rope.

With sword, bow, and mace, Arjuna moved gracefully through the arena, his steps tracing circles like a celestial dancer. Each movement, each strike, was poetry in motion, a testament to his unparalleled skill. The spectators, their eyes fixed on this divine spectacle, were spellbound.

As the exhibition neared its end, and the spectators' excitement began to wane, a new sound, ominous and mighty, reached their ears—the slapping of arms, a portent of great strength and power. The assembly turned as one towards the gate, and there, standing like a colossus, was Drona, encircled by the five sons of Pritha, the Pandavas. The air crackled with anticipation, and Duryodhana, swift as a panther, leaped to his feet, his hundred brothers surrounding him like an impenetrable shield. Mace in hand, he resembled Purandara, the lord of the heavens, encircled by his celestial host, ready to battle the forces of darkness.

In that charged moment, the fate of kingdoms hung in the balance, and the arena crackled with an electrifying energy,

Vaisampayana's words, like the murmur of ancient spirits, flowed through the air. The assembly's gaze turned to the entrance. A formidable figure, bedecked in natural armor and radiant earrings, strode into the spacious arena. Karna, the conqueror of hostile realms, was a man of extraordinary birth, for he was born of Pritha in her maidenhood. He was a portion of the Sun itself, his energy and prowess akin to the might of lions, bulls, and the leaders of elephant herds. He shone with the brilliance of the Sun, the beauty of the Moon, and the fiery vigor of flames.

Towering like a golden palm tree, the son of the Sun was blessed with a youthful vigor that could challenge even the fiercest of lions. His handsome features and countless accomplishments only added to his splendor. With a voice deep as the roar of a tempest, he addressed his unknown brother, Partha, the son of the Asura subduer, Paka (Indra). "O Partha," he declared, "I shall perform feats before this awe-struck multitude, surpassing all that you have ever done. Behold them and be amazed."

As Karna's voice resounded like the roll of distant thunder, the spectators, struck by the strength of his presence, rose from their seats in unison. Duryodhana, the epitome of delight, embraced Karna with his brothers. "Welcome, mighty-armed warrior," he proclaimed. "I consider myself fortunate to have you by my side. Live as you please, and command me and the kingdom of the Kurus."

Karna, his spirit aflame with a love for battle, responded, "When you have said it, consider it already done. I desire only your friendship. Grant me the honor of a single combat with Arjuna." Duryodhana replied, "Enjoy the pleasures of life with me. Be my benefactor, and place your feet on the heads of our enemies."

The discord between Karna and Arjuna was palpable. Arjuna, stung by the feeling of disgrace, spoke with fury. "Karna," he said, "that path you intrude upon is your own. It will lead you to your death, for I shall slay you."

Karna, unshaken, retorted, "This arena belongs to all, not just you, Phalguna. Kings are recognized for their might, and warriors should abide by their strength. Let us resolve this with our arrows, and may the victor reign supreme."

In response to the clamor of the assembly, the two warriors advanced for the combat, and their mentors and supporters stood at their sides. The firmament itself seemed to come alive, enveloped in clouds that gleamed with flashes of lightning. The multicolored bow of Indra, lord of the heavens, appeared, shedding its radiant light. Clouds swirled like a gathering storm, with white cranes circling in the sky. As Indra watched the arena with fatherly affection, the sun, beaming with pride, dispelled the clouds to reveal his offspring.

Partha, shrouded by the clouds, stood in anticipation, while Karna, surrounded by the sun's rays, appeared resplendent. The sons of Dhritarashtra stood beside Karna, while Bharadwaja, Kripa, and Bhishma remained with Partha. The assembly and the female spectators were divided, each silently taking sides.

Kunti, daughter of Bhoja, overcome with emotion, fell into a swoon. Vidura, well-versed in his duties, revived her by sprinkling her with sandal paste and cool water. As she regained consciousness, Kunti, her eyes filled with dread, saw her two sons clad in armor, standing on the precipice of an epic battle, and she could do nothing to protect them.

Kripa, the learned warrior, addressed Karna, inquiring about his lineage and his parentage. Karna's countenance paled at the question, like a lotus crushed by the pelting rains of the monsoon. Duryodhana, ever the eager leader, came to Karna's defense. "The scriptures state that kingship can belong to three classes: those of royal lineage, heroes, and those who lead armies. Phalguna is unwilling to fight those who are not kings. I shall, therefore, install Karna as the king of Anga."

In that moment, with golden seats, parched paddy, flowers, and water vessels, Karna was officially crowned as the king of Anga by Brahmanas versed in the ancient rites. The royal umbrella cast its shade over his regal figure, while yak-tails waved around him,

THE SOURCE OF CONFLICT

marking the momentous occasion. The spectators, their jubilant cheers ringing out, observed the coronation with admiration and delight.

As Duryodhana and Karna embraced each other in jubilation, their joy knew no bounds. They pledged their unbreakable friendship, and Karna, his heart filled with aspiration, made a fateful request. "O repressor of foes," he said, "let me have a single combat with Arjuna." Duryodhana, agreeing to this bold request, welcomed Karna with open arms, sealing a friendship that would forever change the course of the Kurukshetra war.

Adhiratha, his sheet loosely draped, stepped forth, perspiring and trembling, leaning heavily on a staff for support. Karna, having left his bow aside, bowed his head in reverence upon seeing his foster father, the charioteer. Overwhelmed by filial affection, Karna's eyes brimmed with tears, the remnants of his recent coronation still glistening on his wet head.

The charioteer, his feet quickly covered with the edge of his sheet, embraced Karna, his heart overflowing with love. Seeing Arjuna insulted by Karna and Duryodhana and wanting to stand up for his brother stirred Bhimasena, the Pandava of immense strength, to speak up. "O son of a charioteer," he taunted, "you do not deserve to face Partha in battle. Accept the whip, for that is more fitting for your lineage. As a dog is unworthy of the ghee placed before the sacrificial fire, so are you undeserving of the throne of Anga."

Karna, his lips slightly quivering, heaved a deep sigh and cast his eyes toward the sun. Duryodhana, the fierce-hearted prince, rose wrathfully from among his brothers. Addressing Bhimasena, he roared, "Vrikodara, your words are unfitting! Might is the essence of a Kshatriya, and even one of humble birth deserves to be faced in combat. The lineage of heroes, like the source of a majestic river, is often unknown. The fire that engulfs the world rises from water. The thunderbolt that annihilates the Danavas was crafted from a mortal's bone named Dadhichi. Guha, the illustrious deity combining the essence of all others, has a lineage shrouded in mystery. Some claim him to be the progeny of Agni, others of Krittika, some of Rudra, and yet others of Ganga. We have heard of Kshatriyas ascending to the status of Brahmanas. Viswamitra and others, born Kshatriyas, attained the eternal Brahman. Drona, the preceptor and the foremost among warriors, emerged from a water pot, and Kripa of the Gotama lineage sprang from a clump of heath. Your own births, Pandava princes, are known to me. Can a she-deer give birth to a tiger like Karna, radiant as the sun, adorned with auspicious marks, and born with natural armor and ear-rings? This prince among men is fit to rule not just Anga but the entire world, given his strength and my oath to serve him. If anyone here cannot bear what I have done for Karna, let him mount his chariot and bend his bow with his feet!"

Duryodhana's words stirred a tumultuous murmur of approval among the spectators, their voices blending into a cacophony. The sun sank beneath the horizon, casting a shadow over the arena, but Duryodhana, seizing Karna's hand, led him away, illuminated by the glow of countless lamps. The Pandavas, accompanied by Drona, Kripa, and Bhishma, retreated to their dwellings. People dispersed, their whispers carrying the names of Arjuna, Karna, and Duryodhana as the victors of the day. In the midst of this, Kunti, recognizing her son in Karna due to the auspicious marks adorning his person, and witnessing him enthroned as the ruler of Anga, felt a surge of motherly pride.

Duryodhana, having secured Karna, banished his fears spawned by Arjuna's prowess. The valiant Karna, skilled in the art of warfare, endeared himself to Duryodhana with honeyed words, while Yudhishthira found himself awestruck, believing that there was no warrior on Earth comparable to Karna. The night fell, and the echoes of the day's events lingered in the air like the fading resonance of a battle cry.

Chapter 25

DRONAS REVENGE

Vaisampayana's voice resonated with the weight of history as he continued his tale. The great warrior Drona, his eyes alight with the fire of determination, beheld the Pandavas and the valiant son of Dhritarashtra, all accomplished in arms. In his heart, he knew that the moment had come to demand the preceptorial fee he had long awaited. Gathering his pupils, the mighty preceptor Drona spoke with a commanding voice, "Seize Drupada, the king of Panchala, in battle and bring him unto me. That shall be the most acceptable fee."

The warriors, undeterred by the daunting task set before them, answered in unison, "So be it," their voices carrying the echo of their unwavering resolve. Swiftly, they mounted their chariots, ready to bestow upon their revered teacher the fee he sought. With Drona leading the way, they marched forth, their steps resonating with purpose. Among them were Duryodhana, Karna, the mighty Yuyutsu, Duhsasana, Vikarna, Jalasandha, and Sulochana—heroes of the Kshatriya lineage, their hearts aflame with valor.

The warriors, riding in chariots of unparalleled craftsmanship, followed by a formidable cavalry, approached the capital of the great Drupada. The very earth trembled beneath their feet as they entered the hostile city, their eyes ablaze with determination.

Meanwhile, within the city, King Yajnasena, armed to the teeth, stepped forth from his palace, his brothers by his side. The Kuru army, relentless in their pursuit, assailed him with a torrent of arrows, their war cries reverberating through the air. Undeterred, Yajnasena, his resolve unyielding, approached the Kurus on his resplendent chariot, launching a relentless onslaught of arrows upon them.

Amidst this chaos, Arjuna, observing the prowess of his comrades, spoke to his preceptor Drona, the embodiment of wisdom and martial prowess. "Let them display their valor first," he said, his voice steady and determined. "We shall join the fray once they have demonstrated their might. None among them can vanquish the mighty king of Panchala. I will personally face him."

Thus, Arjuna, accompanied by his brothers and surrounded by the energy of impending battle, waited just outside the city, his eyes fixed on the unfolding chaos. Drupada, witnessing the overwhelming Kuru forces, charged into the battle, unleashing a tempest of arrows that struck fear into the hearts of the enemy.

Drupada's agility on the battlefield was unmatched, his movements swift as he fought single-handedly, yet the Kurus, gripped by panic, believed they faced multiple incarnations of the Panchala king. Drupada's arrows rained upon the Kurus like a relentless storm, their impact causing the very ground to shake. The citizens of Panchala, inspired by their king's bravery, unleashed a hail of missiles from their homes, adding to the tumultuous onslaught.

Duryodhana, Vikarna, Suvahu, Dirghalochana, and Duhsasana, their fury kindled, retaliated fiercely, their arrows slicing through the air. However, the unyielding king Drupada, invincible in battle, continued to crush the Kuru ranks, his arrows finding their mark with unerring precision. The Kauravas, now facing the full force of Drupada's wrath, wavered and fled, their cries of distress mingling with the clash of arms.

Undeterred, Bhimasena, the formidable Pandava, charged ahead, his mace raised high like the scepter of an angry god. His powerful blows fell upon the Kuru elephants, shattering their skulls and sending them crashing to the ground. The battlefield echoed with the dying trumpets and cries of the fallen beasts, like the bellowing of thunderclouds.

Arjuna, the resolute son of Pandu, displayed his own unmatched prowess. His bow sang in the air as he released a relentless storm of arrows upon the enemy. The twang of his bowstring reverberated across the battlefield, striking terror into the hearts of his foes. His arrows found their targets with deadly accuracy, piercing the Kuru soldiers and leaving a trail of fallen warriors in their wake.

The battle reached a fevered pitch as Arjuna, driven by the desire to protect his preceptor, unleashed his divine skill upon the enemy. Satyajit, the brave general of Panchala, confronted him, his eyes burning with determination. The clash between the two warriors was like the clash of titans, their arrows creating a dazzling display of light and shadow. Satyajit, formidable though he was, found himself overpowered by Arjuna's might, his bow shattered, and his horses slain.

Undeterred, Arjuna pressed on, his eyes blazing with fury. He pierced Satyajit's chest with a shower of arrows, leaving the Panchala warrior grievously wounded. Satyajit, realizing the futility of further combat, withdrew from the fight, his spirit unbroken despite his defeat.

Seeing Arjuna's unmatched valor, the Panchala troops began to flee, their morale shattered. Arjuna, his spirit undiminished, captured the valiant Drupada, the king of Panchala, and led him back to the Pandava camp. The city of Drupada lay in ruins, its once-proud streets now filled with the echoes of battle and the cries of the fallen.

Arjuna, his eyes burning with righteousness, addressed his preceptor, Drona, "This illustrious king, Drupada, is a relative of the Kuru heroes. Let us not destroy his soldiers. Let us fulfill our preceptor's wish and offer him this victory as the fee he deserves."

Thus, the mighty Bhimasena refrained from further slaughter, and the Pandavas, having achieved their objective, spared the remaining soldiers of Panchala. With King Drupada in their custody, they made their way back, their steps filled with the assurance of victory.

Drona, his eyes reflecting the satisfaction of a long-awaited triumph, turned to Drupada and spoke with a mixture of firmness and compassion, "Your kingdom and capital lie in ruins, humiliated and bereft of wealth. Fear not for your life, for I, Drona, am ever forgiving. Our childhood camaraderie has not been forgotten, and my affection for you has only grown. I offer you my friendship once more, and half your kingdom shall be restored. I, Drona, now rule the northern territories, while you, O Panchala, shall be the sovereign of all lands to the south of the Bhagirathi."

Drupada, his heart brimming with gratitude and admiration, replied, "Your nobility and unmatched valor are evident. I am deeply moved by your magnanimity, O Brahmana. I accept your friendship wholeheartedly."

With these words, the enmity of yore was buried, and a new Chapter began—one where friendship and mutual respect would reign. Drupada, once a mighty king, now embraced his role as a loyal ally, while Drona, the preceptor, stood tall as the revered master of his pupils, his preceptorial fee finally fulfilled. Thus, the tale of bravery, camaraderie, and the undying spirit of Kshatriya dharma echoed across the battlefield, leaving behind a legacy etched in the annals of time.

Chapter 26

THE HOUSE OF LAC

Vaisampayana continued, "Then the son of Suvala, King Duryodhana, along with Duhsasana and Karna, hatched a wicked conspiracy with the sanction of Dhritarashtra, the king of the Kurus. Their malevolent plan was to burn Kunti and her five sons to death. However, the wise Vidura, who could read the intentions of others by observing their expressions, discovered their evil plot solely by looking at their faces. Vidura, a man of noble character devoted to the welfare of the Pandavas, concluded that Kunti and her children should escape from their enemies. For this purpose, he had a boat prepared that could withstand the wind and waves, and he addressed Kunti, saying, 'This Dhritarashtra has been born to ruin the fame and lineage of the Kuru clan. His malevolent nature is about to lead him to forsake eternal virtues. O fortunate one, I have readied a strong boat on the river. Escape with your children to avoid the deathtrap set for you.'

Kunti, upon hearing this, felt deep sorrow but, along with her children, she boarded the boat and crossed the Ganges as advised by Vidura. The Pandavas, taking with them the wealth they had been given by their enemies while at Varanavata, ventured deep into the forest. Meanwhile, in the house of lac prepared for the destruction of the Pandavas, an innocent Nishada woman who had entered for some reason, along with her children, was burnt to death. The wicked Purochana, the architect of the lacquer house, also met the same fate.

In this way, the sons of Dhritarashtra and their advisors were deceived as they believed the Pandavas had been consumed in the fire. The citizens of Varanavata, witnessing the house of lac in flames (and assuming the Pandavas had perished), were filled with immense grief. They sent messengers to King Dhritarashtra to convey the news, and the messengers told the king, 'Your great desire has been fulfilled! You have finally burnt the Pandavas to death! Now enjoy the kingdom with your children. O King of the Kurus, the realm is now yours.' Upon hearing this, Dhritarashtra, along with his sons and relatives, including Vidura and Bhishma, feigned grief and performed the final rites for the Pandavas.

Janamejaya then said, 'O wise Brahmana, I wish to hear in detail the story of the burning of the house of lac and the Pandavas' escape from it. The actions of the Kauravas, acting on the advice of the wicked Kanika, were indeed cruel. Please narrate this story to me; I am consumed by curiosity to hear it.'

Vaisampayana said, 'O King, listen as I narrate in full the story of the burning of the house of lac and the Pandavas' escape. Seeing that Bhimasena excelled everyone in strength and Arjuna was highly skilled in weaponry, the wicked Duryodhana became filled with jealousy and distress. With the counsel of Karna and Sakuni and motivated by jealousy, Duryodhana conspired to destroy the Pandavas. The Pandavas, however, foiled every one of these treacherous schemes. At Vidura's advice, they refrained from discussing these incidents and maintained a calm demeanor.

The citizens, witnessing the talents and virtues of the eldest Pandava, openly discussed him and his qualifications for ruling the kingdom. They said, 'Dhritarashtra, born blind, could never attain the throne, even though he was highly knowledgeable. How can he become king now? Bhishma, having previously renounced the kingdom, would never take the throne again. We should perform the installation of the young, accomplished, virtuous, and learned Yudhishthira, the eldest Pandava. By worshipping Bhishma and Dhritarashtra, well-versed in moral conduct, the realm will undoubtedly prosper.'

Hearing this, Duryodhana, consumed by jealousy, rushed to Dhritarashtra. When he found Dhritarashtra alone, he saluted him and, deeply distressed by the growing popularity of Yudhishthira, spoke to the king, 'O Father, I have heard the people say ill-omened things. They bypass you and Bhishma, favoring Yudhishthira for the throne. Bhishma will approve of this, as he will not rule the kingdom himself. It appears that the citizens are plotting against us. If Yudhishthira inherits the kingdom as the legacy of Pandu, his son will follow, and his son's son after him, and so on. Consequently, we and our children will be disregarded and fall into poverty. Therefore, O King of the world, make plans so that we do not suffer continuous distress and dependence on others for our sustenance. If you had obtained the throne earlier, we would undoubtedly have succeeded you, regardless of the people's opinions.'"

Vaisampayana continued, "King Dhritarashtra, blind to the world, heard his son's words and recollected all that Kanika had done. His mind, burdened with sorrow, wavered like a ship tossed upon turbulent waves. Duryodhana, Karna, Sakuni, and Duhsasana held a secret meeting. Prince Duryodhana, addressing his father, said, 'Father, through clever means, send the Pandavas to the town of Varanavata. Once they are there, we will have nothing to fear.' Upon hearing these words, Dhritarashtra pondered for a moment and responded, 'Pandu was always devoted to virtue and respectful to his relatives, particularly to me. He cared little for worldly pleasures and willingly gave up everything, including the kingdom, to me. His son is as virtuous and accomplished as him and enjoys widespread fame. He is supported by allies. How can we forcibly exile him from his rightful kingdom? The citizens and their descendants, who were all supported and protected by Pandu, will surely rebel against us and slay us along with our friends and relatives because of Yudhishthira.'

"Duryodhana replied, 'Your words are true, Father. However, we can win the people's favor by bestowing wealth and honors upon them. With the treasury and the ministers under our control, let us gently exile the Pandavas to Varanavata. Once the kingdom is mine, Kunti and her children can return.'

"Dhritarashtra responded, 'This thought has crossed my mind as well, Duryodhana, but I have never expressed it due to its sinful nature. Bhishma, Drona, Kshattri, and Gautama (Kripa) will never permit the exile of the Pandavas. In their eyes, we and the Pandavas are equals. They will not differentiate between us. If we mistreat the Pandavas, we risk facing death at the hands of the Kurus, these noble individuals, and the entire world.'

"Duryodhana argued, 'Bhishma remains neutral, showing no excessive favoritism to either side. Aswatthaman, Drona's son, supports us. Where the son is, the father follows. Kripa, the son of Saradwat, will side with Drona and Aswatthaman. He will never forsake his nephew. Vidura depends on us for his livelihood, even though he secretly supports the enemy. If he sides with the Pandavas, he alone cannot harm us. Father, exile the Pandavas to Varanavata without fear. Take the necessary steps to send them there today. By doing so, you will extinguish the grief that consumes me like a blazing fire, robbing me of sleep and piercing my heart like a terrible dart.'"

Vaisampayana spoke, "Then, Prince Duryodhana, accompanied by his brothers, began to gradually sway the people to his side through generous bestowals of wealth and honors. Meanwhile, cunning counselors, following Dhritarashtra's instructions, one day began to extol the charms of Varanavata in the court. They proclaimed, 'The festival of Pasupati (Siva) has commenced in the town of Varanavata. The assembly of people is grand, and the procession is the most delightful spectacle ever witnessed on earth. Adorned with every imaginable ornament, it captivates the hearts of all spectators.' Thus spoke those counselors, guided by Dhritarashtra, painting Varanavata in the most alluring hues. While they narrated the wonders of the town, the Pandavas felt the desire to visit this enchanting place.

When King Dhritarashtra discerned the awakening curiosity in the Pandavas, the son of Ambika addressed them, saying, 'My men often extol Varanavata as the most delightful town in the world. Therefore, if you wish to witness that festival, go to Varanavata with your followers and friends. Enjoy yourselves there like the celestials. Give pearls and gems to the Brahmanas and musicians gathered there. Delight in the festivities as much as you desire, sporting there for some time, and return to Hastinapura again.'

Vaisampayana continued, 'Yudhishthira, fully comprehending Dhritarashtra's motives and recognizing his own vulnerability, replied to the king, saying, 'So be it.' Then, addressing Bhishma, the son of Santanu, wise Vidura, Drona, Valhika, the Kaurava, Somadatta, Kripa, Aswatthaman, Bhurisravas, and the other counselors, Brahmanas, ascetics, priests, citizens, and the illustrious Gandhari, he spoke slowly and humbly, 'At the command of Dhritarashtra, we, with our friends and followers, are going to the delightful and populous town of Varanavata. Cheerfully bestow your blessings upon us, so that acquiring prosperity, we may remain untainted by sin.' Addressed thus by the eldest of Pandu's sons, the Kaurava chiefs joyously pronounced blessings, saying, 'May all the elements bless your journey, and may not the slightest evil befall you.'

The Pandavas, having performed propitiatory rites to secure their share of the kingdom and completed their preparations, set forth for Varanavata.

Vaisampayana spoke, "The malevolent Duryodhana was greatly pleased when the king, O Bharata, had uttered those words to the Pandavas. And, O bull of Bharata's race, Duryodhana, then, in private, summoned his counselor, Purochana, seizing his right hand, and said, 'O Purochana, this world, brimming with wealth, is mine, but it is yours as much as mine. It is your duty, therefore, to safeguard it. You are my most reliable counselor with whom to consult. Therefore, O sire, heed my advice and annihilate my enemies through a cunning stratagem. Do as I command. The Pandavas, sent by Dhritarashtra, are on their way to Varanavata, where, under Dhritarashtra's orders, they will revel in the festivities. Act in a way that will enable you to reach Varanavata today in a chariot drawn by swift mules. Once there, construct a quadrangular palace near the arsenal, abundant in materials and furnishings. Guard the mansion well with vigilant eyes. Utilize hemp, resin, and all other inflammable substances available in building the house. Form a plaster for the walls by mixing earth with clarified butter, oil, fat, and a substantial amount of lac. Surround the house with hemp, oil, clarified butter, lac, and wood in a manner that the Pandavas, even with scrutiny, cannot detect them or suspect the house's combustible nature. Erect such a mansion, and after worshipping the Pandavas with utmost reverence, make them reside in it with Kunti and all their companions. Furnish the place with seats, conveyances, and beds of the finest craftsmanship for the Pandavas, ensuring that Dhritarashtra has no cause for complaint. Manage everything so that the people of Varanavata remain unaware until our objective is achieved. Once you are assured that the Pandavas are resting inside, trusting and unafraid, set fire to the mansion, starting from the outer door. The Pandavas will thus be consumed in the flames, yet the world will believe they perished in an accidental conflagration of their home."

Saying, 'So be it' to the Kuru prince, Purochana swiftly journeyed to Varanavata in a chariot drawn by fleet mules. Arriving there without delay, obedient to Duryodhana's instructions, he executed everything the prince had commanded him to do

Vaisampayana spoke, "As the Pandavas readied their chariots, harnessing steeds swift as the wind, they, in deep sorrow, touched the feet of Bhishma, King Dhritarashtra, the illustrious Drona, Kripa, Vidura, and the other venerable elders of the Kuru lineage. With respectful salutations to the elderly, embraces for their peers, farewells for the children, and regards for all the esteemed ladies of their household, the Pandavas, mindful of their vows, departed for Varanavata. Vidura, the wise sage, and other Kurus, along with the distressed citizens, followed the Pandavas for some distance, expressing their anguish. The citizens and country folk, accompanying the Pandavas, lamented openly, saying, 'King Dhritarashtra, of wicked soul, sees not with the same eye. He pays no heed to virtue. Yudhishthira, Bhima, and Arjuna would never commit the sin of rebellion. If they remain quiet, what can the valiant son of Madri do? Dhritarashtra, having inherited the kingdom from his father, could not tolerate them. How can Bhishma, who endures the exile of the Pandavas to that wretched place, permit such a grave injustice? Both Vichitravirya and the royal sage Pandu cherished us like fathers. Now that Pandu, the lion among men, has ascended to heaven, Dhritarashtra cannot endure the presence of his own sons.

We, who do not endorse this exile, shall leave this excellent town and our homes where Yudhishthira goes.'

To these distressed citizens, Yudhishthira, also grieving, replied after some reflection, 'The king is our father, deserving of respect, our spiritual guide, and our superior. It is our duty to carry out whatever he commands with unsuspicious hearts. You are our friends. Bless us by walking around and then return to your abodes. When the time comes for you to act on our behalf, then accomplish what is agreeable and beneficial to us.' Following Yudhishthira's words, the citizens circled the Pandavas, imparted their blessings, and returned to their homes.

Once the citizens ceased following them, Vidura, well-versed in moral principles, desiring to awaken Yudhishthira to the imminent dangers, addressed him with these words. Using the language of the Mlechchhas, Vidura, skilled in that tongue, spoke to Yudhishthira, who was also conversant with it, making his words unintelligible to all except Yudhishthira. He said, 'One must be aware of the schemes his foes devise in accordance with political science and act to avoid danger. Knowing that there are sharp weapons capable of cutting the body, though not made of steel, and understanding the means to ward them off, one can never be harmed by enemies. The man who takes a weapon not made of steel (an inflammable abode) given by his foes can escape from fire by making his abode like that of a jackal, having many outlets. By wandering, a man may acquire knowledge of paths, and by the stars, he can ascertain direction. He who keeps his five senses under control can never be oppressed by his enemies.'

Having spoken thus, Vidura concluded his advice, and Yudhishthira, the just, replied, 'I have understood.' Vidura, having instructed the Pandavas and accompanied them this far, walked around them, bid them farewell, and returned to his abode. Kunti approached Yudhishthira and said, 'The words exchanged between you and

Vidura were unclear to us, spoken in a language as if nothing was said. If it is not improper, I would like to know everything that transpired between you and him.'

Yudhishthira replied, 'The virtuous Vidura informed me that the mansion prepared for our stay in Varanavata was constructed with inflammable materials. He said to me, 'The path of escape will not be unknown to you,' and added, 'Those who can control their senses can acquire the sovereignty of the whole world.' To Vidura's counsel, I replied, 'I have understood thee.'"

Vaisampayana continued, "The Pandavas departed on the eighth day of the month of Phalguna, under the ascendant star Rohini, and upon reaching Varanavata, beheld the town and its people."

Vaisampayana continued, "The citizens of Varanavata, upon learning of the arrival of the sons of Pandu, filled with joy, poured out of the city in a multitude of vehicles, following the Sastras, carrying auspicious items to welcome the eminent guests. Approaching the sons of Kunti, the people surrounded them, uttering blessings and prayers, their voices echoing like the war cries of warriors. Yudhishthira, encircled by the citizens, resembled a radiant god wielding the thunderbolt amidst the celestials. Adorned in garments of splendor, the Pandavas, honored by the citizens and returning the reverence, entered Varanavata, adorned with every conceivable ornament. They first visited the abodes of the Brahmanas, then the residences of the town officials, and further proceeded to those of the Sutas, Vaisyas, and Sudras. Adored by the citizens, the Pandavas finally arrived at the palace prepared for them, escorted by Purochana, the cunning architect.

For ten nights, the Pandavas, robed in opulence, lived there, honored by Purochana and the inhabitants of Varanavata. After this duration, Purochana revealed to them a mansion named 'The Blessed Home,' though in truth, it was a cursed abode. Yielding to Purochana's urging, the Pandavas, dressed in costly attire, entered that dwelling like celestial Guhyakas entering Siva's palace on Mount Kailasa. Observing the house, the virtuous Yudhishthira remarked to Bhima that it was indeed constructed with inflammable materials. Detecting the scent of fat, clarified butter, and lac, he told Bhima, 'O chastiser of foes, this house is truly built with inflammable materials! It is evident! The enemy, with skilled artists, has crafted this mansion using hemp, resin, heath, straw, and bamboo, all soaked in clarified butter. Purochana, acting under Duryodhana's instructions, stays here, intending to burn me alive when he perceives my trustfulness. Yet, Vidura, with great intelligence, aware of the danger, has forewarned me. Our youngest uncle, ever desiring our well-being, has disclosed that this perilous house was constructed in secret by Duryodhana's conspirators.'

Hearing this, Bhima responded, 'If you are aware that this house is so combustible, sir, it would be prudent for us to return to where we initially lodged.' Yudhishthira replied, 'It seems to me that we should remain here, appearing unsuspecting but vigilant, seeking a certain means of escape. If Purochana discerns our suspicions from our demeanor, he might swiftly set the house ablaze. Purochana cares little for infamy or sin. He remains here, following Duryodhana's orders. If we flee in fear of the flames, Duryodhana, aspiring for dominion, will undoubtedly orchestrate our demise through spies. Devoid of rank and power, bereft of friends and allies, and lacking in wealth, will he not employ suitable means to annihilate us? Let us, therefore, outsmart this villain Purochana and that other villain Duryodhana, living our days with caution, our senses alert, and at times concealing our true identities. Let us adopt a wandering life, becoming familiar with all paths, and create a secret underground passage in our chamber. If we act with discretion and privacy, fire shall never claim us. Let us reside here, actively working for our safety, all the while keeping our intentions concealed from Purochana and the citizens of Varanavata.'

Vaisampayana continued, "A confidant of Vidura, adept in the craft of mining, clandestinely approached the Pandavas, whispering, 'Sent by Vidura, I am a skilled miner, ready to serve the Pandavas. What task shall I undertake for you? Vidura, in his trust, commanded me, 'Go to the Pandavas and work for their welfare.' Purochana, on the fourteenth night of this dark fortnight, will ignite the door of your dwelling with the intent of burning you alive, O sons of Pandu. This nefarious plot is the design of that malevolent wretch, Dhritarashtra's son. O Pandu's son, Vidura also spoke to you in the Mlechchha tongue, to which you responded in kind. I recount these details as my credentials."

Hearing this, Yudhishthira, the truthful scion of Kunti, replied, "O amiable one, I recognize you as a dear and trustworthy friend of Vidura, loyal and ever devoted to him. Vidura knows everything, and as he is, so are we yours. Consider us akin to him. Make no distinction between us and him. Protect us as Vidura always safeguards us. I am aware that Purochana, at the behest of Dhritarashtra's son, has devised this highly flammable abode for me. That wicked wretch, laden with wealth and allies, ceaselessly pursues us. Save us, with a little effort, from the impending inferno. If we are consumed here, Duryodhana's wicked desire will be fulfilled. This mansion is his well-stocked arsenal. It stands adjacent to the lofty ramparts of the arsenal, devoid of any exit. Vidura knew of Duryodhana's unholy plot from the beginning, and it was he who warned us beforehand. The danger that Kshattri foresaw is now at our doorstep. Save us from it without Purochana's knowledge." On hearing these words, the miner declared, 'So be it,' and began the careful excavation, crafting a spacious subterranean passage. The entrance of this passage was concealed in the center of the house, flush with the floor and concealed with planks. To avoid Purochana's scrutiny, the entrance was cleverly covered. The Pandavas, keeping arms ready within their chambers, slept at night, and during the day, engaged in hunting throughout various forests. Living in this mansion, they deceived Purochana, projecting an appearance of trust and contentment while remaining ever vigilant and discontented. None in Varanavata, save Vidura's friend, the adept miner, knew of these schemes of the Pandavas."

Vaisampayana spoke, "Seeing the Pandavas dwelling there merrily and unsuspecting for a full year, Purochana rejoiced greatly. Observing his elation, Yudhishthira, the virtuous son of Kunti, addressed Bhima, Arjuna, and the twins, Nakula and Sahadeva, saying, 'The ruthless villain has been thoroughly deceived. I believe the time for our escape has arrived. By setting fire to the arsenal and reducing Purochana to ashes, leaving his lifeless form behind, let the six of us depart unnoticed by all!' A violent wind began to blow in the night. Bhima ignited the house where Purochana lay asleep. Pandu's son then set fire to the lac-covered door of the house and kindled the mansion in various places. When the Pandavas were assured that the house was ablaze, those vanquishers of enemies, along with their mother, swiftly entered the subterranean passage without delay. Subsequently, the heat and roar of the flames grew intense, awakening the townsfolk. Observing the house in conflagration, citizens with mournful countenances remarked, 'The vile Purochana, guided by Duryodhana's counsel, constructed this house to annihilate his employer's kin. He has indeed set it ablaze. Shame on Dhritarashtra's biased heart! He has, as if an adversary, incinerated the blameless heirs of Pandu! Woe unto the sinful and malevolent Purochana, who, intending harm, has met his own demise.'

Vaisampayana continued, 'The citizens of Varanavata lamented in this manner, surrounding the house for the entire night. Meanwhile, the Pandavas, accompanied by their mother, discreetly emerged from the subterranean passage and fled unnoticed. Yet, hindered by fatigue and trepidation, those warriors, along with their mother, were unable to advance swiftly. Bhimasena, however, possessed of formidable strength and celerity, carried his brothers and mother upon his mighty frame. Placing his mother on his shoulder and the twins on his flanks, with Yudhishthira and Arjuna held firmly in both his arms, the mighty Vrikodara embarked on his journey, cleaving through the darkness, breaking trees with his powerful chest, and imprinting the earth with his forceful tread."

Chapter 27

DEMON IN THE FOREST

Vaisampayana continued, "As mighty Bhima advanced, the entire forest, with its trees and branches, appeared to tremble, resonating with the clash against his breast. His powerful strides created a wind reminiscent of the gusts that blow during the months of Jyaishtha and Ashadha (May and June). Bhima, endowed with the swiftness of Garuda or Marut (the god of wind), forged ahead, forging a path for himself by trampling down trees and creepers in his wake. He effortlessly shattered the large trees and plants, adorned with flowers and fruits, standing in his path. The force with which Bhima proceeded was so great that it caused the Pandavas to lose consciousness. Frequently navigating challenging streams, the Pandavas disguised themselves along the journey, fearing the sons of Dhritarashtra.

Bhima, carrying his brothers and mother on his back, reached a dreadful forest as evening approached. In this desolate forest, where fruits, roots, and water were scarce, the cries of birds and beasts echoed ominously. The increasing darkness intensified the ferocious sounds, and untimely winds toppled many trees, large and small, and withered creepers with dry leaves and fruits. Afflicted by fatigue, thirst, and drowsiness, the Kaurava princes were unable to proceed further. They sat down in the forest, devoid of food and drink. Kunti, tormented by thirst, repeatedly expressed her suffering to her sons, 'Though I am amidst my five sons, I am burning with thirst!' Responding to her plea, Bhima, in his compassion, resolved to go in search of water. Guided by the sweet cries of aquatic fowls, he headed towards a lake, bathing and quenching his thirst. Expressing his affection for his brothers, Bhima brought water by soaking his upper garments.

Returning swiftly over the four miles, he reached his mother. Upon seeing her, Bhima was overwhelmed with sorrow and sighed like a serpent. Distraught at the sight of his mother and brothers sleeping on the bare ground, Bhima lamented, 'Alas! Wretched am I to witness my brothers lying on the ground. What more painful sight could I behold? These princes who, at Varanavata, could not sleep on soft and luxurious beds, now lie on the bare ground! What could be more distressing than this? The virtuous Yudhishthira, deserving the sovereignty of the three worlds, lies fatigued like an ordinary man on the bare ground! Arjuna, with the darkish hue of blue clouds, unparalleled among men, sleeps on the ground like an average person! The twins, as beautiful as the twin Aswins among the celestials, are asleep on the bare ground! What could be more agonizing than this? Oh, the one without envious and malicious relatives lives happily in this world, akin to a single tree in a village. Such a tree, standing alone in a village, becomes sacred and is worshipped by all for its uniqueness. Those with numerous relatives, virtuous and heroic, also live joyfully in the world without sorrow, like tall trees thriving in the same forest. However, we, forced into exile by the wicked Dhritarashtra and his sons, escaped a fiery death by sheer good fortune. After eluding that fire, we now find refuge in the shade of this tree. Having already endured so much, where else can we go? O sons of Dhritarashtra, lacking foresight, revel in your temporary success. The gods are surely smiling upon you. But you villains still breathe because Yudhishthira hasn't commanded me to take your lives. Otherwise, today, filled with wrath, I would send you, O Duryodhana, along with your children, friends, brothers, Karna, and deceitful Sakuni, to the realms of Yama (Pluto)! But what can I do when the virtuous King Yudhishthira, the eldest of the Pandavas, is not yet angered by you?'

Having uttered these words, Bhima, agitated by wrath, clenched his palms and sighed deeply. Stirred once again by anger, like a rekindled fire suddenly blazing up, Vrikodara gazed upon his brothers, sleeping trustfully on the ground. Distraught by grief at the sight of his mother and brothers asleep on the bare ground, Vrikodara began to lament, 'Wretched am I to witness my brothers lying on the ground. What more painful sight could I behold? These princes, who at Varanavata, could not sleep on soft and luxurious beds, now lie on the bare ground! What could be more distressing than this? The virtuous Yudhishthira, deserving the sovereignty of the three worlds, lies fatigued like an ordinary man on the bare ground! Arjuna, with the darkish hue of blue clouds, unparalleled among men, sleeps on the ground like an average person! The twins, as beautiful as the twin Aswins among the celestials, are asleep on the bare ground! What could be more agonizing than this? Oh, the one without envious and malicious relatives lives happily in this world, akin to a single tree in a village. Such a tree, standing alone in a village, becomes sacred and is worshipped by all for its uniqueness. Those with numerous relatives, virtuous and heroic, also live joyfully in the world without sorrow, like tall trees thriving in the same forest. However, we, forced into exile by the wicked Dhritarashtra and his sons, escaped a fiery death by sheer good fortune. After eluding that fire, we now find refuge in the shade of this tree. Having already endured so much, where else can we go? O sons of Dhritarashtra, lacking foresight, revel in your temporary success. The gods are surely smiling upon you. But you villains still breathe because Yudhishthira hasn't commanded me to take your lives. Otherwise, today, filled with wrath, I would send you, O Duryodhana, along with your children, friends, brothers, Karna, and deceitful Sakuni, to the realms of Yama (Pluto)! But what can I do when the virtuous King Yudhishthira, the eldest of the Pandavas, is not yet angered by you?'

Having uttered these words, Bhima, agitated by wrath, clenched his palms and sighed deeply. Stirred once again by anger, like a rekindled fire suddenly blazing up, Vrikodara gazed upon his brothers, sleeping trustfully on the ground. Distraught by grief at the sight of his mother and brothers asleep on the bare ground, Vrikodara began to lament, 'Wretched am I to witness my brothers lying on the ground. What more painful sight could I behold? These princes, who at Varanavata, could not sleep on soft and luxurious beds, now lie on the bare ground! What could be more distressing than this? The virtuous Yudhishthira, deserving the sovereignty of the three worlds, lies fatigued like an ordinary man on the bare ground! Arjuna, with the darkish hue of blue clouds, unparalleled among men, sleeps on the ground like an average person! The twins, as beautiful as the twin Aswins among the celestials, are asleep on the bare ground! What could be more agonizing than this? Oh, the one without envious and malicious relatives lives happily in this world, akin to a single tree in a village. Such a tree, standing alone in a village, becomes sacred and is worshipped by all for its uniqueness. Those with numerous relatives, virtuous and heroic, also live joyfully in the world without sorrow, like tall trees thriving in the same forest. However, we, forced into exile by the wicked Dhritarashtra and his sons, escaped a fiery death by sheer good fortune. After eluding that fire, we now find refuge in the shade of this tree. Having already endured so much, where else can we go? O sons of Dhritarashtra, lacking foresight, revel in your temporary success. The gods are surely smiling upon you. But you villains still breathe because Yudhishthira hasn't commanded me to take your lives. Otherwise, today, filled with wrath, I would send you, O Duryodhana, along with your children, friends, brothers, Karna, and deceitful Sakuni, to the realms of Yama (Pluto)! But what can I do when the virtuous King Yudhishthira, the eldest of the Pandavas, is not yet angered by you?'

Having uttered these words, Bhima, agitated by wrath, clenched his palms and sighed deeply. Stirred once again by anger, like a rekindled fire suddenly blazing up, Vrikodara gazed upon his brothers, sleeping trustfully on the ground. Distraught by grief at the sight of his mother and brothers asleep on the bare ground, Vrikodara began to lament, 'Wretched am I to witness my brothers lying on the ground. What more painful sight could I behold? These princes, who at Varanavata, could not sleep on soft and luxurious beds, now lie on the bare ground! What could be more distressing than this? The virtuous Yudhishthira, deserving the sovereignty of the three worlds, lies fatigued like an ordinary man on the bare ground! Arjuna, with the darkish hue of blue clouds, unparalleled among men, sleeps on the ground like an average person! The twins, as beautiful as the twin Aswins among the celestials, are asleep on the bare ground! What could be more agonizing than this? Oh, the one without envious and malicious relatives lives happily in this world, akin to a single tree in a village. Such a tree, standing alone in a village, becomes sacred and is worshipped by all for its uniqueness. Those with numerous relatives, virtuous and heroic, also live joyfully in the world without sorrow, like tall trees thriving in the same forest. However, we, forced into exile by the wicked Dhritarashtra and his sons, escaped a fiery death by sheer good fortune. After eluding that fire, we now find refuge in the shade of this tree. Having already endured so much, where else can we go? O sons of Dhritarashtra, lacking foresight, revel in your temporary success. The gods are surely smiling upon you. But you villains still breathe because Yudhishthira hasn't commanded me to take your lives. Otherwise, today, filled with wrath, I would send you, O Duryodhana, along with your children, friends, brothers, Karna, and deceitful Sakuni, to the realms of Yama

"Vaisampayana continued, 'Not far from the place where the Pandavas lay in slumber, a Rakshasa named Hidimva lurked on a gnarled Sala tree. Possessed of terrifying energy and prowess, his grim visage bore sharp, elongated teeth that hinted at his insatiable appetite for human flesh. His form, with long shanks and a grotesque belly, boasted of wild, red locks and beard, and his shoulders resembled the broad neck of a sinister tree. Ears pointed like arrows, and eyes glowing red with malevolence, Hidimva, the cannibal, surveyed the sons of Pandu with an insatiable hunger, his sinister gaze casting shadows in the moonlit woods. Longing for human flesh, Hidimva's dry and grizzly locks twitched, and his hungry eyes lingered on the Pandavas, an ominous yawn punctuating his gruesome desire.

Addressing his sister, Hidimva spoke, 'O sister, a banquet of delectable morsels has ventured into my domain after an agonizingly long wait! The scent of these mortals tantalizes my senses, and today, after an eternity, my fangs will sink into the most succulent human flesh. My eight teeth, honed to pierce any substance, shall revel in this feast. I will assail their throats, rupture their veins, and relish copious quantities of hot, fresh, and frothy human blood. Go, ascertain who lies dormant in these woods. The pungent fragrance of mankind delights my nostrils. Slaughter them all, bring them to me; they rest within my territory. Fear them not, for you have my protection. Fulfill my command, and together we shall revel in tearing their bodies apart, savoring their flesh before a rhythmic dance to various measures ensues!'

Abiding by her brother's sinister decree, Hidimva, the female fiend, ventured towards the Pandavas. As she beheld them, with Bhimasena sitting vigilantly awake, an unholy passion ignited within her monstrous heart. Transforming into a creature of unsettling beauty adorned with grotesque ornaments, she approached Bhima, her movements a ghastly mockery of a modest gait. In a voice that resonated with the eerie calm before a storm, she uttered, 'O bull among men, who dares intrude into my brother's territory? What celestial beings lie in slumber here, and who is this lady of otherworldly allure, trusting the darkness as if she were in her own sanctum? Do you not fathom that this forest is the accursed abode of Hidimva, the Rakshasa? I reveal the truth; I have been dispatched by that malevolent creature, my brother, with a dark intent—to feast upon your flesh. Yet, beholding you, radiant as a celestial, I am compelled to claim you as my own. O you, who comprehend the nuances of duty, it is now for you to decide what is fitting. Cupid's arrows have pierced my heart and body, and I implore you to make me yours. I shall liberate you all from the clutches of my cannibal brother. Be my consort, O sinless one, and together, we shall reside in realms inaccessible to mortals, where I, at my whim, shall navigate the very air. In those desolate realms, you shall find unbridled ecstasy in my company.'

Hearing her haunting words, Bhima responded, 'O Rakshasa woman, who could forsake his sleeping mother and brothers, entrusting them as fodder for a Rakshasa, like a Muni with passions subdued? What man like me would indulge his lust, forsaking his slumbering kin for the insatiable appetites of a fiend?'

The Rakshasa woman murmured, 'Awaken them, and I shall offer you pleasures beyond imagination. I vow to deliver you from my cannibal brother.'

Bhima retorted, 'O Rakshasa woman, I shall not awaken my brothers and mother, for I dread your wicked brother. Rakshasas cower before the might of my arms. Neither men, nor Gandharvas, nor Yakshas can withstand my ferocity. O amiable one, you may stay or depart at your leisure, or dispatch your cannibal brother, O delicate one. I remain undeterred.'"

"Vaisampayana said, 'Hidimva, chief of the Rakshasas, furious at his sister's delay, descended swiftly from the gnarled Sala tree and hastened towards the Pandavas. With eyes blazing red, arms as sturdy as the trunks of ancient trees, and hair standing on end, he presented a terrifying spectacle. His mouth, wide open like the entrance to a dark cavern, showcased long, sharp-pointed teeth that hinted at his insatiable hunger. As he approached, Hidimva's grim countenance, resembling a mass of dark clouds, filled the air with dread.

Observing her brother's swift descent, Hidimva, the Rakshasa woman, felt a surge of fear. Addressing Bhima, she pleaded, 'O mighty one, the wicked cannibal approaches in wrath. I implore you, heed my counsel. Deal with your brothers and mother as I instruct. With my Rakshasa powers, I can transport you through the skies. Place your kin on my hips, and I shall carry you all far beyond his reach. Awaken them and let me rescue you from this impending danger.'

Bhima, with a reassuring smile, replied, 'Fear not, fair one. As long as I am here, no Rakshasa can harm these. I shall confront and vanquish this monster before your very eyes. This Rakshasa is no match for my might; he shall crumble before the strength of my arms. Witness these powerful limbs, each akin to an elephant's trunk. See these thighs, resembling iron maces, and this broad, adamantine chest. O charming one, you shall witness today the might of Indra himself. Do not despise me, thinking I am just a man.'

Hidimva responded, 'O tiger among men, O celestial beauty in human form, I do not hold you in contempt. Yet, I have witnessed the prowess that Rakshasas exhibit against men.'

Vaisampayana continued, 'As Bhima spoke, the wrathful Rakshasa, driven by hunger and hatred, overheard their conversation. Beholding his sister transformed into an enchanting human figure, adorned with celestial ornaments and delicate attire, Hidimva suspected her ulterior motives. Enraged, he accused her, 'Have you become so senseless, O Hidimva, that you fear not my wrath? Fie on you, unchaste woman! Are you now enticed by lust, seeking to inflict harm upon me? You are ready to tarnish the honor of all Rakshasas, our ancestors! Those who assist you in this vile endeavor shall meet their demise at my hands. I shall slay them all, beginning with you.' With these words, Hidimva, eyes ablaze with anger and teeth grinding against teeth, advanced menacingly towards his sister.

Witnessing this confrontation, Bhima intervened, 'Stop—Stop! O wicked cannibal, what need is there to awaken my brothers who are in peaceful slumber? O vile creature, face me first, for it is unbecoming to slay a woman, especially when she has been wronged. She is not to blame; the deity of desire has influenced her actions. You have no right to harm her for this transgression. O fiend, you shall not slay a woman while I am here. Confront me, and I shall fight you alone. Today, I will send you to the abode of Yama. Your head, pressed by my might, shall shatter like a mountain crushed by an elephant. After I slay you, let the herons, hawks, and jackals feast upon your torn limbs.'

Hidimva, unyielding, retorted, 'What purpose does your boasting serve? Accomplish what you claim, then boast. Therefore, delay not. You may be strong and powerful, but your true strength will be tested in our battle. Until then, I shall spare your brothers. Let them rest undisturbed. I will slay you first, and after drinking your blood, I shall deal with them and finally with this sister of mine who has wronged me.'

With a grim determination, Bhima declared, 'O Rakshasa woman, I shall not awaken my brothers and mother. Fear not your wicked brother. Rakshasas tremble before my might. Men, Gandharvas, and Yakshas alike cannot withstand my ferocity. O amiable one, stay or depart at your will, or send your cannibal brother. I remain undeterred.'"

"Vaisampayana said, 'Awakened from their sleep, those tigers among men, along with their mother, marveled at the extraordinary beauty of Hidimva. Kunti, gazing upon her with wonder, addressed her sweetly and sought to understand her origin and purpose. She inquired, 'O celestial beauty, who art thou, and whose daughter with the splendor of the celestials? What brings thee to this place, and from whence dost thou come? If thou art a forest deity or an Apsara, reveal thy identity and the reason for thy presence. Why dost thou linger here?'

Hidimva replied, 'O resplendent lady, this extensive forest, with the hue of blue clouds, is the dwelling of a Rakshasa named Hidimva. Recognize me as the sister of that Rakshasa chief. Honored dame, at the behest of my cruel brother, I was sent to slay you and all your children. However, upon arriving here, I beheld your mighty son. O blessed lady, the deity of love, who pervades the essence of every being, swayed my heart, and I mentally chose your mighty son as my husband. Though I endeavored to carry you away, I could not, as your son opposed it. In response to the delay, the cannibal arrived here with the intent of killing your children. Yet, your valiant son forcefully dragged him away. Witness now, that couple—man and Rakshasa—both endowed with great strength and prowess, locked in combat, resonating through the entire region with the echoes of their fierce struggle.'

Vaisampayana continued, 'Upon hearing her words, Yudhishthira, Arjuna, Nakula, and Sahadeva, along with their mother, rose to their feet and witnessed Bhima and the Rakshasa locked in combat. The two warriors, displaying great strength, dragged and grappled with each other, resembling two mighty lions vying for dominance. The dust they raised in their struggle mirrored the smoke of a forest conflagration, and in the midst of that dust, their colossal bodies appeared like two tall cliffs shrouded in mist.

Arjuna, observing Bhima appearing somewhat strained in the fight, smilingly spoke, 'Fear not, Bhima of mighty arms! Unaware of the fierce Rakshasa, we were asleep. Now, I stand ready to assist you. Allow me to slay this Rakshasa, while Nakula and Sahadeva guard our mother.' Bhima, hearing Arjuna's words, replied, 'Behold this encounter like a stranger. Do not worry about the outcome. Once within the range of my arms, he shall not escape with his life.'

Arjuna, then said, 'Why keep this Rakshasa alive for so long? O oppressor of foes, we need to leave. We cannot stay here any longer. The eastern horizon is reddening, and the morning twilight approaches. Rakshasas become stronger with the break of day. Hasten, O Bhima! Do not toy with your adversary; slay the fierce Rakshasa quickly. During these twilights, Rakshasas employ their deceptive powers. Utilize the full strength of your arms.'

Vaisampayana continued, 'Enraged by Arjuna's words, Bhima summoned the immense might of Vayu, his father, employed during the universal dissolution. Filled with rage, he hoisted Hidimva's body high in the air, whirling it a hundred times. Addressing the Rakshasa, Bhima said, 'O Rakshasa, your intelligence is in vain, and your growth on unholy flesh is futile. Today, you deserve an unholy death, and I shall reduce you to nothing. I will make this forest blessed, free from thorns and obstacles. O Rakshasa, you shall no longer prey on humans for your food.' At this moment, Arjuna, with a smile, said, 'O Bhima, if you find it challenging to overcome this Rakshasa in combat, allow me to assist you. Otherwise, slay him yourself without delay. Alternatively, O Vrikodara, permit me to handle the Rakshasa alone. You are fatigued and have nearly concluded the matter. Rest well, for you deserve it.'

Hearing Arjuna's words, Bhima, aflame with anger, forcefully dashed the Rakshasa to the ground and slew him like an animal. The dying Rakshasa emitted a fearsome yell that reverberated through the entire forest, resembling the deep sound of a wet drum. Bhima, seizing the lifeless body with his hands, bent it double, breaking it in the middle, much to the joy of his brothers. Arjuna, offering his worship to Bhima, the illustrious warrior, addressed him again, 'O revered one, I believe there is a town not far from this forest. Let us depart quickly so that Duryodhana cannot trace us.'

The mighty warriors, the sons of Kunti, assented, and along with their mother, proceeded from the forest, followed by Hidimva, the Rakshasa woman."

"Vaisampayana continued, 'Seeing Hidimva following them, Bhima addressed her, 'Rakshasas employ deceptions that are impenetrable to take revenge on their enemies. Therefore, O Hidimva, go in the direction your brother has gone.' Yudhishthira, observing Bhima's anger, advised, 'O Bhima, tiger among men, even when angered, do not slay a woman. O Pandava, upholding virtue is a higher duty than preserving life. You have already slain Hidimva, who came to kill us. This woman is the sister of that Rakshasa. What harm can she cause us, even if she is angry?'

"Hidimva, saluting Kunti and Yudhishthira, with joined palms, spoke respectfully, 'O revered lady, you are aware of the pain women endure from the god of love. Blessed dame, the anguish caused by

Bhimasena's rejection torments me. I have endured this insufferable pain, anticipating the time when your son could alleviate it. That time has come, as I expected to find happiness. Abandoning my friends, relations, and the customs of my race, I have chosen your son, this mighty hero, as my husband. I assure you, O illustrious lady, that if rejected by this hero or by you, I will no longer endure this life. Therefore, O fair lady, in your kindness, consider me either as a foolish woman or your obedient servant. O illustrious dame, unite me with your son, my husband. Endowed with the form of a celestial, let me depart with him wherever I desire. Trust me, O blessed lady, I will return your son to you every day at nightfall. Whenever you think of me, I will promptly come to you and transport you wherever you command. I will rescue you from all dangers and carry you over impassable and rugged terrains. When you wish to travel swiftly, I will carry you on my back. O, be merciful to me and persuade Bhima to accept me. It is said that in times of distress, one should protect life by any means necessary. The one seeking to fulfill this duty should not hesitate about the means. In times of distress, maintaining virtue is the highest virtue. Indeed, distress is the greatest danger to virtue and virtuous men. Virtue protects life; therefore, virtue is called the giver of life. Hence, the means to secure virtue or fulfill a duty can never be censured.'

"Hearing Hidimva's words, Yudhishthira said, 'It is true, O Hidimva, as you say. There is no doubt about it. But, O slender-waisted one, you must act as you have said. Bhima will, after he has purified himself, prayed, and performed the customary propitiatory rites, attend to you until the sun sets. During the day, enjoy your time with him as you wish, O swift one! However, you must bring Bhimasena back here every day at nightfall.'

"Vaisampayana continued, 'Bhima, agreeing to everything Yudhishthira said, addressed Hidimva, 'Listen, O Rakshasa woman! I truly pledge that I will remain with you until you have a son.'

Hidimva, saying, 'So be it,' took Bhima on her body and swiftly traveled through the air. She sported with Bhima in picturesque mountain peaks, sacred regions filled with herds and melodies of birds, and islands adorned with lotuses and lilies. Assuming the most beautiful form, she indulged in their enjoyment, ensuring Bhima's happiness. Likewise, in inaccessible forest regions, mountain caves, lakes filled with lotuses, sylvan streams with scenic banks, and on sea shores glittering with gold and pearls, she continued to delight Bhima. In beautiful towns, gardens, woods sacred to the gods, and on hillsides, in regions inhabited by Guhyakas and ascetics, on the banks of Manasarovara with fruits and flowers in abundance, she, with the speed of thought, played with Bhima, making him happy. Hidimva continued this enjoyment with Bhima in various places, and in due time, she conceived and gave birth to a mighty son fathered by the Pandava. This child, with terrifying eyes, a large mouth, straight arrow-like ears, and other formidable features, was a fearsome sight. With copper-brown lips, sharp teeth, a powerful roar, mighty arms, and extraordinary strength, the child displayed nothing human in appearance, despite being born of a man. Possessing a long nose, broad chest, calves that swelled frightfully, swift motion, and immense strength, the child exhibited no human traits. Although still a child, he immediately grew into a youth the moment he was born. The mighty hero quickly acquired proficiency in the use of all weapons. Rakshasa women give birth the same day they conceive and can change their forms at will. This bald-headed child, the mighty bowman, bowed to his mother and father immediately after birth. His parents then gave him the name 'Ghatotkacha' as his head resembled a water pot. Ghatotkacha, deeply devoted to the Pandavas, became a great favorite, almost one of them.

"Hidimva, aware that her time with her husband had come to an end, bade farewell to the Pandavas, making a new appointment with them. She then went wherever she pleased. Ghatotkacha, also, promising his father that he would come when summoned for any task, saluted them and departed towards the north. Indeed, it was the illustrious Indra who, by lending a portion of himself, created the mighty chariot-warrior Ghatotkacha as a suitable adversary for Karna, endowed with unrivaled energy, due to the divine weapon given to Karna (which was destined to kill the person against whom it was hurled)."

Chapter 28

BHIMA FIGHTS AN ANCIENT EVIL

In the rugged age of myth and might, Sri Vyasa, a harbinger of boundless auspicious virtues, descended upon the Pandavas with a mission veiled in haste—the annihilation of Bhakasura, a relentless juggernaut fortified by the unassailable boons of Shiva, impervious to death's embrace.

The Pandavas found respite in the hermitage of Shaalihotra, a sage steeped in ancient wisdom. There, disguised as Brahmana youths, they immersed themselves in the study of Veda, VedAnga, and Nitishastra—a preparation for navigating the intricate tapestry of the world's rules.

Vyasa, a master weaver in the cosmic loom, left them under the guardianship of a Brahmana, revealing them as his disciples. An unspoken promise lingered—Vyasa would return when the cosmic clock chimed the opportune hour.

In the pursuit of a clandestine existence, Bhima, the thunderous embodiment of Vayu's might, stood apart. His approach to alms, an unrestrained demand rather than a supplication, unsettled the heart of Yudhishthira. Fear nestled within the recesses of the wise elder's mind—an apprehension that Duryodhana's hounds might sniff out the scent of the Pandavas through Bhima's resolute adherence to Dharma and his indomitable strength.

Bhima, clad in the guise of a Brahmana, wielded a pot, a gift from a grateful potter, a vessel vast as a house. The potter's debt, born from the fiery jaws of a conflagration, was repaid by Bhima's singular feat—lifting the house from its very foundations. A colossal token of gratitude, the pot became Bhima's bowl for alms, a symbol of his valor and benevolence.

Yudhishthira, torn between admiration and trepidation, beseeched Bhima to abstain from the daily ritual of begging. Bhima's position as a Brahmana, a cloak for their true identity, allowed him to seek alms according to law, but Yudhishthira, vigilant against potential exposure, pleaded with Bhima to remain with their mother.

A singular trait, however, marked Bhima's demands—though thunderous, they did not terrify. An anomaly in the realm of warfare, his voice, a roar akin to nature's fury, resonated without inducing fear.

The pot, a symbol of Bhima's valor, recounted a tale of a fiery night and a potter's desperate plea. Bhima, the savior, rushed to the potter's aid, lifting the house from impending doom, and securing it in a sanctuary of safety. The potter, an indebted soul, reciprocated with a gift—a pot, colossal in size, a reflection of his gratitude.

THE SOURCE OF CONFLICT

Yudhishthira, while honoring Bhima's unwavering allegiance to Dharma and recognizing his prowess, harbored a fear—the fear that this very allegiance might inadvertently unveil the Pandavas to Duryodhana's watchful eyes. Thus, he implored Bhima to remain concealed, to eat the sustenance brought by Arjuna and the others, sparing the world from the tempest of Bhima's demands.

Bhima, yielding to Dharmaraja's counsel, agreed without hesitation. As others ventured into the shadows to beg for alms, Bhima, the tempest in repose, stood sentinel at home, guarding secrets and fate alike, alongside his mother

In the eon of savage valor, where myths intertwine with the clash of celestial forces, the Pandavas, cloaked in the guise of Brahmana youths, found refuge in the sacred abode of Shaalihotra, a sage steeped in the ancient lore. Their sojourn, shrouded in disguise, unfolded against the backdrop of divine mysteries and the pulsating rhythms of Dharma.

As Bhima, the thunder-wielding colossus among them, roared through the streets demanding alms in a tone that echoed defiance, Yudhishthira, the sage-hearted leader, hesitated. The pot Bhima carried, a relic of a fiery night's heroism, was both a symbol of gratitude and a potential herald of their true identity. Yudhishthira, harboring a prudent fear of Duryodhana's keen eyes, beseeched Bhima to remain concealed, lest their enemies unveil the shadows that concealed the Pandavas.

Meanwhile, the other brothers, navigating the labyrinth of Dharma, stood in silent vigilance outside homes, accepting alms without uttering a word. Bhima's absence during these moments was a deliberate choice, a sign of respect for the delicate sanctity of the homes where women and children dwelled.

In the serenity of their temporary refuge, a Brahmana and his family, hosts to the Pandavas, wailed in despair. Their predicament unfolded in anguished echoes—a recurring tribute demanded by Bhakasura, a demon whose strength defied the very gods. The pact with this fiend, a deal struck in fear, required every household to offer a cartful of sustenance, two bulls, and the cart's driver every thirteen years, lest the demon wreak havoc upon their lives.

The Brahmana, writhing in the clutches of this diabolical agreement, faced the dire prospect of losing a family member. The poignant exchange between husband and wife revealed a tragic dilemma, each member of the family volunteering to be the sacrificial lamb to the demon's insatiable appetite.

Kunti, eavesdropping on the poignant discourse, heard the lamentations and the desperation that enveloped the family like a shroud. The specter of doom loomed large, and the Brahmana's son, a mere toddler, held a straw of grass, vowing to confront the demon with this seemingly feeble weapon.

When Kunti, the sage-minded matron, intervened, the Brahmana unraveled the tale of Bhakasura's indomitable might, recounting his retreat during the era of Sri Ramachandra and his subsequent tyranny over the terrified populace. Kunti, far from recoiling in fear, embraced the opportunity that destiny had thrust upon her.

In an audacious move, she offered one of her five sons as a sacrifice to the demon, propelling Bhima into the crucible of imminent danger. Yudhishthira, confronted with the audacity of his mother's decision, questioned the rationale behind sending Bhima—their bulwark of strength—into the jaws of peril.

Kunti, with the wisdom of ages and a mother's unshakable resolve, revealed the impervious nature of Bhima's existence, a force that not even celestial kings or demonic rulers could obliterate. She recollected the seismic event of his birth—the shattering of Shatashrunga Mountain—and affirmed that Bhima was none other than Vayudevaru incarnate, a force that defied annihilation.

Yudhishthira, persuaded by the unassailable conviction of his mother, relented, and on the morrow, Bhimasena embarked on a perilous journey to face Bhakasura. His destination, the demon's forest, lay in the looming shadows, and Bhima's heart swelled with a strange brew of joy and duty.

In the sylvan depths where the scent of impending battle mingled with the heady aroma of festal food, Bhima, voracious and mighty, consumed a mountainous heap of rice, reveling in the delicacies prepared for the demon's tribute. As Bhakasura, a behemoth of malevolence, approached with a tree uprooted in fury, Bhima, undaunted, halted his blows with a single hand.

A clash of titans ensued, with Bhima invoking the strength of his lineage to quell the onslaught. Bhakasura, the harbinger of doom, faced the tempest of Bhima's wrath. The clash culminated with Bhima, an indomitable force, tearing the demon asunder, liberating the city from the shadow of Bhakasura's tyranny.

Bhima, his valor etched in the annals of destiny, placed Bhakasura's lifeless form at the city's entrance, a stark testimony to the triumph of virtue over malevolence. As the crimson hues of victory painted the horizon, Bhimasena, bathed in the aftermath of his monumental feat, returned to his kin, who rejoiced in the resounding echoes of triumph.

With gratitude, offerings were made to the divine, and Bhima, with the sanctified teachings of Sri Hari echoing in his heart, stood as a testament to the indomitable spirit of righteousness. Guided by the wisdom of Vedavyasa, the Pandavas, having fulfilled their destined act, departed from the city, leaving behind the echoes of valor and the fragrance of victory in the air.

Chapter 29

THE GHANDARVA CHITRANGADA

In the deep recesses of the darkened forest, where shadows danced to the whims of the twilight, the Pandavas and Kunti trod cautiously. Arjuna, brandishing a torch to pierce the encroaching darkness, led the way. As they approached the sacred Ganga, a challenge echoed through the air, and their gaze fell upon a luminous being standing proudly on the opposite bank.

This ethereal being, Chitraratha, a Ghandarva king with wings aglow like the golden orb of the sun, stood taller than Bhima. Beside him, bewitching beauties draped in golden ornaments and silken garments adorned the scene. The Ghandarva's voice carried a regal pride as he proclaimed the twilight as the realm of Ghandarvas and Rakshasas, warning that anyone who dared venture near the Ganges during this sacred time could lawfully meet their demise at the hands of his kind.

Identifying himself as Angaparana, the Parama-Upadeva Ghandarva King, Chitraratha declared his dominion over the forest named Angaparana, a realm where he reveled in the company of his many wives. He boasted of his friendship with Kuvera, the lord of wealth, and issued a stark warning against any intruders disturbing his nocturnal pleasures.

In response to this arrogant proclamation, Arjuna, resolute and unyielding, refuted Chitraratha's claims, asserting that the holy Ganga was open to all, day or night. He scorned the Ghandarva for his misguided notion of strength, declaring that only the weak would cower before such threats. The fiery exchange set the stage for a clash of wills.

With a swift motion, Chitraratha, a general in the army of Indra, armed himself with a jewel-encrusted bow and unleashed arrows of formidable power. Yet, Arjuna, armed with both skill and defiance, skillfully deflected the arrows with the mere touch of his torch, rendering the celestial missiles impotent.

Unfazed by the Ghandarva's show of power, Arjuna invoked the Agniastra, a divine fireball, and hurled his torch. The ensuing explosion charred Chitraratha's magnificent chariot and left the proud Ghandarva king unconscious. Arjuna seized the fallen king by his adorned hair and presented him before his brothers.

Witnessing the plight of her husband, Kumbhinasi, the Ghandarva's wife, approached Yudhishthira, imploring for her husband's life. Yudhishthira, the epitome of righteousness, commanded Arjuna to release the defeated foe, stating that a vanquished enemy, protected by his women, should not be harmed.

Chitraratha, grateful for his life spared by the Pandavas, awoke and acknowledged the valor of his conqueror. In gratitude, he offered Arjuna a unique Siddhi, a spiritual sight to witness the entirety of the universe. Additionally, he promised a gift of a hundred Ghandarva horses, capable of soaring through the skies.

However, Arjuna, true to his Kshatriya code, refused to accept gifts in exchange for sparing a life. He asserted that warriors earned their prowess through their own might, not through alms. In a gesture of goodwill, Arjuna agreed to accept the Ghandarva's knowledge and horses in exchange for his Agniastra.

As the newfound friends embraced, Arjuna inquired about the reason for the confrontation. Chitraratha revealed that the interruption occurred while he was engaged in intimate moments with his wife. Duty-bound as a husband, he fought to display his prowess before his spouse. He also admonished Arjuna for not having a spiritual guru and a Brahmin guide.

Arjuna, respecting the Ghandarva's wisdom, promised to find a priest to guide him in his future household duties. The forest, once fraught with the tension of battle, now resonated with the echoes of newfound friendship and the exchange of knowledge.

Chapter 30

SWAYAMVARA OF DRAUPADI

Here came a time while the Pandavas were traveling that they happened upon a group of excited Brahmanas who were heading to Panchala. They told the Pandavas that they must come with them for a great swayamvara festival was being held and all were invited.

Vaisampayana continued, "In response to the Brahmanas' words, Yudhishthira, the eldest among the Pandavas, spoke with grace, 'O venerable Brahmanas, we are grateful for your counsel. With our mother by our side, we set forth from Ekachakra, and indeed, we shall accompany you to the kingdom of Panchala to witness the grand Swayamvara festivities.'

The Brahmanas, pleased by Yudhishthira's decision, shared further details about the impending event. 'The illustrious Yajnasena, also known as Drupada, has a daughter named Draupadi, whose beauty is unparalleled. She has emerged from the very heart of the sacrificial altar, possessing faultless features, youth, and intelligence. Draupadi's slender-waisted form emits a fragrance akin to the blue lotus, spreading for miles around. She is the sister of Dhrishtadyumna, the valiant warrior born with natural armor, sword, bow, and arrows, emerging from the sacred fire like a second Fire god.

'This maiden of unmatched beauty will choose her husband from the assembled princes during the Swayamvara. We are all headed there to witness this auspicious event, equivalent to a celestial celebration. Kings and princes, renowned for their sacrifices, devotion to study, holiness, and martial prowess, will gather. Eager to win Draupadi's hand, they will offer great wealth, cattle, food, and other opulent gifts. As we partake in this grand spectacle and enjoy the festivities, Krishna may, by fate, choose a suitor among you, my handsome brothers, who are akin to celestial beings. Engage in the athletic competitions, earn glory, and bring back the wealth bestowed upon the deserving.'

"With these words, Yudhishthira affirmed their decision to join the Brahmanas in witnessing Draupadi's Swayamvara, an extraordinary jubilee that promised a confluence of royal might, cultural richness, and divine grace."

Vaisampayana narrated, "As per the Brahmanas' advice, the Pandavas embarked on a journey towards the southern Panchala, the realm ruled by King Drupada. Along the way, they encountered the venerable sage Dwaipayana, known for his pure soul and impeccable righteousness. After exchanging salutations with the revered sage, the Pandavas sought his guidance. Directed by Dwaipayana, they continued their journey to Drupada's kingdom, progressing at a leisurely pace, exploring scenic woods, and pausing by enchanting lakes.

Upon reaching Panchala, the Pandavas, accompanied by their mother, quietly settled in the dwelling of a potter, adopting a humble life. Disguised in the guise of Brahmanas, they chose to remain unnoticed during their stay in Drupada's capital.

King Drupada, harboring the desire to bestow his daughter upon Arjuna, devised a challenging task. He commissioned the creation of an incredibly stiff bow, reserved for Arjuna's strength alone. Erecting a celestial contraption in the sky, Drupada hung a target, declaring, 'He who can string this bow and shoot the mark above the machine with these adorned arrows shall win my daughter.'

Drupada's proclamation spread far and wide, attracting kings, princes, and renowned sages to witness the grand Swayamvara. Even Duryodhana and the Kuru princes, accompanied by Karna, joined the gathering. The capital buzzed with excitement, adorned with fragrant flowers, and resonated with the sounds of trumpets. The citizens eagerly took their seats in the beautifully adorned amphitheater, anticipating the Swayamvara ceremony.

The grand amphitheater, surrounded by opulent mansions, stood as a testament to Drupada's grandeur. Enclosed by high walls and adorned with canopies of various hues, the arena exuded a divine fragrance. The mansions, adorned with diamonds and precious gems, provided a breathtaking spectacle. White and pristine, they resembled the necks of swans, their fragrance perceptible for miles.

As the kings assembled within these mansions, preparing for the event, the citizens marveled at the splendor of the monarchs. The Pandavas, unrecognizable in their Brahmana guise, silently observed the unfolding spectacle.

On the sixteenth day, the daughter of Drupada, Draupadi, entered the amphitheater, resplendent in her adornments, carrying a golden dish and a garland of flowers. The priest initiated the sacred fire, and the Brahmanas performed rituals while musicians played melodious tunes. Dhrishtadyumna, with a voice resonant as thunder, stood beside his sister and proclaimed the challenge. He announced that the one who could shoot the target with five sharpened arrows through the machine's orifice would win Draupadi's hand.

As the arena fell silent, Dhrishtadyumna addressed Draupadi, reciting the lineage, achievements, and names of the assembled kings, who awaited the challenge to prove their worthiness."

Vaisampayana continued, "The youthful princes, adorned with earrings and exuding pride in their beauty, prowess, lineage, knowledge, wealth, and youth, stood up, brandishing their weapons. Intoxicated by the arrogance of their accomplishments, they resembled Himalayan elephants in rut, their crowns seemingly split from excess temporal exuberance. Driven by the god of desire, they rose from their royal seats, each claiming, 'Krishna shall be mine.' The assembled Kshatriyas, eager to win Drupada's daughter, mirrored celestial beings gathered around the mountain goddess Uma.

Infused with desire, the princes descended into the amphitheater, each eyeing Krishna with jealousy, their hearts consumed by the shafts of Kamadeva. Celestials, including Rudras, Adityas, Vasus, Aswins, and Marutas, graced the event, along with the Daityas, Suparnas, Nagas, and revered sages. Halayudha (Valadeva), Janardana (Krishna), and the leaders of the Vrishni, Andhaka, and Yadava tribes, adhering to Krishna's guidance, observed the proceedings.

Identifying the Pandavas, Krishna whispered to Valadeva, 'There is Yudhishthira; there is Bhima with Jishnu (Arjuna); and those are the twin heroes.' Rama, with a glance of satisfaction, acknowledged Krishna's insight. Meanwhile, other heroes, sons and grandsons of kings, eyes and hearts fixated on Krishna, looked upon Draupadi alone, oblivious to the Pandavas.

The Pandavas, too, captivated by Draupadi, were struck by Kama's arrows. The celestial atmosphere resonated with the sounds of musical instruments, the hum of countless voices, and the fragrance of celestial flowers, as the divine assembly of Rishis, Gandharvas, and celestial beings unfolded.

The princes, adorned with crowns, garlands, and bracelets, showcased their might one by one, attempting to string the bow. However, the bow's extraordinary stiffness thwarted their efforts. Some were tossed to the ground, their strength drained, while others lay motionless, their crowns and ornaments disheveled.

Witnessing the failed attempts, Karna stepped forward, but even he couldn't string the bow. Subsequently, the mighty king of the Chedis, Sisupala, and then Jarasandha, faced similar failures. Salya, the king of Madra, also fell short in his attempt.

As the hopeful monarchs, having abandoned their ambitions, looked despondent, Arjuna, the son of Kunti, approached the bow. Determined to prove his prowess, he aimed to string the bow and placed the arrows on the bowstring."

Vaisampayana continued, "When all the monarchs had given up on stringing the bow, Arjuna, with the complexion of Indra's banner, emerged from the crowd of Brahmanas. As Partha approached the bow, the principal Brahmanas, shaking their deer-skins, raised a clamor, some displeased and others well-pleased. Those possessing intelligence foresaw potential ridicule for the entire Brahmana community if an unpracticed youth, untested in arms, failed where celebrated Kshatriyas like Salya had faltered.

Some wise Brahmanas whispered, 'This Brahmana youth, strong as an elephant, with shoulders, arms, and thighs resembling the mighty creature, patient like the Himavat, walking with the grace of a lion, and demonstrating the prowess of an elephant in rut, might achieve

THE SOURCE OF CONFLICT

this feat. He exudes strength and determination; otherwise, he wouldn't voluntarily attempt it. Brahmanas, regardless of their physical prowess, possess immense inner strength. Let us not underestimate him; instead, let him attempt and succeed.'

Arjuna, standing like a mountain, circled the bow, bowed to Lord Isana, the bestower of boons, and remembering Krishna, took up the challenge. The bow, unyielding to accomplished Kshatriyas, succumbed effortlessly to Arjuna's might, strung in the blink of an eye. Taking the five arrows, he shot the mark, causing it to fall through the hole in the machine. The firmament resounded with a loud uproar, the amphitheater echoed with clamor, celestial flowers rained down on Partha's head, and Brahmanas joyously waved their garments. The unsuccessful monarchs lamented, and the gods showered flowers. Musicians played in harmony, bards and heralds sang the hero's praises, and Drupada rejoiced, eager to support Arjuna with his forces if needed.

Amidst the celebration, Yudhishthira, accompanied by the twins, left the amphitheater for their temporary residence. Krishna, witnessing Arjuna's success, approached him with a white robe and a garland of flowers. Arjuna, having won Draupadi in the amphitheater, was revered by all Brahmanas. Shortly after, he left the arena, with Draupadi following, now his wife.

Vaisampayana continued, "When King Drupada expressed his intention to bestow his daughter on the Brahmana who had successfully shot the mark, the invited monarchs, glancing at each other, were suddenly filled with wrath. They exclaimed, 'Drupada has ignored us and, treating the assembled monarchs with disdain, wishes to give his daughter, the first of women, to a Brahmana! He planted the tree but now intends to cut it down before it bears fruit. This wretch shows us no respect; therefore, let us slay him. He deserves neither our respect nor the reverence due to age. We should kill this insolent man, along with his son. He invited us all, entertained us with excellent food, and now he disrespects us. Is there no monarch here equal to him in this assembly of kings, comparable to the celestial conclave? The Vedic declaration clearly states that the Swayamvara is for Kshatriyas, not Brahmanas. If the damsel does not wish to select any one of us as her husband, let's throw her into the fire and return to our kingdoms. As for this Brahmana, though he has done injury to the monarchs out of officiousness or avarice, he should not be killed. Our kingdoms, lives, treasures, sons, grandsons, and all our wealth exist for Brahmanas. Something must be done so that, out of fear of disgrace and the desire to maintain the proper order, future Swayamvaras do not end this way.'

"Agreeing with each other, those mighty monarchs, armed with weapons like spiked iron maces, rushed at Drupada to slay him on the spot. Fearing for his life, Drupada sought the protection of the Brahmanas. However, Bhima and Arjuna, the powerful sons of Pandu, stood ready to confront the wrathful monarchs who were charging like rutting elephants. Bhima, with strength comparable to thunder, uprooted a large tree and stripped it of its leaves, holding it like Yama with his fierce mace. Alongside him, Arjuna, equal to Indra in achievements, prepared to face the assailants.

Observing his brother's feat, Arjuna, the intelligent one with extraordinary prowess, marveled. Addressing his brother Valadeva, Krishna of superhuman intelligence and inconceivable feats, said, 'The hero wielding the large bow, four cubits in length, is Arjuna, no doubt. That's my assertion, for I am Vasudeva. The other hero who swiftly tore up the tree and is ready to repel the monarchs is Vrikodara. None other than Vrikodara could accomplish such a feat today. The youth with lotus-petal eyes, a height of four cubits, a lion-like gait, fair complexion, a prominent shining nose, who left the amphitheater a little earlier, is Dharma's son, Yudhishthira. The two youths resembling Kartikeya are, I suspect, the sons of the twin

Aswins. I heard that the sons of Pandu, along with their mother Pritha, escaped the house of lac when it was set ablaze.'

Then, Halayudha, with a complexion like rain-laden clouds, spoke to his younger brother Krishna with great satisfaction, 'I am pleased to hear, through sheer good fortune, that our father's sister Pritha and the foremost of the Kaurava princes have all escaped death!'"

Vaisampayana continued, "Those mighty Brahmanas, adorned with deer-skins and water-pots made of coconut shells, reassured Arjuna, saying, 'Fear not, we will fight the foe!' Smilingly, Arjuna addressed the Brahmanas, 'Stand aside as spectators. I shall check those angry monarchs by showering arrows like snakes with mantras.' Taking up the bow he had received as dower and accompanied by his brother Bhima, Arjuna stood firm as a mountain. The heroic brothers fearlessly confronted the approaching kings, rushing at them like elephants charging a hostile elephant.

As the kings rushed in, they loudly declared, 'The slaughter of one desiring to fight is permitted in battle.' Saying this, they charged against the Brahmanas. Karna, full of anger, rushed at Arjuna for the fight, while Salya, the mighty king of Madra, advanced against Bhima like an elephant charging another for the sake of a she-elephant in heat. Duryodhana and others skirmished lightly and carelessly with the Brahmanas.

Witnessing Karna approaching, Arjuna drew his bow and pierced him with sharp arrows. The force of those whetted arrows, carrying fierce energy, made Karna momentarily faint. Regaining consciousness, Karna attacked Arjuna with greater vigor. The two warriors, desiring to vanquish each other, fought fiercely, becoming nearly invisible in the exchange of arrows. They exchanged words, intelligible only to heroes, boasting about the strength of their arms and the efficacy of their weapons. Enraged by the unparalleled strength and energy of Arjuna's arms, Karna fought with even greater intensity.

Addressing his opponent, Karna said, 'O foremost of Brahmanas, I am pleased to see the energy of your arms and the weapons capable of achieving victory. Are you the embodiment of the science of weapons, or are you Rama with superhuman powers, or are you Indra himself, or are you Indra's younger brother Vishnu, also called Achyuta? Have you assumed the form of a Brahmana and come to fight with me, disguising yourself from fear of disgrace? Only the husband of Sachi, Kiriti, the son of Pandu, or someone equal to them, is capable of fighting me when I am angry on the battlefield.' Responding to Karna, Arjuna said, 'O Karna, I am neither the personification of the science of arms nor Rama with superhuman powers. I am just a Brahmana, the foremost among all warriors and wielders of weapons. By the grace of my preceptor, I have become proficient in the Brahma and the Paurandara weapons. I am here to defeat you in battle. Wait a little, O hero.'"

"Vaisampayana continued, 'Hearing these words, Karna, the son of Surya, ceased fighting, understanding that Brahman energy is invincible. Meanwhile, on another part of the field, the mighty heroes Salya and Vrikodara, both skilled in battle and possessed of great strength, challenged each other and engaged in combat like two rutting elephants. They struck each other with their clenched fists and knees, pushing and dragging each other, throwing each other down face downward or on the sides. The sounds of their combat, hard as the clash of two masses of granite, echoed through the lists. After a brief exchange, Bhima, lifting Salya on his arms, hurled him to a distance without causing him much harm. Witnessing this feat, the surrounding monarchs were alarmed, and they quickly surrounded Bhima, exclaiming, 'These Brahmanas are indeed extraordinary warriors! We should find out who they are and where they come from. Who can stand against Karna, the son of Radha, except Rama,

Drona, or Kiriti, the son of Pandu? Who can face Duryodhana in battle except Krishna, the son of Devaki, Kripa, the son of Saradwan, or Valadeva and Vrikodara, the sons of Pandu? Let us find out who these warriors are before we engage in battle with them.'

Krishna, observing Bhima's feat, believed them to be the sons of Kunti. Addressing the assembled monarchs gently, he said, 'This maiden has been rightly acquired by the Brahmana.' Encouraging them to abandon the fight, Krishna successfully convinced the kings to cease hostilities. The accomplished Brahmanas then refrained from further combat. The monarchs, bewildered by the unexpected turn of events, returned to their kingdoms, and those who had come from afar left, saying, 'The festive scene has ended with the victory of the Brahmanas. The princess of Panchala has become the bride of a Brahmana.' Surrounded by Brahmanas adorned with deer-skins and other wild animal garments, Bhima and Arjuna, with difficulty, passed through the crowd. Mangled by the enemy and followed by Krishna, they looked like the full moon and the sun emerging from behind the clouds.

Meanwhile, Kunti, seeing that her sons were late in returning from their alms-gathering, was filled with anxiety. She worried about various misfortunes that might have befallen them, imagining the sons of Dhritarashtra recognizing her sons and slaying them or powerful Rakshasas deceiving and killing them. She even questioned whether Vyasa, the illustrious sage who had directed her sons to go to Panchala, had been guided by perverse intelligence. In the late afternoon, Jishnu, accompanied by a group of Brahmanas, finally entered the abode of the potter, resembling the sun appearing on a cloudy day."

Vaisampayana continued, "Upon returning to the potter's abode, the sons of Pritha approached their mother and represented Yajnaseni to her as the alms they had obtained that day. Kunti, not seeing her sons, replied, 'Enjoy what you have obtained.' Shortly after, when she saw Krishna, she regretted her words, saying, 'Oh, what have I said?' Anxious to avoid sin and considering how everyone could be extricated from the situation, she took Draupadi by the hand and approached Yudhishthira. She said, 'The daughter of King Yajnasena, represented to me by your younger brothers as the alms they had obtained, I, in ignorance, told them to enjoy it. O king, tell me how my speech may not become untrue, how sin may not touch the daughter of the King of Panchala, and how she may not become uneasy.'

Vaisampayana continued, 'Addressed thus by his mother, the intelligent king Yudhishthira, reflecting for a moment, consoled Kunti and said, 'By you, O mother, has Yajnaseni been won. Therefore, it is proper that you should wed her. O bull of the Kuru race, ignite the sacred fire and take her hand with due rites.'

Arjuna, hearing this, replied, 'O king, do not involve me in sin. Your command is not conformable to virtue. This is the path followed by the sinful. You should wed first, then the strong-armed Bhima, then myself, then Nakula, and lastly, Sahadeva. Both Vrikodara and I, along with the twins and this maiden, await your commands. Command us as you wish.'

Hearing these words of Arjuna, filled with respect and affection, Yudhishthira cast his eyes upon Draupadi. Draupadi also looked at all the Pandavas. Looking at each other, the princes began to think only of Draupadi. After they had looked at her, the God of Desire invaded their hearts, crushing all their senses. The unparalleled beauty of Panchali, modeled by the Creator himself, captivated the hearts of every creature. Yudhishthira, understanding what was going on in their minds, recollected the words of Krishna-Dwaipayana. The king, fearing division among the brothers, addressed them, 'The auspicious Draupadi shall be the common wife of us all.'

Vaisampayana continued, 'The sons of Pandu, upon hearing these words from their eldest brother, revolved them in their minds with great cheerfulness. Yudhishthira, reflecting upon this, consoled Kunti, and addressing Dhananjaya, said, 'By you, O Phalguna, has Yajnaseni been won. Therefore, it is proper that you should wed her. Ignite the sacred fire and take her hand with due rites.'

Arjuna, hearing this, replied, 'O king, do not make me a participator in sin. Your command is not conformable to virtue. That is the path followed by the sinful. You should wed first, then the strong-armed Bhima, then myself, then Nakula, and lastly, Sahadeva. Both Vrikodara and I, along with the twins and this maiden, all await your commands. O monarch, command us as you wish.'

Hearing these words of Arjuna, filled with respect and affection, Yudhishthira cast his eyes upon Draupadi. Draupadi also looked at all the Pandavas. Looking at each other, the princes began to think only of Draupadi. After they had looked at her, the God of Desire invaded their hearts, crushing all their senses. The unparalleled beauty of Panchali, modeled by the Creator himself, captivated the hearts of every creature. Yudhishthira, understanding what was going on in their minds, recollected the words of Krishna-Dwaipayana. The king, fearing division among the brothers, addressed them, 'The auspicious Draupadi shall be the common wife of us all.'

Vaisampayana continued, 'Hearing these words of their eldest brother, the Pandavas began to revolve them in their minds with great cheerfulness. Krishna, suspecting the five persons he had seen at the Swayamvara to be none other than the Kuru princes, came accompanied by Valadeva to the potter's house where they had taken up quarters. On arriving there, Krishna and Valadeva beheld Yudhishthira, the son of Kunti, of well-developed and long arms, and his younger brothers surrounding him with splendor like fire. Approaching Yudhishthira, Vasudeva touched his feet, saying, 'I am

Krishna,' and Valadeva did the same. The Pandavas, beholding Krishna and Valadeva, expressed great delight, and the princes of the Yadu race then touched the feet of Kunti, their father's sister. Ajatasatru, the son of Kunti, beholding Krishna, inquired about his well-being, asking, 'How, O Vasudeva, have you been able to trace us while we are living in disguise?' Vasudeva, smilingly answering, said, 'O king, fire, even if covered, can be known. Who else among men than the Pandavas could exhibit such might? O resisters of all foes, O sons of Pandu, by sheer good fortune have you escaped from that fierce fire. And it is by sheer good fortune alone that the wicked son of Dhritarashtra and his counselors have not succeeded in accomplishing their wishes. Blessed be you! May you grow in prosperity like a fire in a cave, gradually growing and spreading all around. Lest any of the monarchs recognize you, let us return to our tent.' Obtaining Yudhishthira's leave, Krishna of unfailing prosperity, accompanied by Valadeva, hastily went away from the potter's abode."

Chapter 31

THE MARRIAGE OF DRUPADI

Vaisampayana recounted the tale in a voice like rolling thunder, echoing through the hall, "Dhrishtadyumna, the lunar prince, spoke with cheer in the presence of his father, revealing the valiant youth who had won Krishna's favor. With fiery eyes, clad in deer-skin, he stood, a celestial in beauty, surrounded by reverent Brahmanas, their homage a testament to his feat. His prowess, a force of nature, akin to Indra amidst the celestial beings and sages.

Krishna, unfazed, followed the youth, gripping his deer-skin, resembling a she-elephant drawn to the herd's leader. The enraged monarchs, unable to bear the sight, stood frozen as a mighty hero, tearing up a tree, descended upon them like Yama himself, scattering life like leaves in the wind.

In the aftermath, the heroes—resembling the Sun and the Moon—departed, Krishna in tow, to the abode of a potter on the city's outskirts. A flame-like lady, their possible mother, sat surrounded by three other fiery men. They paid homage, and after eleemosynary visits, Krishna distributed alms, saving a portion for herself.

Beds of kusa grass, deer-skins, and voices deep as black clouds filled the night. The heroes, neither Vaisyas nor Sudras nor Brahmanas but bulls amongst Kshatriyas, discussed military matters. Drupada's son, overhearing their discourse, saw the fructification of hope.

The king, overjoyed, sent his priest to unveil the identity of these warriors. The priest, applauding them, delivered Drupada's message. Yudhishthira, respecting the priest, offered worship, acknowledging the king's desire for Draupadi to wed Arjuna. Drupada's priest waited for their response.

Yudhishthira, commanding reverence, spoke, assuring that Arjuna had won Draupadi as per the king's stipulations. The priest, accepting the offered worship, sat joyously. Yudhishthira explained Drupada need not grieve, as the desires had found fulfillment in the heroic feat.

As Yudhishthira concluded, another messenger rushed in, proclaiming, 'The nuptial feast is ready,' sealing the fate of the lunar princess and the sons of Pandu."

Vaisampayana's narrative unfolded with the messenger's words resonating through the air like the clash of battle, "King Drupada, in anticipation of his daughter's nuptials, hath readied a feast fit for kings. Come hither after your daily rites. Krishna's union awaits. Tarry not, and ride these cars adorned with golden lotuses drawn by noble steeds worthy of kings. Enter the abode of the Panchalas with regal grace."

The Kuru princes, dismissing the priest, guided Kunti and Krishna to share a car. Riding these splendid vehicles, they moved towards Drupada's abode, a procession befitting royalty. Meanwhile, having heard Yudhishthira's words through his priest, King Drupada, eager to discern the order of these heroes, meticulously prepared a vast assortment of articles as mandated by the wedding ordinances for each of the four orders.

He gathered fruits, sanctified garlands, coats of mail, shields, carpets, cattle, seeds, and diverse implements for agriculture. In addition, Drupada collected items from various arts, implements for various sports, excellent coats of mail, shining shields, fine-tempered swords, and ornate chariots and horses. The armory showcased first-class bows, adorned arrows, missiles glistening with gold, darts, rockets, battle-axes, and various war utensils. Beds, carpets, luxurious fabrics, and an array of other fine things adorned the collection.

As the party arrived at Drupada's abode, Kunti, accompanied by virtuous Krishna, entered the inner chambers of the king. Joyful hearts of the king's ladies worshipped the Kuru queen. Drupada and his ministers, son, friends, and attendants were elated upon seeing the lion-like men with deer-skin upper garments, bull-like eyes, broad shoulders, and arms hanging like mighty snakes.

Seated with grace and fearlessness on costly seats, the heroes, one after another by age, observed the utensils of war after dining on the sumptuous feast. Drupada and his son, along with chief ministers, recognized the royal blood coursing through the veins of the sons of Kunti, filling their hearts with unbridled joy.

Vaisampayana's tale echoed through the royal hall as the illustrious King of Panchala, his voice dipped in the respect befitting Brahmanas, addressed Yudhishthira. Drupada's inquiry rang out, its cadence echoing through the chamber, "Shall we know you as Kshatriyas or Brahmanas? Or are you celestial beings disguised as

Brahmanas, wandering the earth, seeking Krishna's hand? Remove our doubts, O chastiser of enemies! Shall we not rejoice when our doubts are dispelled? Have the fates smiled upon us? Speak the truth willingly! Monarchs are better adorned with truth than sacrifices or tank dedications. Do not speak falsely. O celestial-like beauty, O foe-chastising one, your reply shall guide the arrangements for my daughter's wedding, aligning with your order."

Yudhishthira responded with calm assurance, "Do not despair, O king; let joy fill your heart! Your cherished desire is fulfilled. We are Kshatriyas, sons of Pandu. I am the eldest, and these are Bhima and Arjuna. They won your daughter amidst the monarchs' assembly. The twins and Kunti await where Krishna is. Grieve not, for we are Kshatriyas. Your daughter, O monarch, like a lotus, has moved from one lake to another. You are our revered superior, and we have spoken the truth."

Drupada, his eyes gleaming with ecstasy, struggled to contain his emotions. Finally, with great effort, he responded, inquiring about the Pandavas' escape from Varanavata. Yudhishthira recounted the details, censuring Dhritarashtra, and Drupada pledged to restore Yudhishthira to his rightful throne.

Now, the atmosphere shifted, and Drupada turned his attention to the impending marriage. Kunti, Krishna, Bhima, Arjuna, and the twins were treated with respect and hospitality, residing under Drupada's care. The monarch, reassured by the events, approached Yudhishthira, expressing his desire for Arjuna to marry Krishna that very day.

In response, Yudhishthira revealed his own need for marriage. Drupada, open to any suggestion, proposed that Yudhishthira could marry Krishna or choose one of his brothers. Yudhishthira declared Krishna to be the common wife of them all, following the directive of their mother. Drupada, taken aback, cautioned against such a practice, stating it was contrary to moral and Vedic principles. Yudhishthira, adhering to the path laid by illustrious predecessors, upheld their mother's command and stated it was virtuous. Drupada, uneasy, asked them to deliberate and decide.

The discussion continued between Yudhishthira, Kunti, and Dhrishtadyumna. Amidst their deliberation, the island-born Vyasa arrived, a sage wandering in his journey. The tale paused, awaiting the unfolding events that Vyasa's presence would bring.

Vaisampayana's narration unfolded as all present, including the Pandavas, the illustrious King of Panchala, and others, rose to salute the revered Rishi Krishna (Dwaipayana). The atmosphere in the hall became charged with respect as they greeted the sage, and, after exchanging pleasantries, Vyasa seated himself on a golden carpet.

Drupada, curious about the matter of polyandry, respectfully inquired about the practice. With a calm demeanor, he questioned Vyasa, "How can one woman become the wife of many men without being defiled by sin? Tell me the truth about this."

Vyasa, acknowledging the outdated nature of the practice and expressing his interest in their opinions, invited each to share their views.

Drupada, the first to speak, declared, "The practice is sinful, opposed to both usage and the Vedas. Nowhere have I seen many men having one wife. The illustrious ones of former ages never had such a usage amongst them. The wise should never commit a sin."

Dhrishtadyumna, articulating the subtleties of morality, expressed his reservations. "How can the elder brother, if of good disposition, approach the wife of his younger brother? The ways of morality are subtle, and we cannot determine what is conformable to it. I cannot say, 'Let Draupadi become the common wife of five brothers.'"

Yudhishthira, guided by the principles of virtue and his mother's command, defended the practice. "My tongue never utters an untruth, and my heart never inclines to what is sinful. When my heart approves of it, it can never be sinful. It is said that obedience to a superior is ever meritorious, and our mother has commanded us to enjoy Draupadi as we do anything obtained as alms."

Kunti, supporting Yudhishthira's stance, expressed her fear of untruth and questioned how she could be saved from its consequences.

Vyasa, acknowledging the virtue in Yudhishthira's words, proposed to explain the establishment of this practice and why it should be regarded as old and eternal. He assured Drupada that what Yudhishthira had spoken was in line with virtue.

With that, Vyasa, the master Dwaipayana, rose and led Drupada to a private chamber. The Pandavas, Kunti, and Dhrishtadyumna waited anxiously, anticipating the sage's return and the unraveling of the discourse on the practice of polyandry.

Vaisampayana narrated how the celestial Sri (goddess of grace), by the will of the god Sankara (Mahadeva), was preordained to be the common wife of the Pandavas in her future life. In a previous life, this goddess had performed severe ascetic penances and desired a husband with every virtue. Lord Sankara, pleased with her penance, granted her the boon but specified that she would have five husbands. When the maiden expressed her preference for one husband, Sankara, pleased with her devotion, granted her wish and assured her that this would happen in her future life.

This celestial maiden, having undergone ascetic penances and received the boon, was born as Draupadi, the daughter of Drupada. Her birth was a result of the sacrificial rites performed by Drupada.

Vyasa revealed to Drupada that Draupadi was the faultless maiden who had been destined to be the common wife of the five Pandavas.

Vyasa explained to Drupada that Draupadi's extraordinary beauty and virtues were divinely ordained. She had been born for the sake of the Pandavas, and her destiny was intertwined with theirs. The goddess Sri, waited upon by celestial beings, had taken birth as Draupadi in the course of Drupada's grand sacrifice. Vyasa instructed Drupada to understand and accept the divine plan and to act according to his desires.

Hearing this revelation from Vyasa, Drupada was deeply moved and pleased. He acknowledged the divine ordainment of Draupadi's destiny and the connection between her and the Pandavas. Vyasa, having fulfilled his role as the revealer of truths, left the assembly, leaving Drupada to contemplate the divine events that had unfolded.

This episode showcases the intricate web of destiny, divine interventions, and the cosmic design that shapes the lives of the characters in the Mahabharata.

The wedding ceremonies of Draupadi with the Pandavas were conducted with great grandeur and joy. King Drupada, having heard the divine truth from Vyasa, fully accepted the ordained destiny and made preparations for the auspicious occasion. The wedding took place on a day when the moon entered the constellation Pushya, considered highly auspicious.

The illustrious Vyasa instructed Yudhishthira to take Draupadi's hand first, and the brothers, adorned with jewels and perfumed with sandal-paste, entered the wedding hall in due order. The priest Dhaumya, well-versed in the Vedas, performed the wedding rituals, igniting the sacred fire and officiating the union of Yudhishthira with Krishna. The brothers, one by one, took Draupadi's hand, walking around the sacred fire as part of the wedding ceremony.

After the weddings were completed, Dhaumya, having fulfilled his role as the officiating priest, took leave of Yudhishthira and left the palace. Following the ceremonies, King Drupada generously bestowed wealth, cars, elephants, and female servants upon the Pandavas as part of the wedding gifts. Each prince received a hundred cars with golden standards, a hundred auspiciously marked elephants, and a hundred young and adorned female servants.

The Pandavas, having obtained Draupadi as their common wife and received abundant wealth and gifts, lived joyously in the capital of the Panchalas. The grandeur of the wedding festivities and the blessings of celestial beings marked the beginning of a new Chapter in the lives of the Pandavas.

Chapter 32

CONSPIRACY AND DIVISION

Amidst the shifting sands of fate and the whispers of spies, the news unfurled like a dark banner across the realms: Draupadi, she of peerless beauty and fiery spirit, had bound her destiny to the sons of Pandu. The echo of Arjuna's triumph, the foremost archer among victors, resounded through the land, stirring both awe and unease.

Bhima, the mighty warrior, whose very presence struck terror into the hearts of foes, had shown his prowess by hurling Salya, the king of Madra, to the earth, and uprooting a tree in a display of unmatched strength. These deeds, wrought in the flames of battle, marked the Pandavas as champions among men.

The monarchs, hearing of Draupadi's choice and the Pandavas' disguise as Brahmanas, were confounded. Their minds, still reeling from the tale of Kunti and her sons consumed in the lac-house conflagration, now grappled with the resurrection of the exiled princes. In their bewilderment, they turned their gaze to Bhishma and Dhritarashtra, questioning the schemes that had led to this tumultuous moment.

As the monarchs dispersed, bearing the weight of this revelation, Duryodhana's heart grew heavy with despair. The realization that Draupadi had chosen Arjuna as her lord cast a shadow over his soul. With downcast eyes and faltering steps, he returned to Hastinapura, haunted by the specter of the Pandavas' return and the memory of their escape from the fiery trap.

Duhsasana, his cheeks burning with shame, whispered to his brother, lamenting their fate. He spoke of Arjuna's disguise and the hand of destiny that had thwarted their plans. In their sorrow, they entered Hastinapura, their hearts heavy with the burden of defeat.

But amidst the turmoil, Vidura, ever wise and vigilant, saw opportunity in the chaos. He rejoiced at the Pandavas' triumph and the alliances they had forged with Drupada and his allies. To Dhritarashtra, he spoke words of hope, urging him to embrace the newfound strength of their kin.

Yet, Dhritarashtra, blinded by his love for his sons, misunderstood Vidura's meaning, thinking Draupadi had chosen Duryodhana as her husband. He ordered jewels to be crafted for her adornment, unaware of the truth that lay hidden beneath the surface.

When Vidura revealed the reality of Draupadi's choice and the Pandavas' resurgence, Dhritarashtra's joy turned to apprehension. But Duryodhana and Karna, seizing the opportunity, approached him with words of dissent, urging him to act against the Pandavas before their strength grew too great.

THE SOURCE OF CONFLICT

In the shadowed halls of Hastinapura, the seeds of discord were sown anew, as father and sons grappled with the shifting tides of destiny and the specter of impending conflict loomed ever closer.

"Dhritarashtra, his mind a labyrinth of conflicting desires, replied with cautious deliberation, 'I seek your counsel, yet I am wary of revealing my intentions to Vidura. Thus, I feigned approval of the Pandavas in his presence, lest he discern my true motives. Now, with Vidura absent, speak freely, O Suyodhana, and you, Radheya, reveal your schemes.'

"Duryodhana, his eyes glinting with cunning, proposed a web of deceit to ensnare the Pandavas. 'Let us sow seeds of discord between the sons of Kunti and Madri,' he suggested, or 'Bribe Drupada and his kin to forsake Yudhishthira's cause.' His schemes, intricate and venomous, wove a tapestry of treachery.

"Karna, however, with the wisdom born of battle, challenged Duryodhana's stratagems. 'Your methods are flawed,' he declared. 'The Pandavas, shielded by destiny, cannot be swayed by mere manipulation. They have tasted the bitterness of exile and are bound by a common wife. No spies can unravel their unity, nor can we drive a wedge between Krishna and her husbands.'

"'Our best course,' Karna continued, 'is to confront them openly, to meet strength with strength. Strike them while they are vulnerable, before Drupada's allegiance strengthens their ranks. Let our prowess be our weapon, for no subtlety can pierce the armor of fate.'

"Dhritarashtra, impressed by Karna's resolve, lauded his wisdom. 'Your words ring true,' he acknowledged. 'But let us seek counsel from Bhishma, Drona, and Vidura, that we may devise a strategy worthy of our cause.'

"And so, the king summoned his trusted advisors, setting the stage for a council of war where alliances would be forged and destinies decided.

"Upon being asked for his opinion, Bhishma, the venerable grandsire, spoke with the authority of age and wisdom. 'O Dhritarashtra,' he began, 'I cannot condone a quarrel with the Pandavas. As Pandu was to me, so are they, sons of Kunti and sons of Gandhari alike. I must protect them as I would your own sons, for they are as dear to me. Let us not forget, O king, that the kingdom belongs to them as much as it does to any of us. Therefore, let us offer them half the realm peacefully. This is the rightful inheritance of the Pandavas, and it is in the best interest of all.

'If we act otherwise, we shall bring dishonor upon ourselves. Consider, O Duryodhana, the value of a good name. It is said that one lives as long as their fame endures. Let us not tarnish our reputation by denying the rightful claims of the Pandavas. We are fortunate that they survived the fire, and that Kunti yet lives. Let us not repeat the mistakes of the past, but instead, let us rectify them by granting the Pandavas their due share.'

"After Bhishma had spoken, Drona, the preceptor, offered his counsel. 'O Dhritarashtra,' he said, 'it is my belief that we should heed the wise words of Bhishma. Let us send emissaries to Drupada with gifts and proposals for alliance. By securing the Pandavas' return to Hastinapura, we can avoid conflict and ensure the prosperity of the Kuru lineage. This, I believe, is the path to our collective welfare.'

"Karna, however, countered with skepticism, questioning the motives of his elders. 'Bhishma and Drona,' he argued, 'have been swayed by their own interests, blinded by their affection for the Pandavas. But their advice, though well-intentioned, is misguided. Destiny, not counsel, determines our fate. Let us not be deluded by false promises of peace. Our strength lies in our unity, not in compromise.'

"Drona, stung by Karna's accusations, retorted, 'Your words betray your own wickedness, Karna. Bhishma and I have spoken with the welfare of all in mind, not out of favoritism. Our counsel, though hard to hear, is necessary for the survival of the Kurus. If we ignore it, we risk our own downfall.'

"Vidura, ever the voice of reason, interjected, 'O monarch, Bhishma and Drona speak from a place of wisdom and integrity. Let us not dismiss their counsel lightly. The Pandavas' claim to the kingdom is just, and denying them their rights will only bring calamity upon us all. We must act with fairness and foresight, for the sake of our lineage and our people.'"

"With these words, the council weighed the options before them, torn between the dictates of duty and the clamor of ambition."

Hearing the speeches of Bhishma, Drona, and Vidura, Dhritarashtra acknowledged the truth in their words. He recognized the rightful claim of the Pandavas to the kingdom and expressed his joy at their return. Dhritarashtra spoke with gratitude, acknowledging the fortune that had preserved the Pandavas and brought about the alliance with Drupada:

"The learned Bhishma, the illustrious Rishi Drona, and yourself, O Vidura, have spoken the truth and what is most beneficial to me. Indeed, as the sons of Kunti are the children of Pandu, so are they my children according to the ordinance. Just as my sons are entitled to this kingdom, so are the sons of Pandu certainly entitled to it. Therefore, hasten to bring the Pandavas along with their mother, treating them with affectionate consideration. Also, bring Krishna of celestial beauty along with them. It is from sheer good fortune that the sons of Pritha are alive, and from good fortune alone have they obtained the daughter of Drupada. Our strength has increased, and my great grief has been alleviated by this good fortune!"

Following Dhritarashtra's instructions, Vidura proceeded to Drupada's abode, where he conveyed the king's message and presented jewels and wealth to Draupadi, the Pandavas, and Drupada's household. Drupada, in agreement with Vidura's proposal, permitted the Pandavas to return to their ancestral kingdom.

Drupada said, 'It is even so as you, O Vidura of great wisdom, have said. I too have been exceedingly happy in consequence of this alliance. It is highly proper that these illustrious princes should return to their ancestral kingdom. But it is not proper for me to say this myself. If Yudhishthira, Bhima, Arjuna, and the twins themselves desire to go, along with Krishna and if Rama and Krishna are of the same mind, then let the Pandavas go thither.'"

Upon Drupada's agreement, Yudhishthira, Bhima, Arjuna, and the twins, along with Krishna, expressed their readiness to comply. Vasudeva affirmed their decision, stating that they should abide by Drupada's wisdom. Finally, Drupada, acknowledging Krishna's and Vasudeva's support, reiterated his agreement with the plan.

The Pandavas, accompanied by Krishna and Vidura, then embarked on their journey to Hastinapura. Upon their arrival, they were received with honor by Dhritarashtra and Bhishma. Dhritarashtra reiterated his desire for peace and proposed that the Pandavas take up residence in Khandavaprastha, offering them half the kingdom. The Pandavas accepted his proposal and departed for Khandavaprastha.

Upon reaching Khandavaprastha, they beautified the land and built the city of Indraprastha, which became a flourishing center of prosperity and culture. The joy of the Pandavas grew as they settled into their new kingdom, surrounded by the blessings of the people and the beauty of their surroundings.

Thus, through the wisdom and goodwill of their elders, the Pandavas found a new home and a new beginning, marking the start of a prosperous Chapter in their lives

Chapter 33

THE STORY OF TILOTTAMA

Janamejaya asked, "What did the Pandavas do after they got their kingdom? How did Draupadi, their wife, handle being married to all of them? And why didn't they fight among themselves, even though they all loved Krishna? I want to know everything about how they treated each other after they got married."

Vaisampayana replied, "The Pandavas, after winning their kingdom, lived happily in Khandavaprastha with Krishna's help. Yudhishthira, always truthful and wise, ruled the land well with his brothers' help. They defeated all their enemies and lived happily together, governing their kingdom. One day, the wise sage Narada visited them. Yudhishthira respectfully welcomed him and offered him a seat. After Narada was seated, Yudhishthira worshipped him and told him about the kingdom. Narada was pleased and blessed him. Then, at

THE SOURCE OF CONFLICT

Narada's command, Yudhishthira sat down. He informed Krishna about Narada's arrival, and Draupadi, after purifying herself, respectfully came to Narada along with the Pandavas. She worshipped the sage and stood before him with folded hands, properly veiled. Narada blessed her and asked her to leave. After Draupadi left, Narada advised the Pandavas, especially Yudhishthira, to maintain unity among themselves because Draupadi was their common wife. He reminded them of the story of Sunda and Upasunda, who ended up killing each other due to disunity over a woman named Tilottama. He warned the Pandavas not to let such a thing happen among them."

Yudhishthira then asked Narada about the story of Sunda and Upasunda, their dissension, and why they killed each other over Tilottama. He also asked about Tilottama's background, whether she was an Apsara or a celestial's daughter. He expressed a strong desire to hear all the details of the story.

Vaisampayana continued, "When Yudhishthira asked about Sunda and Upasunda, Narada began to tell them a story from long ago. He said, 'There was a powerful demon named Nikumbha, born in the Asura race of Hiranyakasipu. Nikumbha had two sons, Sunda and Upasunda, who were also mighty demons with great strength and wicked hearts. They were like two peas in a pod, always together and always agreeing with each other. They were so alike that they seemed like one person split into two. Both brothers were determined to conquer the three worlds, so they went to the Vindhya mountains and did intense penance. They endured hunger, thirst, and severe hardships for a long time, practicing self-control and meditation.

During their penance, the mountains heated up because of their intense austerities, and the gods became worried. They tried to distract the brothers with temptations, sending beautiful women and precious gifts, but Sunda and Upasunda stayed focused on their goals. Even when the gods tried to trick them with illusions, showing them their loved ones in distress, the brothers remained steadfast. Finally, Lord Brahma himself appeared before them and offered to grant them a boon. The brothers asked for great strength, knowledge of all weapons and illusions, and the ability to change their forms at will. But when they asked for immortality, Brahma refused, saying that they had performed their penance for selfish reasons.

Sunda and Upasunda then asked to be protected from everything in the universe except each other. Brahma granted their request, and they returned to their kingdom as invincible beings. They cut off their matted hair, wore crowns, and lived in luxury, making the moon rise over their city every night. Everyone in their kingdom was happy, celebrating with feasts and music every day, not even noticing how time passed.'"

Narada's story revealed how Sunda and Upasunda became invincible but also foreshadowed the tragic outcome of their wish for protection from each other.

Narada continued his tale, saying, "After the festivities, Sunda and Upasunda, eager to rule the three worlds, prepared for war. With the support of their allies, elders, and ministers, they departed under the constellation Magha, leading a mighty army armed with weapons. Their journey was accompanied by songs of victory from bards, filling them with confidence.

Furious and unstoppable, the demon brothers ascended to the heavens, where they found that the gods had fled to Brahman for protection. Sunda and Upasunda swiftly conquered Indra's realm, defeated Yakshas, Rakshasas, and other celestial beings, and even subdued the Nagas and ocean dwellers. They then turned their attention to earth, ordering their soldiers to slaughter Brahmins and sages performing sacrifices, seeing them as enemies of the Asuras.

The brothers' cruelty knew no bounds. They killed Brahmins, destroyed sacred rituals, and drove Rishis into hiding. Even the most powerful ascetics, terrified by their actions, fled for their lives. With their sacred places desecrated and religious ceremonies halted, the earth plunged into darkness. People stopped farming, and towns lay deserted. The once vibrant land became a wasteland, littered with the remains of the slaughtered.

Sunda and Upasunda, assuming various forms, hunted down and killed the remaining Rishis, leaving no one to challenge their reign of terror. With sacrifices and rituals abandoned, the heavens mourned the loss of their divine rites. The brothers established their dominion in Kurukshetra, unopposed and unrivaled."

Narada continued his story, saying, "Witnessing the atrocities of Sunda and Upasunda, the celestial sages, Siddhas, and wise Rishis, filled with sorrow, sought the aid of the Grandfather of the universe, Brahma. They described in detail the wicked deeds of the demon brothers and pleaded for a solution.

Listening to their plea, Brahma pondered for a moment before deciding on a course of action. He summoned Viswakarman, the divine architect, and instructed him to create a maiden of unparalleled beauty capable of ensnaring the hearts of all.

Following Brahma's command, Viswakarman meticulously crafted a celestial maiden, gathering the most exquisite features from the gems of the universe. This maiden, named Tilottama, surpassed all other women in beauty, captivating the gaze and hearts of all who beheld her.

When Tilottama came into existence, she humbly asked Brahma for her purpose. Brahma directed her to go to the Asura brothers, Sunda and Upasunda, and use her beauty to incite discord between them.

Obeying Brahma's command, Tilottama set out, circling the celestial assembly. As she passed by the gods and sages, their gazes lingered on her mesmerizing form. Even Mahadeva, despite his efforts to remain composed, found himself entranced by her beauty. His longing gaze caused additional faces and eyes to appear on his divine form.

As Tilottama departed for the Asura city, the celestial beings felt assured that her mission would succeed. With the task entrusted to Tilottama, the divine assembly disbanded, returning to their respective realms."

Narada continued his narration, saying, "As the Asura brothers, intoxicated by their power and pleasures, reveled in their conquests, Tilottama, adorned in a single red silk garment, approached them while gathering wild flowers. Enchanted by her unparalleled beauty, Sunda and Upasunda, driven by lust and claiming her as their own, soon found themselves embroiled in a heated dispute.

Sunda, asserting his superiority as the first to hold her hand, clashed with Upasunda, who claimed her as his sister-in-law. The argument quickly escalated into violence, with both brothers attacking each other with fierce maces, fueled by passion and pride. Struck by each other's blows, they fell to the ground, their bodies bathed in blood, like fallen suns from the sky.

Witnessing the tragic outcome, the other beings present fled in fear, seeking refuge in the nether regions. The Grandsire, accompanied by celestial beings and great sages, arrived at the scene. Pleased with Tilottama's role, Brahma granted her a boon, bestowing upon her unparalleled splendor and confining her to the realm of the Adityas, where her radiance would be too dazzling for mortal eyes to behold.

Having witnessed the destructive power of desire and discord, Narada advised the Pandavas to establish a rule to prevent conflicts over Draupadi. Following his counsel, the Pandavas decided that if one of them was found alone with Draupadi, the others would retreat to the forest and live as Brahmacharis for twelve years.

Gratified by their decision, Narada departed, leaving the Pandavas to uphold their newfound rule. Thus, guided by the wisdom of Narada, the Pandavas ensured harmony and unity among themselves, avoiding disputes over their shared wife, Draupadi."

Chapter 34

Arjunas Journeys

Vaisampayana continued the narrative, saying, "The Pandavas, having established their rule and brought many kings under their sway through their valor, lived in joy and prosperity. Draupadi, the beloved wife of the five brothers, found great delight in their company, and they, in turn, cherished her with affection. Due to their virtuous conduct, the entire Kuru dynasty flourished, free from sin and filled with happiness.

However, one day, a Brahmana arrived at Khandavaprastha, distraught and grief-stricken, as his cattle had been stolen by robbers. He implored the Pandavas to help him retrieve his property, lamenting the loss of his sacrificial butter to thieves. The Brahmana beseeched them to rescue his stolen cattle, invoking the duty of kings to protect their subjects and uphold righteousness.

THE SOURCE OF CONFLICT

Arjuna, upon hearing the Brahmana's distress, was moved to action. However, the chamber where their weapons were kept was occupied by Yudhishthira and Draupadi. Despite the urgency of the situation, Arjuna hesitated to enter the chamber alone or disobey the established rule by entering with the Brahmana. After much deliberation, Arjuna resolved to prioritize virtue over personal consequences, even if it meant incurring sin or exile.

Armed with his bow and riding his war-chariot, Arjuna pursued the thieves and defeated them in battle, recovering the Brahmana's cattle. Returning triumphant to the capital, Arjuna was hailed as a hero and honored by all. However, mindful of the established rule, Arjuna expressed his intention to go into exile for transgressing the rule regarding the privacy of Yudhishthira and Draupadi.

Yudhishthira, upon hearing Arjuna's decision, was deeply distressed and urged him to abandon his plan, assuring him that there was no fault in his actions. Yudhishthira emphasized that according to propriety, it was the elder brother who transgressed by entering the chamber of the younger brother with his wife. However, Arjuna remained steadfast in his commitment to truth and virtue, refusing to compromise his principles.

With Yudhishthira's reluctant permission, Arjuna prepared to embark on his forest exile for twelve years, determined to uphold his vow and principles."

Vaisampayana continued, "As Arjuna embarked on his forest exile, accompanied by Brahmanas and various devotees, he journeyed through picturesque forests, lakes, rivers, and provinces, finally arriving at the source of the holy Ganges. Entranced by the beauty of the surroundings, Arjuna decided to settle in that serene region.

Now, let me tell you of an extraordinary incident that occurred while Arjuna resided there. In the company of learned Brahmanas, Arjuna performed numerous sacred rites, including the daily Agnihotra ceremonies, which enhanced the beauty and sanctity of the area where the Ganges descended into the plains. One day, after completing his ablutions and offering oblations to his ancestors in the river, Arjuna was unexpectedly seized and dragged underwater by Ulupi, the daughter of the Naga king.

Taken to the underwater palace of Kauravya, Arjuna found himself face to face with a sacrificial fire lit in his honor. Despite being surprised by Ulupi's actions, Arjuna dutifully performed his sacrificial rites before the fire, earning the favor of the fire god Agni. Following the rituals, Arjuna addressed Ulupi with a smile, inquiring about her identity and the ownership of the beautiful region.

Ulupi revealed herself as the daughter of Naga king Kauravya and expressed her desire for Arjuna, driven by the god of desire. However, Arjuna, bound by his vow of celibacy for twelve years, explained his predicament and sought a way to fulfill her desire without compromising his virtue.

Understanding Arjuna's dilemma, Ulupi reminded him of the agreement amongst the Pandavas regarding their exile for inadvertently entering the chamber where Draupadi was present. She assured Arjuna that fulfilling her desire would not violate his vow or duty. Additionally, she appealed to his sense of compassion, urging him to save her from distress and promising her worship and protection in return.

Moved by Ulupi's plight and her reasoning, Arjuna, guided by virtue, acquiesced to her request, spending the night in the Naga king's palace. In the morning, accompanied by Ulupi, Arjuna returned to the banks of the Ganges, where she granted him a boon, making him invincible in water, before bidding him farewell and returning to her underwater abode."

THE SOURCE OF CONFLICT

Vaisampayana continued, "Arjuna, having narrated his experiences to the Brahmanas accompanying him, proceeded towards the breast of Himavat. He visited various sacred peaks such as Agastyavata, Vasishtha's peak, and Bhrigu's peak, where he performed purifying ablutions and donated generously to Brahmanas. Traveling further to the sacred asylum called Hiranyavindu, Arjuna continued his journey accompanied by the Brahmanas towards the east, exploring many regions and holy waters along the way.

He visited the forest of Naimisha and saw rivers like Utpalini, Nanda, Apara Nanda, Kausiki, Gaya, and Ganga, performing purification rituals and donating cows to Brahmanas. Arjuna then traveled through the regions of Vanga and Kalinga, performing similar rituals and charity. Upon reaching the gate of the kingdom of Kalinga, the Brahmanas bid farewell to him, and Arjuna continued his journey with a few attendants towards the ocean.

Crossing the country of the Kalingas, Arjuna proceeded to Manipura, where he beheld the beautiful princess Chitrangada, daughter of King Chitravahana, in her father's palace. Arjuna expressed his desire to marry her to the king, introducing himself as Dhananjaya, the son of Pandu and Kunti. The king revealed the unique lineage of his family, where each successive descendant was blessed with only one child. He explained that Chitrangada was his only child and had been appointed as a Putrika, a daughter designated to perpetuate the family line by bearing a son for her husband.

Arjuna accepted the king's condition and married Chitrangada, staying in Manipura for three years. When Chitrangada bore a son, Arjuna embraced her and took leave of the king, resuming his wanderings."

Vaisampayana continued, "Arjuna, the bull of Bharata's race, then proceeded to the sacred waters on the banks of the southern ocean, where ascetics resided. He found five such regions adorned with ascetics, but those waters were avoided by all due to the presence of five large crocodiles dwelling there. These sacred waters were named Agastya, Saubhadra, Pauloma, Karandhama, and Bharadwaja.

Arjuna, curious about why these waters were shunned, asked the ascetics residing there about the reason. They informed him that the waters were inhabited by crocodiles that would seize any ascetic bathing there.

Undeterred by their warnings, Arjuna went to the Saubhadra water. As soon as he plunged in, a crocodile seized his leg. However, Arjuna, the mighty warrior, dragged the crocodile to the shore where it transformed into a beautiful damsel adorned with ornaments. Surprised by this transformation, Arjuna asked the damsel about her identity and why she had committed such a dreadful act.

The damsel revealed herself as Varga, an Apsara beloved to the celestial treasurer Kuvera. She explained that she and her companions had tried to tempt a Brahmana ascetic who was deeply immersed in meditation. Despite their efforts, the Brahmana remained steadfast in his devotion and cursed them to become crocodiles for a hundred years."

Vaisampayana continued, "Varga continued her narrative, saying, 'We were distressed by the curse and sought forgiveness from the Brahmana ascetic, acknowledging our wrongdoing. Moved by our words, the virtuous Brahmana explained that his curse would last only for a limited period of a hundred years. He assured us that after that time, a noble individual would rescue us, and the waters where we dwelled would become known as Nari-tirthas, sanctified by our sufferings and deliverance.

"After the Brahmana's words, we saluted him and left the region, pondering on our fate. Suddenly, we encountered the celestial sage Narada, who, upon learning our plight, directed us to the sacred waters bordering the southern ocean, where Arjuna, the son of Pandu, would deliver us from our curse. Thus, following Narada's advice, we came to these waters and have now been freed by you, O hero. But my four companions are still trapped in the other waters here. I beseech you to rescue them as well.'

"Vaisampayana continued, 'Arjuna, endowed with great prowess, then joyfully liberated all of them from the curse. As they emerged from the waters, they regained their true forms, looking as they did before. Arjuna, having freed the sacred waters from their danger and granted the Apsaras their freedom, desired to see Chitrangada once more. He thus proceeded to the city of Manipura, where he beheld his son Vabhruvahana on the throne. After reuniting with Chitrangada and his son, Arjuna continued his journey towards the sacred spot called Gokarna.'"

Chapter 35

ARJUNA AND SUBADRA

When the sons of the Vrishni House honed their archery skills under the tutelage of Drona at Hastinapura, Arjuna's comrade was Gada, cousin to the lion-hearted Krishna. It was Gada who first whispered of Krishna's sister, Subhadra, to Arjuna. Tales of her unparalleled beauty kindled a flame in Arjuna's heart, a love unspoken yet fierce, forged in the fires of imagination.

With Subhadra's image burning bright in his mind, Arjuna, cunning as a serpent, sought ways to lay eyes upon her without drawing notice. Clad in the guise of a yati, trident in hand and ash-daubed body concealed beneath garlands of rudraksha, he tread the streets of Prabhasa, a silent shadow in the night's embrace. Beneath the sprawling branches of a banyan tree, he sat, feigning deep contemplation, while the heavens wept torrents upon the earth.

Krishna, ever the omniscient, caught wind of a sadhu's presence in Prabhasa and sensed the heartache hidden within his dearest friend's bosom. Amidst the dark hours, in the company of his beloved Satyabhama, Krishna erupted into fits of laughter, tears streaming down his cheeks. When questioned by his consort, he divulged the secret of Arjuna's pilgrimage to Prabhasa, driven by thoughts of Subhadra's enchanting visage.

Through the deluge, Krishna made his way to the banyan's sheltering embrace, where Arjuna awaited, his soul laid bare. In tender reunion, Krishna probed Arjuna's wanderings, a sly smile playing upon his lips as he jested about Arjuna's supposed renunciation of worldly ties for the ascetic life.

"My lord," Arjuna implored, "you know my heart's desire. Aid me in winning fair Subhadra's hand." Krishna, ever the schemer, pledged his support, guiding Arjuna to the sacred hill of Raivataka, there to await his fortune.

Days passed, and atop the hill, amidst a feast of revelry, Arjuna beheld Subhadra, radiant as the dawn, escorted by her retinue. His heart stirred, his eyes aflame with passion, he sought Krishna's counsel.

"My friend," Krishna whispered, "your yearning betrays the guise you wear." Arjuna, unable to contain his longing, implored Krishna's aid in winning Subhadra's love and hand in marriage.

With a chuckle, Krishna revealed a plan fit for heroes—a love born in secrecy, nurtured in the shadows, to blossom in the light of dawn. Thus, Arjuna, the valiant warrior, donned the guise of a yati once more, his heart a battleground for love's conquest.

In the temple's courtyard, Arjuna sat in silent meditation, his soul laid bare before the gods. As Subhadra and her retinue departed, Balarama and his kin, oblivious to Arjuna's ruse, beheld the yati in awe.

Balarama, struck by the yati's noble countenance, welcomed him to Dwaraka with reverence, eager to host this sage whose wisdom belied his youth. And so, Arjuna, the Pandava prince, embarked on a journey of love and deception, guided by the hand of fate and the whispers of Krishna's cunning

As Krishna approached the gathering, Balarama, ever the picture of solemnity, motioned for him to pay homage to the revered yati. But beneath Krishna's facade of reverence lurked a mischievous grin, hidden from Balarama's watchful gaze.

With practiced humility, Krishna prostrated before the supposed sage, accepting the holy ashes with a knowing twinkle in his eye. Balarama, oblivious to the subtle game afoot, regaled Krishna with tales of the yati's supposed virtues and travels.

When asked for a suitable lodging for the yati, Krishna's lips twitched with suppressed mirth. "Forgive my impertinence, esteemed elder," he replied with feigned deference. "But I dare not speak in your presence, lest my words betray my unworthiness."

Balarama, pleased by Krishna's apparent humility, suggested the gardens near Subhadra's apartments as an ideal sanctuary for the yati. Little did he know the wheels of Krishna's prank had already been set in motion.

But Krishna's facade faltered as he expressed faux concern. "Brother, I must caution against such proximity between the yati and our dear Subhadra," he warned, his voice dripping with mock apprehension.

THE SOURCE OF CONFLICT

"His youthful charm and eloquence may lead our innocent sister astray."

Enraged by Krishna's disparaging remarks, Balarama defended the yati's honor with fervor, unaware of the jest being played upon him.

With a sly smile, Krishna accepted the task of escorting the yati to Subhadra's care, his heart dancing with anticipation at the unfolding prank. Taking Arjuna's hand, he led him past Rukmini and Satyabhama, whispering their true identities with a wink and a nod.

Finally, they reached Subhadra's side, where Krishna delivered Arjuna into her unsuspecting hands. With a final glance filled with playful mischief, Krishna departed, leaving behind a trail of laughter and anticipation in his wake.

As Krishna escorted Arjuna to Subhadra's side, the air crackled with unspoken tension, each step a dance between destiny and desire.

Subhadra, her gaze like a summer breeze, alighted upon the veiled figure beside Krishna. "Who is this sage, brother?" she inquired, her voice a melody of curiosity.

Krishna, ever the master of subtlety, replied with a cryptic smile, "A traveler seeking solace in our humble abode, dear sister. He comes with tales as vast as the horizon and wisdom as deep as the ocean."

Arjuna, concealed beneath his ascetic garb, felt the weight of Subhadra's gaze upon him, her eyes like twin flames dancing in the night. "Greetings, noble lady," he murmured, his voice a river of hidden longing.

Subhadra, sensing a mystery shrouded in the guise of the yati, inclined her head in respectful acknowledgment. "May your stay bring peace to our home, revered sage," she replied, her words laden with unspoken questions.

With a parting glance filled with silent understanding, Krishna withdrew, leaving Arjuna and Subhadra to navigate the currents of fate that swirled between them like an unseen tempest.

Alone amidst the fragrant blooms of the palace gardens, Arjuna and Subhadra stood in silent communion, their hearts tethered by the invisible threads of destiny, their words a whispered promise of love yet unspoken.

Arjuna found solace in the tranquil gardens of Subhadra's abode, where she dutifully tended to his needs. But despite her attentive care, Arjuna's heart remained heavy with unspoken longing. Subhadra, unaware of his true identity, puzzled over his somber demeanor as she went about her daily routines.

In the bustling streets of Dwaraka, Arjuna's legend loomed large, his name synonymous with bravery and beauty. Everywhere one turned, tales of his valor and grace echoed through the air. In the archery school, his name was invoked as the epitome of skill and prowess, while young boys boasted of their prowess by comparing themselves to the illustrious Pandava. Elders bestowed blessings upon the youth, hoping they would emulate Arjuna's greatness, and mothers prayed to bear sons as noble as he.

Subhadra, steeped in the lore of Arjuna's exploits, found herself drawn to the enigmatic yati who seemed to gaze upon her with fervent intensity. His longing glances stirred a curiosity within her, prompting her to seek his company despite her confusion.

As days turned into weeks, Subhadra found herself captivated by the yati's tales of distant lands and exotic landscapes. She spent hours listening to his melodious voice, entranced by his eloquence. One day, she broached the subject of Indraprastha, hoping to glean some information about her beloved Arjuna.

With a knowing smile, Arjuna seized the opportunity to reveal his true identity. Drawing her close with gentle words, he confessed his love for her, leaving Subhadra speechless with shock and disbelief. Unable to meet his gaze, she retreated to her chamber, her heart in tumult.

Subhadra's sickness soon became the talk of the town, prompting Krishna to intervene. Sensing the need for distance between the young lovers, he dispatched Rukmini to attend to the yati's needs, much to Arjuna's disappointment.

Meanwhile, Devaki, worried about her daughter's condition, sought counsel from Balarama and Krishna. Sensing an opportunity to unite the lovers, Krishna proposed a pilgrimage to the nearby island to seek the blessings of Lord Rudra.

Before departing, Krishna whispered to Subhadra of his plan to orchestrate her wedding with Arjuna upon their return. With renewed hope, Subhadra awaited her beloved's arrival.

Twelve days later, Arjuna approached Subhadra, his heart brimming with anticipation. Reminding her of Krishna's plan, he pleaded for her consent to a gandharva marriage. Overwhelmed with emotion, Subhadra remained silent, tears streaming down her cheeks.

With tender reassurance, Arjuna promised to whisk her away to Indraprastha, urging her to prepare a chariot for their clandestine departure. Subhadra, efficient in the art of charioteering, swiftly complied, ensuring all was in readiness.

As Arjuna shed his yati guise and donned princely attire, the lovers prepared to embark on their journey. With Subhadra at the reins and Arjuna by her side, they set forth, leaving behind the city of Dwaraka in pursuit of their shared destiny.

As Arjuna and Subhadra made their escape from Dwaraka, the vigilant watchmen of the city sounded the alarm, but their efforts to halt the chariot proved futile. Recognizing the miscreant as Arjuna, they sent out a warning, signaling imminent danger to the Vrishnis.

Led by the enraged Balarama, the Vrishnis hastened back to the city, demanding answers from Krishna, who remained eerily silent. Accused of orchestrating the incident, Krishna defended himself, reminding Balarama of his earlier warnings against bringing Arjuna and Subhadra together. Despite Krishna's attempts to calm him, Balarama's fury only intensified, his wrath like the wrath of Death itself.

Approaching Balarama with gentle persuasion, Krishna urged him to reconsider his anger. Emphasizing Subhadra's willing departure with Arjuna, Krishna appealed to his brother's reason, highlighting Arjuna's noble lineage and unmatched prowess as a fitting match for their sister. Reluctantly, Balarama acquiesced, swayed by Krishna's logic and wisdom.

Setting aside their anger, the Vrishnis resolved to pursue Arjuna and Subhadra, but their efforts proved fruitless as the lovers had already ventured too far. Instead, they decided to await Arjuna's arrival in Indraprastha, where they would formally unite him with Subhadra through sacred rites.

Meanwhile, as Arjuna and Subhadra approached the gates of the city, Arjuna's thoughts turned to the formidable Draupadi, fearing her reaction to his romantic escapade. Advising Subhadra to win Draupadi's favor first, he instructed her to adopt the guise of a gopi, a look that suited her divine beauty.

Arriving at the palace, Subhadra, radiant in her rustic attire, introduced herself to Draupadi as Krishna's sister, instantly captivating her with her charm. Draupadi, delighted by Subhadra's presence, blessed her with words of affection, unaware of her identity.

Amidst the joyful chatter, news of Arjuna's return echoed through the streets, signaling his triumphant homecoming. Reuniting with his brothers, Arjuna recounted his adventures and his newfound love for Subhadra, whom he proudly introduced to Draupadi.

With Draupadi's approval, Subhadra's acceptance into the fold was sealed, and soon, the Vrishnis arrived in Indraprastha, bearing lavish gifts and blessings for the newlyweds. Celebrating their union with grandeur and festivity, the Vrishnis eventually bid farewell, leaving Krishna behind to share in the joy of the Pandavas' abode.

Chapter 36

KANDAVA FOREST

Vaisampayana narrated, "The Pandavas, upon establishing themselves in Indraprastha as per Dhritarashtra and Bhishma's directive, commenced extending their dominion over other kings. Under the just rule of Yudhishthira, their subjects lived in unparalleled happiness, akin to a soul thriving within a blessed body adorned with auspicious marks and righteous deeds. Yudhishthira, paying homage to virtue, pleasure, and profit in equal measure, embodied a harmonious blend of the three pursuits, radiating as a beacon of righteousness on earth. With Yudhishthira as their king, the monarchs of other realms found stability, their hearts inclining towards spiritual contemplation, while virtue flourished in all directions.

Assisted by his brothers, Yudhishthira shone even brighter, like a grand sacrifice supported by the four Vedas. Learned Brahmanas, led by Dhananjaya, graced the court, akin to celestial beings attending the Lord of Creation. The people, enamored by Yudhishthira's integrity, found solace in his leadership, drawn not only by his royal status but also by genuine affection. Yudhishthira, with his impeccable speech and unwavering truthfulness, endeared himself to all, governing with compassion and wisdom. Alongside his brothers, who subjugated other kings with their valor, Yudhishthira's reign remained unmarred by external threats, fostering peace and prosperity.

"Amidst this tranquil period, Arjuna proposed to Krishna, 'As summer approaches, let us retreat to the banks of the Yamuna. There, amidst friends, we shall indulge in sport and return by evening.' Agreeing with Arjuna's suggestion, Krishna replied, 'Indeed, this is also my desire. Let us partake in the waters' delights in the company of our friends.'

"Thus, with Yudhishthira's consent, Partha and Govinda, accompanied by their friends, embarked on their journey. Arriving at a picturesque location by the Yamuna, adorned with tall trees and luxurious mansions, stocked with delectable delicacies, fragrant flowers, and perfumes, the group eagerly entered the inner chambers. There, they reveled in various activities, guided by Partha and Govinda's instructions.

"Draupadi and Subhadra, under the influence of wine, generously distributed their ornaments and garments to other women, who danced, sang, and reveled in joy. Amidst the music and merriment, Arjuna and Vasudeva retired to a secluded spot nearby, engaging in conversation about past exploits and other subjects of interest. As they conversed, a Brahmana, resplendent like the morning sun, approached them, prompting Arjuna and Vasudeva to rise respectfully, awaiting his words."

Vaisampayana continued, "The Brahmana then addressed Arjuna and Vasudeva, saying, 'You, who are currently staying near Khandava, are the two foremost heroes on earth. I am a voracious Brahmana who always eats much. O Vrishni and Partha, I request you to gratify me by providing me with sufficient food.' Hearing this, Krishna and Arjuna replied, 'Please tell us what kind of food will satisfy you, so that we may endeavor to provide it.' The illustrious Brahmana responded, 'I do not desire ordinary food. Know that I am Agni! Give me the food that suits me. This forest of Khandava is constantly protected by Indra. As long as it is under his protection, I fail to consume it. In this forest resides a Naga named Takshaka, who is a friend of Indra. Indra protects this forest for Takshaka's sake, along with many other creatures. Despite my desire to consume the forest, I am unable to do so due to Indra's prowess. Whenever I blaze forth, he pours water from the clouds to extinguish me. Therefore, I am seeking your help. You both are skilled in weapons. If you assist me, I will surely consume this forest, for that is the food I desire. As you are proficient in excellent weapons, I implore you to prevent the showers from descending and any creatures from escaping when I begin to consume this forest.'

"Janamejaya asked, 'Why did the illustrious Agni desire to consume the forest of Khandava, which was teeming with various living creatures and protected by the chief of the celestials? There must have been a significant reason for Agni's wrathful act. O Brahmana, I wish to hear in detail from you how the Khandava forest was consumed in ancient times. Please narrate the story to me.'

"Vaisampayana replied, 'O chief among men, I shall narrate to you the story of the conflagration of Khandava as told by the Rishis in the Puranas. It is said that there was a celebrated king named Swetaki, who was endowed with great strength and prowess, equal to Indra himself. No one on earth could match him in sacrifices, charity, and intelligence. Swetaki performed numerous sacrifices and bestowed large gifts upon Brahmanas. However, his priests, afflicted by the smoke of continuous sacrifices, abandoned him, refusing to assist in further rituals. Despite his repeated requests, they declined to return, citing the discomfort caused by the perpetual smoke.

"Undeterred, Swetaki sought other priests and completed his rituals. However, he desired to perform a sacrifice lasting a hundred years, yet could not find priests willing to assist. In frustration, he chastised his former priests, but they remained adamant. Ultimately, Swetaki resorted to severe asceticism, undertaking rigorous penance in the mountains of Kailasa to seek the assistance of Lord Shiva.

"Moved by Swetaki's devotion, Shiva appeared before him and granted a boon, promising assistance in the sacrifice on the condition that Swetaki maintain strict observance for twelve years, constantly pouring clarified butter into the fire. Swetaki faithfully fulfilled the conditions, and upon completion, Shiva directed him to seek the assistance of the sage Durvasa.

"Following Shiva's instructions, Swetaki conducted the sacrifice under Durvasa's guidance. After its successful conclusion, he was honored by Brahmanas and citizens alike. However, Agni, having consumed clarified butter continuously for twelve years, suffered from surfeit, losing his brilliance and strength.

"Approaching Lord Brahma, Agni sought relief from his malady. Brahma advised him to consume the inhabitants of the Khandava forest, as it was once burnt to ashes at the gods' behest. Thus, Agni, assisted by Vayu, blazed forth repeatedly in Khandava, each time being thwarted by the forest dwellers' efforts to extinguish the fire."

Vaisampayana continued, "Havyavahana (Agni), in his anger and disappointment, returned to the Grandsire (Brahma) with his ailment uncured, lamenting the inability to consume the Khandava forest. He narrated everything that had transpired. Reflecting for a moment, the illustrious deity said to him, 'O sinless one, I see a way by which you may consume the forest of Khandava in the very sight of Indra. The ancient deities Nara and Narayana have incarnated on earth as Arjuna and Vasudeva. They are currently staying in the forest of Khandava. Seek their aid in consuming the forest. They will prevent the inhabitants of Khandava from escaping, and even thwart Indra from intervening. I have no doubt about this.'

"Hearing these words, Agni swiftly approached Krishna and Arjuna. Having reached them, he conveyed Brahma's message. Arjuna, in response to Agni's plea, expressed his readiness to assist. He stated that while he possessed numerous celestial weapons, he lacked a bow suited to his strength and arrows that would never deplete. Arjuna also desired celestial steeds and a magnificent chariot befitting his prowess. He emphasized the need for adequate means to accomplish the task.

"Thus addressed by Arjuna, Agni, eager to seek Varuna's aid, recollected the god, who promptly appeared before him. Agni respectfully requested Varuna for the bow, quiver, and chariot obtained from King Soma, which were necessary for the task. Varuna agreed and granted Arjuna's request. He gave them a splendid bow that was indestructible and enhanced fame and achievements. It was capable of smiting hostile armies and was equal to a hundred thousand bows. Varuna also provided two inexhaustible quivers and a celestial chariot adorned with flags and banners, drawn by steeds as swift as the wind.

"Arjuna, adorned in armor and armed with his sword, ascended the magnificent chariot with humility and reverence. Taking up the celestial bow Gandiva, he was filled with joy. As Arjuna strung the bow forcibly, the sound made the listeners tremble with fear. Having obtained the bow, quivers, and chariot, Arjuna felt confident in his ability to assist. Meanwhile, Varuna also bestowed upon Krishna a discus with an iron pole, known as Sudarshana, and a mace named Kaumodaki.

"With their weapons in hand, Arjuna and Krishna declared their readiness to assist Agni in consuming the Khandava forest, asserting their ability to vanquish even the celestials and Asuras. Agni, pleased with their readiness, assumed his most energetic form and surrounded the forest on all sides with his seven flames, ready to consume it."

Vaisampayana continued, "Krishna and Arjuna, positioned on opposite sides of the Khandava forest, initiated a great slaughter of its inhabitants. They swiftly moved to prevent any creature from escaping the burning forest. Their chariots and themselves seemed to merge into one, as they coordinated their actions seamlessly. As the forest burned, countless creatures attempted to flee in all directions. Some were injured, some scorched, and some died embracing their loved ones, unable to abandon them. Others, overwhelmed by fear, perished in the flames or fell into the boiling ponds and tanks within the forest.

"The cries of the burning creatures filled the air, resembling the tumult of the churning ocean. The celestial dwellers, witnessing the intense flames, became anxious and sought the chief of the celestials, Indra, for an explanation. They questioned why Agni was consuming the creatures below, expressing concern about the destruction of the world.

"Hearing their concerns and observing Agni's actions, Indra set out to protect the Khandava forest. He covered the sky with numerous clouds and showered rain upon the burning forest, but the rain evaporated before reaching the flames. Undeterred, Indra intensified his efforts, causing heavy downpours that clashed with Agni's flames, enveloping the forest in smoke and lightning.

"Arjuna, invoking his divine weapons, countered Indra's rain with a deluge of his own weapons. He blanketed the sky above Khandava with arrows, preventing any creature from escaping. As the forest burned, Aswasena, son of Takshaka, attempted to flee but was thwarted by Arjuna's arrows. His mother, in a desperate attempt to save him, swallowed him, but Arjuna, seeing this, swiftly severed her head. However, Aswasena managed to escape while Arjuna was momentarily distracted.

"Enraged by the deception, Arjuna continued to prevent any creature from escaping, cutting them into pieces with his arrows. Meanwhile, Krishna also engaged in battle, slaying numerous Asuras with his discus. Indra, witnessing Arjuna's anger, hurled his thunderbolt, but Arjuna countered it with the Vayavya weapon, dispersing the clouds and halting the rain.

"Undeterred, Indra and the other celestials, armed with various weapons, launched a fierce assault on Krishna and Arjuna. However, the two heroes, fearless and invincible, repelled their attacks with thunderous arrows. Despite repeated attempts by the celestials, Krishna and Arjuna stood their ground, displaying unmatched prowess in battle.

"Sakra, impressed by their valor, intensified his efforts, causing a shower of stones. Arjuna, using his arrows skillfully, dispersed the stones. Frustrated, Indra hurled a large peak from Mount Mandara, but Arjuna swiftly destroyed it with his arrows, causing it to fall upon the forest, crushing numerous creatures dwelling within."

Vaisampayana continued, "As the stones fell upon the Khandava forest, its inhabitants, including the Danavas, Rakshasas, Nagas, and various other creatures, fled in fear. They saw Krishna and Arjuna with their weapons ready, and their hearts trembled. The roar of the falling stones mingled with the roar of fire, creating a terrifying cacophony that echoed through the heavens.

"In order to destroy them, Krishna hurled his formidable discus, cutting the forest-dwellers into pieces. The Asuras, smeared with blood and fat, resembled dark clouds in the evening sky as they fell into the mouth of Agni. Krishna, relentless in his slaughter, slew Pisachas, Nagas, and Rakshasas by the thousands, while his discus, always returning to his hand, continued its deadly work.

"The form of Krishna, usually gentle and divine, now appeared fierce as he unleashed destruction upon the forest-dwellers. None among the assembled celestials could defeat Krishna and Arjuna in battle. Witnessing their unmatched prowess, the gods, realizing the futility of their efforts, withdrew from the scene.

"Indra, filled with joy and admiration, praised Krishna and Arjuna for their valor. However, an incorporeal voice assured Indra that his friend Takshaka had escaped unharmed, and declared Krishna and Arjuna to be invincible, worthy of worship by all beings.

"Upon hearing this, Indra, acknowledging the truth of the words, abandoned his anger and departed for heaven, followed by the other celestial beings. Krishna and Arjuna, seeing the celestials retreat, roared triumphantly and continued to assist in the forest's destruction.

"Arjuna, with his skillful archery, prevented any creature from escaping, while Krishna, with his discus, slaughtered the forest-dwellers mercilessly. The flames of Agni, fueled by the fat and blood of the slain creatures, rose high without producing smoke, gratifying the fire-god immensely.

"Suddenly, Krishna spotted Maya, an Asura, attempting to escape from Takshaka's abode. Agni, driven by Vayu, pursued Maya with the intent to consume him. Maya sought protection from Arjuna, who reassured him and prevented Krishna from harming him. Moved by Arjuna's compassion, Krishna spared Maya, and Agni refrained from burning him.

"Protected by Krishna and Arjuna, Agni continued to burn the Khandava forest for fifteen days. In the end, only six creatures were spared: Aswasena, Maya, and four birds called Sarngakas."

Chapter 37

Maya Sabha

Vaisampayana spoke, his voice resonating with the weight of ancient sagas, as he recounted the tale of Maya Danava's encounter with Arjuna, the mighty son of Kunti, in the presence of the revered Vasudeva.

"Arjuna," Maya said, his demeanor humble yet tinged with the pride of his lineage, "you have saved me from the wrath of Krishna in his fury and from the fiery clutches of Agni himself. Tell me, O son of Kunti, what boon may I grant you in return for your noble deeds?"

Arjuna, his bearing noble and resolute, replied, "Great Asura, your offer alone is a boon in itself. I ask nothing more of you. Go forth and pursue your desires without hindrance. Yet, if you seek to repay me, let your kindness be directed towards Krishna. That will suffice as recompense for my actions."

But Maya, the skilled architect among the Danavas, pressed on, his heart filled with gratitude and a desire to serve. "O bull among men," he said, "I wish to offer my talents in service to you. As a master craftsman, I long to create something worthy of your greatness."

Arjuna, unmoved by personal gain, deferred to Krishna, the master of all creation, to determine the course of action. And Krishna, in his wisdom, commanded Maya to construct a grand palace for Yudhishthira the just, a hall so magnificent that it would stand as a testament to the divine and defy imitation by mortal hands.

Upon hearing Krishna's decree, Maya's heart swelled with joy, and he set about his task with fervor. With his skills honed over countless ages, he fashioned a palace fit for kings and gods alike, a structure that would inspire awe and wonder in all who beheld it.

And so, with Krishna and Arjuna as his guides, Maya erected a palace of unparalleled beauty and splendor, its walls adorned with celestial motifs and its halls resplendent with the craftsmanship of the ages. As he toiled tirelessly, Maya poured his heart and soul into his work, driven by a desire to honor the noble sons of Pandu and their righteous king.

When the palace was finally completed, Krishna and Arjuna presented Maya to Yudhishthira, who received him with the respect befitting a master craftsman. And Maya, humbled by the honor bestowed upon him, regaled the sons of Pandu with tales of his ancient lineage and the feats of his forebears.

With the blessings of Krishna and the sons of Pritha, Maya embarked on his task, laying the foundation for a grand palace that would stand as a beacon of dharma for all time. And as he worked, he offered prayers to the gods and performed propitiatory rites, ensuring that his creation would be blessed with prosperity and good fortune for generations to come.

"Vaisampayana spoke, his words echoing through the halls of time like the resonance of ancient epics, as he recounted the departure of Janardana, the worthy of all worship, from the hallowed grounds of Khandavaprastha.

Janardana, deserving of reverence from every corner of creation, dwelt happily in Khandavaprastha for a time, basking in the respectful love and affection bestowed upon him by the noble sons of Pritha. Yet, one day, a desire stirred within him to depart from Khandavaprastha and visit his father.

With due respect, Janardana bid farewell to Yudhishthira and Pritha, offering obeisance to the feet of his aunt Kunti, his father's sister. Pritha, her heart filled with motherly love, embraced him tenderly, while Janardana approached his sister Subhadra, his eyes glistening with tears of affection.

Subhadra, sweet of speech and gentle of heart, returned his salutations and conveyed her heartfelt wishes to their relatives on their paternal side. With blessings and benedictions, Janardana took his leave, his thoughts turning to Draupadi and Dhaumya.

With due reverence, Janardana paid his respects to Dhaumya and sought Draupadi's permission to depart. Then, accompanied by Partha, he went to his cousins, surrounded by the five brothers, shining like the sun amidst the stars.

Preparations were made for the journey, and Janardana, adorned with ornaments and armed with his celestial weapons, purified himself with a bath and worshiped the gods and Brahmanas with offerings and prayers. With every rite observed and every blessing sought, he prepared to set out.

As he stepped out of the inner chambers, Janardana made offerings to the Brahmanas and sought their blessings, bestowing gifts upon them in gratitude. Then, ascending his golden chariot, adorned with the emblem of Garuda and drawn by his swift horses Saivya and Sugriva, he set forth at an auspicious moment, with Yudhishthira at the reins.

Arjuna, ever loyal and devoted, walked beside the chariot, fanning Janardana with a white chamara, while Bhima and the twins followed closely behind. Thus, with the blessings of his kinsmen, Janardana embarked on his journey, his heart filled with love and gratitude.

Halfway on their journey, Janardana beseeched Yudhishthira to bid him farewell, and with tears of affection, he embraced his beloved cousins and took his leave. Yudhishthira, the just, raised Janardana and bid him farewell, watching as he departed like Indra journeying to Amravati.

With hearts heavy with longing, the Pandavas gazed after Janardana until he disappeared from sight, their minds following him even as he vanished from view. Reluctantly, they returned to their city, their thoughts still lingering on their departed friend.

Meanwhile, Janardana, surrounded by his loyal followers, reached Dwaraka with the speed of Garuda, welcomed by his people with joy and celebration. And as he entered his own city, embraced by his family and loved ones, Janardana's heart swelled with happiness, knowing that he was home once more."

Vaisampayana continued, his voice resonating with the grandeur of ancient tales, as he recounted the words of Maya Danava to Arjuna, the foremost of warriors, before his departure.

'My leave I take now,' Maya addressed Arjuna with respect, 'but fear not, for I shall return swiftly. In the northern realms, near the towering peak of Kailasa, amidst the Mainaka mountains, lies a treasure trove of exquisite vanda—rough materials crafted from jewels and gems. Once, during a Danava sacrifice by the banks of the Vindu lake, I gathered this wealth, which now rests within the mansion of Vrishaparva, steadfast in its truth. Should it still exist, I shall retrieve it and return to you, O Bharata. With this bounty, I shall commence the construction of the wondrous palace of the Pandavas, adorned with every imaginable gem and renowned throughout the world.'

Maya's words stirred visions of distant lands, of peaks and lakes, of treasures hidden and waiting to be unearthed. He continued, 'Near the northern slopes of Kailasa, amidst the jeweled heights of Hiranya-sringa, lies the tranquil lake of Vindu. Once, it was graced by the presence of King Bhagiratha, who sought the goddess Ganga, now called Bhagirathee in his honor. Indra, the lord of the gods, performed countless sacrifices there, adorning the banks with gem-studded sacrificial stakes and golden altars. Mahadeva himself resides nearby, revered by thousands of celestial beings. It is a place where gods and sages perform their rites, where virtue and piety flourish.'

With these words, Maya painted a picture of divine splendor, of a realm where gods and mortals mingled, where the very air was suffused with sanctity. He spoke of treasures hidden beneath the waves, of a club and a conch-shell awaiting their rightful owners. And so, guided by Maya's wisdom, Arjuna awaited the return of these treasures, knowing they would adorn the palace of the Pandavas in all its glory.

With his departure, Maya journeyed to the north-east, his heart set on reclaiming the wealth guarded by Yakshas and Rakshasas. And in due time, he returned, bearing the club and the conch-shell, along with a wealth of crystalline articles that once belonged to King Vrishaparva.

With these treasures in hand, Maya set to work, constructing a palace fit for kings, a masterpiece of celestial craftsmanship. Its golden walls shimmered in the sunlight, its archways adorned with precious jewels. Within its halls, a peerless tank sparkled with lotuses of dark-colored gems, while artificial woods exuded a fragrant aroma, pleasing to the senses.

In just fourteen months, Maya's vision took shape, and the palace stood complete, a testament to his skill and ingenuity. With pride, he reported its completion to Yudhishthira, knowing that it would serve as a beacon of splendor for generations to come."

Chapter 38

NARADA RISHI SPEAKS

Vaisampayana spoke: Then Yudhishthira, the indomitable king, strode into the grand palace. He had first ensured that ten thousand Brahmanas were fed on sumptuous fare of milk and rice, enriched with clarified butter, honey, fruits, roots, pork, and venison. The Brahmanas, hailing from lands far and wide, were delighted with a feast fit for the gods—food seasoned with sesame, vegetables called jibanti, and rice soaked in butter. They were further gratified with endless preparations of meat, countless viands fit to be sucked, and a plethora of drinks. To each Brahmana, he gifted a thousand kine, and their voices, raised in blessing, echoed to the very heavens: "What an auspicious day!"

With the gods worshipped through music and rare perfumes, Yudhishthira, the son of Dharma, entered the palatial hall. Athletes, mimes, prize-fighters, bards, and encomiasts showcased their talents, striving to please the illustrious king. Amidst the celebrations, Yudhishthira and his brothers reveled in the splendor of the palace, akin to Indra in his celestial abode.

Seated in that magnificent hall were not just the Pandavas, but also revered Rishis and kings from many realms: Asita, Devala, Satya, Sarpamali, Mahasira; Arvavasu, Sumitra, Maitreya, Sunaka, and Vali; Vaka, Dalvya, Sthulasira, Krishna-Dwaipayana, and Suka; Sumanta, Jaimini, Paila, and Vyasa's own disciples, including ourselves; Tittiri, Yajanavalkya, and Lomaharshana with his son; Apsuhomya, Dhaumya, Animandavya; and Kausika; Damoshnisha and Traivali, Parnada, and Varayanuka, Maunjayana, Vayubhaksha, Parasarya, and Sarika; Valivaka, Silivaka, Satyapala, and Krita-srama; Jatukarna, Sikhavat, Alamva, and Parijataka; the exalted Parvata, and the great Muni Markandeya; Pavitrapani, Savarna, Bhaluki, and Galava. Janghabandhu, Raibhya, Kopavega, and Bhrigu; Harivabhru, Kaundinya, Vabhrumali, and Sanatana; Kakshivat, Ashija, Nachiketa, Aushija, Gautama; Painga, Varaha, Sunaka, and Sandilya of great ascetic merit; Kukkura, Venujangha, Kalapa, and Katha—all these virtuous and learned sages, masters of Vedas and Vedangas, conversant in morality and pure conduct, graced Yudhishthira with their presence and gladdened him with their sacred discourses.

And there too were mighty Kshatriyas: Mujaketu, Vivarddhana, Sangramjit, Durmukha, the powerful Ugrasena; Kakshasena, lord of the Earth, Kshemaka the invincible; Kamatha, king of Kamvoja, and the fearsome Kampana who made the Yavanas tremble like the thunderbolt-wielding god terrifies the Asuras; Jatasura, king of the Madrakas, Kunti, Pulinda king of the Kiratas, and the kings of Anga and Vanga, and Pandrya, king of Udhara, and Andhaka; Sumitra, Saivya the slayer of foes; Sumanas, king of the Kiratas, and Chanur, king of the Yavanas; Devarata, Bhoja, Bhimaratha, Srutayudha, king of Kalinga, Jayasena, king of Magadha; and Sukarman, Chekitana,

Puru the foe-slayer; Ketumata, Vasudana, Vaideha, Kritakshana; Sudharman, Aniruddha, Srutayu of great strength; invincible Anuparaja, handsome Karmajit; Sisupala with his son, king of Karusha; and the valiant youths of the Vrishni race, all equal in beauty to the celestials: Ahuka, Viprithu, Sada, Sarana, Akrura, Kritavarman, and Satyaka, son of Sini; and Bhismaka, Ankriti, and the mighty Dyumatsena, those chiefs of bowmen, the Kaikeyas and Yajnasena of the Somaka race—all these Kshatriyas, strong and wealthy, honored Yudhishthira, son of Kunti, in that grand hall, eager to bring him joy. Princes too, trained under Arjuna, dressed in deer-skins, and mighty Vrishnis: Pradyumna, Samva, Yuyudhana, Sudharman, Aniruddha, Saivya—all gathered to honor Yudhishthira, the lord of the Earth.

And there was Tumvuru, the friend of Dhananjaya, and Gandharva Chittasena with his ministers, alongside other Gandharvas and Apsaras, skilled in music and dance, who sang celestial tunes in captivating voices. These divine beings delighted the sons of Pandu and the Rishis in that grand hall. Amidst such celestial splendor and mighty gatherings, Yudhishthira, steadfast in his vows and devoted to truth, was revered like Brahma himself, surrounded by the heavenly hosts.

Vaisampayana spoke: "As the noble Pandavas sat in their grand hall, surrounded by the chief Gandharvas, there entered the celestial Rishi Narada, a sage of immeasurable wisdom and power. Narada, master of the Vedas and Upanishads, revered by the gods and learned in the ancient histories and Puranas, stood before them. He knew the truths of moral science and the intricacies of logic, and was adept in the six Angas: pronunciation, grammar, prosody, explanation of terms, religious rites, and astronomy. His mind, sharp and resolute, could reconcile contradictions and apply principles to specific cases with unmatched clarity. A paragon of intelligence, with an infallible memory, he possessed a mastery over every branch of learning and was skilled in the arts of both Sankhya and Yoga philosophies.

Accompanied by the luminous Parijata, Raivata, Saumya, and Sumukha, the Rishi arrived with the speed of thought, his presence filling the hall with joy. Paying homage to Yudhishthira, the Pandavas' eldest, Narada blessed him and wished him victory. Yudhishthira, knowledgeable in the rules of duty, rose with his brothers, greeted the sage with humility, and offered him a seat with due ceremony. He bestowed upon Narada cows, arghya offerings, and precious gems, showing his reverence with a full heart. Pleased by this reception, Narada, worshipped by the Pandavas and other great Rishis, addressed Yudhishthira with wisdom concerning religion, wealth, pleasure, and salvation.

"Narada said: 'Do you, O chief of men, spend your wealth on rightful causes? Does your heart find joy in virtue, and do you relish the pleasures of life without being overwhelmed by them? Are you steadfast in the noble conduct of your ancestors towards all subjects, be they good, indifferent, or bad? Do you never compromise religion for wealth, or both for the sake of fleeting pleasures? Devoted to the welfare of all, do you judiciously balance your time among religion, wealth, pleasure, and salvation?

Are you vigilant in the six attributes of kingship: eloquence, resourcefulness, intelligence in dealing with foes, memory, and political acumen? Do you use the seven means: sowing dissension, chastisement, conciliation, gifts, incantations, medicine, and magic? Do you assess your strength and weaknesses, and that of your enemies, with keen insight? Is your kingdom fortified with treasure, food, arms, water, engineers, and archers, ready against any threat?

Do you have wise ministers skilled in their duties, loyal to you, and uncorrupted? Are your spies, known only to you, watching friends, foes, and strangers alike? Do you act swiftly on your resolutions, ensuring your plans remain secret until accomplished? Are your officers of state, governors, generals, priests, physicians, and astrologers dedicated and capable? Is your commander brave, intelligent, patient, well-born, and devoted to you? Do you reward those who serve you well and support the families of those who have died for your cause?

Are you fair and accessible to all your subjects, treating them as a father would his children? Do you take counsel with wise advisors, avoiding the ills of procrastination and negligence? Are your actions aligned with the eternal principles of the Vedas and the practices of your forebears? Do you protect and cherish the blind, the dumb, the lame, the deformed, the friendless, and the homeless ascetics?

Narada continued, 'A king, who governs with justice and wisdom, securing the prosperity and happiness of his people, ensures his kingdom's stability and his own fame. By adhering to these principles, he gains not only this world but also the heavenly realms.'

Vaisampayana spoke, "At the conclusion of Narada's words, King Yudhishthira the Just worshipped him duly. Commanded by him, the monarch began to reply succinctly to the questions the Rishi had posed.

'Yudhishthira said, "O holy one, the truths of religion and morality you have elucidated are just and proper. As for myself, I strive to observe those ordinances to the best of my power. Indeed, the acts that were properly performed by monarchs of yore are to be regarded as bearing proper fruit, and undertaken from solid reasons for the attainment of proper objects. O master, we desire to walk in the virtuous path of those rulers who had their souls under complete control."

Vaisampayana continued, "Yudhishthira, son of Pandu, possessed of great glory, received with reverence the words of Narada. Having answered the Rishi thus, he reflected for a moment. Perceiving a proper opportunity, the monarch, seated beside the Rishi, asked Narada, sitting at his ease and capable of traversing every world at will, in the presence of that assembly of kings, 'Possessed of the speed of mind, you wander over various and many worlds created in days of yore by Brahma, beholding everything. Tell me, if you have ever beheld an assembly room like mine, or superior to it!' Hearing these words of Yudhishthira the Just, Narada smilingly answered the son of Pandu in these sweet accents:

'Narada said, "O child, O king, I have neither seen nor heard of any assembly room built of gems and precious stones like this of yours, O Bharata. However, I shall describe unto you the rooms of the King of the Departed (Yama), of Varuna (Neptune) of great intelligence, of Indra, the King of Gods, and also of him who has his home in Kailasha (Kuvera). I shall also describe unto you the celestial Sabha of Brahma that dispels every kind of uneasiness. All these assembly rooms exhibit in their structure both celestial and human designs and present every kind of form that exists in the universe. They are ever worshipped by the gods and the Pitris, the Sadhyas, by ascetics offering sacrifices with souls under complete command, by peaceful Munis engaged without intermission in Vedic sacrifices with presents to Brahmanas. I shall describe all these to you if you, O bull of the Bharata race, have any inclination to listen to me!"

Vaisampayana continued, "Thus addressed by Narada, the high-souled King Yudhishthira the Just, with his brothers and all those foremost of Brahmanas seated around him, joined his hands in entreaty. The monarch then asked Narada, 'Describe unto us all those assembly rooms. We desire to listen to you. O Brahmana, what are the articles with which each of the Sabhas are made of? What is the area of each, and what is the length and breadth of each? Who waits upon the Grandsire in that assembly room? And who also upon Vasava, the Lord of the celestials, and upon Yama, the son of

Vivaswana? Who waits upon Varuna and upon Kuvera in their respective assembly rooms? O Brahmana Rishi, tell us all about these. We all together desire to hear you describe them. Indeed, our curiosity is great.' Thus addressed by the son of Pandu, Narada replied,

'Narada said, "O monarch, hear ye all about those celestial assembly rooms one after another."

Vaisampayana continued, "As Narada began to weave his tale, the air grew thick with ancient secrets, and the assembly leaned in, their hearts beating with the anticipation of wonders untold. The stars themselves seemed to pause in their courses to listen to the celestial stories that would unfold."

Narada spoke, "The celestial assembly room of Sakra shines with a light unmatched. He has earned it through the fruit of his own deeds. Possessed of the splendor of the sun, it was constructed by Sakra himself, O scion of the Kuru race. Capable of traveling anywhere at will, this celestial hall measures a full one hundred and fifty yojanas in length, a hundred yojanas in breadth, and five yojanas in height. Dispelling the frailties of age, grief, fatigue, and fear, it is auspicious and bestows good fortune, furnished with rooms and seats, and adorned with celestial trees, making it delightful beyond measure.

There, in that assembly room, O son of Pritha, sits the Lord of the Celestials on an excellent throne, with his wife Sachi, endowed with beauty and affluence. Assuming an indescribable form, with a crown upon his head and bright bracelets on his arms, attired in robes of purest white and decked with floral wreaths of many hues, he sits surrounded by beauty, fame, and glory. The illustrious deity of a hundred sacrifices is daily attended, O monarch, in that assembly by the Marutas, each leading the life of a householder in the bosom of his family.

The Siddhyas, celestial Rishis, the Sadhyas, the gods, and Marutas, all of brilliant complexion and adorned with golden garlands, always wait upon and worship the illustrious chief of the immortals, that mighty represser of all foes. O son of Pritha, the celestial Rishis, pure of soul, with sins washed off and resplendent as fire, endowed with energy and free from sorrow and anxiety, and all performers of the Soma sacrifice, also attend and worship Indra.

Among them are Parasara and Parvata, Savarni and Galava; Sankha, the Muni Gaursiras, Durvasa, Krodhana, Swena, the Muni Dhirghatamas; Pavitrapani, Savarni, Yajnavalkya, Bhaluki; Udyalaka, Swetaketu, Tandya, and Bhandayani; Havishmat, Garishta, King Harischandra; Hridya, Udarshandilya, Parasarya, Krishivala; Vataskandha, Visakha, Vidhatas, and Kala. Karaladanta, Tastri, Vishwakarman, and Tumuru; and other Rishis, some born of women, others subsisting on air, and others yet living on fire—these all worship Indra, the wielder of the thunderbolt, the lord of all worlds.

Sahadeva, Sunitha, Valmiki of great ascetic merit; Samika of truthful speech, Prachetas ever fulfilling their promises, Medhatithi, Vamadeva, Pulastya, Pulaha, and Kratu; Maruta and Marichi, Sthanu of great ascetic merit; Kakshivat, Gautama, Tarkhya, the Muni Vaishwanara; the Muni Kalakavrikhiya, Asravya, Hiranmaya, Samvartta, Dehavya, Viswaksena of great energy; Kanwa, Katyayana, Gargya, Kaushika—all are present there along with the celestial waters and plants; faith, intelligence, the goddess of learning, wealth, religion, pleasure; lightning, O son of Pandu; the rain-charged clouds, the winds, and all the loud-sounding forces of heaven; the eastern point, the twenty-seven fires conveying the sacrificial butter, Agni and Soma, the fire of Indra, Mitra, Savitri, Aryaman; Bhaga, Viswa, the Sadhyas, the preceptor (Vrihaspati), and also Sukra; Vishwavasu, Chitrasena, Sumanas, and Taruna; the Sacrifices, the gifts to Brahmanas, the planets, and the stars, O Bharata, and the mantras uttered in sacrifices—all these are present there.

And, O King, many Apsaras and Gandharvas, through various dances and music, both instrumental and vocal, the practice of auspicious rites, and feats of skill, gratify the lord of the celestials—Satakratu—the illustrious slayer of Vala and Vritra. Besides these, many other Brahmanas and royal and celestial Rishis, all resplendent as fire, decked in floral wreaths and ornaments, frequently come to and leave that assembly, riding on celestial cars of various kinds. Vrihaspati and Sukra are present there on all occasions. These and many other illustrious ascetics of rigid vows, and Bhrigu and the seven Rishis, equal, O king, unto Brahma himself, come to and leave that assembly house, riding on cars as beautiful as the car of Soma, and themselves looking as bright therein as Soma himself.

This, O mighty-armed monarch, is the assembly house called Pushkaramalini, of Indra of a hundred sacrifices that I have seen. Listen now to the account of Yama's assembly house.

Narada spoke, "O Yudhishthira, I shall now describe the assembly house of Yama, the son of Vivaswat, built by Viswakarma. Listen well, O son of Pritha. Bright as burnished gold, that hall, O monarch, spans an area far greater than a hundred yojanas. Possessed of the sun's brilliance, it provides all one could desire. Neither overly cool nor excessively warm, it delights the heart. In that assembly house, there is no grief, no weakness of age, neither hunger nor thirst. No evil feelings find a place there; nothing disagreeable exists. Every object of desire, celestial or human, is present in that mansion.

All manner of enjoyable articles, and sweet, juicy, agreeable, and delicious edibles, both licked and sucked, are found there in abundance, O chastiser of enemies. The floral wreaths in that mansion carry the most delightful fragrances, and the trees around it bear fruits desired by all. There are both cold and hot waters, sweet and agreeable. In that mansion, many royal sages of great sanctity and

Brahmana sages of great purity cheerfully wait upon, and worship Yama, the son of Vivaswat.

Yayati, Nahusha, Puru, Mandhatri, Somaka, Nriga; the royal sage Trasadasyu, Kritavirya, Sautasravas; Arishtanemi, Siddha, Kritavega, Kriti, Nimi, Pratarddana, Sivi, Matsya, Prithulaksha, Vrihadratha, Vartta, Marutta, Kusika, Sankasya, Sankriti, Dhruva, Chaturaswa, Sadaswormi, and King Kartavirya; Bharata and Suratha, Sunitha, Nisatha, Nala, Divodasa, and Sumanas, Amvarisha, Bhagiratha; Vysawa, Vadhraswa, Prithuvega, Prithusravas, Prishadaswa, Vasumanas, Kshupa, and Sumahavala, Vrishadgu, and Vrishasena, Purukutsa, Dhwajin, and Rathin; Arshtisena, Dwilipa, and the high-souled Ushinara; Ausinari, Pundarika, Saryati, Sarava, and Suchi; Anga, Rishta, Vena, Dushmanta, Srinjaya, and Jaya; Bhangasuri, Sunitha, and Nishada, and Bahinara; Karandhama, Valhika, Sudymna, and the mighty Madhu; Aila and the mighty king of earth, Maruta; Kapota, Trinaka, Shadeva, and Arjuna also. Vysawa; Saswa and Krishaswa, and king Sasavindu; Rama, the son of Dasaratha, and Lakshmana, and Pratarddana; Alarka, and Kakshasena, Gaya, and Gauraswa; Rama, the son of Jamadagnya, Nabhaga, and Sagara; Bhuridyumna and Mahaswa, Prithaswa, and Janaka; king Vainya, Varisena, Purujit, and Janamejaya; Brahmadatta, and Trigarta, and king Uparichara; Indradyumna, Bhimajanu, Gauraprishta, Nala, Gaya; Padma and Machukunda, Bhuridyumna, Prasenajit; Aristanemi, Sudymna, Prithulauswa, and Ashtaka; a hundred kings of the Matsya race, a hundred of the Vipa, and a hundred of the Haya races; a hundred kings named Dhritarashtra, eighty kings named Janamejaya; a hundred monarchs called Brahmadatta, and a hundred kings named Iri; more than two hundred Bhishmas, and a hundred Bhimas; a hundred Prativindhyas, a hundred Nagas, and a hundred Palasas, and a hundred named Kasa and Kusa; that king of kings, Santanu, and thy father, Pandu, Usangava, Sata-ratha, Devaraja, Jayadratha; the intelligent royal sage Vrishadarva with his ministers;

and a thousand other kings known by the name of Sasa-vindu, who have died, having performed many grand horse-sacrifices with large presents to the Brahmanas—these holy royal sages of grand achievements and great knowledge of the Sastras wait upon and worship the son of Vivaswat in that assembly house.

Agastya and Matanga, Kala, and Mrityu (Death), performers of sacrifices, the Siddhas, and many Yogins; the Pitris (belonging to the classes called Agniswattas, Fenapa, Ushampa, Swadhavat, and Verhishada), as well as those with forms; the wheel of time, and the illustrious conveyer of sacrificial butter; all sinners among humans, and those who died during the winter solstice; Yama's officers who count the allotted days of everyone; the Singsapa, Palasa, Kasa, and Kusa trees and plants in their embodied forms—all, O king, wait upon and worship the god of justice in his assembly house. These and many others are present in the Sabha of the king of the Pitris (manes). Their numbers are so vast that I am incapable of describing them all by name or deed.

O son of Pritha, the delightful assembly house, moving everywhere at the will of its owner, is vast and resplendent with its own effulgence. Built by Viswakarma after a long course of ascetic penances, it stands glorified in all its beauty. Sannyasis of severe ascetic penance, excellent vows, and truthful speech, peaceful and pure and sanctified by holy deeds, of shining bodies and attired in spotless robes, decked with bracelets and floral garlands, with earrings of burnished gold, and adorned with their own holy acts as with the marks of their order (painted over their bodies), constantly visit that Sabha (Assembly). Many illustrious Gandharvas and Apsaras fill every part of that mansion with music, both instrumental and vocal, and with sounds of laughter and dance. O son of Pritha, excellent perfumes, sweet sounds, and garlands of celestial flowers always contribute to making that mansion supremely blessed. Hundreds of thousands of virtuous persons of celestial beauty and great wisdom always wait upon and worship the illustrious Yama, the lord of created beings, in that assembly house. Such, O monarch, is the Sabha of the illustrious king of the Pitris!

I shall now describe to you the assembly house of Varuna, also called Pushkaramalini!

Narada spoke, "O Yudhishthira, the celestial Sabha of Varuna is unparalleled in splendor. Its dimensions rival that of Yama's, with walls and arches of pure white. This magnificent hall, built by Viswakarma, the celestial architect, rests within the waters. It is surrounded by celestial trees made of gems and jewels, yielding exquisite fruits and flowers. Many plants, heavy with blossoms of blue, yellow, black, darkish, white, and red, form excellent bowers around it. Within these bowers, hundreds and thousands of variegated birds of diverse species pour forth their melodies.

The atmosphere of this mansion is extremely delightful, neither cold nor hot. Owned by Varuna, that delightful assembly house of pure white consists of many rooms and is furnished with numerous seats. Varuna sits there, attired in celestial robes, decked in celestial ornaments and jewels, with his queen, adorned with celestial scents and besmeared with pastes of celestial fragrance. The Adityas wait upon and worship the illustrious Varuna, the lord of the waters.

Vasuki and Takshaka, and the Naga called Airavana; Krishna and Lohita; Padma and Chitra endowed with great energy; the Nagas Kamvala and Aswatara; Dhritarashtra and Valahaka; Matimat and Kundadhara and Karkotaka and Dhananjaya; Panimat and the mighty Kundaka; Prahlada and Mushikada, and Janamejaya, all with auspicious marks and mandalas and extended hoods, wait upon and worship Varuna without anxiety of any kind.

And, O king, Vali, the son of Virochana, and Naraka, the subjugator of the Earth; Sanghraha and Viprachitti, and those Danavas called

Kalakanja; Suhanu, Durmukha, Sankha, Sumanas, and Sumati; Ghatodara, Mahaparswa, Karthana, Pithara, Viswarupa, Swarupa, Virupa, Mahasiras; Dasagriva, Vali, Meghavasas, Dasavara; Tittiva, Vitabhuta, Sanghrada, Indratapana—these Daityas and Danavas, all bedecked with ear-rings, floral wreaths, crowns, and attired in celestial robes, blessed with boons, possessed of great bravery, enjoying immortality, and of excellent conduct and vows, wait upon and worship in that mansion the illustrious Varuna, the deity bearing the noose as his weapon.

O king, there are also the four oceans, the river Bhagirathee, the Kalindi, the Vidisa, the Venwa, the Narmada of rapid current; the Vipasa, the Satadu, the Chandrabhaga, the Saraswati; the Iravati, the Vitasta, the Sindhu, the Devanadi; the Godavari, the Krishnavenwa and that queen of rivers, the Kaveri; the Kimpuna, the Visalya and the river Vaitarani; the Tritiya, the Jeshthila, and the great Sone; the Charmanwati, the great river Parnasa; the Sarayu, the Varavatya, the queen of rivers, the Langali, the Karatoya, the Atreyi, the red Mahanada, the Laghanti, the Gomati, the Sandhya, and the Trisrotasi—these and other rivers, sacred and world-renowned places of pilgrimage, as well as other rivers, sacred waters, lakes, wells, springs, and tanks, in their personified forms, wait upon and worship Varuna.

The points of the heavens, the Earth, and all the Mountains, as well as every species of aquatic animal, worship Varuna. Various tribes of Gandharvas and Apsaras, devoted to music, both vocal and instrumental, wait upon Varuna, singing eulogistic hymns unto him. All those mountains noted for their delightfulness and richness in jewels wait in their personified forms in that Sabha, enjoying sweet converse with one another. The chief minister of Varuna, Sunabha by name, surrounded by his sons and grandsons, also attends upon his master, along with the personified form of a sacred water called 'Go.' These all, in their personified forms, worship the deity. O bull of the Bharata race, such is the assembly room of Varuna seen by me before in the course of my wanderings.

Listen now to the account I give of the assembly room of Kuvera."

Narada spoke with a voice echoing through the grand halls, "O Yudhishthira, the celestial Sabha of Vaisravana is unparalleled in splendor. Possessed of great grandeur, the assembly house of Vaisravana spans a hundred yojanas in length and seventy in breadth. This colossal structure was erected by Vaisravana himself, harnessing his ascetic power. Its magnificence rivals the peaks of Kailasa, and it outshines even the brilliance of the Moon.

Supported by the mystical Guhyakas, the mansion appears to hover in the firmament. Its celestial make, adorned with high chambers of gold, renders it extremely handsome. The air is redolent with celestial perfumes, and the halls are variegated with countless costly jewels. Like the peaks of a white cloud mass, it seems to float, painted with celestial gold and streaked with lightning.

Within that mansion, seated on an excellent seat bright as the sun, covered with celestial carpets and furnished with a handsome footstool, sits King Vaisravana. His agreeable person is attired in excellent robes and adorned with costly ornaments and ear-rings of great brilliance, surrounded by his thousand wives. Delicious and cooling breezes, murmuring through forests of tall Mandaras and bearing the fragrance of extensive jasmine plantations, lotuses on the bosom of the river Alaka, and the Nandana-gardens, always minister to the pleasure of the King of the Yakshas.

There, the deities with the Gandharvas, surrounded by various tribes of Apsaras, sing in chorus notes of celestial sweetness. Misrakesi, Rambha, Chitrasena, Suchismita, Charunetra, Gritachi, Menaka, Punjikasthala, Viswachi, Sahajanya, Pramlocha, Urvasi, Ira, Varga, Sauraveyi, Samichi, Vududa, and Lata—these and a thousand other

Apsaras and Gandharvas, all well-skilled in music and dance, attend upon Kuvera, the lord of treasures.

The mansion, always filled with the notes of instrumental and vocal music, as well as the sounds of dance from various tribes of Gandharvas and Apsaras, has become extremely charming and delicious. The Gandharvas called Kinnaras, and others called Naras, and Manibhadra, Dhanada, Swetabhadra, Guhyaka; Kaseraka, Gandakandu, the mighty Pradyota; Kustumvuru, Pisacha, Gajakarna, Visalaka, Varaha-Karna, Tamraushtica, Falkaksha, Falodaka; Hansachuda, Sikhavarta, Vibhishana, Pushpanana, Pingalaka, Sonitoda, Pravalaka; Vrikshavaspa-niketa, and Chiravasas—all these and many other Yakshas, by hundreds and thousands, always wait upon Kuvera.

The goddess Lakshmi, the embodiment of fortune, always stays there, along with Kuvera's son, Nalakuvera. Myself and many others like me often repair thither. Many Brahmana Rishis and celestial Rishis also visit often. Many Rakshasas and Gandharvas, beyond those named, wait upon and worship the illustrious lord of all treasures.

O tiger among kings, the illustrious husband of Uma and lord of created things, the three-eyed Mahadeva, the wielder of the trident and slayer of the Asura called Bhaga-netra, the mighty god with the fierce bow, surrounded by multitudes of spirits in their hundreds and thousands—some dwarfish, some fierce-visaged, some hunch-backed, some with blood-red eyes, some with frightful yells, some feeding upon fat and flesh, and some terrible to behold—all armed with various weapons and endowed with the speed of wind, with the goddess Parvati ever cheerful and untiring, always wait upon their friend Kuvera, the lord of treasures.

Hundreds of Gandharva chiefs, with cheerful hearts and attired in their respective robes—Viswavasu, Haha, Huhu; Tumvuru, Parvatta,

Sailusha; Chitrasena skilled in music, and also Chitraratha—these and innumerable Gandharvas worship the lord of treasures. Chakradhaman, the chief of the Vidyadharas, with his followers, waits upon the lord of treasures. Kinnaras by hundreds, innumerable kings with Bhagadatta as their chief, Druma, the chief of the Kimpurushas, Mahendra, the chief of the Rakshasas, and Gandhamadana accompanied by many Yakshas, Gandharvas, and Rakshasas, all wait upon the lord of treasures. The virtuous Vibhishana also worships his elder brother, the lord Kuvera.

The mountains Himavat, Paripatra, Vindhya, Kailasa, Mandara, Malaya, Durdura, Mahendra, Gandhamadana, Indrakila, Sunava, and the Eastern and Western hills, along with Meru, in their personified forms, all wait upon and worship the illustrious lord of treasures. The illustrious Nandiswaras, Mahakala, and many spirits with arrowy ears and sharp-pointed mouths—Kaksha, Kuthimukha, Danti, and Vijaya of great ascetic merit, and the mighty white bull of Siva roaring deep—all wait in that mansion. Many other Rakshasas and Pisachas also worship Kuvera in that assembly house.

Kuvera, the son of Pulastya, used to worship in all modes and sit, with permission obtained, beside the god of gods, Siva, the creator of the three worlds, that supreme Deity surrounded by his attendants. One day, the exalted Bhava (Siva) made friendship with Kuvera. From that time, O king, Mahadeva always sits in the mansion of his friend, the lord of treasures. Those best of all jewels, those princes of all gems in the three worlds—Sankha and Padma in their personified forms, accompanied by all the jewels of the earth—worship Kuvera.

"This delightful assembly house of Kuvera that I have seen, attached to the firmament and capable of moving along it, is such, O king. Listen now to the Sabha I describe unto thee, belonging to Brahma the Grandsire."

Narada began, his voice a resonant melody that filled the air with ancient wisdom, "Listen to me, O child, as I tell thee of the assembly house of the Grandsire, Brahma, a place so wondrous that none can capture its essence in mere words. In the golden age, the Krita Yuga, the exalted deity Aditya, the Sun, descended from the heavens to the realm of men. Having beheld the celestial assembly house of Brahma, the Self-created, Aditya wandered the Earth in human guise, eager to witness the marvels of this world.

It was then, O son of Pandu, that the god of day shared with me, O bull of the Bharata race, the glories of Brahma's celestial Sabha. Immeasurable, immaterial, and indescribable in form and shape, it delights the heart of every creature with its splendor. Captivated by his account, I yearned to behold it myself and thus implored Aditya, 'O exalted one, guide me to the sacred Sabha of the Grandsire. By what penances or rituals may I earn this vision?'

The deity of a thousand rays, Surya, answered, 'Observe the Brahma vow for a thousand years, with mind absorbed in meditation.' Obediently, I repaired to the breast of the Himavat and commenced the great vow. After its completion, the tireless, radiant Surya led me to Brahma's Sabha.

O king, words cannot encapsulate that Sabha. It changes form within a moment, defying description. Dimensions and shape are beyond comprehension. Ever contributing to the happiness of its occupants, it is neither cold nor warm. Hunger and thirst vanish upon entry. It seems composed of brilliant gems, unsupported by columns, eternal and undeteriorating. Self-effulgent, it surpasses the moon, sun, and fire in splendor, its blaze chastising even the creator of day.

There, in that mansion, dwells the Supreme Deity, the Grandsire Brahma, creator of all, surrounded by creations born of his illusion. With him are Daksha, Prachetas, Pulaha, Marichi, the master Kasyapa, Bhrigu, Atri, Vasistha, Gautama, Angiras, Pulastya, Kratu,

Prahlada, Kardama, and other Prajapatis. The personified forms of Intelligence, Space, Knowledge, Air, Heat, Water, Earth, Sound, Touch, Form, Taste, Scent; Nature, the Modes of Nature, and the elemental causes all stand beside Brahma.

Great Rishis like Agastya, Markandeya, Jamadagni, Bharadwaja, Samvarta, Chyavana, Durvasa, Rishyasringa, and the illustrious Sanatkumara; Asita, Devala, Jaigishavya; Rishava, Ajitasatru, Mani of great energy; the Science of healing; the moon with stars, Aditya with rays, winds, Sacrifices, declarations, and vital principles—all these personified beings attend Brahma. Wealth, Religion, Desire, Joy, Aversion, Asceticism, Tranquillity; the twenty tribes of Gandharvas and Apsaras, and their seven other tribes, the Lokapalas, Sukra, Vrihaspati, Vudha, Angaraka, Sani, Rahu, and other planets; Mantras of the Sama Veda, the Adityas with Indra, Agnis, Marutas, Viswakarman, Vasus, Pitris, and all kinds of sacrificial libations—all reside there in the Sabha.

The goddesses, the Adityas, Vasus, Rudras, Marutas, Aswins, Viswadevas, Sadhyas, and Pitris; Rakshasas, Pisachas, Danavas, Guhyakas; Nagas, Birds, and various animals; all mobile and immobile beings worship the Grandsire. Purandara, Varuna, Kuvera, Yama, and Mahadeva with Uma frequently visit, as does Mahasena, Kartikeya. Narayana and celestial Rishis, Valakhillyas, beings born of females and not, all exist within the realms of this divine assembly.

Eighty thousand Rishis with vital seed drawn up and fifty thousand Rishis with sons are seen there. The Supreme Deity, Brahma, the Self-created of immeasurable intelligence and glory, honors and gratifies gods, Daityas, Nagas, Brahmanas, Yakshas, Birds, Kaleyas, Gandharvas, Apsaras, and all beings. The mansion, ever bustling with visitors, radiates with Brahma's divine possessions, unmatched in grace.

Narada concluded with a reverent bow, "As this Sabha of yours is unrivalled in the world of men, so is Brahma's Sabha, a sight beyond mortal comprehension, unmatched in all the worlds."

Yudhishthira, the king of kings, leaned forward, eyes gleaming with the fervor of a seeker of truth. "O thou foremost of eloquent men," he began, "as thou hast described the different Sabhas unto me, it appears that almost all the monarchs of the earth dwell in the Sabha of Yama. The Nagas, the principal Daityas, and the rivers and oceans reside in the Sabha of Varuna. The Yakshas, the Guhyakas, the Rakshasas, the Gandharvas, the Apsaras, and the deity Yama are in the Sabha of the lord of treasures. And in the Sabha of the Grandsire are gathered all the great Rishis, all the gods, and all branches of learning. Regarding the Sabha of Sakra, you have named all the gods, the Gandharvas, and various Rishis. But, O great Muni, only one king is named, the royal Rishi Harischandra. What deed of valor or ascetic penance with steady vows made him the equal of Indra? And how did you meet my father, the exalted Pandu, now a guest in the realm of the Pitris? Did he share any words with you? I am eager to hear."

Narada, the great sage, nodded solemnly, his eyes reflecting the wisdom of countless ages. "O king of kings, I shall tell thee of Harischandra, his high excellence, and his deeds that rival those of the gods. Harischandra was a mighty emperor, lord of all the kings of the earth. Mounted alone upon a chariot adorned with gold, he brought the entire earth with her seven islands under his dominion through the prowess of his weapons. Having subjugated the whole earth, he made preparations for the grand sacrifice known as the Rajasuya.

At his command, all the kings of the earth brought wealth to that sacrifice. They distributed food and gifts to the Brahmanas. Harischandra, generous beyond measure, gave away wealth five times what each had solicited. At the conclusion of the sacrifice, he bestowed large presents upon the Brahmanas, who, satiated with food, enjoyable articles, and heaps of jewels, proclaimed, 'King Harischandra is superior to all kings in energy and renown.' It was this boundless generosity and virtue that made Harischandra shine more brightly than thousands of other kings.

Having completed his great sacrifice, Harischandra ascended to the sovereignty of the earth, resplendent on his throne. Those monarchs who perform the Rajasuya sacrifice, and those who die without turning their backs on the battlefield, attain the mansion of Indra and live joyfully in his company. Those who surrender their bodies after severe ascetic penances also reach this region and shine there for ages.

Your father, Pandu, beholding the good fortune of Harischandra, has told me something for you. Knowing that I was coming to the world of men, he bowed to me and said, 'Tell Yudhishthira, O Rishi, that he can subjugate the whole earth with his brothers' support and perform the grand Rajasuya sacrifice. He is my son; if he accomplishes this, I may, like Harischandra, soon reach Indra's region and enjoy endless joy in his Sabha.' I promised him, 'O King, I shall convey your message to your son if I visit the world of men.' And now, I have fulfilled my promise.

O son of Pandu, accomplish your father's desires. Perform the Rajasuya sacrifice, and you will ascend to the same exalted region as Indra, accompanied by your deceased ancestors. But know, O king, that this great sacrifice is fraught with obstacles. A class of Rakshasas called Brahma Rakshasas seek to obstruct all sacrifices, always searching for loopholes. A slight misstep could plunge the earth into chaos. Reflect upon this, O king, and do what is for thy good. Be vigilant in protecting your subjects and grow in prosperity. Satisfy the Brahmanas with gifts of wealth.

I have answered all your questions in detail. With your leave, I will now depart for the city of the Dasarhas."

Vaisampayana, the narrator, continued, "O Janamejaya, having said this to the son of Pritha, Narada departed, accompanied by the Rishis who had come with him. And after Narada had gone, King Yudhishthira, with his brothers, began to ponder the grand sacrifice called Rajasuya."

Chapter 39

KRISHNA GIVES COUNSEL

Vaisampayana recounted, "Yudhishthira, having heard the sage Narada's words, began to sigh heavily. Engulfed in thoughts of the Rajasuya, the king found no peace of mind. Hearing of the glory of ancient monarchs and knowing the celestial rewards awaiting those who perform such sacrifices, especially the revered Harischandra, Yudhishthira resolved to undertake the grand Rajasuya sacrifice.

In his great Sabha, Yudhishthira worshipped his counselors and others present, and was in turn worshipped by them. He discussed the merits of the Rajasuya sacrifice, weighing its benefits and challenges. Yudhishthira, a king of unparalleled energy and prowess, was dedicated to the welfare of all his subjects. He cast aside anger and arrogance, always adhering to righteousness. His kingdom echoed with praises of 'Blessed be Dharma! Blessed be Dharma!'

Known as Ajatasatru, the one with no enemies, Yudhishthira nurtured his kingdom like his own family. Bhima ruled justly, while Arjuna protected the realm with his ambidextrous skill. Sahadeva administered justice impartially, and Nakula displayed natural humility. Under their rule, the kingdom flourished, free from disputes and fear. Prosperity reigned, with abundant rainfall, thriving trade, and contented subjects.

During Yudhishthira's reign, there was no extortion, no harsh collection of rents, no fear of disease or calamity. Thieves and cheats were unheard of, and royal favorites behaved justly. Kings from afar paid homage, and traders willingly paid their taxes. Even those indulging in luxuries contributed to the kingdom's prosperity. Yudhishthira's dominion grew, and his subjects were more devoted to him than to their own kin.

Vaisampayana continued, "King Yudhishthira, the wise and virtuous, summoned his counselors and brothers to discuss the Rajasuya sacrifice. His ministers, acknowledging his worthiness, urged him to perform the sacrifice, likening him to the emperor Varuna. They assured him that the time was right and that he was capable of such an undertaking. The Ritwijas and Rishis, skilled in the Sama Veda, supported this view, emphasizing the sacrifices' rewards.

The king, however, reflecting on his responsibilities and the welfare of his people, sought further counsel. He knew that wise decisions come from thorough deliberation. Yudhishthira, with his mind firmly resolved, decided to seek the guidance of Krishna, the foremost of all beings. Krishna, with his immeasurable energy and wisdom, was deemed the most suitable to decide on this matter.

Yudhishthira sent a swift messenger to Dwaravati, where Krishna resided. Upon receiving the message, Krishna, drawn by his swift horses, arrived at Indraprastha accompanied by Indrasena. Yudhishthira welcomed Krishna with paternal affection, as did Bhima and the twins. Krishna, after conversing cheerfully with Arjuna, was informed of Yudhishthira's desire to perform the Rajasuya sacrifice.

Yudhishthira said, 'I wish to perform the Rajasuya sacrifice, but mere desire is not enough. You, O Krishna, know the means to accomplish it. Only one who is worshipped everywhere, a king of kings, can achieve this feat. My friends and counselors urge me to undertake this sacrifice, but I seek your guidance. Counselors often overlook difficulties, speak from self-interest, or advise based on personal gain. But you, O Krishna, are above such motives, having conquered desire and anger. It is fitting for you to tell me what is most beneficial to the world.'

Krishna spoke with a voice like thunder on a distant mountain. "O great king, thou art indeed worthy of the Rajasuya sacrifice. Thy qualities surpass those of many, O Bharata. Still, there are things thou must hear.

The Kshatriyas of today pale in comparison to those Rama, son of Jamadagni, exterminated. These warriors of old ruled by ancient laws handed down through generations, and only a few amongst them are worthy of the Rajasuya sacrifice.

The descendants of Aila and Ikshwaku each boast a hundred dynasties, scattered over the earth. Among them are the mighty Bhojas and Yayati's lineage, revered by all Kshatriyas. But today, these great tribes are oppressed by the might of Jarasandha, who has subdued them with his relentless power.

Jarasandha, the sovereign of Mathura, seeks to divide us. Only a king who holds dominion over all, with the might to command the universe, can claim the title of emperor. Sisupala, endowed with great energy, serves as his generalissimo. Vaka, the king of the Karushas, using his powers of illusion, is Jarasandha's disciple. Hansa and Dimvaka, with their immense energy, have sought his shelter, as have Dantavakra, Karusha, Karava, and Meghavahana.

Bhagadatta, the king of the Yavanas, possessing a gem of incredible wonder and ruling the west, has bowed to Jarasandha. Though he regards thee with affection, seeing thee as a father sees his child, he serves Jarasandha. Only Purujit, thy maternal uncle, slayer of foes, remains loyal to thee out of affection.

Paundraka Vasudeva, who foolishly emulates my divine signs, has also joined Jarasandha. Bhishmaka, the mighty king of the Bhojas, friend of Indra, conqueror of the Pandyas and Kratha-Kausikas, serves the king of Magadha despite our kinship. The eighteen tribes of the Bhojas, the Surasenas, Bhadrakas, Vodhas, Salwas, Patachchavas, Susthalas, Mukuttas, and Kulindas, along with the Kuntis, have fled in fear. The Matsyas, Sannyastapadas, Panchalas, and Kosalas have also abandoned their lands, seeking refuge.

Kansa, strengthened by marrying Jarasandha's daughters, persecuted his relatives. The Bhojas sought our protection, and with the aid of my brother Balarama, we slew Kansa. However, this act drew Jarasandha's wrath, forcing us to flee Mathura.

In the western town of Kusasthali, amidst the mountains of Raivata, we found refuge. There, we rebuilt its fortifications, making it impregnable. Guarded by valiant heroes, even women could defend it. With eighteen thousand warriors and my family, we established our stronghold.

Our defenders, including Ahuka's hundred sons, Charudeshna, Chakradeva, Satyaki, Balarama, my son Samva, Kritavarman, Anadhrishti, Samika, Samitinjaya, Kanka, Sanku, Kunti, and many more, are invincible. We live in peace, fortified against Jarasandha.

But Jarasandha, with his allies Hansa and Dimvaka, remains a formidable foe. These allies, once thought dead, have made him nearly invincible. Only by vanquishing Jarasandha can the Rajasuya sacrifice be achieved.

Jarasandha, driven by his vow to sacrifice a hundred kings, has imprisoned monarchs like animals. To perform the Rajasuya, thou must first liberate these kings and defeat Jarasandha. This is my counsel, O sinless one. Reflect upon it and decide what thou deemest best. Only through this path can the Rajasuya be accomplished.

Yudhishthira, his voice grave and steady, said, "Wise Krishna, your words are unparalleled, their wisdom unmatched. No one else can settle doubts as you do. There are many kings in the provinces, all striving for their own benefit, yet none have achieved the imperial dignity. The title of emperor is not easily attained. He who truly knows the strength and valor of others never praises himself unjustly.

The man who proves his worth in battle against his enemies is deserving of honor. O supporter of the Vrishni race, human desires and propensities are as vast and varied as the earth adorned with countless jewels. Just as experience is gained by traveling far from home, so is salvation attained by striving for lofty principles, beyond ordinary desires and tendencies. I value peace of mind as the highest goal here, for from it my prosperity will come.

If I undertake this sacrifice, I fear I shall not achieve the highest reward. Many in our race believe one of us will become the foremost among all Kshatriyas. Yet, we have all been daunted by the fear of Jarasandha. O Krishna, your might is my refuge. When even you fear

Jarasandha's power, how can I see myself as stronger than him? O Keshava, I often wonder if Jarasandha can be slain by you, by Rama, by Bhima, or by Arjuna. Yet, you are my highest authority in all matters."

Bhima, ever quick with words, responded, "A king who is without effort, or who is weak and without resources yet engages a stronger foe, perishes like an ant-hill. However, even a weak king can defeat a stronger enemy through vigilance and the application of strategy. Krishna holds the key to strategy, I possess strength, and Arjuna brings victory. Together, like the three fires that complete a sacrifice, we shall bring about the death of the king of Magadha."

Krishna then spoke, his voice calm but firm, "One who seeks to fulfill his desires without foresight is immature. No one forgives a foe who is self-serving and short-sighted. In the Krita age, emperors like Yauvanaswin abolished taxes, Bhagiratha treated his subjects kindly, Kartavirya harnessed ascetic energy, Bharata wielded strength and valor, and Maruta thrived through prosperity. But you, Yudhishthira, deserve the imperial dignity through all these qualities: victory, protection of your people, virtue, prosperity, and policy.

Know, O Yudhishthira, that Jarasandha, son of Vrihadratha, is a contender for this dignity. A hundred dynasties of kings cannot oppose him. He, therefore, may be regarded as an emperor due to his strength. Kings bearing jewels worship Jarasandha with tributes, but he is never satisfied. He attacks even those crowned with jewels, taking tribute from all. He has nearly a hundred kings under his sway.

How can a weak monarch challenge him? These monarchs, confined in the temple of Shiva, suffer as sacrifices to the god. A Kshatriya who dies in battle is always honored. Why should we not meet Jarasandha in battle? He has already imprisoned eighty-six kings; only fourteen remain to complete his hundred. Once he has those, he will begin his cruel ritual. The one who stops him will gain immense renown and become emperor of all Kshatriyas."

Yudhishthira, the wise and cautious, spoke with a voice tinged with concern. "Krishna, you who are as my mind, and Bhima and Arjuna, who are as my eyes, how can I send you into the lair of Jarasandha, driven by a selfish desire for imperial dignity? Jarasandha's might is immense, his host formidable and valiant. Even Yama, the god of death, might falter before him. What chance do we have against such a foe? This endeavor could lead to great misfortune. I believe it is best to abandon this task. My heart is troubled, and the Rajasuya sacrifice seems an insurmountable challenge."

Then, Vaisampayana recounted how Arjuna, the wielder of the unparalleled bow, possessing inexhaustible quivers, and a magnificent chariot with a glorious banner, spoke up. "Brother, I have acquired a bow, weapons, arrows, allies, dominions, fame, and strength. These are rare and difficult to attain, even when greatly desired. Men of wisdom always extol noble lineage, but might is paramount.

Born into a race known for valor, one without bravery is scarcely worth consideration. However, one with valor, even from a lesser lineage, surpasses the former. A true Kshatriya is one who enhances his fame and wealth by subduing his foes. Even without other virtues, valor alone can bring victory. Conversely, one with all virtues but without valor achieves little. All merits accompany valor in an incipient state. Concentration, effort, and destiny are the three pillars of victory. Yet, even the valorous may fail if careless, and strength sometimes succumbs to folly. A king seeking victory must avoid both carelessness and folly.

For our sacrifice, if we slay Jarasandha and rescue the captive kings, there is no nobler act. If we shrink from this challenge, the world will see us as unworthy. We are indeed capable, O king. Why doubt our competence? The Munis attain peace easily, just as we will attain the imperial dignity by defeating our enemy. Thus, we must fight."

Vasudeva, the ever-wise, addressed Yudhishthira, his voice firm and unwavering. "Arjuna has spoken like one truly born of the Bharata race, especially as a son of Kunti. We know not when death shall claim us, be it in the night or day. Immortality has never been achieved by avoiding battle. It is the duty of men to face their enemies as per the sacred ordinances, for this brings peace to the heart. Aided by sound strategy and not thwarted by Destiny, any endeavor can succeed. When two equally matched forces clash, one must prevail, for both cannot win. A battle driven by poor strategy leads to defeat or ruin. If both sides are equal, the outcome is uncertain. Why, then, should we not, with wise strategy, confront our foe directly and destroy him like a river's current uproots a tree? If we mask our faults and exploit our enemy's weaknesses, success is assured. The wise do not engage powerful enemies openly; they strike at opportune moments. This is my belief. If we accomplish our goal by secretly infiltrating the enemy's abode and striking him down, we will avoid disgrace. Jarasandha, that formidable man, enjoys unblemished glory, like a radiant sun in the hearts of all. Yet, I foresee his downfall. To protect our kin, we shall either slay him or attain heaven, slain by him."

Yudhishthira, intrigued yet wary, inquired, "O Krishna, who is this Jarasandha? What are his strengths and valor that he has not been scorched like an insect upon touching you?"

Krishna, with a steady gaze, began his tale. "Listen, O monarch, to who Jarasandha is, his might, his valor, and why he remains unscathed despite offending us. There was a mighty king named Vrihadratha, lord of the Magadhas, proud in battle, commanding three Akshauhinis of troops. Handsome and energetic, affluent and unparalleled in prowess, he bore marks of sacrificial rites upon his person, a second Indra in glory, as radiant as the sun, as forgiving as the Earth, as wrathful as Yama, and as wealthy as Vaisravana. His virtues shone like sunbeams across the land. This formidable monarch wed two beautiful twin daughters of the king of Kasi, promising equal love to both. Living joyfully with his queens, he was like a mighty elephant with two consorts, or the personified ocean between the personified Ganga and Yamuna.

Yet, despite his happiness, no son was born to perpetuate his line. The king sought offspring through various auspicious rites and sacrifices but to no avail. One day, he heard of the sage Chandakausika, son of Kakshivat of the Gautama race, who had ended his penances and settled under a mango tree in Vrihadratha's capital. The king, with his queens, worshipped the sage with precious offerings. Pleased, the sage offered the king a boon. Overcome with despair, the king, with tears, pleaded, 'O holy one, I am ready to forsake my kingdom for the woods. I am cursed with childlessness. What use are kingdom or boons to me without an heir?'

Krishna continued, "Moved by the king's plea, the sage meditated deeply. A ripe, untouched mango fell into his lap. Blessing it with mantras, he gave it to the king, assuring him, 'Your wish is granted. Return home.' The joyous king gave the fruit to his queens, who shared and consumed it. They soon conceived, but each birthed only half a child. Dismayed, the queens abandoned the lifeless halves. The midwives, wrapping the fragments, discarded them discreetly.

A Rakshasa woman named Jara found the halves and, out of curiosity, joined them together. Miraculously, they formed a robust, whole child. Unable to carry the now lively and sturdy child, Jara marveled at her creation. The infant's roars drew the palace's attention, bringing out the king and his anxious queens. Jara, assuming a human form, presented the child to the king, explaining how she had protected and united the fragments, fulfilling the sage's prophecy.

'O Vrihadratha,' she said, 'this is your child, given by me. Born of your queens by the great sage's blessing, I have protected him.' The queens, overjoyed, nourished the child, and the king, grateful, questioned the golden-complexioned Jara, 'Who are you, O auspicious one, who bestows this blessing upon me?'"

Krishna continued, "Hearing these words from the king, the Rakshasa woman replied, 'Blessed be thou, O king of kings. I am capable of assuming any form at will. I am a Rakshasa woman named Jara. I live happily in your house, worshipped by all. Daily, I wander from house to house of men. Indeed, I was created long ago by the Self-create and named Grihadevi (the household goddess). Possessing celestial beauty, I was placed in the world for the destruction of the Danavas. He who with devotion paints a likeness of myself, youthful and surrounded by children, on the walls of his house, will have prosperity in his abode. Without it, a household must sustain decay and destruction. O lord, a likeness of myself is painted on the walls of your house, surrounded by numerous children. There, I am daily worshipped with scents, flowers, incense, edibles, and various objects of enjoyment. Thus worshipped in your house, I daily think of how to return the favor. It happened that I saw the fragmentary bodies of your son. When I united them, a living child was formed. O great king, this happened due to your good fortune alone. I was merely an instrument. I am capable of swallowing the mountain of Meru itself, what then of a child? I am gratified by the worship I receive in your house and therefore bestowed this child upon you.'

Krishna continued, 'Having spoken these words, Jara disappeared then and there. The king, having obtained the child, re-entered the palace. He performed all the rites of infancy for the child and ordered a festival in honor of the Rakshasa woman. Equal unto Brahma himself, the monarch then named his child Jarasandha, meaning "united by Jara." The son of the king of Magadha, endowed with great energy, began to grow in bulk and strength, like a fire into which clarified butter has been poured. Increasing day by day like the moon in the bright fortnight, the child enhanced the joy of his parents.'

Krishna said, 'Some time after this, the great ascetic Chandakausika again came into the country of the Magadhas. Filled with joy at the Rishi's advent, King Vrihadratha, accompanied by his ministers, priests, wives, and son, went out to receive him. Worshipping the Rishi with water for his feet and face, and offerings of Arghya, the king offered his entire kingdom and his son for the Rishi's acceptance. The sage, accepting the worship, addressed the ruler of Magadha with a well-pleased heart, "O king, I knew all this by spiritual insight. Hear now what this son of yours will be in the future, his beauty, excellence, strength, and valor. Without doubt, this son of yours, growing in prosperity and prowess, will surpass all. Like birds that can never match the speed of Garuda, other monarchs will not equal him in energy. All who stand against him will surely be destroyed. Weapons hurled at him, even by celestials, will fail to harm him. He will outshine all crowned heads. Like the sun dimming other luminous bodies, your son will rob all monarchs of their splendor. Powerful kings with vast armies will perish upon approaching him, like insects in fire. This child will absorb the growing prosperity of all kings, like the ocean receives swollen rivers in the rainy season. Supporting both good and evil, like the earth, he will uphold all four orders of men. All the kings of the earth will live in obedience to him, just as every creature depends on Vayu. This prince of Magadha, the mightiest of men, will see with his own eyes the god of gods, Rudra or Hara, the slayer of Tripura. Saying this, the Rishi dismissed King Vrihadratha, thinking of his own business.'

THE SOURCE OF CONFLICT

Vaisampayana continued, 'After re-entering his capital, the lord of the Magadhas installed Jarasandha on the throne. Vrihadratha, along with his two wives, retired into an ascetic asylum in the woods. After some time, having practiced ascetic penances, he ascended to heaven with his wives. Jarasandha, endowed with numerous boons as prophesied by Kausika, ruled his kingdom like a father. When King Kansa was slain by Vasudeva, enmity arose between Jarasandha and Krishna. From Girivraja, Jarasandha hurled a mace towards Mathura, where Krishna resided. The mace fell near Mathura, ninety-nine yojanas away. The citizens, seeing this, informed Krishna. The place where the mace fell is called Gadavasan. Jarasandha had two powerful allies, Hansa and Dimvaka, both invincible by weapons. Wise and skilled in politics and morality, they were unmatched in counsel. Jarasandha, with these allies, was more than a match for the three worlds. It was for this reason that the Kukkura, Andhaka, and Vrishni tribes, out of policy, refrained from fighting him.'"

Krishna said, "Both Hansa and Dimvaka have fallen, and Kansa, along with all his followers, has been slain. Therefore, the time has come for the destruction of Jarasandha. He is invincible in battle, even by all the celestials and Asuras combined. However, we believe he can be defeated in a personal struggle with bare arms. I possess the wisdom of policy, Bhima the strength, and Arjuna the triumph; thus, as a prelude to performing the Rajasuya, we will surely achieve the destruction of the ruler of Magadha. When we three approach that monarch in secret, he will undoubtedly engage in an encounter with one of us. From fear of disgrace, covetousness, and pride in his strength, he will certainly summon Bhima to the encounter. Like death itself that slays a person swollen with pride, the long-armed and mighty Bhimasena will bring about the king's destruction. If you trust my heart and have faith in me, then entrust Bhima and Arjuna to me without delay!"

Vaisampayana continued, "Thus addressed by the exalted one, Yudhishthira, seeing Bhima and Arjuna standing with cheerful faces, replied, 'O Achyuta, O slayer of all enemies, say not so. You are the lord of the Pandavas, and we depend on you. What you say, O Govinda, is wise counsel. You never lead those whom Prosperity has abandoned. Under your command, I consider Jarasandha already slain, the monarchs confined by him already freed, and the Rajasuya already accomplished by me. O lord of the universe, O best of persons, act watchfully so this task may be accomplished. Without you, I dare not live, like a sorrowful man afflicted with disease and bereft of the three attributes of morality, pleasure, and wealth. Partha cannot live without Sauri (Krishna), nor can Sauri live without Partha. There is nothing in the world unconquerable by these two, Krishna and Arjuna. This handsome Bhima is also the foremost of all persons endowed with might. Of great renown, what can he not achieve with you two? Troops properly led always perform excellently. A force without a leader is inert, according to the wise. Forces should always be led by experienced commanders. The wise always direct water to low places. Even fishermen cause the water of a tank to run out through holes. (Experienced leaders always lead their forces by noting the loopholes and assailable points of the foe). We will strive to accomplish our purpose by following the leadership of Govinda, conversant with the science of politics, whose fame has spread worldwide. For the successful accomplishment of one's purposes, one should ever place Krishna in the lead, that foremost of persons whose strength lies in wisdom and policy and who possesses knowledge of both method and means. Therefore, let Arjuna, the son of Pritha, follow Krishna, the foremost of the Yadavas, and let Bhima follow Arjuna. Policy, good fortune, and might will then ensure success in a matter requiring valor.'"

Vaisampayana continued, "Thus addressed by Yudhishthira, the trio Krishna, Arjuna, and Bhima, all possessing great energy, set out for

Magadha attired in the garb of Snataka Brahmanas. Their resplendent bodies, blessed by the agreeable speeches of friends and relatives, blazed even more with the wrath felt at the sad lot of their relative kings. The people, seeing Krishna and Arjuna, both never before vanquished in battle, with Bhima in the lead, all ready for the same task, regarded Jarasandha as already slain. For the illustrious pair, Krishna and Arjuna, were masters directing every operation in the universe and all acts related to morality, wealth, and pleasure.

Having set out from the country of the Kurus, they passed through Kuru-jangala and arrived at the charming lake of lotuses. Passing over the hills of Kalakuta, they crossed the Gandaki, the Sadanira (Karatoya), and the Sarkaravarta and other rivers originating in the same mountains. They then crossed the delightful Sarayu and saw the country of Eastern Kosala. Passing over that country, they went to Mithila and then crossed the Mala and Charamanwati. The three heroes crossed the Ganges and the Sone and went on towards the east. At last, they arrived at Magadha in the heart of the country of Kushamva. Reaching the hills of Goratha, they saw the city of Magadha, always filled with kine, wealth, water, and rendered beautiful by the innumerable trees standing there.

Chapter 40

KRISHNA AND THE PANDAVAS GO TO SEE JARASANDHA

Vasudeva spoke, his voice like the rumble of distant thunder, "Behold, O Partha, the magnificent capital of Magadha, standing resplendent in its prime. Here, amidst verdant fields and never-ending waters, flocks and herds flourish. Fine mansions, arrayed in perfect harmony, adorn the city, free from calamity. The towering peaks of Vaihara, Varaha, Vrishava, Rishigiri, and the delightful Chaitya, covered with tall trees casting cool shadows, stand as sentinels, safeguarding the city of Girivraja. Forests of fragrant Lodhras, their branches ablaze with flowers, conceal the mighty breasts of these hills.

It was here, in these ancient forests, that the illustrious Gautama, of unyielding vows, fathered Kakshivat and other celebrated sons upon Ausinari, the daughter of Usinara. Though their race remains under the sway of ordinary human monarchs, this is but evidence of Gautama's kindness to kings. O Arjuna, it was here that the mighty monarchs of Anga, Vanga, and other lands sought Gautama's abode, finding joy and happiness in his presence.

Behold, those forests of Pippalas and Lodhras stand proudly near Gautama's ancient abode. In these woods dwelled Nagas of old: Arvuda, Sakravapin, Swastika, and Manu, who commanded the land of the Magadhas never to suffer drought. Jarasandha, unlike other monarchs, forever seeks to fulfill his ambitions, protected by this delightful and impregnable city. But today, we shall humble his pride by slaying him."

Thus, the brothers of great energy, the hero of the Vrishni race and the two Pandavas, entered the city of Magadha. Approaching Girivraja, full of cheerful and well-fed inhabitants, they neared the gate. Instead of passing through, they attacked the heart of the high Chaityaka peak, revered by the race of Vrihadratha and the citizens of Magadha. Here, Vrihadratha had slain the cannibal Rishava and made three drums from his hide, whose sound echoed for a full month. The brothers, with mighty arms, shattered the celebrated peak, their actions a bold challenge to Jarasandha.

The learned Brahmanas within the city reported evil omens to Jarasandha. To ward off these portents, the king mounted an elephant, performing rites with lighted brands. Possessed of great prowess, he entered into the celebration of a sacrifice, adhering to proper vows and fasts.

Meanwhile, the brothers, unarmed yet powerful, entered the capital in the guise of Brahmanas. They marveled at the beauty of shops brimming with goods, forcibly taking garlands from flower vendors.

Adorned in colorful robes and garlands, they entered Jarasandha's abode like Himalayan lions. The people of Magadha, awestruck by their appearance, watched as they approached the king through three gates.

Jarasandha, rising hastily, greeted them with respect, offering water, honey, kine, and other tokens of welcome. Yet, Partha and Bhima remained silent, observing their vow. Krishna spoke, "O king, these two are bound by a vow and will remain silent until midnight. After that hour, they will converse with thee."

Quartering his guests in the sacrificial quarters, Jarasandha awaited midnight. Then, true to his vow, he approached the disguised Brahmanas. Curious yet respectful, he addressed them, "Welcome, O Brahmanas."

Krishna, skilled in speech, replied, "O king, know us as Snataka Brahmanas. Brahmanas, Kshatriyas, and Vaishyas alike observe this vow. A Kshatriya's strength lies in his arms, not his speech. Thus, we have adorned ourselves with flowers. This is our eternal vow: to enter the foe's abode through a wrong gate and a friend's through the right one. We accept no worship from an enemy."

With these words, the disguised heroes prepared to confront Jarasandha, their true purpose revealed, their resolve unshaken

Jarasandha spoke, his voice a low growl like a lion pondering its prey, "I do not recall ever wronging you. Even with careful scrutiny, I find no injury I have caused. Why, then, do you regard me as a foe? Answer me truthfully, for the honest follow this rule. The mind suffers at the injury to one's pleasure and morality. A Kshatriya who harms an innocent man's pleasure and morality, regardless of his prowess or knowledge, inevitably falls from prosperity and earns the fate of sinners. The practices of Kshatriyas are the most honorable in the three worlds, lauded by those who know morality. Adhering to my order's practices, I have never injured those under my rule. Therefore, your accusation against me is misguided."

Krishna, calm as a cobra ready to strike, replied, "O mighty king, we come at the behest of a leader upholding his royal line's dignity. You have imprisoned many Kshatriyas from across the world. Having committed this grave wrong, how do you see yourself as innocent? How can a king act wrongfully towards other virtuous kings? Yet you, treating other kings with cruelty, intend to sacrifice them to Rudra. O son of Vrihadratha, this sin may taint even us, for we are bound to protect virtue. Human sacrifice to the gods is unseen; why do you seek to sacrifice men to Sankara? You, a fool, treat your equals as animals for sacrifice. None other than you, O Jarasandha, could act so. One always reaps the fruits of their deeds. We, desiring to aid the distressed, have come to end you, the slaughterer of our kin. You think none among the Kshatriyas can match you. This is your error. Which Kshatriya, proud of their lineage, would not ascend to eternal heaven, falling in open battle? Kshatriyas engage in battle with heaven in view, conquering the world. Study of the Vedas, great fame, ascetic penances, and death in battle all lead to heaven. The other acts' fruits are uncertain, but death in battle surely leads to triumph. This is why Indra, through his hundred sacrifices and battles against Asuras, rules the universe. Hostility with you ensures heaven for us, proud as you are of your Magadha host's strength. Do not underestimate others, O king. Valor resides in many. You are known for your valor only until others prove theirs. Your prowess can be borne by us, so I speak thus. O king of Magadha, cast off your pride before equals. Do not lead your kin and army to Yama's realm. Damvodhava, Kartavirya, Uttara, and Vrihadratha met their end for disregarding their superiors. We come to free the captive monarchs. We are not Brahmanas. I am Hrishikesha, also known as Sauri, and these are Pandu's sons. We challenge you. Fight us. Either free the monarchs or join Yama's abode."

Jarasandha, eyes burning with pride, replied, "I never imprison a king without first defeating him. Who here has not been bested in battle? This is a Kshatriya's duty: to subjugate others through prowess, then treat them as subjects. Having gathered these kings to sacrifice to the god, why should I fearfully release them now? Troops against troops, alone against one, two, or three—however it be, I am ready to fight."

Vaisampayana said, "Thus resolved, Jarasandha ordered his son Sahadeva to be installed on the throne. The king, preparing for battle, called upon his generals Kausika and Chitrasena, once known as Hansa and Dimvaka. Sauri, ever true to his word, remembered that Bhima, not he, was destined to slay Jarasandha. With a warrior's prowess and a tiger's valor, Krishna refrained from the kill, leaving the task to Bhima."

Vaisampayana said, "Then, the foremost of all speakers, Krishna of the Yadava race, addressing King Jarasandha, who was resolved upon fighting, said, 'O king, with whom amongst us three do you desire to fight? Who among us shall prepare for battle with you?' Thus addressed, the ruler of Magadha, King Jarasandha of great splendor, expressed his desire to fight with Bhima.

The priest, bringing with him the yellow pigment obtained from the cow, garlands of flowers, and other auspicious articles, as well as various excellent medicines for restoring lost consciousness and alleviating pain, approached Jarasandha, who was panting for battle. The king, on whose behalf propitiatory ceremonies and benedictions were performed by a renowned Brahmana, remembering the duty of a Kshatriya, dressed himself for battle. Taking off his crown and binding his hair properly, Jarasandha stood up like an ocean bursting its continents.

The monarch, possessed of terrible prowess, addressing Bhima, said, 'I will fight with you. It is better to be vanquished by a superior person.' And saying this, Jarasandha, that represser of all foes, rushed with great energy at Bhimasena like the Asura Vala of old who rushed at the chief of the celestials.

The mighty Bhimasena, on whose behalf the gods had been invoked by Krishna, that cousin of his, having consulted with him, advanced towards Jarasandha, impelled by the desire to fight. Then, those tigers among men, those heroes of great prowess, with their bare arms as their only weapons, cheerfully engaged themselves in the encounter, each desirous of vanquishing the other.

Seizing each other's arms and twining each other's legs, at times they slapped their armpits, causing the enclosure to tremble at the sound. Frequently seizing each other's necks with their hands, dragging and pushing with violence, and pressing every limb of their bodies against every limb of the other, they continued to slap their armpits. Sometimes stretching their arms and sometimes drawing them close, now raising them up and now dropping them down, they began to seize each other. Striking neck against neck and forehead against forehead, they caused fiery sparks to come out like flashes of lightning.

Grasping each other in various ways by means of their arms, and kicking each other with such violence as to affect the innermost nerves, they struck at each other's breasts with clenched fists. With bare arms as their only weapons, roaring like clouds, they grasped and struck each other like two mad elephants encountering each other with their trunks. Incensed at each other's blows, they fought on, dragging and pushing each other and fiercely glaring at each other like two wrathful lions. Each striking every limb of the other with his own and using his arms also against the other, they caught hold of each other's waists and hurled each other to a distance.

Accomplished in wrestling, the two heroes clasped each other with their arms, dragging each other closer and pressing with great violence. They performed grand feats in wrestling called

Prishtabhanga, throwing each other down with faces towards the earth and maintaining the one knocked down in that position as long as possible. They also performed feats called Sampurna-murchcha and Purna-kumbha. Twisting each other's arms and limbs as if they were vegetable fibers to be twisted into cords, they struck each other with clenched fists, pretending to aim at particular limbs while the blows descended upon other parts of the body. Thus, the heroes fought with each other.

The citizens, consisting of thousands of Brahmanas, Kshatriyas, Vaisyas, and Sudras, and even women and the aged, gathered to behold the fight. The crowd became so great that it formed a solid mass of humanity with no space between bodies. The sound made by the wrestlers—the slapping of their arms, the seizing of each other's necks, and the grasping of each other's legs—resembled the roar of thunder or falling cliffs.

Both were foremost of mighty men and took great delight in the encounter. Desirous of vanquishing each other, each was alert for any lapse. The mighty Bhima and Jarasandha fought terribly, driving the crowd at times by the motions of their hands, like Vritra and Vasava of old. Dragging and pressing each other, with sudden jerks throwing each other face down and sideways, they mangled each other dreadfully. At times they struck each other with their knee-joints, addressing each other loudly in stinging speeches, and struck each other with clenched fists, the blows descending like masses of stone.

With broad shoulders and long arms, both well-skilled in wrestling encounters, they struck each other with long arms like maces of iron. The encounter commenced on the first lunar day of the month of Kartik (October), and the illustrious heroes fought without intermission or food, day and night, until the thirteenth lunar day. On the night of the fourteenth lunar fortnight, the monarch of Magadha desisted from fatigue.

Janardana, beholding the monarch tired, addressed Bhima of terrible deeds and, as if to stimulate him, said, 'O son of Kunti, a foe that is fatigued cannot be pressed, for if pressed, he may even die. Therefore, do not oppress this king. On the other hand, fight with him with only as much strength as your antagonist has left!' The son of Pandu, thus addressed by Krishna, understood Jarasandha's plight and resolved upon taking his life. The prince of the Kuru race, desirous of vanquishing the hitherto unvanquished Jarasandha, mustered all his strength and courage."

Vaisampayana said, "Thus addressed, Bhima, firmly resolved upon slaying Jarasandha, replied to Krishna of the Yadu race, saying, 'O tiger of the Yadu race, O Krishna, this wretch who still stands before me with sufficient strength and bent upon fighting should not be forgiven by me.' Hearing these words of Vrikodara (Bhima), Krishna, desiring to encourage that hero to accomplish the death of Jarasandha without any delay, answered, 'O Bhima, exhibit today upon Jarasandha the strength you have luckily derived, the might you have obtained from your father, the god Maruta.'

Thus addressed by Krishna, Bhima, that slayer of foes, holding up in the air the powerful Jarasandha, began to whirl him on high. And, O bull of the Bharata race, having so whirled him in the air a full hundred times, Bhima pressed his knee against Jarasandha's backbone and broke his body in twain. And having killed him thus, the mighty Vrikodara uttered a terrible roar. The roar of the Pandava mingling with that death knell of Jarasandha, while he was being broken on Bhima's knee, caused a loud uproar that struck fear into the heart of every creature. All the citizens of Magadha became dumb with terror, and many women were even prematurely delivered. Hearing those roars, the people of Magadha thought that either the

Himavat was tumbling down or the earth itself was being rent asunder.

Then, those oppressors of all foes, leaving the lifeless body of the king at the palace gate where he lay as one asleep, went out of the town. Krishna, causing Jarasandha's car furnished with an excellent flagstaff to be made ready and making the brothers Bhima and Arjuna ride in it, went in and released his imprisoned relatives. Those kings, rescued from a terrible fate, rich in the possession of jewels, approached Krishna and made presents to him of jewels and gems. Having vanquished his foe, Krishna, furnished with weapons and unwounded, accompanied by the kings he had released, came out of Girivraja riding in that celestial car of Jarasandha.

He also who could wield the bow with both hands, Arjuna, who was incapable of being vanquished by any of the monarchs on earth, who was exceedingly handsome in person and well-skilled in the destruction of the foe, accompanied by the possessor of great strength, Bhima, came out of that fort with Krishna driving the car whereon he rode. That best of cars, incapable of being vanquished by any king, ridden in by those warriors Bhima and Arjuna and driven by Krishna, looked exceedingly handsome. Indeed, it was upon that car that Indra and Vishnu had fought of old in the battle with the Asuras in which Taraka, the wife of Vrihaspati, had become the immediate cause of much slaughter.

Riding upon that car, Krishna now came out of the hill-fort. Possessed of the splendor of heated gold, decked with rows of jingling bells and furnished with wheels whose clatter was like the roar of clouds, always victorious in battle, and always slaughtering the foe against whom it was driven, it was the very car upon which Indra had slain ninety-nine Asuras of old. Those bulls among men, the three cousins, having obtained that car, became exceedingly glad. The people of Magadha, beholding the long-armed Krishna along with the two brothers seated in that car of Jarasandha, wondered much.

That car, to which celestial horses were yoked and which possessed the speed of the wind, ridden upon by Krishna, looked exceedingly beautiful. Upon that best of cars was a flag-staff without being visibly attached thereto, a product of celestial skill. The handsome flag-staff, possessed of the splendor of the rainbow, could be seen from the distance of a yojana. Krishna, while coming out, thought of Garuda. Garuda, thought of by his master, came thither in no time, like a tree of vast proportions standing in a village worshipped by all. Garuda, of immense weight of body and living upon snakes, sat upon that excellent car along with the numberless open-mouthed and frightfully-roaring creatures on its flag-staff. Thereupon, that best of cars became still more dazzling with its splendor and was as incapable of being looked at by created beings as the midday sun surrounded by a thousand rays.

O king, such was that best of flag-staffs of celestial make that it never struck against any tree nor could any weapon injure it at all, even though visible to men's eyes. Achyuta, that tiger among men, riding with the two sons of Pandu upon that celestial car, the clatter of whose wheels was like the roar of the clouds, came out of Girivraja. The car upon which Krishna rode had been obtained by King Vasu from Vasava, and from Vasu by Vrihadratha, and from the latter in due course by King Jarasandha.

He of long arms and eyes like lotus-petals, possessing an illustrious reputation, coming out of Girivraja, stopped for some time on a level plain outside the town. All the citizens, with the Brahmanas at their head, hastened thither to adore him with due religious rites. The kings who had been released from confinement worshipped the slayer of Madhu with reverence and addressed him with eulogies, saying, 'O you of long arms, you have today rescued us, sunk in the deep mire of sorrow in the hand of Jarasandha. Such an act of virtue by you, O son of Devaki, assisted by the might of Bhima and Arjuna, is most extraordinary. O Vishnu, languishing as we all were in the terrible hill-fort of Jarasandha, it was verily from sheer good fortune alone that you have rescued us, O son of the Yadu race, and achieved thereby a remarkable reputation. O tiger among men, we bow down to you. O, command us what we shall do. However difficult of accomplishment, your command being made known to us, O lord Krishna, it will at once be accomplished by us.'

Thus addressed by the monarchs, the high-souled Hrishikesa gave them every assurance and said, 'Yudhishthira is desirous of performing the sacrifice of Rajasuya. That monarch, ever guided by virtue, is solicitous of acquiring the imperial dignity. Having known this from me, assist him in his endeavors.' Then, O king, all those monarchs with joyous hearts accepted the words of Krishna, saying, 'So be it!' Saying this, those lords of earth made presents of jewels to him of the Dasarha race. Govinda, moved by kindness towards them, took a portion of those presents.

Then, the son of Jarasandha, the high-souled Sahadeva, accompanied by his relatives and the principal officers of state, and with his priest in front, came thither. The prince, bending himself low and making large presents of jewels and precious stones, worshipped Vasudeva, that god among men. That best of men, Krishna, giving every assurance to the prince afflicted with fear, accepted those presents of great value. Krishna joyfully installed the prince there and then in the sovereignty of Magadha. The strong-armed and illustrious son of Jarasandha, thus installed on the throne by those most exalted of men and having obtained the friendship of Krishna and treated with respect and kindness by the two sons of Pritha, re-entered the city of his father.

That bull among men, Krishna, accompanied by the sons of Pritha and graced with great good fortune, left the city of Magadha laden with numerous jewels. Accompanied by the two sons of Pandu, Achyuta (Krishna) arrived at Indraprastha and, approaching Yudhishthira, joyfully addressed that monarch, saying, 'O best of kings, from good fortune, the mighty Jarasandha has been slain by Bhima, and the kings confined at Girivraja have all been set free. From good fortune also, these two, Bhima and Dhananjaya, are well and have arrived, O Bharata, in their own city unwounded.'

Yudhishthira worshipped Krishna as he deserved and embraced Bhima and Arjuna in joy. The monarch who had no enemy, having obtained victory through the agency of his brothers and the death of Jarasandha, gave himself up to pleasure and merriment with all his brothers. The eldest son of Pandu (Yudhisthira), together with his brothers, approached the kings who had come to Indraprastha, entertained and worshipped them according to their age, and dismissed them all. Commanded by Yudhishthira, those kings with joyful hearts set out for their respective countries without loss of time, riding upon excellent vehicles.

Thus, O king, did that tiger among men, Janardana of great intelligence, cause his foe Jarasandha to be slain through the instrumentality of the Pandavas. O Bharata, that chastiser of all foes, having caused Jarasandha to be slain, took leave of Yudhishthira, Pritha, Draupadi, Subhadra, Bhimasena, Arjuna, and the twins Nakula and Sahadeva. After taking leave of Dhananjaya also, he set out for his own city of Dwarka, riding upon that best of cars of celestial make, possessed of the speed of the mind and given to him by Yudhishthira, filling the ten points of the horizon with the deep rattle of its wheels. O bull of the Bharata race, just as Krishna was on the point of setting out, the Pandavas with Yudhishthira at their head walked round that tiger among men who was never fatigued with exertion.

After the illustrious Krishna, the son of Devaki, had departed from Indraprastha, having acquired that great victory and having also dispelled the fears of the kings, that feat, O Bharata, swelled the fame of the Pandavas. O king, the Pandavas passed their days, continuing to gladden the heart of Draupadi. At that time, whatever was proper and consistent with virtue, pleasure, and profit, continued to be properly executed by King Yudhishthira in the exercise of his duties of protecting his subjects."

Chapter 41

PANDAVAS HEAD OUT TO CONQUER THE WORLD

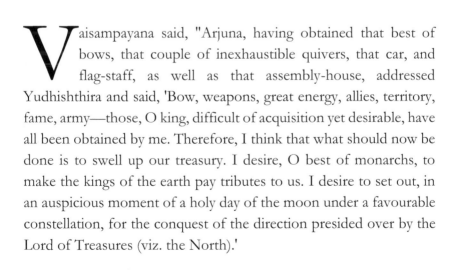

Vaisampayana said, "Arjuna, having obtained that best of bows, that couple of inexhaustible quivers, that car, and flag-staff, as well as that assembly-house, addressed Yudhishthira and said, 'Bow, weapons, great energy, allies, territory, fame, army—those, O king, difficult of acquisition yet desirable, have all been obtained by me. Therefore, I think that what should now be done is to swell up our treasury. I desire, O best of monarchs, to make the kings of the earth pay tributes to us. I desire to set out, in an auspicious moment of a holy day of the moon under a favourable constellation, for the conquest of the direction presided over by the Lord of Treasures (viz. the North).'

Vaisampayana continued, "King Yudhishthira the just, hearing these words of Dhananjaya, replied to him in a grave and collected tone, saying, 'O bull of the Bharata race, set out, having made holy Brahmanas utter benedictions on you, to plunge your enemies in sorrow and to fill your friends with joy. Victory, O son of Pritha, will surely be yours, and you will surely obtain your desires fulfilled.'

Thus addressed, Arjuna, surrounded by a large host, set out in that celestial car of wonderful achievements he had obtained from Agni. Bhimasena also, and those bulls among men, the twins, dismissed with affection by Yudhishthira the just, set out, each at the head of a large army. Arjuna, the son of the chastiser of Paka, then brought under subjugation the North, which was presided over by the Lord of Treasures. Bhimasena overcame the East by force, Sahadeva the South, and Nakula, O king, acquainted with all the weapons, conquered the West. While his brothers were thus employed, the exalted king Yudhishthira the just stayed within Khandavaprastha, enjoying great affluence in the midst of friends and relatives."

Vaisampayana continued, " After Arjuna headed out the first king he met was the mighty Bhagadatta. Arjuna approached and proclaimed the intention of Yudhistera to perform Rajasurya Yajna. Bhagadatta, hearing this, said, 'O thou who hast Kunti for thy mother, as thou art to me, so is Yudhishthira also. I shall do all this. Tell me, what else I may do for thee.' Thus addressed, Dhananjaya replied unto Bhagadatta, saying, 'If thou wilt give thy promise to do this, thou hast done all I desire.' And having thus subjugated the king of Pragjyotisha, Dhananjaya of long arms, the son of Kunti, then marched towards the north—the direction presided over by the Lord of Treasures.

That bull among men, the son of Kunti, then conquered the mountainous tracts and their outskirts, as also the hilly regions. And having conquered all the mountains and the kings that reigned there, and bringing them under his sway, he exacted tributes from all. Winning the affections of those kings and uniting himself with them, he next marched, O king, against Vrihanta, the king of Uluka, making the earth tremble with the sound of his drums, the clatter of his chariot-wheels, and the roar of the elephants in his train. Vrihanta, however, quickly coming out of his city, followed by his army consisting of four kinds of troops, gave battle to Falguna (Arjuna). The fight that took place between Vrihanta and Dhananjaya was terrible. It so happened that Vrihanta was unable to bear the prowess of the son of Pandu. Then that invincible king of the mountainous region, regarding the son of Kunti as irresistible, approached him with all his wealth. Arjuna snatched the kingdom from Vrihanta, but having made peace with him, marched, accompanied by that king, against Senavindu, whom he soon expelled from his kingdom.

After this, he subjugated Modapura, Vamadeva, Sudaman, Susankula, the Northern Ulukas, and the kings of those countries and peoples. Hereafter, at the command of Yudhishthira, O monarch, Arjuna did not move from the city of Senavindu but sent his troops and brought those five countries and peoples under his sway. Arjuna, having arrived at Devaprastha, the city of Senavindu, took up his quarters there with his army consisting of four kinds of forces. Thence, surrounded by the kings and peoples he had subjugated, the hero marched against King Viswagaswa, that bull of Puru's race. Having vanquished in battle the brave mountaineers, who were all great warriors, the son of Pandu then occupied the town protected by the Puru king. Having vanquished in battle the Puru king and the robber tribes of the mountains, the son of Pandu brought the seven tribes called Utsava-sanketa under his sway. That bull of the Kshatriya race then defeated the brave Kshatriyas of Kashmira and also King Lohita along with ten minor chiefs.

Then the Trigartas, the Daravas, the Kokonadas, and various other Kshatriyas, O king, advanced against the son of Pandu. That prince of the Kuru race then took the delightful town of Avisari and then brought under his sway Rochamana ruling in Uraga. Then the son of Indra (Arjuna), putting forth his might, pressed the delightful town of Singhapura that was well-protected with various weapons. Then Arjuna, that bull among the sons of Pandu, at the head of all his troops, fiercely attacked the regions called Suhma and Sumala. Then the son of Indra, endowed with great prowess, after pressing them with great force, brought the Valhikas, always difficult of being vanquished, under his sway.

Then Falguna, the son of Pandu, taking with him a select force, defeated the Daradas along with the Kambojas. Then the exalted son of Indra vanquished the robber tribes that dwelt in the northeastern frontier and those that dwelt in the woods. And, O great king, the son of Indra also subjugated the allied tribes of the Lohas, the eastern Kambojas, and northern Rishikas. The battle with the Rishikas was fierce in the extreme. Indeed, the fight between them and the son of Pritha was equal to that between the gods and the Asuras in which Taraka (the wife of Vrihaspati) had caused so much slaughter. Defeating, O king, the Rishikas in battle, Arjuna took from them as tribute eight horses of the colour of a parrot's breast, as well as other horses of the hues of the peacock, born in northern and other climes and endowed with high speed. At last, having conquered all the Himalayas and the Nishkuta mountains, that bull among men, arriving at the White mountains, encamped on its breast.

Vaisampayana said, "That heroic and foremost of the Pandavas, endowed with great energy, crossed the White mountains and subjugated the country of the Limpurushas ruled by Durmaputra, after a collision involving a great slaughter of Kshatriyas, bringing the region under his complete sway. Having reduced that country, the son of Indra (Arjuna), with a collected mind, marched at the head of his troops to the country called Harataka, ruled by the Guhakas. Subjugating them by a policy of conciliation, the Kuru prince beheld that excellent lake called Manasa and various other lakes and tanks sacred to the Rishis.

The exalted prince, having arrived at the lake Manasa, conquered the regions ruled by the Gandharvas that lay around the Harataka territories. Here the conqueror took numerous excellent horses called Tittiri, Kalmasha, and Manduka as tribute from the country. At last, the son of the slayer of Paka, arriving in the country of North Harivarsha, desired to conquer it. Thereupon certain frontier-guards of huge bodies and endowed with great strength and energy, coming to him with gallant hearts, said, 'O son of Pritha, this country can never be conquered by thee. If thou seekest thy good, return hence. He that entereth this region, if human, is sure to perish. We have been gratified with thee; O hero, thy conquests have been enough. Nor is anything to be seen here, O Arjuna, that may be conquered by thee. The Northern Kurus live here. There cannot be war here. Even if thou enterest it, thou will not be able to behold anything, for with human eyes nothing can be seen here. If, however, thou seekest anything else, O Bharata, tell us, O tiger among men, so that we may do thy bidding.'

Thus addressed by them, Arjuna smilingly said, 'I desire the acquisition of the imperial dignity by Yudhishthira the just, of great intelligence. If your land is shut against human beings, I shall not enter it. Let something be paid unto Yudhishthira by you as tribute.' Hearing these words of Arjuna, they gave him as tribute many cloths and ornaments of celestial make, silks of celestial texture, and skins of celestial origin.

It was thus that tiger among men subjugated the countries that lay to the North, having fought numerous battles with both Kshatriya and robber tribes. And having vanquished the chiefs and brought them under his sway, he exacted from them much wealth, various gems and jewels, horses of the species called Tittiri and Kalmasha, as well as those of the colour of a parrot's wings and those that were like peacocks in hue, all endowed with the speed of the wind. Surrounded, O king, by a large army consisting of the four kinds of forces, the hero came back to the excellent city of Sakraprastha. And Partha offered the whole of that wealth, together with the animals he had brought, unto Yudhishthira the just. Commanded by the monarch, the hero then retired to a chamber of the palace for rest."

Vaisampayana said, "In the meantime, Bhimasena, also endowed with great energy, having obtained the assent of Yudhishthira the just, marched towards the eastern direction. The tiger among the Bharatas, possessed of great valour and ever increasing the sorrows of his foes, was accompanied by a mighty host with the full complement of elephants, horses, and cars, well-armed and capable of crushing all hostile kingdoms.

That tiger among men, the son of Pandu, going first into the great country of the Panchalas, began by various means to conciliate that tribe. Then that hero, that bull of the Bharata race, within a short time, vanquished the Gandakas and the Videhas. That exalted one then subjugated the Dasarnas. There, in the country of the Dasarnas, the king called Sudharman, with his bare arms, fought a fierce battle with Bhimasena. And Bhimasena, beholding that feat of the illustrious king, appointed the mighty Sudharman as the first in command of his forces.

Then Bhima of terrible prowess marched towards the east, causing the earth itself to tremble with the tread of the mighty host that followed him. That hero, who in strength was the foremost of all strong men, defeated in battle Rochamana, the king of Aswamedha, at the head of all his troops. And the son of Kunti, having vanquished that monarch by performing feats that excelled in fierceness, subjugated the eastern region.

Then that prince of the Kuru race, endowed with great prowess, going into the country of Pulinda in the south, brought Sukumara and the king Sumitra under his sway. Then, O Janamejaya, that bull in the Bharata race, at the command of Yudhishthira the just, marched against Sisupala of great energy. The king of Chedi, hearing of the intentions of the son of Pandu, came out of his city. And that chastiser of all foes then received the son of Pritha with respect.

Then, O king, those bulls of the Chedi and the Kuru lines, thus met together, enquired after each other's welfare. Then, O monarch, the king of Chedi offered his kingdom unto Bhima and said smilingly, 'O sinless one, upon what art thou bent?' And Bhima thereupon represented unto him the intentions of king Yudhishthira. And Bhima dwelt there, O king, for thirty nights, duly entertained by Sisupala. And after this, he set out from Chedi with his troops and vehicles."

Vaisampayana said, "That chastiser of all foes, Bhimasena, then vanquished King Srenimat of the country of Kumara and then Vrihadvala, the king of Kosala. The foremost of the sons of Pandu, by performing feats excelling in fierceness, defeated the virtuous and mighty King Dirghayaghna of Ayodhya. The exalted one then subjugated the country of Gopalakaksha, the northern Kosalas, and the king of Mallas. The mighty one, arriving then in the moist region at the foot of the Himalayas, soon brought the whole country under his sway.

That bull of the Bharata race brought under control diverse countries and, endowed with great energy and strength, conquered the country of Bhallata and the mountain of Suktimanta. Bhima of terrible prowess and long arms vanquished in battle the unretreating Suvahu, the king of Kasi, bringing him under complete sway. Then that bull among the sons of Pandu overcame in battle, by sheer force, the great King Kratha reigning in the region lying about Suparsa. The hero of great energy vanquished the Matsya and the powerful Maladas, as well as the country called Pasubhumi.

The long-armed hero then, coming from that land, conquered Madahara, Mahidara, the Somadheyas, and turned his steps towards the north. The mighty son of Kunti subjugated, by sheer force, the country called Vatsabhumi, the king of the Bhargas, the ruler of the Nishadas, Manimat, and numerous other kings. Bhima, with scarcely any exertion and very soon, vanquished the southern Mallas and the Bhagauanta mountains. The hero next vanquished, by policy alone, the Sarmakas and the Varmakas. That tiger among men defeated with comparative ease that lord of the earth, Janaka, the king of the Videhas.

The hero then subjugated strategically the Sakas and the barbarians living in that part of the country. The son of Pandu, sending forth expeditions from Videha, conquered the seven kings of the Kiratas living about the Indra mountain. The mighty hero, endowed with abundant energy, vanquished in battle the Submas and the Prasuhmas. Winning them over to his side, the son of Kunti, possessed of great strength, marched against Magadha. On his way, he subjugated the monarchs known by the names of Danda and Dandadhara. Accompanied by those monarchs, the son of Pandu marched against Girivraja.

After bringing the son of Jarasandha under his sway by conciliation and making him pay tribute, the hero, accompanied by the monarchs he had vanquished, marched against Kansa. Making the earth tremble by means of his troops consisting of the four kinds of forces, the foremost of the Pandavas encountered Karna, the slayer of foes. O Bharata, having subjugated Karna and brought him under his sway, the mighty hero then vanquished the powerful king of the mountainous regions. The son of Pandu slew in a fierce encounter, by the strength of his arms, the mighty king who dwelt in Madagiri.

The Pandava then, O king, subjugated in battle those strong and brave heroes of fierce prowess, viz., the heroic and mighty Vasudeva, the king of Pundra, and King Mahaujah who reigned in Kausika-kachchha, and then attacked the king of Vanga. Having vanquished Samudrasena, King Chandrasena, and Tamralipta, and also the king of the Karvatas and the ruler of the Suhmas, as well as the kings that dwelt on the sea-shore, that bull among the Bharatas conquered all Mlechchha tribes. The mighty son of the wind-god, having thus conquered various countries and exacting tributes from them all, advanced towards Lohity.

The son of Pandu then made all the Mlechchha kings dwelling in the marshy regions on the sea-coast pay tributes of various kinds of wealth, including sandalwood, aloes, clothes, gems, pearls, blankets, gold, silver, and valuable corals. The Mlechchha kings showered upon the illustrious son of Kunti a thick downpour of wealth consisting of coins and gems counted by hundreds of millions. Returning to Indraprastha, Bhima of terrible prowess offered the whole of that wealth unto King Yudhishthira the just."

Vaisampayana said, "Thus Sahadeva, dismissed with affection by King Yudhisthira the just, marched towards the southern direction accompanied by a mighty host. Strong in strength, that mighty prince of the Kuru race, vanquishing completely at the outset the Surasenas, brought the king of Matsya under his sway. The hero then defeated Dantavakra, the mighty king of the Adhirajas, and made him pay tribute, reinstating him on his throne. Sahadeva then brought under his sway Sukumara and King Sumitra, and he next vanquished other Matsyas and the Patacharas.

Endowed with great intelligence, Sahadeva conquered soon enough the country of the Nishadas and also the high hill called Gosringa, and the lord of earth called Srenimat. Subjugating the country called Navarashtra next, the hero marched against Kuntibhoja, who willingly accepted his sway. From there, on the banks of the Charmanwati, Sahadeva encountered the son of King Jamvaka, who had been previously defeated by Vasudeva due to old hostilities. The son of Jamvaka engaged Sahadeva in battle, and after defeating him, Sahadeva continued his march southward.

The mighty warrior then vanquished the Sekas and others, exacting tributes and various kinds of gems and wealth from them. Forming alliances with these tribes, Sahadeva marched towards the countries along the Narmada River. There, he battled and defeated the two heroic kings of Avanti, Vinda and Anuvinda, supported by a mighty host, and exacted much wealth from them.

Proceeding further to the town of Bhojakata, Sahadeva engaged in a fierce encounter with the king of that city for two whole days. Eventually, he vanquished the invincible Bhismaka and defeated in battle the king of Kosala, the ruler of the territories along the Venwa River, as well as the Kantarakas and the kings of the eastern Kosalas. Sahadeva defeated both the Natakeyas and the Heramvaks in battle, subjugating the country of Marudha and reducing Munjagrama through sheer strength.

Continuing his campaign, Sahadeva defeated the mighty monarchs of the Nachinas and the Arvukas, as well as various forest kings in that part of the country. With his great strength, he then brought king Vatadhipa under his subjection. Sahadeva battled the Pulindas next and marched southward. He fought for a day with the king of Pandrya, and after defeating him, continued further south.

Sahadeva then encountered the celebrated caves of Kishkindhya and engaged in a seven-day battle with the monkey-kings Mainda and Dwivida. Despite the fierce battle, the monkey-kings were gratified with Sahadeva and allowed him to pass, showering him with jewels and gems as tribute.

THE SOURCE OF CONFLICT

Proceeding towards the city of Mahishmati, Sahadeva battled with King Nila, a fierce and terrible encounter where Agni himself assisted Nila. The battlefield was enveloped in flames, causing great anxiety to Sahadeva. Janamejaya inquired why Agni would be hostile towards Sahadeva, who was fighting to accomplish a sacrifice.

Vaisampayana continued, "It is said that Agni, residing in Mahishmati, had earned a reputation as a lover. King Nila had a daughter of great beauty who always stayed near her father's sacred fire, causing it to blaze up with vigor. Agni desired the girl, and disguised as a Brahmana, enjoyed her company. When discovered, King Nila ordered punishment, but upon learning the truth, bestowed his daughter upon Agni, who became gracious to the king.

Agni granted Nila's kingdom protection from those unaware of his alliance. Sahadeva, seeing his troops afflicted with fear and surrounded by flames, purified himself and addressed Agni, praising his sanctity and seeking his favor. Agni, testing Sahadeva, eventually granted his assurance and allowed him to proceed. Sahadeva, having accepted the worship from King Nila, made him pay tribute and continued his march southward.

The long-armed hero brought the king of Tripura and the Paurava kingdom under his sway, followed by Akriti of Saurashtra and the kings of Surparaka and Talakata. He subdued numerous Mlechchha tribes along the sea coast, the Nishadas, the Karnapravarnas, and the Kalamukhas, among others. Sahadeva exacted tribute from the Paundrayas, Dravidas, Udrakeralas, Andhras, Talavanas, Kalingas, Ushtrakarnikas, and the cities of Atavi and Yavanas.

At the sea-shore, Sahadeva sent messengers to Vibhishana, who willingly accepted his sway and sent him abundant wealth and treasures. Accepting them, Sahadeva returned to his kingdom victorious.

Thus, that slayer of all foes, Sahadeva, having vanquished numerous kings through conciliation and war, and making them pay tribute, returned to his city. He presented the entire wealth unto King Yudhisthira, considering his mission accomplished and lived happily

Vaisampayana said, "I shall now recite to you the deeds and triumphs of Nakula, and how that exalted one conquered the direction that had once been subjugated by Vasudeva. The intelligent Nakula, surrounded by a large host, set out from Khandavaprastha towards the west, causing the earth to tremble with the shouts and roars of warriors and the rumble of chariot wheels.

First, Nakula assailed the mountainous country of Rohitaka, beloved by Kartikeya, filled with wealth, cattle, and prosperity. He had a fierce encounter with the Mattamyurakas of that region. Moving on, Nakula subjugated the entire desert country, Sairishaka, Mahetta, and engaged in a fierce battle with the royal sage Akrosa.

Continuing his conquests, Nakula subdued the Dasarnas, Sivis, Trigartas, Amvashtas, Malavas, five tribes of the Karnatas, and the Madhyamakeyas and Vattadhanas. He then conquered the Mlechcha tribes known as the Utsava-sanketas and brought under his sway the mighty Gramaniya on the seashore, the Sudras, Abhiras along the Saraswati, fisherfolk tribes, mountain dwellers, the country of the five rivers, the Amara mountains, Uttarayotisha, Divyakutta city, and the tribe of Dwarapala.

By sheer strength, Nakula subdued the Ramathas, Harahunas, and various western kings. Sending messengers to Vasudeva, all the Yadavas accepted Nakula's sway. Proceeding to Sakala, the city of the Madras, Nakula made his uncle Salya accept the Pandavas' sway out of affection. Salya generously entertained Nakula and gifted him with jewels and gems before he departed.

Nakula then subdued fierce Mlechchas on the sea coast, the wild tribes of Palhavas, Kiratas, Yavanas, and Sakas, making them all pay tributes. Returning to his city, Nakula brought back such vast wealth that ten thousand camels could barely carry it. Arriving at Indraprastha, he presented the entire wealth to Yudhishthira.

Thus, Nakula, foremost of the Kurus, conquered the western direction, previously subdued by Vasudeva himself, through his valor and resourcefulness."

Chapter 42

RAJASURYA YAJNA

Vaisampayana said: "Due to the protection offered by Yudhishthira the just, and his consistent truthfulness, along with the control he maintained over all enemies, the subjects of that virtuous monarch thrived in their respective vocations. Because of the equitable taxation and the virtuous rule of the monarch, the clouds in his kingdom poured as much rain as desired by the people, leading to prosperous cities and towns. Indeed, as a result of the king's actions, every affair in the kingdom, especially cattle breeding, agriculture, and trade, flourished significantly. O king, during those days, even robbers and cheats refrained from lying among themselves, nor did the king's favorites. There were no droughts, floods, plagues, fires, or premature deaths during the virtuous reign of Yudhishthira.

Kings approached Yudhishthira only for agreeable services, worship, or tributes that did not impoverish them, not for hostility or battle. The king's treasury was so abundantly filled with wealth obtained virtuously that it could not be exhausted even in a hundred years. Determining the state of his treasury and the extent of his possessions, the son of Kunti set his heart upon performing a sacrifice. His friends and officers, both individually and collectively, approached him and said, 'The time has come, O exalted one, for your sacrifice. Let arrangements be made without delay.'

As they were discussing, Hari (Krishna), the omniscient and ancient one, the soul of the Vedas, the invincible one as described by those knowledgeable, the foremost of all lasting existences in the universe, the origin of all things, and the lord of the past, future, and present, Kesava—the slayer of Kesi, the protector of all Vrishnis, and the dispeller of all fear in times of distress, the smiter of all foes—entered the excellent city of Khandava. Appointing Vasudeva to command the Yadava army and bringing a vast treasure for Yudhishthira, Krishna arrived, surrounded by a mighty host, filling the atmosphere with the rattle of his chariot wheels. Enhancing the limitless wealth of the Pandavas with an inexhaustible ocean of gems he brought, Madhava heightened the sorrows of the Pandavas' enemies. Krishna's presence in the Bharata capital gladdened it, just as the sun brings joy to a dark region or a gentle breeze to still air. Joyfully receiving and respectfully welcoming him, Yudhishthira inquired about Krishna's welfare.

After Krishna was comfortably seated, Yudhishthira, with Dhaumya, Dwaipayana, and other sacrificial priests, along with Bhima, Arjuna, and the twins, addressed Krishna: 'O Krishna, it is because of you that the whole earth is under my sway. Through your grace, I have acquired vast wealth. O son of Devaki, O Madhava, I wish to dedicate that wealth according to the ordinance to superior Brahmanas and the carrier of sacrificial libations. O Krishna of the

Dasarha race, it would be proper for you, mighty-armed one, to grant me permission to celebrate a sacrifice along with you and my younger brothers. Therefore, O Govinda, of long arms, install yourself at that sacrifice; for if you perform the sacrifice, I shall be cleansed of sin. Or, exalted one, grant permission for myself to be installed at the sacrifice along with my younger brothers, for if permitted by you, O Krishna, I shall be able to enjoy the fruit of an excellent sacrifice.'

Vaisampayana continued: "Krishna, extolling Yudhishthira's virtues, said, 'You, O tiger among kings, deserve imperial dignity. Therefore, let the great sacrifice be performed by you. If you perform that sacrifice and obtain its fruit, we shall all regard ourselves as crowned with success. I am always engaged in seeking good. Perform the sacrifice you desire. Employ me also in some office for that purpose, for I shall obey all your commands.' Yudhishthira replied, 'O Krishna, my resolve is already crowned with fruit, and success is surely mine when you, O Harishikesa, have arrived here in accordance with my wish!'

Vaisampayana continued: "Commanded by Krishna, the son of Pandu, along with his brothers, set about collecting materials for the performance of the Rajasuya sacrifice. That chastiser of all foes, the son of Pandu, then commanded Sahadeva, the foremost of warriors, and all ministers, saying, 'Let persons be appointed to collect, without delay, all the articles required for the performance of this sacrifice, as directed by the Brahmanas, and all materials and auspicious necessaries that Dhaumya may order as needed for it, each kind in the proper order. Let Indrasena, Visoka, and Puru with Arjuna for his charioteer be engaged to collect food if they are to please me. Let these foremost of the Kurus also gather every article of agreeable taste and smell that may delight and attract the hearts of the Brahmanas.'

Simultaneously with these words of king Yudhishthira the just, Sahadeva, having accomplished everything, represented the matter to the king. Dwaipayana then appointed as sacrificial priests exalted Brahmanas, who were like the Vedas themselves in embodied forms. The son of Satyavati became the Brahma of that sacrifice. Susaman of the Dhananjaya race became the chanter of the Vedic (Sama) hymns. Yajnavalkya devoted to Brahma became the Adhvaryu, and Paila, the son of Vasu, and Dhaumya became the Hotris. The disciples and sons of these men, all well-acquainted with the Vedas and their branches, became Hotragts. After uttering benedictions and reciting the purpose of the sacrifice, they worshipped the large sacrificial compound as prescribed.

Commanded by the Brahmanas, builders and artisans erected numerous spacious and well-perfumed edifices, resembling the temples of the gods. When these were finished, king Yudhishthira, the virtuous son of Pandu, entered the sacrificial compound, surrounded by thousands of Brahmanas, his brothers, relatives, friends, counselors, and many Kshatriya kings from various countries, and officers of state. Numerous Brahmanas, skilled in all branches of knowledge and versed in the Vedas and their branches, arrived from various regions. At the king's command, thousands of craftsmen built separate, well-provided habitations for those Brahmanas and their attendants, complete with food, clothes, and seasonal fruits and flowers. O king, worshipped by the monarch, the Brahmanas stayed there, conversing on diverse topics and enjoying performances by actors and dancers. The clamour of high-souled Brahmanas, cheerfully eating and talking, was heard continuously. 'Give,' and 'Eat' were the incessant words, day after day. Yudhishthira the just gave each Brahmana thousands of cattle, beds, gold coins, and damsels.

Thus commenced on earth the unrivaled sacrifice of the illustrious son of Pandu, resembling the sacrifice of Sakra in heaven.

Yudhishthira then dispatched Nakula to Hastinapura to bring Bhishma, Drona, Dhritarashtra, Vidura, Kripa, and his well-disposed cousins."

Vaisampayana said, "The ever-victorious Nakula, the son of Pandu, reached Hastinapura and formally invited Bhishma and Dhritarashtra. The elders of the Kuru race, with the preceptor at their head, joyfully accepted the invitation and came to the sacrifice, accompanied by Brahmanas. O bull of the Bharata race, upon hearing of King Yudhishthira's sacrifice, hundreds of other Kshatriyas from various countries, acquainted with the nature of the sacrifice and desiring to behold King Yudhishthira and his sacrificial mansion, arrived with joyous hearts, bringing costly jewels of various kinds.

Dhritarashtra, Bhishma, Vidura of high intelligence, and all the Kaurava brothers with Duryodhana at their head, along with Suvala, the king of Gandhara, and the mighty Sakuni; Achala, Vrishaka, Karna the foremost charioteer, the powerful Salya, the strong Valhika, Somadatta, Bhuri of the Kuru race, Bhurisravas, Sala; Aswatthama, Kripa, Drona, Jayadratha the ruler of Sindhu; Yajnasena with his sons, Bhagadatta the great car warrior king of Pragjyotisha, accompanied by all Mlechcha tribes from the marshy sea-shore regions; many mountain kings, King Vrihadvala, Vasudeva the king of the Paundrayas, the kings of Vanga and Kalinga; Akastha, Kuntala, the kings of the Malavas and the Andhrakas; the Dravidas, Singhalas, the king of Kashmira, Kuntibhoja of great energy, King Gauravahana, all the other heroic kings of Valhika; Virata with his two sons, Mavella of great might; various other kings and princes, and Sisupala of great energy and invincible in battle, accompanied by his son—all of them came to the sacrifice of the son of Pandu. Additionally, Rama, Aniruddha, Kanaka, Sarana, Gada, Pradyumna, Shamva, Charudeshna of great energy, Ulmuka, Nishatha, and the brave Angavaha, along with innumerable other Vrishnis—mighty car-warriors—all came.

These and many other kings from the middle country came, O monarch, to the great Rajasuya sacrifice of the son of Pandu. At the command of King Yudhishthira the just, mansions were assigned to all those monarchs, filled with various kinds of edibles and adorned with tanks and tall trees. The son of Dharma worshipped all those illustrious monarchs as they deserved. Worshipped by the king, they retired to the mansions assigned to them. These mansions, white and high like the cliffs of Kailasa, were delightful to behold and furnished with every kind of furniture. Enclosed on all sides with well-built and high white-washed walls, their windows were covered with gold networks and their interiors were adorned with rows of pearls. Their flights of stairs were easy to ascend, and the floors were covered with costly carpets. Garlands of flowers hung over them, and they were perfumed with excellent aloes. White as snow or the moon, they looked extremely handsome even from a distance of a yojana. Their wide doors and entrances could admit a crowd of people. Adorned with various costly articles and built with various metals, they looked like peaks of the Himavat.

After resting a while in those mansions, the monarchs beheld King Yudhishthira the just, surrounded by numerous Sadasyas (sacrificial priests) and ever performing sacrifices distinguished by large gifts to Brahmanas. That sacrificial mansion, filled with kings, Brahmanas, and great Rishis, looked, O king, as handsome as heaven itself crowded with the gods!"

Vaisampayana said, "Then, O king, Yudhishthira, having approached and worshipped his grandfather Bhishma and his preceptor Drona, addressed Bhishma, Drona, Kripa, Ashwatthama, Duryodhana, and Vivingsati. He said, 'Help me, all of you, in the matter of this sacrifice. This large treasure that is here is yours. Consult with one another and guide me as you desire.'

The eldest of the sons of Pandu, who had been installed at the sacrifice, having said this, appointed each of them to suitable offices. He appointed Dussasana to superintend the department of food and other enjoyable articles. Ashwatthama was asked to attend to the Brahmanas. Sanjaya was appointed to offer return worship to the kings. Bhishma and Drona, both endowed with great intelligence, were appointed to oversee what was done and what was left undone. The king appointed Kripa to look after the diamonds, gold, pearls, and gems, as well as the distribution of gifts to Brahmanas. Other tigers among men were appointed to similar offices. Valhika, Dhritarashtra, Somadatta, and Jayadratha, brought there by Nakula, enjoyed themselves as lords of the sacrifice. Vidura, also known as Kshatta and conversant with every rule of morality, became the disburser. Duryodhana became the receiver of the tributes brought by the kings. Krishna, who was himself the center of all worlds and around whom every creature moved, was engaged at his own will in washing the feet of the Brahmanas, desirous of acquiring excellent fruits.

None came there with tribute less than a thousand in number, weight, or measure, desirous of beholding the sacrificial mansion and King Yudhishthira the just. Everyone honored King Yudhishthira with large presents of jewels, each king flattering himself with the proud belief that the jewels he gave would enable the Kuru king to complete his sacrifice. The sacrificial compound of the illustrious son of Kunti looked extremely handsome, with the multitude of palaces built to last forever and crowded with guards and warriors. These palaces were so high that their tops touched the cars of the gods who came to behold the sacrifice. The compound was also adorned with the cars of the celestials, the dwellings of the Brahmanas, and the mansions made for the kings, resembling the cars of the celestials and adorned with gems, filled with every kind of wealth. The compound was crowded with kings, all endued with beauty and wealth.

Yudhishthira, as though vying with Varuna himself in wealth, commenced the Rajasuya sacrifice, distinguished by six fires and large gifts to Brahmanas. The King gratified everyone with presents of great value and every kind of object one could desire. With an abundance of rice and every kind of food, as well as a mass of jewels brought as tribute, that vast concourse consisted of persons who were all fed to the full. The gods were gratified at the sacrifice by the Ida, clarified butter, Homa, and libations poured by the great Rishis versed in mantras and pronunciation. Like the gods, the Brahmanas were also gratified with the sacrificial gifts, food, and great wealth. All other orders of men were also gratified at that sacrifice and filled with joy."

Vaisampayana said, "On the last day of the sacrifice, when the king was to be sprinkled with the sacred water, the great Brahmana Rishis, ever deserving of respectful treatment, along with the invited kings, entered the inner enclosure of the sacrificial compound. Those illustrious Rishis, with Narada as their foremost, seated at their ease with the royal sages within that enclosure, looked like the gods seated in the mansion of Brahma in the company of the celestial Rishis. Endued with immeasurable energy, those Rishis, having obtained leisure, started various topics of conversation. 'This is so,' 'This is not so,' 'This is even so,' 'This cannot be otherwise,' thus did many of them engage in discussions with one another. Some disputants, by well-chosen arguments, made the weaker position appear stronger and the stronger weaker. Some disputants, endued with great intelligence, attacked the positions urged by others like hawks darting at meat thrown into the air, while some, versed in the interpretations of religious treatises and others of rigid vows, well-acquainted with every commentary and gloss, engaged in pleasant converse. O king, that platform, crowded with gods, Brahmanas, and great Rishis, looked extremely handsome, like the wide expanse of the firmament studded with stars. O monarch, there was no Shudra near that platform of Yudhishthira's mansion, nor anybody without vows.

Narada, beholding the fortunate Yudhishthira's prosperity born of that sacrifice, became highly gratified. Seeing that vast concourse, the Muni Narada, O king of men, became thoughtful. O bull among men, the Rishi began to recollect the words he had heard of old in the mansion of Brahma regarding the incarnation on earth of portions of every deity. Knowing, O son of the Kuru race, that it was a concourse of incarnate gods, Narada thought in his mind of Hari with eyes like lotus-petals. He knew that the creator himself of every object, the exalted one of all gods, Narayana, who had formerly commanded the celestials, saying, 'Be ye born on earth, slay one another, and come back to heaven,' the slayer of all the enemies of the gods, the subjugator of all hostile towns, in order to fulfill his own promise, had been born in the Kshatriya order. Narada knew that the exalted and holy Narayana, also called Sambhu, the lord of the universe, having commanded all the celestials thus, had taken birth in the race of Yadus. That foremost perpetuator of races, having sprung from the line of the Andhaka-Vrishnis on earth, was graced with great good fortune and shone like the moon among stars. Narada knew that Hari, the grinder of foes, whose strength of arm was ever praised by all the celestials with Indra among them, was then living in the world in human form. The Self-Create will himself take away from the earth this vast concourse of Kshatriyas endowed with so much strength. Such was the vision of Narada, the omniscient, who knew Hari or Narayana to be the Supreme Lord whom everyone worshipped with sacrifice. Narada, gifted with great intelligence and the foremost of all persons, conversant with morality, thinking of all this, sat at that sacrifice of the wise king Yudhishthira the just with feelings of awe.

Then Bhishma, O king, addressing king Yudhishthira the just, said, 'O Bharata, let Arghya (an article of respect) be offered to the kings as each of them deserves. Listen, O Yudhishthira, the preceptor, the sacrificial priest, the relative, the Snataka, the friend, and the king are the six that deserve Arghya. The wise have said that when any of these dwell with one for a full year, he deserves to be worshipped with Arghya. These kings have been staying with us for some time. Therefore, O king, let Arghyas be procured to be offered to each of them. Let an Arghya be presented first to the foremost among those present.'

Hearing these words of Bhishma, Yudhishthira said, 'O Grandsire, O thou of the Kuru race, whom thou deemest the foremost among these and to whom the Arghya should be presented by us, O tell me.'

Vaisampayana continued, "Then, O Bharata, Bhishma, the son of Santanu, judged by his intelligence that on earth Krishna was the foremost of all. He said, 'As is the sun among all luminous objects, so is the one (Krishna) who shines like the sun among us all, in consequence of his energy, strength, and prowess. This sacrificial mansion is illuminated and gladdened by him as a sunless region by the sun, or a region of still air by a gust of breeze.' Thus commanded by Bhishma, Sahadeva, endued with great prowess, duly presented the first Arghya of excellent ingredients to Krishna of the Vrishni race. Krishna also accepted it according to the forms of the ordinance."

Chapter 43

ENVIOUS SISHUPALLA

Vaisampayana said, "But Sisupala could not bear to see that worship offered unto Vasudeva. And this mighty king of Chedi, reproving in the midst of that assembly both Bhishma and Yudhishthira, censured Vasudeva thereafter."

Sisupala said, "O thou of the Kuru race, this one of the Vrishni race does not deserve royal worship as if he were a king in the midst of all these illustrious monarchs. O son of Pandu, this conduct of thine in thus willingly worshipping him with eyes like lotus-petals is not worthy of the illustrious Pandavas. Ye sons of Pandu, ye are children; ye know not what morality is, for that is very subtle. Bhishma, this son of Ganga, is of little knowledge and hath transgressed the rules of morality by giving ye such counsel. And, O Bhishma, if one like thee, possessed of virtue and morality, acteth from motives of interest, he is deserving of censure among the honest and the wise. How does he of the Dasarha race, who is not even a king, accept worship before these kings, and how is it that he hath been worshipped by ye? O bull of the Kuru race, if thou regardest Krishna as the oldest in age, here is Vasudeva, and how can his son be said so in his presence? Or, if thou regardest Vasudeva as your well-wisher and supporter, here is Drupada; how then can Madhava deserve the first worship? Or, O son of Kuru, regardest thou Krishna as preceptor? When Drona is here, how hast thou worshipped him of the Vrishni race? Or, O son of Kuru, regardest thou Krishna as the Ritwija? When old Dwaipayana is here, how hath Krishna been worshipped by thee? Again, when old Bhishma, the son of Santanu, that foremost of men who is not to die save at his own wish is here, why, O king, hath Krishna been worshipped by thee? When the brave Aswatthaman, versed in every branch of knowledge, is here, why, O king, hath Krishna, O thou of the Kuru race, been worshipped by thee? When that King of kings, Duryodhana, that foremost of men, is here, as also Kripa the preceptor of the Bharata princes, why hath Krishna been worshipped by thee? How, O son of Pandu, passing over Druma, the preceptor of the Kimpurusas, hast thou worshipped Krishna? When the invincible Bhishmaka and king Pandya possessed of every auspicious mark, and that foremost of kings--Rukmi and Ekalavya and Salya, the king of the Madras, are here, how, O son of Pandu, hast thou offered the first worship unto Krishna? Here also is Karna ever boasting of his strength amongst all kings, and really endued with great might, the favourite disciple of the Brahmana Jamadagnya, the hero who vanquished in battle all monarchs by his own strength alone. How, O Bharata, hast thou, passing him over, offered the first worship unto Krishna? The slayer of Madhu is neither a sacrificial priest nor a preceptor, nor a king. That thou hast nonetheless worshipped him, O chief of the Kurus, could only have been from motives of gain. If, O Bharata, it was your wish to offer the first worship unto the slayer of Madhu, why were these monarchs brought here to be insulted thus? We have not paid tributes to the illustrious son of Kunti from fear, from desire of gain, or from having been won over by conciliation. On the other hand, we have paid him tribute simply because he hath been desirous of the imperial dignity from motives of virtue. And yet he it is that thus insulteth us. O king, from what else, save motives of insult, could it have been that thou hast worshipped Krishna, who possesseth not the insignia of royalty, with the Arghya in the midst of the assembled monarchs? Indeed, the reputation for virtue that the son of Dharma hath acquired, hath been acquired by him without cause, for who would offer such undue worship unto one that hath fallen off from virtue? This wretch born in the race of the Vrishnis unrighteously slew of old the illustrious king Jarasandha. Righteousness hath today been abandoned by Yudhishthira and meanness only hath been displayed by him in consequence of his having offered the Arghya to Krishna. If the helpless sons of Kunti were affrighted and disposed to meanness, thou, O Madhava, ought to have enlightened them as to their claims to the first worship? Why also, O Janardana, didst thou accept the worship of which thou art unworthy, although it was offered unto thee by those mean-minded princes? Thou thinkest much of the worship unworthily offered unto thee, like a dog that lappeth in solitude a quantity of clarified butter that it hath obtained. O Janardana, this is really no insult offered unto the monarchs; on the other hand, it is thou whom the Kurus have insulted. Indeed, O slayer of Madhu, as a wife is to one that is without virile power, as a fine show is to one that is blind, so is this royal worship to thee who art no king. What Yudhishthira is, hath been seen; what Bhishma is, hath been seen; and what this Vasudeva is hath been seen. Indeed, all these have been seen as they are!"

Having spoken these words, Sisupala rose from his excellent seat, and accompanied by the kings, went out of that assembly.

THE SOURCE OF CONFLICT

Vaisampayana said, "Then King Yudhishthira hastily pursued Sisupala, his voice soft and conciliatory as he addressed the fuming monarch. 'O lord of earth,' he said, 'your words are not befitting. Such utterances are sinful and cruel, unworthy of one of your stature. Do not insult Bhishma by questioning his understanding of virtue. Look around; these kings, many older and wiser than you, all approve of the honor given to Krishna. It behooves you to accept this decision with patience, like them. Bhishma knows Krishna truly; you, O ruler of Chedi, know him not as well as this elder of the Kuru race.'

Bhishma then spoke, his voice resonating through the hall. 'He who denies worship to Krishna, the eldest in the universe, deserves neither kind words nor conciliation. The greatest of Kshatriya warriors, who spares a vanquished foe, becomes the guru of the defeated. I see no ruler here who has not been bested by the power of this son of the Satwata race. Krishna, of undefiled glory, deserves worship not just from us, but from the three worlds. Countless warriors have fallen before his might. The limitless universe itself is founded in him. Thus, we honor Krishna as the best and the eldest. Your words are ill-advised, O king of Chedi. I have served many learned elders and heard from them of Krishna's countless virtues and deeds. We do not honor him out of caprice or personal gain, but for his fame, heroism, and success. Every young and old soul here has been considered. We choose Hari for his supreme virtues.

In this assembly, the one superior in knowledge among Brahmanas, in strength among Kshatriyas, in wealth among Vaisyas, and in years among Sudras deserves worship. Krishna excels in Vedic knowledge and strength, surpassing all in the world of men. He embodies liberality, cleverness, Vedic knowledge, bravery, modesty, achievements, intelligence, humility, beauty, firmness, contentment, and prosperity. These dwell eternally in Achyuta. Therefore, O kings, you should approve of the honor given to Krishna, a preceptor, father, and guru, worthy of the Arghya and deserving of universal worship. Hrishikesa is the sacrificial priest, the guru, the sought-after son-in-law, the learned Snataka, the king, and the friend. Thus, Achyuta is honored by us.

Krishna is the origin and dissolution of the universe. The universe of both mobile and immobile beings sprang from him. He is the unmanifest primal cause, the eternal creator beyond all creatures' comprehension. Hence, his unfading glory deserves the highest worship. Intellect, sensibility, the five elements—air, heat, water, ether, earth—and all beings are established in Krishna. The sun, the moon, constellations, planets, directions—all are founded in Krishna. Just as the Agnihotra is foremost among sacrifices, the Gayatri among meters, the king among men, the ocean among rivers, the moon among constellations, the sun among luminous bodies, Meru among mountains, and Garuda among birds, so is Kesava foremost in all worlds, including the celestial realms.

This Sisupala is but a boy, ignorant of Krishna's greatness, and speaks out of turn. This ruler of Chedi will never perceive virtue as those seeking high merit do. Among the elders and youths here, who does not regard Krishna as deserving of worship? If Sisupala finds this honor undeserved, let him do what he deems proper.'

Vaisampayana said, "The mighty Bhishma fell silent, his words hanging in the air like a weighty pall. Then Sahadeva, his face set in grim resolve, spoke to Sisupala with words that cut like tempered steel. 'If among you there is any king who cannot bear to see Kesava, the slayer of Kesi, the possessor of immeasurable energy, worshipped by me, then let this my foot rest upon the heads of all such mighty ones. Let anyone who dares, answer me. And let those kings who possess true wisdom approve the worship of Krishna, who is the preceptor, the father, the guru, and who rightly deserves the Arghya and the worship bestowed upon him.'

When Sahadeva thus displayed his foot, a hush fell over the assembly of proud monarchs. Not one dared to challenge him. Then, as if the heavens themselves took note, a shower of flowers rained down upon Sahadeva's head, and an incorporeal voice rang out, 'Excellent, excellent.' Narada, clad in black deer-skin, speaking of both the future and the past, and dispelling all doubts with his knowledge of the worlds, declared, 'Those who refuse to worship the lotus-eyed Krishna should be considered as dead though they walk the earth, and should never be spoken to on any occasion.'

Vaisampayana continued, "Sahadeva, aware of the distinction between a Brahmana and a Kshatriya, honored those who deserved respect and completed the ceremony. But as Krishna received the first worship, Sisupala, eyes blazing red with fury, addressed the gathered rulers of men. 'When I am here to lead you all, what are you thinking now? Let us array ourselves for battle against the assembled Vrishnis and Pandavas.' Stirring the kings to a fever pitch, the bull of the Chedis began conspiring to disrupt the sacrifice.

The invited monarchs, with Sisupala at their head, seethed with anger, their faces pale with rage. 'We must act so that the final sacrificial rite performed by Yudhishthira and the worship of Krishna are not seen as having our approval,' they vowed, their minds clouded by fury and pride. Driven by their belief in their own might and stung by the perceived insult, the kings repeated their oaths. Though their friends tried to calm them, their faces burned with the fury of lions deprived of their prey.

Krishna, seeing the vast sea of monarchs, with its countless waves of troops, understood that a storm was brewing, a tempest of battle that threatened to unleash its fury upon the sacrificial ground."

Vaisampayana said, "Beholding that vast assembly of kings, wrathful and seething like the sea at the time of universal dissolution, Yudhishthira turned to the aged Bhishma, the wisest among men and the grandsire of the Kurus, akin to Indra, the slayer of foes, seeking counsel from Vrihaspati. 'This ocean of kings is agitated by wrath. Grandsire, tell me what I should do. How can I ensure that my sacrifice is not obstructed and my subjects remain unharmed?'

King Yudhishthira, ever just and conversant with morality, sought guidance, and Bhishma, the grandsire of the Kurus, replied, 'Fear not, O tiger of the Kurus. Can the dog slay the lion? I have discerned a path that is both beneficial and easy to follow. As dogs in a pack bark at a sleeping lion, so are all these lords of earth. Like dogs before a lion, they rage before the sleeping lion of the Vrishni race. Achyuta is now like a sleeping lion. Until he awakens, this chief of the Chedis, this lion among men, makes these monarchs appear fierce. But know, O child, that this Sisupala, possessed of little intelligence, seeks to lead these kings to the realm of Yama through the agency of the one who is the soul of the universe. Surely, Vishnu desires to reclaim the energy residing in Sisupala. The intelligence of this wicked-minded king of the Chedis, and of all these monarchs, has become perverse. Indeed, the minds of those whom this tiger among men wishes to take unto himself become perverse, just like that of the king of the Chedis. Yudhishthira, know that Madhava is the creator and destroyer of all beings of the four species in the three worlds.'

Vaisampayana continued, "Then the ruler of Chedis, having heard Bhishma's words, addressed the grandsire with stern and rough words.

Sisupala snarled, his eyes blazing with a fiery wrath. "Old and infamous wretch of the Kuru race, are you not ashamed, trying to terrify these mighty kings with your falsehoods? You, who are supposed to be the wisest among the Kurus, living a life of celibacy, should be ashamed of yourself for preaching such misguided morality. You are like a blind guide leading other blind men, dragging the Kurus into disgrace with your empty words. Once again, you have

THE SOURCE OF CONFLICT

pained our hearts with your tales of Krishna's supposed feats, like the slaying of Putana.

Arrogant and ignorant as you are, you seek to praise Krishna—why does your deceitful tongue not split into a hundred pieces? How dare you, who claim wisdom, extol that cowherd, who even fools can revile? If Krishna killed a vulture in his infancy, what of it? What is remarkable about his other feats, Bhishma, like his killing of Aswa and Vrishava, who were mere novices in battle? If this one toppled a wooden cart with a kick, what wonder is there in that? And what is so great about his holding up a hill like Govardhan, which is no more than an anthill?

You speak of his feats on the mountaintop, of him devouring large amounts of food—many have laughed at your words. And, Bhishma, what of the fact that he killed Kansa, who had offered him food? You, an infamous Kuru, are ignorant of true morality. Have you not heard from the wise that weapons should not be raised against women, cows, Brahmanas, those whose food one has taken, or those whose shelter one has enjoyed? All these teachings seem lost on you, Bhishma. In your blind praise of Krishna, you describe him as superior in wisdom and age, as if we know nothing. If, by your words, one who has slain women and cows deserves worship, then what is left of morality? How can such a one be praised, Bhishma?

You claim that Krishna is the foremost of wise men, the lord of the universe. Hearing this, Janardana believes these falsehoods. But they are lies. Like a chanter whose verses fall on deaf ears, so does Krishna's supposed greatness. Each creature acts according to its nature, like the bird Bhulinga picking meat from a lion's teeth while preaching caution.

Your nature is indeed base, Bhishma. There is no doubt. The Pandavas, who see Krishna as deserving worship and follow you, are equally corrupt. Possessing knowledge of virtue, you have strayed from the path of the wise. You are sinful. Who, Bhishma, knowing himself to be virtuous and wise, would act as you have, under the guise of virtue?

If you understand morality, if your mind is truly wise, then blessed are you. But why, Bhishma, did you abduct the virtuous Amva, who had given her heart to another, if you are so full of wisdom and virtue? Your brother Vichitravirya, in keeping with the ways of the honest and virtuous, did not marry her, knowing her heart's condition. And in your very sight, sons were begotten on your brother's widow by another man, following the ways of the honest. Where is your virtue, Bhishma? Your celibacy, whether from ignorance or impotence, is fruitless. You, who claim to know virtue, seem blind to true wisdom.

Worship, gifts, study, sacrifices with generous offerings to Brahmanas—none of these equals the merit of having a son. The merit from countless vows and fasts becomes fruitless for the childless. You are old, childless, and a false expounder of morality. Like the deceitful swan, you will die at the hands of your kin. Others wise in knowledge have spoken of this long ago. I shall recount it fully.

Once, an old swan lived on the sea-coast, preaching morality but acting otherwise, instructing the feathered tribes. 'Practice virtue and avoid sin,' he would say. The birds, trusting him, brought him food out of virtue. But this sinful swan, attentive only to his own needs, ate the eggs of those who trusted him. When their eggs dwindled, a wise bird grew suspicious and caught him in the act. In sorrow, the wise bird told the others, and they, seeing the swan's deceit, slew him.

Your behavior, Bhishma, mirrors that old swan. These kings might slay you in their anger, like the birds slew the deceitful swan. Those who know the Puranas recite a proverb: 'O you who live on wings, though your heart is corrupt, you preach virtue; yet your sinful act of devouring the eggs betrays your words.'"

Sisupala sneered, his voice dripping with disdain. "That mighty king Jarasandha, who refused to fight Krishna, declaring 'He is a mere slave,' earned my highest respect. What praise can there be for the treacherous act committed by Krishna, Bhima, and Arjuna in Jarasandha's death? Disguised as a Brahmana, Krishna entered Jarasandha's domain through deceit, masking his true intentions. When Jarasandha offered this deceiver water to wash his feet, Krishna shed his Brahmanahood under false pretenses of virtue. And when Jarasandha invited Krishna, Bhima, and Dhananjaya to dine, it was Krishna who arrogantly refused.

If Krishna is indeed the lord of the universe, as you claim, why does he not uphold the dignity of a Brahmana? It astounds me that, despite your misguidance, the Pandavas still view you as honorable. But perhaps it is not so surprising, considering they follow a counselor like you, O Bharata, who is feeble in spirit and weighed down by age."

Vaisampayana continued, "At these harsh and scornful words from Sisupala, Bhimasena, that foremost of mighty men, was consumed by anger. His eyes, naturally large and lotus-like, flared wide and turned the color of molten copper. The assembled monarchs saw the three deep lines of rage on his forehead, resembling the Ganga's currents on the triple-peaked mountain. Bhimasena's teeth ground together in fury, his face transforming into a visage of Death itself, poised to devour all at the end of the Yuga. As the hero, brimming with wrath, prepared to leap, Bhishma, the mighty-armed grandsire, seized him, much like Mahadeva holding back Mahasena.

Bhishma's wise counsel soon quelled Bhima's rage, the chastiser of foes yielding to his grandsire's words, just as the ocean respects its shores even in the tumult of the rainy season. Yet, even though Bhima was pacified, Sisupala, reliant on his own valor, showed no fear. Bhima's threatening leaps were met with Sisupala's indifference, like a lion ignoring the rage of a lesser beast.

The proud king of Chedi, undeterred by Bhima's fearsome wrath, laughed and taunted, 'Release him, O Bhishma! Let all the assembled kings witness him consumed by my might like an insect in the fire.' Hearing the audacious words of Sisupala, Bhishma, the wisest of the Kurus and the most sagacious of men, addressed Bhima with these words."

Bhishma spoke, his voice a steady anchor amidst the gathering storm of emotions. "This Sisupala was born in the lineage of the king of Chedi, marked by omens both wondrous and dreadful. With three eyes and four hands, he entered the world, his cries akin to the braying of an ass. His birth struck terror into the hearts of his parents and kin. In their fear, they resolved to abandon him. But then, an incorporeal voice echoed, soothing their anxieties. It declared, 'This son of yours, O king, will grow to be fortunate and unmatched in strength. Fear not for his life. He is destined for greatness, and his end is not yet written. The one who will slay him with weapons has also been born.'

At these words, the mother, her heart bound by maternal love, beseeched the unseen speaker, 'I bow to thee, exalted being, whether god or spirit. Reveal to me who will be the slayer of my son.' The invisible voice replied, 'He upon whose lap this child is placed, causing his superfluous arms to fall away like five-headed serpents, and at whose sight his third eye will vanish, shall be his slayer.'

Hearing this prophecy, kings from all corners of the earth journeyed to Chedi, drawn by the marvel of the child with three eyes and four arms. Each monarch, received with honor by the king of Chedi, held the child upon his lap, yet the prophecy did not come to pass. From the distant city of Dwaravati, the mighty Yadava heroes, Sankarshana and Janardana, came to see their father's sister, the queen of Chedi.

THE SOURCE OF CONFLICT

Paying their respects to all, including the king and queen, they took their seats with dignity.

The queen, with a heart full of joy and anticipation, placed the child on the lap of Damodara. Instantly, the superfluous arms fell away, and the third eye vanished. Overwhelmed by fear and awe, the queen begged Krishna for a boon. 'O mighty-armed Krishna, I am consumed by dread. Grant me a boon, for you are the protector of the fearful and the dispeller of anxieties.'

Krishna, with compassion in his eyes, replied, 'Fear not, O noble one. You are wise and just. What boon do you seek? Speak, and I shall fulfill it to the best of my ability.'

The queen, trembling, said, 'O you of great strength, pardon the offenses of Sisupala for my sake. This is the boon I ask.'

Krishna, ever magnanimous, responded, 'O aunt, even when he deserves death, I shall forgive a hundred offenses of his. Do not grieve.'

Bhishma continued, "Thus, O Bhima, this vile king Sisupala, emboldened by the boon granted by Govinda, dares to challenge you. His heart is wicked, and his pride will be his downfall.'"

Bhishma spoke, his voice like the rumble of distant thunder, "The summons of the ruler of Chedi, challenging you to fight, Bhima, though you are a pillar of unwavering strength, is not truly his own doing. Surely, it is the design of Krishna himself, the lord of the universe. What king on earth would dare to insult me so brazenly as this wretch has today, unless driven by some divine purpose? Sisupala, mighty though he may seem, is but a vessel for a fragment of Hari's energy. It is clear that the Lord seeks to reclaim this part of his own essence. Thus, this king of Chedi, wicked and roars with such arrogance, thinking little of us all."

Vaisampayana continued, "Hearing these words of Bhishma, the king of Chedi could restrain his wrath no longer. He replied in anger, 'Let our enemies possess the prowess that Kesava has, whom you, like a bard reciting hymns, incessantly praise, rising repeatedly from your seat. If your heart delights so much in praising others, then praise these kings instead of Krishna. Praise Darada, the ruler of Valhika, who split the earth at birth. Praise Karna, the king of Anga and Vanga, who equals Indra in strength, who wields a mighty bow, who was born with celestial earrings and a coat of mail that shines like the rising sun. Praise him who bested the invincible Jarasandha in wrestling, tearing and mangling that mighty monarch. O Bhishma, praise Drona and his son Aswatthaman, the mightiest warriors, the best of Brahmanas, either of whom, if angered, could annihilate the world. I see no king on earth equal to Drona or Aswatthaman. Why do you not praise them?

Passing over Duryodhana, the mighty-armed king of kings, unmatched on the earth, and Jayadratha, master of weapons and great prowess, and Druma, the renowned preceptor of the Kimpurushas, and Kripa, the learned preceptor of the Bharata princes, why do you sing the praises of Kesava? Passing over Rukmin, the illustrious king, and Bhishmaka, and Dantavakra, and Bhagadatta, celebrated for his many sacrificial stakes, and Jayatsena of Magadha, and Virata, and Drupada, and Sakuni, and Vrihadvala, and Vinda and Anuvinda of Avanti, and Pandya, Sweta, Uttama, Sankhya, the proud Vrishasena, the mighty Ekalavya, and the great charioteer Kalinga, why do you sing of Kesava? And, O Bhishma, if you are so inclined to praise others, why not praise Salya and the other rulers of the earth? O king, what can I do when it seems you have never heard the teachings of virtuous elders? Have you never learned that self-praise and slander are not the ways of respectable men? None approve of your conduct, O Bhishma, in constantly praising Krishna, who is unworthy of such honor. How do you, by your own will, elevate the cowherd of Bhoja,

Kansa's servitor, to the lord of the universe? Perhaps, O Bharata, your inclination does not match your true nature, like the bird Bhulinga, as I have mentioned before.

There is a bird called Bhulinga, living beyond the Himalayas. Always preaching caution, it says, 'Never act rashly,' yet it itself acts recklessly, picking flesh from between the lion's teeth while it eats. Assuredly, O Bhishma, you are like that bird. Your survival depends on the goodwill of these kings. Always acting contrary to the counsel of the wise, none is like you in this regard."

Vaisampayana continued, "Hearing these harsh words from the ruler of Chedi, Bhishma, O king, said in the hearing of all, 'Truly, I live at the pleasure of these kings, but I regard them as not worth even a straw.' As soon as Bhishma spoke, the kings flamed with wrath. Some stood with their hair standing on end, and others began to reproach Bhishma. Some, wielders of large bows, exclaimed, 'This wretched Bhishma, though old, is exceedingly boastful. He does not deserve our pardon. Let us kill this wretch, or burn him in a fire of grass or straw.'

Hearing these words, Bhishma, the grandsire of the Kurus, wise and unperturbed, addressed those lords of earth, 'Words may answer words endlessly. Therefore, listen to me, ye lords of earth. Whether I am slain like an animal or burned in a fire of grass and straw, I still place my foot upon your heads. Here stands Govinda, unyielding and eternal. Let him who seeks a swift death challenge Madhava, the dark-hued wielder of the discus and mace, and join in the divine body of this god!'"

Vaisampayana said, "Hearing these words of Bhishma, the ruler of Chedi, endowed with exceeding prowess, desirous of combating Vasudeva, addressed him and said, 'O Janardana, I challenge thee. Come, fight with me until I slay thee today along with all the Pandavas. For, O Krishna, the sons of Pandu, who have disregarded the claims of all these kings to worship thee, who art no king, deserve to be slain by me along with thee. This is my opinion, O Krishna, that they who have foolishly worshipped thee, as if thou deservest it, although thou art unworthy of worship, being only a slave and a wretch and no king, deserve to be slain by me.' Having said this, that tiger among kings stood there roaring in anger.

Krishna then addressed all the assembled kings in the presence of the Pandavas, speaking these words in a soft voice: 'Ye kings, this wicked-minded one, who is the son of a daughter of the Satwata race, is a great enemy of us of the Satwata race; and though we never seek to injure him, he ever seeks our evil. This wretch of cruel deeds, hearing that we had gone to the city of Pragjyotisha, came and burnt Dwaraka, although he is the son of my father's sister. While King Bhoja was sporting on the Raivataka hill, this one attacked the attendants of that king, slew many, and led away many others in chains to his own city. Sinful in all his actions, this wretch stole the sacrificial horse of my father's horse-sacrifice, which had been let loose under the guard of armed men, to obstruct the sacrifice. Prompted by sinful motives, he ravished the reluctant wife of the innocent Vabhru (Akrura) while she was traveling from Dwaraka to the country of the Sauviras. This injurer of his maternal uncle, disguising himself as the king of Karusha, ravished the innocent Bhadra, the princess of Visala, the intended bride of King Karusha. I have patiently borne all these sorrows for the sake of my father's sister. It is fortunate that all this has occurred today in the presence of all the kings. Behold today the hostility this one bears towards me, and know all the injuries he has inflicted upon me. For his excessive pride displayed in the presence of all these monarchs, he deserves to be slain by me. I can no longer pardon him today for the injuries he has done me. Desiring a speedy death, this fool sought Rukmini. But the fool obtained her not, like a Sudra failing to obtain the Vedas.'

Vaisampayana continued, 'Hearing these words of Vasudeva, all the assembled monarchs began to reprove the ruler of Chedi. But the powerful Sisupala, laughing aloud, replied, 'O Krishna, art thou not ashamed to say in this assembly, before all these kings, that Rukmini (thy wife) had been coveted by me? O slayer of Madhu, who else would say in the midst of respectable men that his wife had been intended for someone else? O Krishna, pardon me if thou pleasest, or pardon me not. But angry or friendly, what canst thou do unto me?'

While Sisupala was speaking thus, the exalted slayer of Madhu summoned the discus that humbles the pride of the Asuras. As soon as the discus came into his hands, Krishna, skilled in speech, loudly proclaimed, 'Listen, ye lords of earth, why this one has hitherto been pardoned by me. As asked by his mother, a hundred offenses of his were to be pardoned by me. This was the boon she had asked, and this I granted her. That number, ye kings, is now complete. I shall now slay him in your presence, ye monarchs.' Having said this, the chief of the Yadus, slayer of all foes, instantly cut off the head of the ruler of Chedi with his discus. The mighty-armed Sisupala fell down like a cliff struck by thunder. The assembled kings then beheld a fierce energy, like the sun in the sky, issue from the body of the king of Chedi, and that energy, worshipping Krishna, entered his body. All the kings, beholding this energy entering the mighty-armed chief of men, regarded it as wonderful.

When Krishna had slain the king of Chedi, the sky, though cloudless, poured showers of rain, and blasting thunders were hurled, and the earth trembled. Some of the kings sat silently, gazing at Janarddana, while others rubbed their palms in rage or bit their lips. Some applauded Krishna in private, others were incensed, and some sought to mediate. The great Rishis, with pleased hearts, praised Kesava and departed. All the high-souled Brahmanas and mighty kings praised Krishna.

Yudhishthira then commanded his brothers to perform the funeral rites of Sisupala, the brave son of Damaghosha, with proper respect. The Pandavas obeyed his command. Yudhishthira then, with all the kings, installed the son of Sisupala as the sovereign of the Chedis.

That sacrifice of the Kuru king, blessed with prosperity, became exceedingly handsome and pleasing to all. Commenced auspiciously, with all impediments removed, and furnished with abundance of wealth, corn, and food, it was properly supervised by Kesava. Yudhishthira completed the great sacrifice in due time. Janarddana, the exalted Sauri, with his bow Saranga, his discus, and mace, guarded the sacrifice until its completion. The Kshatriya monarchs, having approached Yudhishthira after the conclusion of the sacrifice, said, 'By good fortune, thou hast come out successful. Thou hast obtained the imperial dignity and great religious merit. We have been worshipped by thee to the full extent of our desires. We now wish to return to our own kingdoms. It behooveth thee to grant us permission.'

Hearing these words, Yudhishthira worshipped each king as deserved and commanded his brothers, saying, 'These monarchs came to us willingly. They now wish to return, bidding me farewell. Follow these excellent kings to the confines of our dominions.' The Pandava princes followed the kings as each deserved. Dhrishtadyumna followed King Virata, Dhananjaya followed the mighty charioteer Yajnasena, Bhimasena followed Bhishma and Dhritarashtra, Sahadeva followed Drona and his son, and Nakula followed Suvala and his son. The sons of Draupadi and the son of Subhadra followed the kings of the mountainous countries. Other Kshatriyas followed other Kshatriyas, and Brahmanas by thousands also departed, duly worshipped.

After all the kings and Brahmanas had gone, Vasudeva addressed Yudhishthira, saying, 'O son of the Kuru race, with thy leave, I desire to return to Dwaraka. By great good fortune, thou hast accomplished the foremost of sacrifices, the Rajasuya!' Yudhishthira replied, 'Owing to thy grace, O Govinda, I have accomplished the great sacrifice. Without thee, my heart never feels any delight. How can I, therefore, give thee leave to go? But thou must return to Dwaraka.' The virtuous Hari of worldwide fame, thus addressed by Yudhishthira, cheerfully went with his cousin to Pritha and said, 'O aunt, thy sons have obtained the imperial dignity, vast wealth, and success. Be pleased. Commanded by thee, I desire to go to Dwaraka.' Kesava bade farewell to Draupadi and Subhadra, then performed his ablutions and daily rites, and made the Brahmanas utter benedictions. The mighty-armed Daruka arrived with a chariot of excellent design. Beholding the Garuda-bannered chariot, Krishna, with eyes like lotus leaves, respectfully circled it, ascended, and set out for Dwaravati. Yudhishthira and his brothers followed Vasudeva on foot. Krishna, stopping the chariot for a moment, said, 'O king of kings, cherish thy subjects with vigilance and patience. Be the refuge and support of thy relatives.' Krishna and Yudhishthira took leave and returned to their respective homes. After Krishna had gone to Dwaravati, Duryodhana and Sakuni, bulls among men, continued to live in the celestial assembly house.

Chapter 44

THE PORTENT OF DOOM FORETOLD

Vaisampayana spoke, "When that foremost of sacrifices, the Rajasuya, so arduous and majestic, had reached its zenith, Vyasa, the ancient sage surrounded by his disciples, presented himself before Yudhishthira. The King of Dharma, upon beholding him, swiftly rose from his seat, flanked by his stalwart brothers. With reverence, he worshipped the Rishi, his grandfather, offering water to cleanse his feet and a seat of honor.

The illustrious Vyasa, once settled on a lavish carpet inlaid with gold, addressed Yudhishthira, 'Take thy seat.' And after the king had taken his place, the sage, ever truthful, said, 'O son of Kunti, fortune favors you. Thou hast achieved the imperial sway, an honor so few attain. The Kauravas have thrived under thy rule. Emperor, I have been duly worshipped; I seek your leave to depart.'

Yudhishthira, thus addressed by the venerable Rishi of dark hue, saluted him and touched his feet, saying, 'O revered one, a doubt plagues me deeply. O bull among sages, none but you can dispel it. The exalted Narada mentioned that the Rajasuya sacrifice would herald three kinds of portents: celestial, atmospheric, and terrestrial. O grandsire, have these portents ceased with the fall of the king of the Chedis?'

Vaisampayana continued, "Hearing these words of the king, the exalted Vyasa, son of Parasara, spoke, 'For thirteen years, O king, these portents will unfold into cataclysmic events, leading to the annihilation of the Kshatriyas. O scion of Bharata, thou shalt be the unwitting cause of this devastation, brought about by the sins of Duryodhana and the might of Bhima and Arjuna. In your dreams, towards the end of this period, thou shalt behold the blue-throated Bhava, the destroyer of Tripura, meditating, his bull by his side, drinking from a human skull. Tall and white as the Kailasa cliff, armed with trident and bow, garbed in tiger skin, he gazes unceasingly towards the southern direction, the domain of the Pitris. This shall be your vision tonight. Do not despair, for no one can escape the grasp of Time. Blessed be thou! I now depart to Kailasa. Rule with vigilance and patience, enduring all trials.'"

Vaisampayana continued, "Having spoken thus, Vyasa, the island-born sage, accompanied by his disciples, departed towards Kailasa. Left alone, the king, gripped by anxiety and grief, brooded over the Rishi's words. He pondered, 'Indeed, what the Rishi foretold shall come to pass. Can we thwart fate by sheer effort?' Then, with resolute calm, Yudhishthira addressed his brothers, 'Tigers among men, you have heard the Rishi's prophecy. I have decided to accept my fate, as I am destined to be the cause of the Kshatriya's downfall. Dear ones, if Time decrees so, what purpose have I to live?'

Hearing this, Arjuna replied, 'O king, do not surrender to despair, which clouds reason. Muster your courage and do what is beneficial.'

Firm in his resolve, Yudhishthira responded, 'Blessed be ye. Hear my vow from this day forth. For thirteen years, I shall speak no harsh word to my brothers or any king. I shall live by their commands, practicing virtue. If I hold to this vow, making no distinction between my children and others, discord shall not arise. Disagreement breeds war. By avoiding conflict and doing what pleases others, I shall escape ill repute.'

The Pandavas, ever supportive of their eldest brother, approved his words. Yudhishthira, having pledged this vow, performed the customary rites, satisfying the priests and the gods. After the monarchs departed, Yudhishthira, accompanied by his brothers and ministers, entered his palace. Meanwhile, King Duryodhana and Sakuni, son of Suvala, remained in the splendid assembly hall."

Thus, the stage was set for the inexorable march of destiny, where the grand designs of fate would unfold, and heroes would rise and fall like the tides of an unending sea.

Chapter 45

THE JEALOUSY OF DURYODHANA

Vaisampayana said, "That bull among men, Duryodhana, continued to dwell in the assembly house of the Pandavas. Accompanied by Sakuni, the Kuru prince wandered through the mansion, beholding many celestial designs unseen before in Hastinapura. One day, as Duryodhana roamed the mansion, he came upon a crystal surface. Mistaking it for a pool of water, the king, from ignorance, drew up his clothes. Realizing his mistake, he wandered the mansion in sorrow.

Later, mistaking a crystal lake adorned with lotuses for solid ground, he fell into it, clothes and all. Beholding Duryodhana's plight, Bhima laughed aloud, joined by the palace menials. At the king's command, the servants brought him dry, handsome clothes. Duryodhana's repeated blunders—mistaking solid ground for water and vice versa, and striking his head against a crystal door he thought open—drew more laughter from Bhima, Arjuna, and the twins. Concealing his humiliation, Duryodhana did not even cast a glance at them.

After enduring these humiliations, Duryodhana, with the Pandavas' leave, returned to Hastinapura. His heart, tormented by the sight of the Pandavas' prosperity, inclined towards sin. Reflecting on the wealth displayed at the Rajasuya sacrifice and his numerous errors, he grew pale and sorrowful.

As he journeyed to his city, Duryodhana brooded on the Pandavas' happiness and the homage paid to them by all the kings of the earth. The sight of their splendor and prosperity left him deeply afflicted. So absorbed was he in his thoughts that he did not speak a word to Sakuni, who addressed him repeatedly.

Sakuni, seeing his nephew's distraction, said, 'O Duryodhana, why do you proceed thus?'

Duryodhana replied, 'O uncle, the whole earth sways under Yudhishthira's rule, thanks to Arjuna's might. That sacrifice of the son of Pritha rivaled that of the great Indra himself. Filled with jealousy, I burn day and night, drying up like a shallow tank in summer. When Sisupala was slain by Krishna, no one dared defend him. That improper act was forgiven by all because of Yudhishthira's power. So many monarchs brought wealth for Yudhishthira, paying tribute like obedient subjects! Witnessing Yudhishthira's splendor, my heart burns with jealousy, though it is unworthy of me.

Reflecting thus, Duryodhana, as if burnt by fire, addressed the king of Gandhara again, 'I shall throw myself into a flaming fire, swallow poison, or drown in water. I cannot live seeing my enemies prosper while I am destitute. What man of vigor can bear to see his foes in prosperity while he languishes? Therefore, I, who endure this torment, am neither man nor woman. Witnessing their sovereignty and affluence, I am consumed by jealousy. Alone, I cannot achieve such royal splendor, nor do I see allies to aid me. Thus, I contemplate self-destruction. Seeing the Pandavas prosper and remembering the laughing menials, my heart burns as if on fire. Therefore, O uncle, know me as deeply grieved and jealous, and speak of it to Dhritarashtra.'

Thus, Duryodhana's heart, consumed by envy and despair, set the stage for the tragic events that would follow, driven by the inexorable forces of fate and his own burning jealousy."

Sakuni spoke with a voice as smooth and treacherous as a serpent's hiss, "O Duryodhana, cast aside this jealousy gnawing at your heart like a ravenous beast. The sons of Pandu enjoy their fortunes, granted by destiny and their own prowess. Mighty king, all your schemes and machinations have fallen to naught against their indomitable spirit and luck. These lion-hearted men, escaping every snare, now bask in the glory of their deeds and alliances. Draupadi, queen of unparalleled beauty, stands by their side, along with Drupada and his valiant sons, and the formidable Vasudeva. United, they are a force that could conquer the very heavens. Their kingdom, earned by right and strengthened by their valor, thrives. Why let this fester in your soul?

Recall how Dhananjaya, blessed by Agni, wields the legendary Gandiva, the inexhaustible quivers, and celestial weapons. With these, and his unmatched skill, he has subjugated kings far and wide. What grievance can you hold against their well-earned triumphs? When Arjuna saved the demon architect Maya from the flames, he was gifted that magnificent assembly hall. Its beauty is beyond mortal craftsmanship, protected by the grim Kinkaras at Maya's command. This should stir no bitterness in your breast.

You claim to lack allies, but this is untrue, O son of Kuru. Your brothers stand ready, obedient to your will. Drona, master of the great bow, along with his fierce son, Radha's son Karna, the warrior

Gautama (Kripa), myself and my kin, and the resolute king Saumadatti—these are your stalwart allies. With our combined might, the earth itself could be brought under your dominion."

Duryodhana, his eyes burning with a dark flame, replied, "With you and these formidable warriors, I shall indeed subjugate the Pandavas. If their power can be broken, then the world, its kings, and that opulent assembly house will be mine."

Sakuni, with a knowing smile, said, "Arjuna and Vasudeva, Bhimasena and Yudhishthira, Nakula and Sahadeva, and the mighty Drupada with his sons—none can match them in open battle. Not even the gods dare challenge them, for they are peerless warriors. But, O king, I know a way to bring Yudhishthira to his knees. Hearken to my plan."

Duryodhana leaned in, eager and desperate, "Reveal this path to victory, one that does not endanger our loyal men."

Sakuni's eyes gleamed with cunning, "Yudhishthira, the son of Kunti, has a weakness—a love for the game of dice, though he is not skilled in its art. If challenged, he cannot refuse. I, however, am a master of the dice, unmatched in all the realms. Challenge him to a game. I shall ensure his defeat, and with it, his kingdom and his riches shall be yours."

Duryodhana's lips curled into a cruel smile, "But, O son of Suvala, it is you who must present this plan to Dhritarashtra, the chief of the Kurus. I lack the words to persuade him."

Thus, the seeds of treachery were sown, in the shadows of ambition and jealousy, setting the stage for a game that would alter the fate of empires and heroes

Vaisampayana said: "O king, impressed with the grandeur of the Rajasuya sacrifice of King Yudhishthira, Sakuni, son of Suvala, understood Duryodhana's dark intentions as they departed from the assembly house. Wishing to please him, Sakuni approached the wise but blind Dhritarashtra, finding him seated upon his throne. He spoke thus: 'O great king, bull of the Bharata race, know that Duryodhana, your eldest son, has grown pale, emaciated, and a prey to deep anxiety. Why do you not, after due inquiry, ascertain the grief that burdens his heart, grief caused by his foes?'

Dhritarashtra replied, 'Duryodhana, what is the reason for your great affliction, son of the Kuru race? If it is fit for me to hear, tell me the reason. Sakuni here says you have lost color, become pale and emaciated, and are consumed by anxiety. I know not what grief torments you. All my wealth is at your disposal. Your brothers and all our kin never do anything against your wishes. You wear the finest apparel and eat the best food prepared with meat. The best horses carry you. What then has made you so pale and emaciated? Costly beds, beautiful damsels, mansions adorned with excellent furniture, and delightful pastimes await you at your command, like the very gods themselves. Why then do you grieve, son, as if destitute?'

Duryodhana, his voice seething with barely concealed rage, replied, 'I live like a wretch, eating and dressing myself with no joy, consumed by fierce jealousy. He indeed is a man who, unable to bear the pride of his foes, lives only to vanquish them and liberate his people from their tyranny. Contentment, pride, compassion, and fear—these are destructive to prosperity. One who acts under their influence achieves nothing. Beholding Yudhishthira's prosperity, I find no gratification in my own. The splendor of Kunti's son makes me burn with envy. His affluence torments me, even unseen. Thus, I have grown pale and melancholy. Yudhishthira supports eighty-eight thousand Brahmanas with thirty slave-girls each. Thousands more Brahmanas eat daily at his palace from golden plates. The king of Kambhoja sends innumerable deer skins and blankets as tribute. Thousands of elephants and camels wander his grounds. Kings bring him heaps of jewels and gems. Such wealth I have never seen or heard of before. Witnessing this, I find no peace. Hundreds of Brahmanas wait at his palace gates with vast tributes but are turned away. Ocean himself brings him nectar superior to that produced for Sakra. Vasudeva bathed the son of Pritha with sea water in golden jars adorned with gems. All this I witnessed, becoming feverish with jealousy. The jars were taken to the Eastern and Southern oceans and to the Western sea on men's shoulders. Arjuna even exacted tribute from the Northern regions, unreachable except by birds. A hundred thousand Brahmanas were fed daily, announced by the chorus of conches. Hearing those conches, my hair stood on end. The palatial compound, filled with monarchs, resembled a starry firmament. Kings brought every kind of wealth, distributing food like Vaisyas. The prosperity I beheld in Yudhishthira is unmatched by even the chief of the celestials. Witnessing it, my heart burns, robbing me of peace.

Hearing Duryodhana's words, Sakuni replied, 'Hear how you may attain this prosperity, O son of truth and prowess. I am a master of dice, unmatched in the world. I know the success of every throw, when to stake and when to refrain. The son of Kunti loves the game but lacks skill. Summon him to play, and I shall defeat him repeatedly through deception. I promise to win all his wealth, and you shall enjoy it.'

Vaisampayana continued: King Duryodhana, thus addressed by Sakuni, immediately said to Dhritarashtra, 'This Sakuni, master of dice, can win the wealth of the sons of Pandu. Grant him permission, O king.'

Dhritarashtra replied, 'I always follow the counsel of Kshatta, my wise minister. After consulting with him, I will decide. Endowed with foresight, he will determine what is good and proper for both parties, keeping morality in view.'

Duryodhana, his face darkening, said, 'If you consult Kshatta, he will dissuade you. If you desist, I will kill myself. Once I am dead, you and Vidura will be happy, enjoying the whole earth. What need have you of me?'

Vaisampayana continued: Dhritarashtra, hearing these despairing words from Duryodhana, succumbed to his son's demand. He commanded his servant, 'Have artisans erect a magnificent palace with a hundred doors and a thousand columns. Adorn it with jewels and precious stones. Report to me when it is complete.'

Having decided to pacify Duryodhana, Dhritarashtra sent for Vidura, whose counsel he never ignored. Though aware of gambling's evils, the king was drawn to it. Vidura, sensing impending doom, quickly came to Dhritarashtra, bowed, and said, 'O exalted king, I do not approve this resolution. It behooves you to act to prevent any dispute between your children over this gambling match.'

Dhritarashtra replied, 'If the gods are merciful, no dispute will arise. Let this friendly challenge proceed. Fate has ordained it. With Drona, Bhishma, and you near, nothing evil will happen. Go swiftly to Khandavaprastha, bring Yudhishthira here. My mind is set. I regard Fate as supreme.'

Vidura, realizing the doom of his race, went sorrowfully to the wise Bhishma

Chapter 46
THE CAUSE OF THE GAME OF DICE

Janamejaya said, "O foremost among those versed in the Vedas, how did that fateful game of dice transpire, bringing such sorrow upon my grandsires, the sons of Pandu? Which kings were present in that assembly, and who among them sanctioned the game, and who opposed it? O sinless one, chief of the regenerate, I desire you to recount in detail this event, which led to the world's destruction."

Santi said, "Thus addressed by the king, Vyasa's disciple, endowed with great energy and conversant with the entire Vedas, narrated all that had occurred."

Vaisampayana said, "O best of the Bharatas, great king, if you wish to hear, then listen as I recount everything again in detail.

Upon consulting Vidura, Dhritarashtra, son of Amvika, called Duryodhana aside and spoke to him in private, 'O son of Gandhari, have nothing to do with dice. Vidura does not speak well of it. Possessed of great wisdom, he will never give me advice that is not for my good. I regard what Vidura says as exceedingly beneficial. Do that, O son, for it is for your good also. Indeed, Vidura knows all the mysteries of the science of political morality that the illustrious and learned Vrihaspati, the celestial Rishi who is the spiritual guide of Vasava, unfolded to the wise chief of the immortals. O son, I always accept Vidura's advice. As the wise Uddhava is esteemed among the Vrishnis, so is Vidura, possessed of great intelligence, regarded among the Kurus. Therefore, O son, have nothing to do with dice. Dice sows dissension, and dissension ruins kingdoms. Therefore, O son, abandon this idea of gambling. You have received from us what a father and mother should give to their son: ancestral rank and possessions. You are educated and clever in every branch of knowledge, and have been brought up with affection in your paternal home. Born the eldest among your brothers, living in your own kingdom, why regard yourself as unhappy? O mighty-armed one, you enjoy the best food and attire, which ordinary men cannot obtain. Why then do you grieve? Ruling your vast ancestral kingdom, swelling with people and wealth, you shine as splendidly as the chief of the celestials in heaven. You are wise. It behooves you to tell me what is the root of this grief that has made you so melancholy.'

Duryodhana replied, 'I am a sinful wretch, O king, because I eat and dress while beholding the prosperity of our foes. It is said that a man is a wretch if he is not filled with jealousy at the sight of his enemy's prosperity. O exalted one, this kind of prosperity does not gratify me. Beholding the blazing prosperity of the son of Kunti, I am deeply pained. My vitality must be strong, for I live despite seeing the whole earth under Yudhishthira's sway. The Nipas, Chitrakas, Kukkuras, Karaskaras, and Lauha-janghas live in Yudhishthira's palace like bondsmen. The Himavat, the ocean, the regions on the seashore, and countless other regions that yield jewels and gems have all acknowledged the superiority of Yudhishthira's mansion in terms of wealth. Considering me the eldest and worthy of respect, Yudhishthira received me respectfully and appointed me to receive the jewels and gems brought as tribute. O Bharata, the excellence and number of these invaluable jewels are beyond compare. My hands grew weary from receiving that wealth. When I was tired, those who brought the valuable items waited until I could resume. Maya, the Asura architect, brought jewels from the lake Vindu and constructed a crystal lake-like surface for the Pandavas. Seeing the (artificial) lotuses, I mistook it for water. As I lifted my clothes to cross, Vrikodara (Bhima) laughed at me, thinking I had lost my head at the sight of my enemy's wealth. If I had the strength, I would kill Vrikodara without delay. But if we attempt to slay Bhima now, our fate will be like Sisupala's. O Bharata, that insult burns me. Again, mistaking a similar lake full of water for a crystal surface, I fell into it. Bhima, Arjuna, and Draupadi, accompanied by other women, laughed at me. That pains my heart greatly. My wet clothes were replaced by menials at the king's command, adding to my sorrow. In another mistake, I struck my forehead against stone, injuring myself while attempting to pass through what seemed like a door but was not. The twins Nakula and Sahadeva, seeing me hit my head, supported me, expressing concern. Sahadeva said, as if smiling, 'This is the door, O king. Go this way!' Bhimasena laughed aloud, saying, 'O son of Dhritarashtra, this is the door.' In that mansion, I saw gems whose names I had never heard before. For these reasons, my heart aches so."

Duryodhana continued, "Listen now, O Bharata, to the most costly articles I beheld, one after another, brought by the kings of the earth to the sons of Pandu. Beholding that wealth of the foe, I lost my senses and scarcely recognized myself. Hear as I describe that wealth, consisting of both manufactured goods and agricultural produce.

"The king of Kamboja presented innumerable skins of the finest kings, woolen blankets embroidered with threads of gold, and three hundred horses of the Titteti and Kalmasha breeds, each with noses like parrots. He also gave three hundred camels and an equal number of she-asses, all fattened with olives and Pilusha. Countless Brahmanas, engaged in cattle rearing and other lowly occupations, came with three hundred million tributes but were denied entry into the palace. Hundreds of wealthy Brahmanas, living on lands gifted by Yudhishthira, arrived with their golden Kamandalus filled with clarified butter, yet they too were refused entry.

"Sudra kings from the coastal regions brought hundreds of thousands of serving girls from Karpasika, adorned with golden ornaments, along with Ranku deer skins fit even for Brahmanas. Vairamas, Paradas, Tungas, Kitavas, and others from riverine and coastal regions, along with tribes born in woodlands and across the ocean, came with goats, kine, asses, camels, vegetables, honey, blankets, jewels, and gems of various kinds, all refused entry at the gate.

"Great warrior King Bhagadatta of Pragjyotisha, ruler of mlechchas, arrived with Yavanas, bearing a tribute of horses known for their swiftness. Unable to enter, Bhagadatta left, leaving behind swords with ivory handles adorned with diamonds and other gems. Tribes from various regions, some with two eyes, some with three, and others with foreheads adorned with eyes, such as Aushmikas, Nishadas, Romakas, and even cannibals, stood at the gate, denied entry. They brought ten thousand asses of diverse hues and enormous size, famed for their speed and docility, bred on the Vankhu coast. Many kings offered Yudhishthira vast quantities of gold and silver, gaining admission into his palace.

"Tribes with single-legged inhabitants presented wild horses—some red as cochineal, others white, some like the hues of the rainbow or evening clouds, all swift as thought. They also bestowed superior gold upon the king. I witnessed Chins, Sakas, Uddras, barbarous tribes from the woods, Vrishnis, Harahunas, dusky tribes of the Himavat, Nipas, and coastal dwellers, all waiting at the gate, denied entry.

"Valhikas presented ten thousand asses of impressive stature with black necks, capable of running two hundred miles daily, in various forms, well-trained and renowned worldwide. They also brought numerous woolen blankets from Chin, skins of Ranku deer, jute and insect-spun clothes not made of cotton, possessing lotus-like colors and smooth textures, along with thousands of soft sheepskins. They offered sharp swords, scimitars, hatchets, and finely-edged battle-axes from western lands, alongside thousands of perfumes, jewels, and gems, yet were denied entry.

"Sakas, Tukhatas, Tukharas, Kankas, Romakas, and horned men brought large elephants, ten thousand horses, and billions in gold, also refused entry. Kings from the east presented countless valuable items, including luxurious carpets, vehicles, beds, armors adorned with jewels, gold, and ivory, various weapons, diverse-shaped chariots with well-trained horses draped in tiger skins, and vibrant blankets for elephant caparisons. They brought jewels, gems, long and short arrows, and other weapons, finally gaining entry into the sacrificial palace of the illustrious Pandavas!"

Duryodhana continued, "O sinless one, listen as I describe the vast wealth in various forms of tribute presented to Yudhishthira by the kings of the earth. The Khashas, Ekasanas, Arhas, Pradaras, Dirghavenus, Paradas, Kulindas, Tanganas, and other tribes dwelling near the river Sailoda amidst the bamboo groves of Kichaka, brought gold measured in dronas, mined by ants and thus named after these creatures. Mountain tribes of great strength brought soft black and moon-white Chamaras, honey from Himavat and Mishali champaka flowers, garlands from northern Kuru lands, and various plants from Kailasa, yet were refused entry.

"I saw numerous Kirata chiefs armed with cruel weapons, living on fruits, roots, and clad in skins, from the northern slopes of Himavat, the sun-rising mountains, Karusha region on the sea-coast, and both sides of Lohitya mountains. They brought sandalwood, black aloe, valuable skins, gold, perfumes, ten thousand native serving-girls, beautiful animals, birds from distant lands, and gold of splendid hue, yet were denied entry. Kairatas, Daradas, Darvas, Suras, Vaiamakas, Audumvaras, Durvibhagas, Kumaras, Paradas with Vahlikas, Kashmiras, Ghorakas, Hansakayanas, Sivis, Trigartas, Yauddheyas, Madra and Kaikeya rulers, Amvashtas, Kaukuras, Tarkshyas, Vastrapas with Palhavas, Vashatayas, Mauleyas including Kshudrakas, Malavas, Paundrayas, Kukkuras, Sakas, Angas, Vangas, Punras, Sanavatyas, Gayas—all these noble Kshatriyas brought tribute in hundreds and thousands.

"Vangas, Kalingas, Magadhas, Tamraliptas, Supundrakas, Dauvalikas, Sagarakas, Patrornas, Saisavas, and countless Karnapravaranas were instructed by gatekeepers that with good tribute they could enter. Each gave a thousand elephants with tusks like ploughshafts, draped in gold-adorned blankets resembling lotuses, dark as rocks, and always musty, bred near Kamyaka lake, clad in defensive armor, exceedingly patient, and of the finest breed. After presenting these, they gained entry.

"Chitraratha, the Gandharva king and Indra's friend, gifted four hundred horses as swift as the wind. Gandharva Tumvuru joyfully gave a hundred mango-leaf-colored horses adorned with gold. The celebrated Sukaras, Mlechcha tribe king, presented numerous excellent elephants. Virata of Matsya offered two thousand gold-decked elephants. King Vasudana from Pansu gave twenty-six elephants and two thousand horses, all bedecked in gold, youthful, and robust, along with other wealth. Yajnasena offered fourteen thousand serving-girls, ten thousand serving-men with wives, hundreds of excellent elephants, twenty-six elephant-yoked chariots, and his entire kingdom. Vasudeva of Vrishni race enhanced Arjuna's honor with fourteen thousand excellent elephants. Krishna, Arjuna's very soul, and Arjuna, capable of sacrificing for Krishna, share an inseparable bond.

"Kings of Chola and Pandya, though they brought numerous jars of gold filled with fragrant sandal juice from Malaya hills, sandal and aloe wood from Dardduras hills, brilliant gems, and fine cloths inlaid with gold, were not permitted entry. King of Singhalas gave sea-born lapis lazuli gems, heaps of pearls, and hundreds of elephant coverlets, accompanied by dark-skinned men with copper-red eyes and gem-adorned clothes. Countless Brahmanas, Kshatriyas, Vaisyas, serving Sudras, and even Mlechchas came out of love for Yudhishthira. Men of all races and orders from diverse lands made Yudhishthira's abode a microcosm of the world.

"Seeing these kings presenting such excellent and valuable gifts to our enemies, I wished for death out of sorrow. Now, O king, I will tell you about the servants of the Pandavas, who receive food both cooked and raw from Yudhishthira. There are a hundred thousand billion mounted elephants and cavalry, a hundred million chariots, and countless foot soldiers. At one place, provisions are being measured, at another cooked, and at another distributed. Festive notes resound everywhere. In Yudhishthira's mansion, not a single person lacks food, drink, or ornaments. Eighty-eight thousand Snataka Brahmanas leading domestic lives, each with thirty serving-girls, pray daily for the destruction of his foes, supported by the king. Ten thousand other ascetics, leading withdrawn lives, daily dine on golden plates. Yajnaseni, though not having eaten herself, ensures everyone, even the deformed and dwarfs, are fed. Only the Panchalas, due to marital ties, and Andhakas and Vrishnis, due to friendship, do not pay tribute to Kunti's son."

Duryodhana continued, "Those kings revered across the world, devoted to truth and strict vows, learned in Vedas, sacrifices, eloquent, pious, modest, virtuous, renowned, and coronated, all waited upon and worshiped Yudhishthira. I saw many thousands of wild kine with vessels of white copper for milking, brought as sacrificial gifts to be given to Brahmanas. For Yudhishthira's bathing after the sacrifice, kings eagerly brought jars of water in a state of purity. King Vahlika brought a chariot adorned with pure gold. King Sudakshina yoked four white Kamboja horses, Sunitha fitted the lower pole, the ruler of Chedi placed the flagstaff, the southern king stood with the coat of mail, Magadha's ruler held garlands and headgear, Matsya's king brought gold-clad side-fittings, Ekalavya provided shoes, Avanti's king brought various waters for the final bath, Kasi's king presented the bow, and Salya offered a sword with gold-adorned hilt and straps. Dhaumya, Vyasa, Narada, and Asita's son Devala performed the ceremony of sprinkling sacred water over Yudhishthira, with other Rishis including Jamadagni's son.

"Satyaki held the umbrella, Arjuna and Bhima fanned the king, while the twins held chamaras. The Ocean himself brought Varuna's big conch in a sling, made by Viswakarman with a thousand Nishkas of gold, presented by Prajapati to Indra in a previous Kalpa. Krishna bathed Yudhishthira with this conch, causing me to swoon at its sight. People travel to Eastern, Western, and Southern seas, but birds reach the Northern sea. Yet the Pandavas extend their dominion there, as hundreds of conches brought thence were blown at the mansion, signaling auspicious joy. Hearing these conches, my hair stood on end, weaker kings fell unconscious, and Dhrishtadyumna, Satyaki, Pandu's sons, and Krishna laughed. Arjuna cheerfully gifted five hundred bullocks with gold-plated horns to the principal Brahmanas.

"Yudhishthira, having completed the Rajasuya sacrifice, attained prosperity unmatched by Harishchandra, Rantideva, Nabhaga, Jauvanaswa, Manu, Prithu, Bhagiratha, Yayati, or Nahusha. Seeing Yudhishthira's unparalleled prosperity, like that of Harishchandra's, I find no reason to live, O Bharata! Like a blind man's yoke, our dominance is slipping away, with the younger rising while the elder fades. Seeing this, O chief of Kurus, I cannot find peace even in reflection. Thus, plunged into grief, I grow pale and emaciated."

Dhritrashtra spoke, his voice stern yet laced with a father's concern, "You are my eldest son, born of my foremost wife. Hence, son, cast aside your envy towards the Pandavas. Jealousy is a serpent that gnaws at the soul, filling one's days with sorrow and nights with the restless anguish of the damned. Mighty scion of the Bharata line, know this: Yudhishthira harbors no deceit, his wealth matches yours, he counts your friends as his own, and he harbors no ill will towards you. Why, then, should you begrudge him?

King, in the realm of allies and friends, you are Yudhishthira's equal. Why covet, in your folly, the riches of your brother? Abandon this jealousy. Do not let grief consume you. Lion among Bharatas, if it is the glory of performing great sacrifices you desire, let the priests prepare for you the grand Saptatantu. The monarchs of the earth shall then, with joy and reverence, present to you treasures, gems, and adornments. Coveting another's wealth is beneath you, a deed for the base and ignoble.

True happiness belongs to those who are content with their own lot, who toil in their own sphere, protecting what is theirs without yearning for what belongs to others. This is the mark of true greatness. One who remains steadfast in calamity, skilled in their trade, ever diligent and humble, shall always find prosperity. The sons of Pandu are as your own limbs. Would you sever your own arms in a fit of madness? Do not plunge this family into strife over the riches of your kin. King, harbor no envy towards the sons of Pandu. Your wealth rivals theirs in its entirety. There is great sin in quarreling with one's own blood.

Those who are your grandsires are theirs as well. Give generously at sacrifices, fulfill every noble desire, revel in the company of women, and find joy and peace in your life.

Duryodhana, his voice sharp and edged with frustration, spoke thus, "One who lacks intellect but has merely heard many things can scarcely grasp the true essence of the scriptures, much like a spoon that has no perception of the taste of the soup it touches. You know everything, yet you confound me. We are tied to each other like boats fastened together. Are you neglecting your own interests, or do you harbor hostile feelings towards me? Your sons and allies are doomed to destruction, for you describe as attainable in the future what should be done in the present moment. He who follows a guide acting under the instructions of others often stumbles. How then can his followers hope to find the right path?

King, you possess mature wisdom, you have had the opportunity to listen to the words of the ancients, and your senses are under your control. It is not fitting for you to confound those of us who seek our own interests. Vrihaspati has said that the customs of kings differ from those of common people. Therefore, kings should always attend to their own interests with vigilance. Success is the sole criterion that should guide the conduct of a Kshatriya. Whether the means are virtuous or sinful, what scruples can there be in the duties of one's own order? One who wishes to seize the blazing prosperity of his foe should, like a charioteer taming his steeds with a whip, bring every direction under his control.

Weapons, those accustomed to handling them say, are not merely instruments that cut, but means, whether overt or covert, to defeat a foe. Who is a foe and who a friend does not depend on one's appearance or size. He who causes pain to another is to be regarded as a foe by the one who is pained. Discontent is the root of prosperity. Therefore, King, I desire to be discontented. The one who strives for prosperity is truly wise. No one should be attached to wealth and affluence, for hoarded wealth may be plundered. Such are the customs of kings.

During a time of peace, Indra cut off Namuchi's head after having given a pledge to the contrary, approving this eternal practice towards the enemy. Like a snake that swallows frogs and other creatures living in holes, the earth swallows a peaceful king and a Brahmana who never leaves his home. King, no one is by nature another's foe. He is a foe who has common pursuits with another. Neglecting a growing foe from folly allows one's vitals to be cut off as by a disease cherished without treatment. A foe, however insignificant, if allowed to grow in power, will swallow one like white ants eating at the root of a tree.

O Bharata, O Ajamida, let not the prosperity of the foe be acceptable to you. This policy of neglecting the foe should always be borne in mind by the wise. He who always wishes for the increase of his wealth grows naturally in the midst of his relatives, just as the body grows from the moment of birth. Prowess brings rapid growth. Coveting the prosperity of the Pandavas, I have not yet made it my own. Currently, I am prey to doubts about my ability. I am determined to resolve these doubts. I will either obtain their prosperity or perish in battle. King, when my mind is in such a state, what do I care for life, as the Pandavas daily grow while our possessions remain stagnant?

Sakuni, his eyes glinting with a dark promise, declared, "O foremost of victorious men, I will snatch the prosperity of Yudhishthira, son of Pandu, the sight of which grieves you so. Summon Yudhishthira, son of Kunti. With my skill at dice, I can vanquish him without causing harm. Understand, O Bharata, that betting is my bow, the dice are my arrows, the marks on them my bowstring, and the dice-board my chariot."

Duryodhana, his voice firm with determination, said, "This Sakuni, skilled in dice, is ready, O king, to seize the prosperity of the son of Pandu through dice. You should give him permission."

Dhritarashtra, hesitant and wary, replied, "I am obedient to the counsels of my brother, the illustrious Vidura. Consulting with him, I will decide what should be done in this matter."

Duryodhana, dismissing his father's caution, retorted, "Vidura is always working for the good of the sons of Pandu. His feelings towards us are different. He will undoubtedly dissuade you from this plan. No man should embark on a task relying solely on another's counsel, for the minds of two people seldom agree. The fool who avoids all risks wastes away like an insect in the rainy season. Neither sickness nor death waits for prosperity. Therefore, as long as there is life and health, one should strive to accomplish one's goals."

Dhritarashtra, troubled but resigned, said, "Son, hostility with those who are strong is never wise. Hostility changes feelings, and that itself is a weapon, though not made of steel. You see a great blessing in this plan, but it brings the terrible consequences of war. What you propose is fraught with mischief. Once begun, it will lead to sharp swords and pointed arrows."

Duryodhana, undeterred, replied, "Men of ancient times invented the use of dice. There is no destruction in it, no striking with weapons. Let Sakuni's words be heeded, and let your command be issued for the speedy construction of the assembly house. Gambling will open the door to happiness. With this aid, we will attain good fortune. The

Pandavas will become your equals; therefore, gamble with the Pandavas."

Dhritarashtra, his voice heavy with foreboding, said, "Your words do not convince me. Do what you find agreeable, O ruler of men. But you will have to repent for acting on these words. Words that are fraught with such immorality can never bring prosperity. This was foreseen by the wise Vidura, ever treading the path of truth and wisdom. The great calamity, destructive of the Kshatriyas, comes as destined by fate."

Vaisampayana continued: "Having said this, the weak-minded Dhritarashtra saw fate as supreme and unavoidable. The king, deprived of reason by fate and obedient to his son's counsels, commanded his men loudly, saying, 'Construct, without delay, an assembly house of the most beautiful description, to be called the Crystal-Arched Palace with a thousand columns, decked with gold and lapis lazuli, furnished with a hundred gates, and two miles in length and breadth.' Hearing his command, thousands of skilled artisans erected the palace with great speed and filled it with every kind of article. They soon informed the king that the palace was complete, delightful, and handsome, furnished with countless gems and covered with many-colored carpets inlaid with gold. Then King Dhritarashtra, summoning Vidura, his chief minister, said, 'Go to Khandavaprastha, bring Prince Yudhishthira here without delay. Let him come with his brothers to behold my magnificent assembly house, furnished with countless jewels and gems, and costly beds and carpets, and let a friendly match at dice commence here.'"

Vaisampayana spoke, "King Dhritarashtra, understanding his son's inclinations and knowing that Fate is inevitable, followed the course I've described. However, Vidura, that foremost of intelligent men, disapproved of his brother's words and spoke thus, 'I do not approve of this command, O king. Do not act so. I fear this will lead to the destruction of our race. When your sons lose their unity, dissension will surely follow. This, I apprehend, will arise from this match at dice.'

Dhritarashtra, resigned and fatalistic, replied, 'If Fate is not hostile, this quarrel will not grieve me. The whole universe moves at the will of its Creator, under the controlling influence of Fate. It is not free. Therefore, Vidura, go to King Yudhishthira at my command and bring that invincible son of Kunti here soon.'"

Chapter 47

THE GAMBLING MATCH BEGINS

Vaisampayana spoke, "Vidura, compelled against his will by King Dhritarashtra, set out with swift and strong horses for the abode of the wise sons of Pandu. Possessed of great intelligence, Vidura traveled swiftly to the capital of the Pandavas. Arriving at the city of King Yudhishthira, he entered the palace, worshipped by numerous Brahmanas. Reaching the palace, which resembled the mansion of Kuvera, the virtuous Vidura approached Yudhishthira, the son of Dharma. The illustrious Yudhishthira, devoted to truth and without enemies, respectfully greeted Vidura and inquired about Dhritarashtra and his sons.

Yudhishthira asked, 'O Kshatta, you seem troubled. Do you come here in peace and happiness? Are the sons of Dhritarashtra obedient to their father? Are the people content under Dhritarashtra's rule?'

Vidura replied, 'The illustrious king and his sons are well and happy. Surrounded by relatives, he reigns like Indra himself. The king is content with his obedient sons and has no grief. He seeks his own aggrandizement. Dhritarashtra has commanded me to inquire about your well-being and to invite you to Hastinapura with your brothers. He wishes you to see his newly erected palace and engage in a friendly dice match. We would be pleased if you accept, as the Kurus are already there. You will find skilled gamblers and cheats that Dhritarashtra has brought. This is why I have come. Let the king's command be agreeable to you.'

Yudhishthira said, 'O Kshatta, gambling can lead to quarrels. Who, knowing this, would consent to it? What do you think is best for us? We all follow your advice.'

Vidura said, 'I know gambling is the root of misery, and I tried to dissuade the king. However, he sent me to you. Knowing this, O wise one, do what you think is beneficial.'

Yudhishthira said, 'Besides the sons of Dhritarashtra, what other dishonest gamblers are there? Tell us who they are and with whom we must play, staking hundreds upon hundreds of our possessions.'

Vidura replied, 'O monarch, Sakuni, the king of Gandhara, is adept at dice and skilled in deceit. He, along with Vivingati, King Chitrasena, Satyavrata, Purumitra, and Jaya, are there.'

Yudhishthira said, 'These are some of the most desperate and deceitful gamblers. However, the universe moves at the will of its Creator, under Fate's control. It is not free. I do not desire to gamble at Dhritarashtra's command. A father always wishes to benefit his son. You are our master, Vidura. Tell me what is proper. If Sakuni does not summon me, I will not gamble. But if he challenges me, I will not refuse, as that is my vow.'

Vaisampayana continued, "King Yudhishthira, having said this to Vidura, ordered preparations for his journey without delay. The next day, the king, accompanied by his relatives, attendants, and the women of the household with Draupadi in their midst, set out for Hastinapura. 'Like a brilliant star falling before our eyes, Fate deprives us of reason, and man, bound as if by a cord, submits to Providence,' said Yudhishthira as he set out with Vidura, without deliberating on Dhritarashtra's summons. The son of Pandu and Pritha, riding in a splendid car given by the king of Valhika and dressed in royal robes, set out with his brothers. The king, blazing with royal splendor, with Brahmanas walking before him, departed from his city, summoned by Dhritarashtra and driven by Fate.

Arriving at Hastinapura, he went to Dhritarashtra's palace. He approached Bhishma, Drona, Karna, Kripa, and the son of Drona, embracing each one. The mighty-armed hero then approached Somadatta, Duryodhana, Salya, and the other kings. He greeted Dusshasana and his other brothers, then Jayadratha, and all the Kurus. The mighty-armed one, surrounded by his brothers, entered Dhritarashtra's chamber. Yudhishthira then beheld the reverend Gandhari, obedient to her lord, surrounded by her daughters-in-law like Rohini by the stars. Saluting Gandhari and blessed by her, he then beheld his old uncle, the wise Dhritarashtra. The king smelt the heads of the five Pandavas, including Bhimasena, and all the Kurus became exceedingly glad. Commanded by the king, the Pandavas retired to their chambers, furnished with jewels and gems.

Once in their chambers, the women of Dhritarashtra's household, led by Dussala, visited them. The daughters-in-law of Dhritarashtra, seeing the splendid beauty and prosperity of Yajnaseni, became cheerless and filled with jealousy. The Pandavas conversed with the ladies, performed their daily exercises, and then the religious rites of the day. They adorned themselves with fragrant sandal paste and sought good luck and prosperity through gifts and benedictions from

Brahmanas. After enjoying the best food, they retired to their chambers for the night. The Kurus were put to sleep with music by beautiful women. Awoken by bards with sweet music, they rose from their beds, and after performing the usual rites, entered the assembly house, where they were greeted by those ready for gambling."

Vaisampayana continued, "The sons of Pritha, with Yudhishthira at their head, entered the assembly house and approached all the kings present. They worshipped those who deserved it, saluted others as appropriate according to age, and then seated themselves on clean seats furnished with costly carpets. Once they were seated, Sakuni, the son of Suvala, addressed Yudhishthira, saying, 'O king, the assembly is full. All have been waiting for you. Let us, therefore, cast the dice and set the rules of play, O Yudhishthira.'

Yudhishthira replied, 'Deceitful gambling is sinful. There is no Kshatriya prowess in it, nor any morality. Why, then, O king, do you praise gambling so? The wise do not applaud the pride that gamesters feel in deceitful play. O Sakuni, vanquish us, not like a wretch, by deceitful means.'

Sakuni said, 'A high-souled player who knows the secrets of winning and losing, who is skilled in baffling deceit, and who is united in all the diverse operations of gambling, truly knows the play and endures everything that happens. O son of Pritha, it is the stakes, which may be lost or won, that may harm us. That is why gambling is regarded as a fault. Let us, therefore, O king, begin the play. Fear not. Let the stakes be fixed. Delay not!'

Yudhishthira said, 'The sage Devala, the son of Asita, always instructs us about acts that lead to heaven, hell, or other regions, and he has said that it is sinful to play deceitfully with a gamester. Victory in battle without cunning or stratagem is the best sport. Gambling, however, is not such a sport. Respectable people do not use the language of the Mlechchas, nor do they adopt deceitful behavior.

Honest men carry on war without crookedness and cunning. Do not, O Sakuni, playing desperately, win of us that wealth with which we strive to benefit the Brahmanas. Even enemies should not be vanquished by desperate stakes in deceitful play. I do not desire happiness or wealth by means of cunning. The conduct of a gamester, even if without deceitfulness, should not be applauded.'

Sakuni said, 'O Yudhishthira, it is from a desire of winning, not an honest motive, that one high-born person approaches another in a contest of superiority. Similarly, a learned person approaches another in a contest of learning with a desire of defeating, which is also not an honest motive. But such motives are not regarded as truly dishonest. Similarly, a person skilled at dice approaches one who is not so skilled to vanquish him. One conversant with the truths of science approaches another that is not from a desire of victory. But such a motive is not truly dishonest. Similarly, one skilled in weapons approaches one who is not so skilled; the strong approach the weak. This is the practice in every contest. The motive is victory, O Yudhishthira. If you regard my motives as dishonest, if you are afraid, then desist from play.'

Yudhishthira said, 'Summoned, I do not withdraw. This is my established vow. O king, Fate is all-powerful. We all are under the control of Destiny. With whom in this assembly am I to play? Who can stake equally with me? Let the play begin.'

Duryodhana said, 'O monarch, I shall supply jewels, gems, and every kind of wealth. Sakuni, my uncle, will play on my behalf.'

Yudhishthira said, 'Gambling for one's sake by the agency of another seems contrary to rule. You, O learned one, will admit this. If you are still bent on it, let the play begin.'"

Vaisampayana continued, "When the game started, all the kings, led by Dhritarashtra, took their seats in the assembly. Bhishma, Drona,

THE SOURCE OF CONFLICT

Kripa, and the wise Vidura, all with heavy hearts, sat behind them. The kings, each strong and noble, sat on beautifully crafted, colorful seats, some individually and others in pairs. The mansion shone brightly with the presence of these kings, resembling heaven filled with fortunate celestials. They were all knowledgeable in the Vedas, brave, and had radiant appearances. And so, the friendly game of dice began.

Yudhishthira said, 'O king, I stake this excellent wealth of valuable pearls, obtained from the ocean long ago, adorned with pure gold. What will you stake against it, O great king?'

Duryodhana said, 'I have many jewels and much wealth. But I am not proud of them. Win this stake if you can.'

Vaisampayana continued, 'Then Sakuni, who was very skilled with dice, took them and, after casting them, said to Yudhishthira, 'Look, I have won!'"

Yudhishthira said, "You won this stake by unfair means, Sakuni. But don't be so proud. Let's play with larger stakes. I have many beautiful jars each filled with a thousand Nishkas in my treasury, inexhaustible gold, and much silver and other minerals. This is the wealth I will stake."

Vaisampayana continued, "Sakuni said to Yudhishthira, 'I have won!'"

Yudhishthira said, "This sacred and victorious royal car, which gladdens the heart and has carried us here, equal to a thousand cars, covered with tiger-skin, and furnished with excellent wheels and flag-staffs, drawn by eight noble steeds as white as the moonbeam, is my next stake."

Vaisampayana continued, "Hearing this, Sakuni, using his unfair methods, said to Yudhishthira, 'I have won!'"

Yudhishthira said, "I have a hundred thousand young serving-girls, adorned with golden bracelets and ornaments, skilled in dancing and singing, who serve the celestials, the Snataka Brahmanas, and kings at my command. With this wealth, I will stake."

Vaisampayana continued, "Sakuni, using his unfair methods, said to Yudhishthira, 'I have won!'"

Yudhishthira said, "I have thousands of young serving-men, always dressed in silken robes, wise and intelligent, who serve guests day and night. With this wealth, I will stake."

Vaisampayana continued, "Sakuni, using his unfair methods, said to Yudhishthira, 'I have won!'"

Yudhishthira said, "I have a thousand elephants, adorned with golden garlands, with fine white tusks as thick as plough-shafts, capable of carrying kings and bearing every kind of noise in battle, each with eight she-elephants. With this wealth, I will stake."

Vaisampayana continued, "Sakuni, laughing, said, 'I have won!'"

Yudhishthira said, "I have as many chariots as elephants, furnished with golden poles and flag-staffs, and well-trained horses and warriors who receive a thousand coins monthly. With this wealth, I will stake."

Vaisampayana continued, "Sakuni, pledged to enmity, said to Yudhishthira, 'I have won!'"

Yudhishthira said, "The horses of the Tittiri, Kalmasha, and Gandharva breeds, which Chitraratha gave to Arjuna, are my next stake."

Vaisampayana continued, "Sakuni, using his unfair methods, said to Yudhishthira, 'I have won!'"

Yudhishthira said, "I have ten thousand chariots and vehicles with the finest draught animals, and sixty thousand warriors, all brave and strong. With this wealth, I will stake."

Vaisampayana continued, "Sakuni, using his unfair methods, said to Yudhishthira, 'I have won!'"

Yudhishthira said, "I have four hundred jewels of great value, each equal to five draunikas of the purest gold. With this wealth, I will stake."

Vaisampayana continued, "Sakuni, using his unfair methods, said to Yudhishthira, 'I have won!'"

Chapter 48

VIDURA SPEAKS

It is known that among the Bhojas, they abandoned a son unworthy of their race for the good of the citizens. The Andhakas, the Yadavas, and the Bhojas united and abandoned Kansa. Later, at the command of the tribe, Krishna killed Kansa, and the people were happy for a hundred years. So too, at your command, let Arjuna kill this Duryodhana. With this wretch gone, the Kurus can be happy and live in peace. Trade this crow, Duryodhana, for the peacocks, the Pandavas; and this jackal for the tigers. For the sake of a family, an individual may be sacrificed; for the sake of a village, a family; for the sake of a province, a village; and for the sake of one's soul, the whole earth may be sacrificed. This is what the wise Kavya, knowing the thoughts of all creatures, told the great Asuras to make them abandon Jambha at birth.

A king once brought wild birds that vomited gold into his house, but later killed them out of greed, losing both present and future gains. Blinded by temptation, he destroyed his own prosperity. Do not, O king, pursue the Pandavas out of greed, like that king. Otherwise, you will regret it, just like the person who killed the birds. Like a flower-seller who plucks flowers from cherished trees every day, continue to take benefits from the Pandavas without destroying them. Do not burn them to their roots like a destructive fire-producing breeze. Do not lead your sons and troops to the region of Yama (death), for who can fight the sons of Pritha together? Not even the chief of the celestials with all his might can defeat them.'"

Vidura said, "Gambling is the root of conflicts. It causes division and its consequences are terrible. Yet, Dhritarashtra's son Duryodhana, by engaging in it, is creating fierce enemies for himself. The descendants of Pratipa and Santanu, along with their fierce troops and allies the Vahlikas, will be destroyed because of Duryodhana's sins. Duryodhana, in his intoxication, is driving away luck and prosperity from his kingdom, like an enraged bull breaking its own horns. A brave and wise person who ignores his own foresight and follows another's misguided advice will end up in terrible affliction, like someone entering the sea in a boat guided by a child.

Duryodhana is gambling with Yudhishthira, and you are thrilled that he is winning. But such success leads to war, which results in the destruction of men. This fascination with gambling, which you have embraced, only leads to dire outcomes. You have brought great affliction upon yourself with these actions. Your quarrel with Yudhishthira, who is closely related to you, is something you approve of, even if you didn't foresee it.

Listen, sons of Santanu and descendants of Pratipa, who are present in this Kaurava assembly, to these words of wisdom. Do not enter the terrible fire ignited by this wretch. When Yudhishthira, the son of Pandu, driven by his frustration with the dice, and Bhima, Arjuna, and the twins, give way to their wrath, who will protect you in that hour of chaos? O great king, you are a mine of wealth yourself. You can earn as much wealth through other means as you seek to gain through gambling. What do you achieve by winning the Pandavas' wealth? Win the Pandavas themselves, who will be worth more to you than all their wealth combined.

We all know the skill of Suvala in gambling. This hill-king knows many deceitful methods in the game. Let Sakuni return to where he came from. Do not, O Bharata, engage in conflict with the sons of Pandu!"

Duryodhana said, "O Vidura, you constantly boast about our enemies and disparage the sons of Dhritarashtra. It's clear whom you favor. You show favoritism by wishing success for those close to you and defeat for others. Your words reveal your true intentions, even more hostile than what you conceal in your heart. We've nurtured you like a serpent on our lap, yet you wish ill upon us like a cat. The wise say there's no greater sin than harming one's master. Are you not afraid of this sin? We've gained great advantages by defeating our enemies. Stop speaking ill of us. You always seek peace with our foes, and that's why you hate us. Speaking unforgivable words makes a person an enemy. Praising the enemy should not involve revealing secrets of one's own party, yet you cross that line. Why do you obstruct us like this, you parasite? Speak only what is necessary. Don't meddle in others' affairs or assume you're our leader. Stop your harsh words, Vidura. We don't seek your counsel. Cease irritating those who have already suffered enough from you. There is only one Controller, and He directs all, including me. I act according to His guidance, like water flowing downhill. Those who try to control others by force become enemies. Wise advice, however, is tolerated. Like one who sets fire to camphor, I act guided by my own intelligence. One shouldn't harbor someone who befriends their foes, is jealous of their protector, or is malevolent. Go wherever you please, Vidura. Even a well-treated unchaste wife forsakes her husband."

Vidura turned to Dhritarashtra and said, "O king, tell us impartially, like a witness, what you think of those who dismiss their servants for offering them instruction. Kings' hearts are indeed fickle. They grant protection at first, then strike with clubs later. Prince Duryodhana, you see yourself as intellectually mature, and you regard me as a child. But one who first accepts a friend and then finds fault with them is childish. An evil-hearted man can never be guided to righteousness, just as an unchaste wife cannot be guided in a noble household. Certainly, instruction is not welcomed by this bull of the Bharata race, just as a sixty-year-old husband is unwelcome to a young bride. If you wish to hear only agreeable words about your deeds, good or bad, consult women, idiots, cripples, or similar persons. Sinful people who speak pleasing words are common, but rare are those who speak or listen to harsh yet necessary truths. A true ally of a king acts virtuously regardless of what pleases or displeases the ruler, speaking uncomfortable truths when needed. O great king, embrace humility, bitter and pungent like medicine—sobering, sober, and corrective. Drink it and regain your clarity. I always wish prosperity and fame for Dhritarashtra and his sons, regardless of what happens. I bow to you now and take my leave. Let the Brahmanas wish me well. Son of Kuru, remember this lesson: the wise should never provoke those who are as venomous as adders."

"Sakuni sneered, his eyes glinting with malice. 'Yudhishthira, you've lost enough of the Pandavas' wealth. If there's anything left that you haven't gambled away to us, son of Kunti, speak now.'

"Yudhishthira's voice held a steely edge, his resolve unyielding. 'I know riches untold lie within my grasp. But why ask, Sakuni? Let's wager—tens of thousands, millions upon millions, billions and trillions and beyond, I stake it all. With my wealth, O king, I'll gamble.'

"Vaisampayana recounted how Sakuni, dice in hand, grinned wickedly as he cheated. 'I've won,' he declared.

"Undeterred, Yudhishthira spoke with conviction. 'I possess immeasurable herds, horses, milch cows, and more, stretching from Parnasa to the Sindu's eastern bank. This is my stake.'

"But Sakuni, fueled by deceit, proclaimed triumph again. 'I've won,' he insisted.

"'My kingdom, my lands, and all who dwell therein, save the Brahmanas—I stake them,' Yudhishthira asserted.

"Yet Sakuni, with foul play, claimed victory once more. 'I've won,' he taunted.

"Yudhishthira, pointing to his brothers, adorned in royal splendor, declared, 'These princes, resplendent in their jewels and ornaments—they are my stake.'

"Sakuni's laughter was harsh. 'They are mine now,' he gloated.

"Undeterred by the treachery, Yudhishthira's gaze turned to Nakula, proud and noble. 'He is my stake,' he announced firmly.

"Sakuni mocked, 'Nakula is already in our grasp. With whom will you play now?'

"As the dice rolled, Sakuni claimed, 'I've won.'

"Sahadeva, known for his justice and wisdom, became Yudhishthira's next stake, despite his unworthiness for such a game.

"But Sakuni's deceit knew no bounds. 'I've won,' he declared again.

THE SOURCE OF CONFLICT

"'The sons of Madri, dear to me,' Yudhishthira said, 'are my stake now.'

"'You sow discord among us,' Yudhishthira accused, his voice heavy with scorn.

"Sakuni shrugged. 'A man drunk with victory falls into his own pit of damnation. You, O king, older and wiser, should know this truth. Gamesters rave in their frenzy, words they'd never utter in waking or in dreams.'

"Yudhishthira's resolve hardened. 'He who leads us across the sea of battle, he who stands triumphant over foes, Arjuna—him I stake now.'

"But Sakuni, with his dice of deceit, laughed triumphantly. 'I've won,' he proclaimed.

"Next came Bhima, unmatched in might and valor, the thunderbolt-wielder, leader of the Pandavas. 'I stake Bhimasena,' Yudhishthira declared boldly.

"Sakuni, relentless in his treachery, declared, 'He's mine now.'

"Sakuni continued, 'You've lost much, O son of Kunti—wealth, horses, elephants, and now your brothers. Is there anything left?'

"Yudhishthira, with grim determination, stated, 'I alone remain, eldest of my brothers, dear to them all. If won by you, I will abide by the fate of the conquered.'

"Sakuni's smile was malicious. 'You've agreed to be won. It's a sin you've embraced. But there's still wealth left, O king. Your self-loss is a sin in itself.'

"Vaisampayana recounted how Sakuni, skilled in his deceit, boasted to the assembly of kings, claiming victory over each Pandava one by one. Then Sakuni turned to Yudhishthira, his eyes gleaming with triumph. 'There remains one stake dear to you—Draupadi, princess of Panchala. Stake her, and perhaps you can win yourself back.'

"Yudhishthira's voice rang out clear and defiant. 'I stake Draupadi, neither tall nor short, neither thin nor fat, with her blue curls and eyes like autumn lotuses, radiant as Lakshmi herself. She is the epitome of grace, virtue, and beauty, fit for any man's desires. With her as my stake, O son of Suvala, I challenge you.'

"As Yudhishthira spoke these words, cries of dismay filled the assembly. Bhishma, Drona, Kripa—all were gripped with unease. Vidura, head in hands, sat in silent despair. Dhritarashtra's heart swelled with secret joy, while Karna and Dussassana laughed aloud, tears flowing from others in the gathering. Meanwhile, Sakuni, intoxicated with his deceit, announced with glee, 'I've won,' and seized the dice once more.

Chapter 49

THE ASSAULT OF DRAUPADI

"Duryodhana sneered, his voice dripping with malice. 'Fetch Draupadi, beloved wife of the Pandavas. Make her sweep our chambers, compel her,' he commanded, eyes flashing with cruelty. 'Let the unfortunate woman serve where our maidens do.'

"But Vidura's voice thundered with righteous anger. 'Do you not comprehend, you fool,' he retorted, 'that with each harsh word you utter, you bind yourself tighter in the coils of your own destruction? Can't you see you're dancing on the edge of a precipice, surrounded by tigers eager to pounce? Venomous snakes await your misstep! Hold your tongue, lest you find yourself in Yama's realm!'

"'Krishna cannot be enslaved,' Vidura continued, his words cutting like a blade. 'She was staked by the King after he had lost himself, no longer master of his fate. Duryodhana, like a dying bamboo bearing fruit, you claim this prize through deceit. Drunk on your own arrogance, you fail to see how dice sow enmity and terror. A man should never wield harsh words or subjugate foes with deceitful games. Such speech, condemned by the Vedas, leads straight to hell.'

"'Words can wound deeper than any blade,' Vidura admonished, his voice heavy with sorrow. 'The wise never unleash such venom upon others. Only base men, like curs, bark harshly at all they meet—those who dwell in forests, those leading household lives, ascetics in their devotions, and those steeped in knowledge.'

"'Alas,' Vidura lamented, 'Dhritarashtra's son knows not that dishonesty is a gateway to hell's darkest depths. Many among the Kurus, led by Dussasana, have followed him down this treacherous path of deceit in this accursed game of dice. Though gourds may sink and stones may float, and even boats may founder in water, this foolish king of the Kurus heeds not my counsel, a lifeline to save him from ruin. Without doubt, his folly shall spell the doom of our entire clan.'

"'When the words of wisdom, offered by friends as life's guide, fall on deaf ears,' Vidura concluded solemnly, 'and temptation reigns supreme, it foretells an imminent and catastrophic end for all the Kurus.'

"Vaisampayana continued, 'Intoxicated with pride, the son of Dhritarashtra spoke out boldly, 'Curse on you, Kshatta!' His eyes scanned the hall, fixing on Pratikamin, commanding amidst the council of elders, 'Go, Pratikamin, fetch Draupadi here. You need not fear the Pandavas. Vidura quakes alone, never wishing us well!'

"Pratikamin, of the Suta caste, hastened at the king's behest, his mission clear. He entered the Pandavas' abode, a mouse daring the lion's den, and approached Yajnaseni, queen of the sons of Pandu.

THE SOURCE OF CONFLICT

'Yudhishthira, drunk on dice, has lost you, O Draupadi,' he announced. 'Come now to Dhritarashtra's abode. I shall escort you and assign you to menial tasks.'

"Draupadi's voice sliced through the air, sharp with indignation. 'Why, Pratikamin, do you say so?' she demanded. 'What prince stakes his wife in a game? Surely the king was blinded by dice! Could he find no other prize?'

"'When all else was lost,' Pratikamin replied, 'Ajatasatru, son of Pandu, staked you. The king first wagered his brothers, then himself, and then you, princess.'

"'Go back,' Draupadi commanded, 'and ask that gambler in the assembly: whom did he lose first, himself or me? Find out, then return.'

"Returning to the assembly, the messenger relayed Draupadi's words to all present, including Yudhishthira, who sat silent amidst the kings, unable or unwilling to respond.

"Duryodhana grinned triumphantly. 'Let the Princess of Panchala come forth,' he declared. 'Let all hear the exchange between her and Yudhishthira.'

"Once more, the messenger, distressed, went to Draupadi's chambers. 'The assembly summons you,' he said. 'It seems the Kauravas' end draws near. Duryodhana intends to bring you before them. The king may no longer protect his prosperity.'

"'So be it,' Draupadi acknowledged, her voice calm. 'Fate decrees it so. Happiness and sorrow visit both wise and foolish alike. But morality reigns supreme. Let it not abandon the Kauravas. Return to the assembly, convey my words to those elders versed in morality. I shall abide by their decision.'

"The Suta returned, conveying Draupadi's message. But the assembly sat in silence, faces downcast, aware of Duryodhana's resolve.

"Meanwhile, Yudhishthira, bound by his promise and distressed, sent a trusted envoy to Draupadi. He instructed her to present herself before her father-in-law, clad in a single garment, her eyes wet with tears. Yet, torn by dilemma, the Pandavas could not decide their next move.

"Duryodhana, his heart gleeful, turned to Pratikamin and commanded, 'Bring her here! Let the Kauravas answer her question openly.' The Suta, though fearful of Draupadi's wrath, hesitated not, posing the query to the assembly, 'What message shall I convey to Krishna?'

"Duryodhana scoffed, 'Dussasana, go yourself and fetch the daughter of Yajnasena. Fear not Bhima. Our foes are at our mercy. What harm can they do?'

"Dussasana rose with fiery eyes, storming into the warriors' abode. 'Come, Krishna,' he demanded harshly. 'You belong to us now. Come to the assembly, princess of Panchala. You are ours, won fair and square. Attire or not, you are our slave, to serve as we please.'

"Driven by anguish, Draupadi rose in distress, her face pale, hands trembling. She fled to Dhritarashtra's harem, pursued by Dussasana, who seized her long blue locks without mercy. Those very locks, sanctified in the Rajasuya sacrifice, were now a trophy in Dussasana's grip, defying the Pandavas' valor.

"Dragged forcibly, her attire disheveled, Draupadi spoke out in anguish, 'Not in this state,' she implored. 'I cannot appear thus before these learned elders, devoted to sacrifices and knowledge. Spare me this shame!'

"Dussasana laughed cruelly, 'Slave! Slave!' His mockery echoed through the hall, echoed by Karna's laughter and Sakuni's approval. All in the assembly, save these three and Duryodhana, watched in silent sorrow as Draupadi suffered.

"Bhishma spoke, 'O blessed one, morality is subtle. I cannot judge this matter. A man may stake what is his, including his wife, as per Kshatriya customs. Yudhishthira accepted his loss. Therefore, I cannot decide.'

"Draupadi retorted, 'The king was coerced into the game, tricked by deceitful, desperate gamblers. How can this be deemed voluntary? All Kuru lords here, ponder my words. Give me a fair answer.'

"Distressed and helpless, Draupadi's piteous cry pierced the assembly. Her gaze fell on her enraged lords, fanning the flames of their wrath. They endured the loss of kingdom, wealth, and jewels with less agony than they did this assault on their honor.

"Dussasana, relentless, continued to drag Draupadi forward, hurling harsh words at her. Enraged beyond measure, Bhima's eyes fixed on Yudhishthira, burning with unspoken fury."

"Bhima roared, his voice echoing through the hall like thunder on a stormy night. 'Yudhishthira, gamblers keep their houses filled with loose women, yet even they wouldn't stoop to stake them. But the treasures bestowed upon us by the king of Kasi, the gems, weapons, and our very kingdom—all have fallen into the hands of our enemies. I've held my anger, my king, for you are our lord. But this—staking Draupadi—this is a deed of ultimate shame. This innocent woman does not deserve such treatment. She belongs to you, having chosen the Pandavas as her lords. My wrath burns for her sake. Sahadeva, fetch me fire!'

Arjuna, his voice like a quiet storm before the eruption, spoke next. 'Bhima, never have I heard such words from you. These foes have stained your honor. Yet we must uphold our virtue. We cannot abandon our eldest brother's path. Yudhishthira was ensnared in this dice game by deceitful hands. It was a test of our honor.'

'If I did not know the king's plight was a Kshatriya's duty,' Bhima thundered, 'I would have seized those hands and burnt them in a pyre!'

Vaisampayana recounted, 'Vikarna, son of Dhritarashtra, could hold back no longer. 'Answer, kings of the assembly!' he demanded. 'Draupadi has posed her question. Silence will damn us all. Why do Bhishma and Dhritarashtra stay silent? Where is Vidura's wisdom now? Answer, kings, and cast aside greed and rage!'

But the assembly remained mute, until Vikarna spoke again, rubbing his hands in frustration like a coiled serpent. 'If you won't judge, then hear my judgment,' he declared boldly. 'Hunting, drinking, gambling, and chasing women—these are the vices of kings. Pandu's son, caught in this vice, staked Draupadi, our shared wife. Suvala's son goaded him, yet they all agreed. Draupadi cannot be rightfully won.'

The hall erupted in protest. Vikarna's bold words were met with both applause and scorn. Enraged, Karna rose, his voice a sharp blade. 'Vikarna, you speak foolishly!' he bellowed. 'Draupadi was rightfully won, included in the stake with the Pandavas' possessions. She's not a chaste woman; she has many husbands. Bringing her here in one cloth is no surprise.'

Duryodhana's brother, driven by fury, lunged forward, shouting, 'This boy Vikarna speaks like an old man! He knows nothing of true honor! Draupadi was staked rightfully. Why doubt it?'

THE SOURCE OF CONFLICT

Vaisampayana continued, "As the attire of Draupadi was being violently dragged, her heart turned towards Hari, and she cried out in anguish, 'O Govinda, dweller of Dwaraka, O Krishna, beloved of the cowherdesses of Vrindavana! O Kesava, Lord of Vraja, destroyer of all afflictions, O Janardhana, see how the Kauravas humiliate me! O Krishna, O Krishna, great yogin, soul of the universe, creator of all things, O Govinda, save me from this distress, from losing my senses amidst the Kurus!' The radiant lady, her beauty undimmed, covered her face, calling out to Krishna, Hari, the lord of the three worlds.

Hearing Draupadi's heartfelt plea, Krishna was deeply moved. With compassion stirring within him, he left his seat and swiftly arrived on foot. Yajnaseni's cry to Krishna, also known as Vishnu, Hari, and Nara, echoed for protection. In that moment, unseen by mortal eyes, the illustrious Dharma intervened, covering her with robes of many hues. Each time one garment was stripped away, another identical one appeared, safeguarding her modesty.

Under the divine protection of Dharma, hundreds of robes continued to manifest, a miraculous cascade of colors amidst the uproar of voices in the assembly. Kings beheld this extraordinary sight, applauding Draupadi's steadfastness and rebuking the actions of Dhritarashtra's son. Bhima, his hands clenched in fury, his lips trembling, then swore a terrible oath before all those gathered kings, vowing to take vengeance on the perpetrators."

Witnessing this miracle, Bhima's rage reached its zenith. 'Kshatriyas of the world!' he thundered. 'I swear an oath! If I do not rend open Dussasanas chest in battle and drink his blood, may I never reach my ancestors' realm!'

The hall echoed with the weight of Bhima's vow, condemning the Kauravas. The kings, stunned, murmured their approval. Vidura, master of morality, silenced the tumult. 'Answer, assembly!' he commanded. 'Draupadi asks, and virtue demands a response. Those who remain silent share the guilt.'

And thus, the fate of Draupadi hung in the balance, amidst the clash of virtue and vice, honor and deceit, in that fateful assembly of kings.

Vaisampayana continued, "Draupadi spoke with firm resolve amidst her affliction, addressing Dussasana, 'Wait a moment, vilest of men, wicked-minded Dussasana. There is a duty I must perform, a sacred act yet undone. Dragged by your brutal strength, my senses failed me. I now bow to the venerable elders of this Kuru assembly, a courtesy I could not extend earlier, not by my fault.'"

As she was forcibly dragged once more, the distressed Draupadi, unjustly treated, fell upon the ground and wept bitterly before the assembly of Kurus,

"'Alas, once before, in the Swayamvara hall, I was seen by assembled kings, never again thereafter. Today, I stand exposed before this gathering. I, whom even the wind and sun could not touch within my palace, am now seized and dragged by this wretch, sanctioned by the Pandavas themselves. Alas, the Kauravas too allow their daughter-in-law, undeserving of such disgrace, to suffer so. It seems the times are troubled. What greater distress for me, a noble and chaste woman, than to be compelled into this public court? Where is the virtue for which these kings were famed? Ancient kings never brought their wives to public courts. Alas, that sacred tradition is lost among the Kauravas! How can it be that the chaste wife of the Pandavas, sister of Prishata's son, friend to Vasudeva, stands before this assembly? Kauravas, I am wedded to the righteous Yudhishthira, of the same lineage as the King. Tell me now, am I a servant or something else? I will accept your judgment willingly. This base wretch, this shame to the Kuru lineage, torments me relentlessly. I cannot bear it any longer. Kings, I beseech you to decide whether you deem me won or unwon. Whatever your verdict, I will abide.'"

Upon hearing her impassioned plea, Bhishma replied, "O blessed one, the path of morality is indeed subtle. Even the wisest often fail to grasp its full extent. What a strong man upholds as moral may not be so esteemed by others, no matter its true nature. The complexity and gravity of your question make it difficult for me to give a definitive answer. Yet, it is clear that the Kurus, ensnared by greed and folly, are hastening the destruction of our lineage. O Princess of Panchala, the family into which you have entered holds fast to virtue and morality, unwavering even in adversity. Your conduct, enduring such hardship yet steadfast in righteousness, befits your noble character. These elders, Drona and others, though learned in morality, sit here like lifeless beings, heads bowed. However, it is Yudhishthira who should decide whether you are won or unwon."

Vaisampayana continued, "In that assembly, the kings present, fearful of Duryodhana, remained silent, neither speaking for nor against Draupadi as she cried out in anguish like a female osprey, appealing repeatedly to them. Duryodhana, observing their silence, smiled faintly and addressed Draupadi, daughter of the King of Panchala, saying, 'O Yajnaseni, the answer to your question lies with your husbands—Bhima of great strength, Arjuna, Nakula, and Sahadeva. Let them speak on your behalf before these respected men. O Panchali, let them declare here that Yudhishthira is not their lord, thus proving him false. By this, you will be released from the bonds of slavery. Let the illustrious son of Dharma, steadfast in virtue and resembling Indra himself, declare whether he is not your lord. Upon his word, accept either the Pandavas or us without delay. Indeed, all the Kauravas here are deeply affected by your distress. Despite their magnanimity, they cannot answer your question, seeing the plight of your unfortunate husbands.'"

Vaisampayana continued, "Upon hearing these words from the Kuru king, the assembly loudly applauded, signaling approval to one another through subtle gestures of eyes and lips. Some present expressed distress with sounds of 'O!' and 'Alas!' In response to Duryodhana's pleasing words, the Kauravas in the assembly rejoiced greatly. The kings turned to look at Yudhishthira, well-versed in moral conduct, eager to hear his response. Every eye was fixed on Arjuna, undefeated in battle, on Bhima, and on the twins, curious about their reaction. As the murmurs of conversation quieted down, Bhima, his strong arms adorned with sandalwood paste, raised his voice,

'If our eldest brother, the righteous Yudhishthira, were not our lord, we would never have tolerated the Kuru clan's actions. He is the master of all our religious merits and our lives. If he considers himself won, then so do we. And if not, who among mortals would escape my wrath after laying hands on Draupadi's locks? Look at these arms of mine, powerful as iron maces! Once ensnared within them, even one who performs a hundred sacrifices would find no escape. Bound by duty and respect for our eldest brother, and despite Arjuna's counsel for restraint, I refrain from acting now. But if commanded by King Yudhishthira, I would slay these wretched sons of Dhritarashtra, using slaps where swords would be too kind, like a lion among lesser beasts.'

Vaisampayana continued, "To Bhima, who spoke these words, Bhishma, Drona, and Vidura said, 'Restrain yourself, O Bhima. You are capable of anything.'"

Vaisampayana continued, "Karna said, 'Among all present here, only three—Bhishma, Vidura, and Drona—seem independent, as they always criticize their master and do not wish for his welfare. O excellent one, slaves, sons, and wives are always dependent; whatever they earn belongs to their master. You are the wife of a slave who possesses nothing of his own. Go now to the inner chambers of King Dhritarashtra and serve his relatives. That is your rightful duty now. O princess, all the sons of Dhritarashtra, not the sons of Pritha, are

THE SOURCE OF CONFLICT

now your masters. Choose another husband who will not reduce you to slavery through gambling. It is well-known that women, especially slaves, are blameless in choosing their husbands freely. Therefore, exercise that right. Nakula, Bhima, Yudhishthira, Sahadeva, and even Arjuna have been won over. O Yajnaseni, you are now a slave. Your slave husbands cannot be your masters any longer. Does the son of Pritha disregard life, strength, and manhood by staking you, the daughter of Drupada, before this assembly?'

"Vaisampayana continued, 'Hearing these words, the wrathful Bhima breathed heavily, a picture of despair. Though bound by duty and respect for the king, his eyes blazed with fury, he said, 'O king, I cannot be angry at the words of this son of a charioteer, for we have truly entered servitude. But, O king, if our enemies had spoken thus had you not staked Draupadi?'

"Vaisampayana continued, 'Hearing Bhima's words, King Duryodhana addressed the silent and bewildered Yudhishthira, saying, 'O king, both Bhima and Arjuna, as well as the twins, are under your control. Answer Draupadi's question. Declare whether you consider Krishna as unwon.' Saying this to the son of Kunti, Duryodhana, desiring to bolster Karna and to humiliate Bhima, quickly revealed his left thigh, strong and adorned with auspicious signs, in Draupadi's view. Seeing this, Bhima's eyes widened with anger as he spoke to Duryodhana amidst the assembled kings, piercing them with his words, 'May Vrikodara not attain the ancestral realms if he does not shatter that thigh of yours in battle.' Bhima's wrath emitted sparks like fire from every sense organ, akin to flames from a blazing tree.

"Vidura then addressed everyone, saying, 'O kings of Pratipa's lineage, behold the danger presented by Bhima. Understand that this calamity threatening the Bharatas has been sent by Destiny itself. The sons of Dhritarashtra have gambled without regard for propriety.

They now debate in this assembly over a lady of the royal household. Our kingdom's prosperity is at an end. Alas, the Kauravas now engage in sinful deliberations. O Kauravas, take to heart this noble precept: When virtue is persecuted, the entire assembly is polluted. If Yudhishthira had staked Draupadi before gambling away himself, he would certainly have been considered her master. But staking something when one possesses nothing of their own is like gaining wealth in a dream. Do not deviate from this undeniable truth spoken by the King of Gandhara.'

"Duryodhana, hearing Vidura, said, 'I am willing to abide by Bhima's, Arjuna's, and the twins' words. Let them declare that Yudhishthira is not their master. Then Draupadi will be freed from slavery.'

"Arjuna then spoke up, saying, 'Our illustrious brother Yudhishthira was indeed our master before he started gambling. But having lost himself, let all the Kauravas decide who his master could be now.'

"Vaisampayana continued, 'At that moment, a jackal cried loudly in the sacrificial hall of King Dhritarashtra's palace. In response, the donkeys brayed loudly, and ominous birds echoed with their cries from all directions. Vidura, understanding the meaning of these dreadful sounds, exclaimed loudly along with Gandhari, 'Auspicious! Auspicious!' Then Bhishma, Drona, and the wise Gautama also joined in. King Dhritarashtra, reflecting with his wisdom, sought to save his kin and friends from destruction as he comforted Draupadi, the princess of Panchala. Addressing her, the monarch said, 'Ask of me any boon, O princess of Panchala, that you desire. Chaste and virtuous, you are the foremost among all my daughters-in-law.'

"Draupadi replied, 'O bull of the Bharata race, if you will grant me a boon, I ask that the noble Yudhishthira, obedient to all duties, be freed from slavery. Let not ignorant children call my son Prativindhya, who possesses great inner strength, the son of a slave.

He was nurtured by kings and born a prince; it is not fitting that he be called the offspring of a slave.'

"Dhritarashtra said to her, 'So be it as you say, O auspicious one. I grant you this boon. Ask another, for my heart inclines to grant you a second. You deserve more than just one boon.'

"Draupadi replied, 'I ask, O king, that Bhima, Arjuna, and the twins, along with their chariots and bows, be freed from bondage and regain their liberty.'

"Dhritarashtra said, 'O blessed daughter, let it be as you desire. Ask for a third boon, for two boons are not sufficient for you. You are virtuous in conduct, the foremost among all my daughters-in-law.'

"Draupadi replied, 'O best of kings, O illustrious one, greed always leads to the loss of virtue. I do not wish for a third boon. Therefore, I dare not ask for one. O king of kings, it is said that a Vaishya may ask for one boon, a Kshatriya woman for two, a Kshatriya man for three, and a Brahmana for a hundred. O king, let my husbands, freed from the wretched state of bondage, attain prosperity through their own virtuous deeds!'"

Chapter 50

THE FINAL DECEIT

Vaisampayana continued, "Yudhishthira said, 'O king, you are our master. Command us as to what we shall do. O Bharata, we wish to always obey you.'

"Dhritarashtra replied, 'O Ajatasatru, blessed be you. Go in peace and safety. Following my command, go and rule your own kingdom with your wealth. And, O child, take to heart this advice from an old man, as nourishing as nutritious food. O Yudhishthira, you understand the subtle path of morality. Possessed of great wisdom, you are also humble and respect the elderly. Intelligence comes with forbearance. Therefore, O Bharata, follow the path of peace. The axe falls on wood, not on stone. You are open to advice, unlike Duryodhana. The best of people do not dwell on the hostility of their foes; they see only the merits, not the faults, of their enemies. They never engage in hostilities themselves. The noble remember only the good deeds of their foes and not their hostile actions. They do good without expecting anything in return. O Yudhishthira, only the worst of people speak harsh words in quarrels; the indifferent reply when such words are spoken by others. But the good and wise do not dwell on such harsh words, caring little whether they were uttered by their foes or not. The good consider their own feelings and understand those of others, remembering only the good deeds and not the hostilities of their foes. You have acted as good men of exemplary conduct do, not exceeding the limits of virtue, wealth, pleasure, and salvation. O child, do not dwell on Duryodhana's harsh words. Look at your mother Gandhari and myself if you seek to remember only what is good. O Bharata, look at me, your father, old and blind, still alive. I allowed this game of dice to proceed out of policy, to observe our friends and assess my children's strengths and weaknesses. O king, those among the Kurus who have you as their ruler and the wise Vidura as their counselor have nothing to grieve about. You embody virtue, Arjuna embodies patience, Bhima embodies prowess, and the twins embody pure reverence for superiors. Blessed be you, O Ajatasatru. Return to Khandavaprastha and let there be brotherly love between you and your cousins. Keep your heart fixed on virtue.'"

Vaisampayana continued, "Thus addressed by his uncle, Yudhishthira, the just, foremost of the Bharatas, having observed all the polite formalities, departed with his brothers for Khandavaprastha. Accompanied by Draupadi and riding on their chariots resembling clouds in hue, they joyfully set out for their splendid city called Indraprastha."

Vaisampayana continued, "O Janamejaya, upon learning that the Pandavas had been commanded by the wise Dhritarashtra to return to their capital, Dussasana hurried to his brother Duryodhana without delay. He spoke with grief, saying, 'O mighty warriors, the wealth we gained with so much effort has been relinquished by our father. He has handed over all that wealth to our enemies.' Hearing this, Duryodhana, Karna, and Sakuni, guided by their pride, joined together. They desired to counteract the Pandavas and approached Dhritarashtra in haste. Privately, they spoke to the wise king, Dhritarashtra, son of Vichitravirya, with pleasing and artful words.

"Duryodhana said, 'O king, have you not heard what the learned Vrihaspati counseled Indra about mortals and politics? He said, "Those enemies who always wrong others by stratagem or force should be slain by every means." Therefore, if we use the wealth of the Pandavas to gratify the kings of the earth and then fight them, what harm can come to us? Once venomous snakes of wrath are placed around one's neck and back for his destruction, can he remove them? Arjuna is already preparing, clad in armor with his Gandiva bow, casting angry glances around. Bhima is readying his chariot, wielding his heavy mace. Nakula holds his sword and Sahadeva his semi-circular shield. Yudhishthira and Sahadeva have made their intentions clear. They mount their fully equipped chariots, urging their horses toward Khandavaprastha, assembling their forces. Persecuted by us, they cannot forgive the insults they endured, especially Draupadi's. We must gamble again with the Pandavas to send them into exile. Either they or we, defeated at dice, will go to the forest for twelve years. The thirteenth year must be spent incognito; if recognized, another twelve years of exile follow. This is our duty. Sakuni knows the entire science of dice. Even if they manage to fulfill this vow, we will establish ourselves firmly in the kingdom, make alliances, gather a vast and invincible army, ensuring that we can defeat the Pandavas if they return. Consider this plan, O slayer of foes.'

"Dhritarashtra replied, 'Bring back the Pandavas, even if they have gone far. Bring them back immediately to resume the dice game.'

"Despite the objections of Drona, Somadatta, Valhika, Gautama, Vidura, Drona's son, Bhurisravas, Bhishma, and Vikarna, who all advocated for peace, Dhritarashtra, favoring his sons, disregarded the counsel of his wise advisors and summoned the sons of Pandu."

Vaisampayana continued, "'O monarch,' Gandhari, deeply affected by her affection for her sons, then addressed King Dhritarashtra with great sorrow. She said, 'When Duryodhana was born, Vidura, of great intelligence, said, "It is advisable to send this disgrace of the race to the other world. He cries repeatedly and discordantly like a jackal. It is certain that he will bring destruction upon our lineage." Take this to heart, O King of the Kurus. Do not sink, due to your own fault, into an ocean of calamity. O lord, do not give your approval to the counsel of these wicked and immature ones. Do not be the cause of the terrible destruction of our lineage. Who would break a completed embankment or rekindle an extinguished fire? O bull of the Bharata race, who would provoke the peaceful sons of Pritha? You remember everything, O Ajamida, but still I remind you of this. The scriptures can never control the wicked-minded for good or ill. And a person of immature understanding will never act with the maturity of years. Let your sons follow you as their leader. Do not let them be separated from you forever by losing their lives. Therefore, at my urging, O King, abandon this disgrace of our lineage. Due to parental affection, you could not do it earlier. Know that the time for the destruction of our lineage through him has come. Do not err, O King. Let your mind, guided by counsel of peace, virtue, and true policy, remain as it naturally is. Prosperity acquired through wicked acts is quickly destroyed, while that which is gained through gentle means takes root and endures from generation to generation.'

"The king, thus addressed by Gandhari, who showed him the path of virtue in such words, replied to her, saying, 'If the destruction of our lineage has come, let it happen naturally. I am not capable of preventing it. Let it be as they, my sons, desire. Let the Pandavas return, and let my sons gamble again with the sons of Pandu.'

Vaisampayana continued, "The royal messenger, according to the commands of the intelligent King Dhritarashtra, approached Yudhishthira, the son of Pritha, who had by that time gone a considerable distance. He addressed the monarch and said, 'These are the words of your father-like uncle, O Bharata, spoken to you, 'The assembly is ready. O King Yudhishthira, son of Pandu, come and cast the dice."

Yudhishthira said, 'Creatures obtain fruits, good and ill, according to the dispensation of the Ordainer of the creation. Those fruits are inevitable whether I play or not. This is a summons to dice; it is also the command of the old king. Although I know that it will prove destructive to me, yet I cannot refuse.'

Vaisampayana continued, "Although an animal made of gold was an impossibility, yet Rama allowed himself to be tempted by a golden deer. Indeed, the minds of men over whom calamities hang become deranged and out of order. Yudhishthira, therefore, having said these words, retraced his steps along with his brothers. Knowing full well the deception practiced by Sakuni, the son of Pritha came back to sit at dice with him again. These mighty warriors once more entered that assembly, afflicting the hearts of all their friends. Compelled by Fate, they again sat down at ease for gambling for their own destruction."

"Sakuni then said, 'The old king has given you back all your wealth. That is well. But, O bull of the Bharata race, listen to me, there is a stake of great value. Either defeated by you at dice, dressed in deer skins we shall enter the great forest and live there for twelve years, passing the whole of the thirteenth year in some inhabited region, unrecognized. If recognized, we shall return to an exile of another twelve years. Or, vanquished by us, dressed in deer skins, you shall, with Krishna, live for twelve years in the woods, passing the whole of the thirteenth year unrecognized in some inhabited region. If recognized, an exile of another twelve years is to be the consequence. On the expiry of the thirteenth year, each is to have his kingdom surrendered by the other. O Yudhishthira, with this resolution, play with us, O Bharata, casting the dice.'

"At these words, those in the assembly, raising their arms, said in great anxiety of mind and from the strength of their feelings, 'Alas, fie on the friends of Duryodhana that they do not apprise him of his great danger. Whether he, O bull among the Bharatas, (Dhritarashtra) understands or not, of his own sense, it is your duty to tell him plainly.'

"Vaisampayana continued, "King Yudhishthira, even hearing these various remarks, from shame and a sense of virtue again sat at dice. Though possessed of great intelligence and fully knowing the consequences, he began to play again, as if knowing that the destruction of the Kurus was at hand.

"And Yudhishthira said, 'How can I, O Sakuni, a king like me, always observant of the duties of his own order, refuse when summoned to dice? Therefore, I play with you.'

"Sakuni answered, 'We have many kine and horses, and milch cows, and an infinite number of goats and sheep, and elephants and treasures, and gold and slaves both male and female. All these were staked by us before, but now let this be our one stake: exile into the woods. Being defeated, either you or we will dwell in the woods for twelve years and the thirteenth year, unrecognized, in some inhabited place. You bulls among men, with this determination, will we play.'

"O Bharata, this proposal about a stay in the woods was uttered but once. The son of Pritha, however, accepted it, and Sakuni took up the dice. And casting them, he said to Yudhishthira, 'Lo, I have won.'"

Vaisampayana said, "Then the vanquished sons of Pritha prepared for their exile into the woods. One after another, casting off their royal robes, they attired themselves in deer-skins. Dussasana, beholding those chastisers of foes dressed in deer-skins and deprived of their kingdom and ready to go into exile, exclaimed, 'The absolute sovereignty of the illustrious king Duryodhana hath commenced. The sons of Pandu have been vanquished and plunged into great affliction. Now have we attained the goal either by broad or narrow paths. For today, becoming superior to our foes in prosperity as also in the duration of rule, we have become praiseworthy of men. The sons of Pritha have all been plunged by us into everlasting hell. They have been deprived of happiness and kingdom forever and ever. They who, proud of their wealth, laughed in derision at the son of Dhritarashtra, will now have to go into the woods, defeated and deprived by us of all their wealth. Let them now put off their variegated coats of mail, their resplendent robes of celestial make, and let them all attire themselves in deer-skins according to the stake they had accepted of the son of Suvala. They who always used to boast that they had no equals in all the world will now know and regard themselves in this their calamity as grains of sesame without the kernel. Although in this dress of theirs the Pandavas seem like unto wise and powerful persons installed in a sacrifice, yet they look like persons not entitled to perform sacrifices, wearing such a guise. The wise Yajnasena of the Somake race, having bestowed his daughter—the princess of Panchala—on the sons of Pandu, acted most unfortunately for the husbands of Yajnaseni—these sons of Pritha are as eunuchs. And O Yajnaseni, what joy will be thine upon beholding in the woods these thy husbands dressed in skins and threadbare rags, deprived of their wealth and possessions. Elect thou a husband, whomsoever thou likest, from among all these present here. These Kurus assembled here are all forbearing and self-controlled and possessed of great wealth. Elect thou one amongst these as thy lord, so that this great calamity may not drag thee to wretchedness. The sons of Pandu now are even like grains of sesame without the kernel, or like show-animals encased in skins, or like grains of rice without the kernel. Why shouldst thou then longer wait upon the fallen sons of Pandu? Vain is the labor used upon pressing the sesame grain devoid of the kernel!'

Vaisampayana said, "The defeated sons of Pritha prepared for their exile into the wilderness. One by one, they shed their royal robes and donned rough deer-skins. Dussasana, seeing those warriors in their humble garb, robbed of their kingdom and ready for exile, sneered, 'The reign of the mighty Duryodhana has begun! The sons of Pandu are defeated and wallowing in misery. We have achieved our goal by any means necessary. Today, we stand superior to our enemies in wealth and power, and we are praised by all. The sons of Pritha are doomed to eternal damnation, stripped of joy and sovereignty forever. Those who once mocked Dhritarashtra's son now must wander the forests, broken and penniless. Let them shed their glittering armor and celestial robes and wear these deer-skins as per the wager they lost to Sakuni. They, who once claimed no equals in the world, must now see themselves as mere husks. Though in their deer-skins they appear as noble ascetics, they are like pretenders unfit for sacrifices. Wise Yajnasena, who gave his daughter, the princess of Panchala, to these sons of Pandu, made a grave mistake. These sons of Pritha are nothing but eunuchs. O Yajnaseni, what joy will you find watching your husbands in the wilderness, dressed in rags, robbed of their riches and pride? Choose a new husband from among these mighty Kurus present here. They are all noble, wealthy, and self-controlled. Spare yourself from misery by selecting a new lord and abandoning these fallen men. The sons of Pandu are like hollow sesame seeds or show animals in disguise. Why should you cling to them any longer? Effort spent on pressing empty sesame seeds is in vain.'

"Dussasana's cruel words echoed in the hall, piercing the hearts of the Pandavas. Bhima, unable to tolerate the insult, advanced like a lion upon a jackal, and roared, 'You wicked scoundrel, how dare you speak such vile words? You boast in the presence of these kings, propped up by the cunning of Sakuni. You may wound us now with your venomous words, but I swear I will tear your heart out in battle and remember this insult. And all those who protect you out of greed or anger, they too will meet their end at my hands.'

Vaisampayana continued, 'As Bhima stood there, restrained by his commitment to virtue, Dussasana, abandoning all shame, danced around the Kurus, mocking, 'O cow! O cow!'

Bhima, seething with rage, shouted, 'Wretch, do you dare to taunt me? You who have gained your victory through deceit, hear me. If Vrikodara, the son of Pritha, does not drink your blood, tearing open your chest in battle, let him never find peace in the afterlife. Mark my words, by killing the sons of Dhritarashtra in battle, before the eyes of all these warriors, I will quench this fury.'

Vaisampayana continued, 'As the Pandavas left the hall, Duryodhana, in a fit of joy, mimicked Bhima's powerful strides. Bhima, half-turning towards him, declared, 'You fool, do you think this gains you any power over me? I will crush you and all your followers and remind you of this day. And as Bhima followed Yudhishthira, he spoke with burning resolve, 'I will kill Duryodhana. Arjuna will kill Karna. Sahadeva will kill that gambler Sakuni. I proclaim here and now, if ever we battle the Kurus, these vows will be fulfilled. I will crush Duryodhana under my mace and plant my foot on his head. As for that wicked Dussasana, I will drink his blood like a lion.'

Arjuna said, 'Bhima, men of honor act, they do not just speak. On the fourteenth year from today, they will see our wrath.'

Bhima responded, 'The earth will drink the blood of Duryodhana, Karna, Sakuni, and Dussasana.'

Arjuna vowed, 'Bhima, I will kill Karna in battle, that malicious, jealous, and foul-mouthed fiend. I will fulfill your wish. With my arrows, I will bring down Karna and his followers. And I will send to Yama all those foolish enough to fight against me. The mountains may move, the sun may lose its shine, the moon its cold glow, but this vow of mine stands firm. On the fourteenth year, if Duryodhana does not return our kingdom with respect, he will face our fury.'

Vaisampayana continued, 'After Arjuna spoke, Sahadeva, the fierce son of Madri, eager to slay Sakuni, with eyes red in anger, declared, 'Disgrace of Gandhara, those you think defeated are sharp arrows waiting to strike. I will accomplish all that Bhima has vowed. If you have any courage, do what you must before that day. I will kill you and all your followers in battle if you remain in the light like a true Kshatriya.'

Then Nakula, the handsomest of men, spoke, 'I will send to Yama all the wicked sons of Dhritarashtra, who, driven by Fate and Duryodhana's whims, insulted Draupadi. At Yudhishthira's command, remembering Draupadi's wrongs, I will make the earth desolate of Dhritarashtra's line.'"

Yudhishthira said, "I bid farewell to all the Bharatas: to my venerable grandsire Bhishma, to King Somadatta, to the great King Vahlika, to Drona, Kripa, and all the other kings. Farewell to Ashwatthama, Vidura, Dhritarashtra, all the sons of Dhritarashtra, Yayutsu, Sanjaya, and all the courtiers. I bid you all farewell, and I promise you this: I shall return and see you again."

Vaisampayana continued, "Overwhelmed with shame, none of those present could speak a word to Yudhishthira. In their hearts, however, they all prayed for the welfare of the wise prince.

Vidura then said, 'Revered Pritha is a princess by birth. It is not right for her to go into the wilderness. She is delicate, old, and accustomed to a life of comfort. Let her stay with me, respected and cared for, in my home. Know this, sons of Pandu, and may you always be safe.'

Vaisampayana continued, 'The Pandavas replied, 'O sinless one, let it be as you say. You are our uncle, and therefore, like our father. We will obey you. You are our most respected elder, and we shall always follow your commands. Please, tell us what else remains to be done.'

Vidura responded, 'O Yudhishthira, noble bull of the Bharata race, know this: one defeated by sinful means need not feel ashamed of such defeat. You know every rule of morality; Arjuna is ever victorious in battle; Bhima is a formidable slayer of foes; Nakula is a skilled gatherer of wealth; Sahadeva is gifted in administration; Dhaumya is a master of the Vedas; and Draupadi is well-versed in virtue and economy. You are united, delighting in each other's company, and no enemy can separate you. Who would not envy you? This period of detachment from the world will be greatly beneficial to you. No enemy, even one as powerful as Indra, will be able to withstand it.

You have been taught by the great Meru Savarni in the mountains of Himavat, by Krishna Dwaipayana in Varanavata, by Rama on the cliffs of Bhrigu, and by Sambhu himself on the banks of the Dhrishadwati. You have listened to the wisdom of the great sage Asita on the hills of Anjana and have been a disciple of Bhrigu on the banks of the Kalmashi. Now, let Narada and your priest Dhaumya guide you. Hold fast to the excellent lessons imparted by the Rishis, especially in matters of the afterlife.

O son of Pandu, you surpass even Pururavas, the son of Ila, in intelligence; all other monarchs in strength; and even the Rishis in virtue. Resolve to win victory, which belongs to Indra; to control your wrath, which belongs to Yama; to give in charity, which belongs to Kuvera; and to master your passions, which belongs to Varuna. Draw inspiration from the moon for joy, from water for sustenance, from the earth for forbearance, from the sun for energy, from the wind for strength, and from the elements for affluence.

May welfare and freedom from ailments be yours. I hope to see you return, Yudhishthira, safe and victorious. Conduct yourself properly in all situations, whether in times of distress or difficulty. With our blessings, go forth. No one can accuse you of any sin. We hope to see you return in safety and success.'

Vaisampayana continued, 'Thus addressed by Vidura, Yudhishthira, with unyielding resolve, bowed low to Bhishma and Drona and, saying, 'So be it,' went away.'"

Made in the USA
Columbia, SC
29 October 2024

45058792R00228